Environmental Issues
and Policies

Pearson Education

We work with leading authors to develop the strongest educational materials in economics, bringing cutting-edge thinking and best learning practice to a global market.

Under a range of well-known imprints, including Financial Times Prentice Hall, we craft high quality print and electronic publications which help readers to understand and apply their content, whether studying or at work.

To find out more about the complete range of our publishing, please visit us on the World Wide Web at:
www.pearsoneduc.com

Environmental Issues and Policies

Stephen Ison

Stephen Peake

Stuart Wall

FINANCIAL TIMES
Prentice Hall

An imprint of **Pearson Education**

Harlow, England · London · New York · Reading, Massachusetts · San Francisco
Toronto · Don Mills, Ontario · Sydney · Tokyo · Singapore · Hong Kong · Seoul
Taipei · Cape Town · Madrid · Mexico City · Amsterdam · Munich · Paris · Milan

Pearson Education Limited

Edinburgh Gate
Harlow
Essex CM20 2JE
England

and Associated Companies throughout the world

Visit us on the World Wide Web at:
www.pearsoneduc.com

First edition 2002

© Pearson Education Limited 2002

ISBN 0273 646249

British Library Cataloguing-in-Publication Data
A catalogue record for this book is available from the British Library

10 9 8 7 6 5 4 3 2 1
06 05 04 03 02

Typeset in 10/12.5 Sabon
Printed by Bell & Bain Ltd., Glasgow

The publisher's policy is to use paper manufactured from sustainable forests.

Contents

Preface: using this book

This book is primarily written for students taking modules involving the environment on a range of undergraduate and postgraduate programmes. Any text on environmental issues and policies must, of necessity, span a wide variety of topic areas and embrace a number of different subject disciplines. In that sense it is clearly difficult to locate its boundaries precisely. What we can be sure about is that we are studying a vibrant, ever-changing set of issues and relationships which will almost certainly have major impacts on all our lives.

This book seeks to bring firmly into centre stage the *anthropogenic* (human-related) perspectives on environmental issues and policy prescriptions, while at the same time seeking to give due attention to the more conventional issues and policies involving natural resources. After discussing some of the ethical, socio-cultural, economic, political, historical and other considerations which can legitimately be applied to an environmental approach, Chapters 2–4 develop some of the theoretical underpinnings which support the discussion in the later chapters. The following chapters then take a topic-by-topic approach to the current debate on issues such as sustainable development, pollution, climate change, natural resource and population constraints, transport, housing and the rural economy. The focus of these chapters, at least from the policy perspective, is mainly, but not exclusively, that of the advanced industrialised economies, and in particular the UK and EU. However, where the global scale is important (as in Chapters 6 and 7 on pollution and climate change respectively) the role of supranational bodies and institutions (e.g. WTO, World Bank, UN, IMF) is introduced. Similarly, the developing economies appear throughout the book wherever appropriate (e.g. Chapter 5 on sustainability), but are the sole focus of attention in Chapter 12. The final chapter concludes by briefly reviewing the environmental policy-making machinery of the EU and uses specific case studies to highlight some of the strengths and weaknesses of the processes involved.

Throughout the book you will find up-to-date case materials to illustrate many of the environmental issues involved. A number of questions will help direct your thoughts to some of the principles underpinning the facts and events presented in each case study; outline answers and responses can be found to each question at the end of the book as a self-check on your lines of reasoning. A number of 'boxes' are presented to take further some of the analysis presented in the text. Each chapter concludes with a brief review of further sources of reading and information, including useful websites. If you turn to the *companion website* to this book some interactive questions (with solutions) can be found to help you self-check the content of each chapter, together with further up-to-date factual and case-study materials on the topics contained in that chapter. You will also find a regularly updated selection of *articles* on the companion website to keep you at the forefront of contemporary developments in the subject matter of that chapter.

Acknowledgements

Author's Acknowledgements

The authors would like to thank Eleanor Wall for all her help in typing the manuscript and in arranging diagramatic and other materials.

Publisher's Acknowledgements

We are grateful to the following for permission to reproduce copyright material:

Table 2.5 from *Environmental Economics* by Turner, R.K., Pearce, D. and I. Bateman (1994), Harlow: FT/Prentice Hall, reproduced with permission of Pearson Education Limited; Figure 5.1 from *Environmental Economics* by Turner, R.K., Pearce, D. and I. Bateman (1994), Harlow: FT/Prentice Hall, reproduced with permission of Pearson Education Limited; Table 6.2 from 'Acid rain precursors: by source 1991 and 1998' in *Social Trends*, no. 31, HMSO © Crown copyright 2000; Figure 8.2 from *Environmental Economics* by Turner, R.K., Pearce, D. and I. Bateman (1994), Harlow: FT/Prentice Hall, reproduced with permission of Pearson Education Limited; Figure 13.6 logo reproduced by permission of EMAS. For further information visit their website at http://europa. eu.int/comm/environment/emas/

Case Study 1.3 from 'Managing the rainforests' © The Economist Newspaper Limited, London (12 May, 2001); Case Study 2.3 from *Environmental Economics: A Critical Overview* by A. Gilpin (2001), reproduced by permission of John Wiley & Sons Limited; Case Study 3.1 from 'Oil and cloud forests don't mix' © The Economist Newspaper Limited, London (23 June, 2001); Case Study 3.3 from 'A renaissance that may not come' © The Economist Newspaper Limited, London (19 May, 2001); Case Study 6.3 from 'A Way with Waste' from *British Economy Survey*, Autumn, vol. 30, no. 1 (2000); Case Study 8.1 from 'New York City's Watershed Protection Plan' in *World Resources 2000–2001: The Fraying Web of Life*, World Resources Institute (2001); Case Study 9.2 from *Royal Commission on Environmental Pollution: Energy – The Changing Climate*, 22nd Report, June, HMSO © Crown Copyright 2000; Case Study 12.2 from 'Rural Poverty and Adaptation' in *World Resources 2000–2001: The Fraying Web of Life*, World Resources Institute (2001).

We are grateful to the Financial Times Limited for permission to reprint the following material:

Case Study 5.1 from 'WTO puts the brakes on anti-dumping bandwagon', © *Financial Times* (6 March, 2001); Case Study 6.2 from 'Renewable energy's renaissance', © *Financial Times* (30 January, 2001); Case Study 8.3 from

'Aluminium smelting faces meltdown in North-west US', © *Financial Times* (19 April, 2001); Case Study 10.2 from 'Living with a fear of flooding', © *Financial Times* (13–14 January, 2001); Case Study 11.1 from 'Low Water', © *Financial Times* (14 August, 2001); Case Study 11.2 from 'Health Food', © *Financial Times* (27 June, 2000); Case Study 12.3 from 'A weather eye on African farmers', © *Financial Times* (2 July, 2001).

In some instances we have been unable to trace the owners of copyright material, and we would appreciate any information that would enable us to do so.

Approaching environmental issues

The chapter begins by reviewing various perspectives of what we mean by 'environmental' issues and concerns. We note that a range of biotic (living) and abiotic (non-living) factors are involved, with some perspectives placing a greater emphasis on human-related issues than others. A more detailed assessment of environmental issues is then conducted from a number of different standpoints, including economic, ethical, sociocultural, political and legal standpoints. It is seen that environmental issues and policies invariably involve a *multi-disciplinary* approach when seeking to fully understand them and to find appropriate policy solutions.

What do we mean by 'Environment'?

Most dictionary definitions of 'environment' will include the conditions or influences under which any animate or inanimate object exists, lives or develops. Gilpin (2000) suggests that these surrounding influences may be placed into three categories:

1 The combination of physical conditions that affect and influence the growth and development of an individual or community.
2 The social and cultural conditions that affect the nature of an individual or community.
3 The surroundings of an inanimate object of intrinsic social value.

The first two of these categories are clearly human related (i.e. *anthropogenic*), although other views on defining the 'environment' sometimes place greater emphasis on the intrinsic worth of natural phenomena, independently of any contribution they might make to the human condition.

This emphasis on humanity as the focus for discussions when considering the environment is well illustrated by the European Commission (EC) which defined the environment as 'The combination of elements whose complex interrelationships make up the settings, the surroundings and the conditions of life of the individual and of society, as they are or as they are felt'.

Even such a human-centred perspective of environmental issues will still pay considerable attention to abiotic (non-living) as well as to biotic (living) factors:

● **Abiotic factors** will include land, water, atmosphere, climate, sound, odours and tastes.

- **Biotic factors** will include fauna, flora, ecology, bacteria and viruses as well as a wide range of interactions of these factors with human beings. This latter point is sometimes extended to include a number of social, cultural and ethical issues which impact on the 'quality of life' of individuals or communities.

Even the third category in Gilpin's list brings human perceptions into play in the context of inanimate objects via the expression 'intrinsic social value'. Others would, however, place greater emphasis on the preservation and conservation of inanimate matter in its natural state irrespective of social valuations.

That the approach to many environmental issues must be broad-based and multi-disciplinary is well illustrated by Box 1.1 on the Earth Charter.

BOX 1.1

Earth Charter

The *Earth Charter* recognises that humanity's environmental, economic, social, cultural, ethical and spiritual problems and aspirations are interconnected. It is a global campaign involving individuals and organisations from around the world, seeking to pursue 'sustainable development' (see Chapter 5) using holistic thinking and collaborative, integrated problem solving.

In the nine or so years since the 'Earth Summit' at Rio, thousands of people in cities, villages, meeting halls, schools and in the open air have been part of the Earth Charter drafting. In March 2000 the final draft of the Earth Charter was released in Paris. The May 2000 Millennium Forum of the non-governmental organisations (NGOs) called on the UN General Assembly to adopt the charter – organisers hope that will happen by 2002, the tenth anniversary of the Rio Earth Summit. In the meantime, the Earth Charter principles are being used in schools, universities and faith communities. They provide a values framework that is being used in government, business and civil society.

Caring for people caring for the Earth
The Earth Charter draws on the seven UN summits held during the 1990s, over 200 NGO declarations and position papers, the insights of science, law and cosmology, and the wisdom of the world's philosophies and religious traditions. It also builds on best practices for sustainable living, both ancient and contemporary. In the words of Steven Rockefeller, Chair of the Earth Charter drafting committee, 'It shifts authority from the outmoded ideologies of the last century to a new ecology of values. While the Earth Charter has an environmental focus, it is based on the conviction that caring for people and caring for Earth are two dimensions of one task. We cannot care for people in a world with collapsing ecosystems,' says Rockefeller. 'And we cannot care for Earth in a world with widespread poverty, injustice and violent conflict.'

The principles of the Earth Charter are summarised below:

(I) *Respect and care for the community of life:*
  1 Respect Earth and life in all its diversity.
  2 Care for the community of life with understanding, compassion, and love.
  3 Build democratic societies that are just, participatory, sustainable and peaceful.
  4 Secure Earth's bounty and beauty for present and future generations.

(II) *Ecological integrity:*
  5 Protect and restore the integrity of the Earth's ecological systems, with special concern for biological diversity and the natural processes that sustain life.

▶

6 Prevent harm as the best method of environmental protection and, when knowledge is limited, apply a precautionary approach.

7 Adopt patterns of production, consumption and reproduction that safeguard Earth's regenerative capacities, human rights and community well-being.

8 Advance the study of ecological sustainability and promote the open exchange and wide application of the knowledge acquired.

(III) *Social and economic justice:*

9 Eradicate poverty as an ethical, social and environmental imperative.

10 Ensure that economic activities and institutions at all levels promote human development in an equitable and sustainable manner.

11 Affirm gender equality and quality as prerequisites to sustainable development and ensure universal access to education, health care and economic opportunity.

12 Uphold the right of all, without discrimination, to a natural and social environment supportive of human dignity, bodily health, and spiritual well-being, with special attention to the rights of indigenous peoples and minorities.

(IV) *Democracy, non-violence and peace:*

13 Strengthen democratic institutions at all levels, and provide transparency and accountability in governance, inclusive participation in decision making, and access to justice.

14 Integrate into formal education and lifelong learning the knowledge, values and skills needed for a sustainable way of life.

15 Treat all living beings with respect and consideration.

16 Promote a culture of tolerance, non-violence and peace.

Economic considerations

One of the central concepts of economics involves allocating scarce resources between alternative uses. This is sometimes captured in the expression that whereas people's 'wants' are unlimited, the 'means' (i.e. the resources available such as land, labour and capital) to satisfy those wants are strictly limited. Choices must therefore be made between alternative uses of these scarce resources, bringing into play the idea of **opportunity cost** (i.e. the next best alternative forgone). For example, planning authorities may have to choose between building a more direct (less expensive) route through an area of natural beauty or a less direct (more expensive) one which circumvents these areas. Farmers may have to choose between growing crops by conventional (high application of fertilisers, pesticides) means or by organic means. In all such cases alternative allocations of scarce resources are forgone when a particular choice is made.

This 'economic' perspective highlights a range of issues involving the environment, not least the 'value' placed on the various alternative resource allocations by the market. Are these market valuations appropriate given the many imperfections we know exist in the market mechanism, such as monopolies, externalities, lack of information, public good characteristics, etc.? If not, how can any adjustments be made to market valuations when prices are arguably too high, too low or do not even exist? These valuation issues are considered in rather more detail in Chapter 2.

The economic perspective also includes a discussion of how individuals and groups set 'targets' for their actions. A range of *motivations* are involved here, some involving the more obvious economic indicators such as profit, revenue, cost and market share, others involving indicators which are arguably non-economic, such as status, power relationships, sociocultural and ethical considerations. Some of these issues are considered in Chapter 1 and others in Chapter 3, which specifically looks at target setting in an environmental context.

Of course achieving whatever targets are set involves, at least at the governmental level, selecting between a range of policy instruments. Some of these policy instruments may be 'market-based', seeking to influence individuals and firms via the price mechanism (e.g. taxes/subsidies). Others may be 'non-market-based' using rules and regulations of the 'command and control' variety. These issues are considered in more detail in Chapter 4.

Clearly both economic and non-economic considerations are important to much of the debate in this text. However, we begin by highlighting some economic considerations before moving on to a variety of non-economic considerations.

The environment and the macroeconomy

The familiar circular flow analysis represents the flow of income (and output) between domestic firms and households. Withdrawals (leakages) from the circular flow are identified as savings, imports and taxes, and injections into the circular flow as investment, exports and government expenditure. When withdrawals exactly match injections, then the circular flow is regarded as being in 'equilibrium', with no further tendency to rise or fall in value.

All this should be familiar from any introductory course in macroeconomics. This circular flow analysis is often considered to be 'open' since it incorporates external flows of income (and output) between domestic and overseas residents via exports and imports. However, many economists would still regard this system as 'closed' in one vital respect, namely that it takes no account of the constraints imposed upon the economic system by environmental factors. Such a 'traditional' circular flow model assumes that natural resources are abundant and limitless, and generally ignores any waste disposal implications for the economic system.

Figure 1.1 provides a simplified model in which linkages between the conventional economy (circular flow system) and the environment are now introduced. The natural environment is seen as being involved with the economy in at least three specific ways:

1 *Amenity services* (A). The natural environment provides consumer services to domestic households in the form of living and recreational space, natural beauty and so on. We call these 'amenity services'.
2 *Natural resources* (R). The natural environment is also the source of various inputs into the production process such as mineral deposits, forests, water resources, animal populations and so on. These natural resources are in turn the basis of both the renewable and non-renewable energy supplies used in production.
3 *Waste products* (W). Both production and consumption are activities which generate waste products or residuals. For example, many productive activities generate harmful by-products which are discharged into the atmosphere or

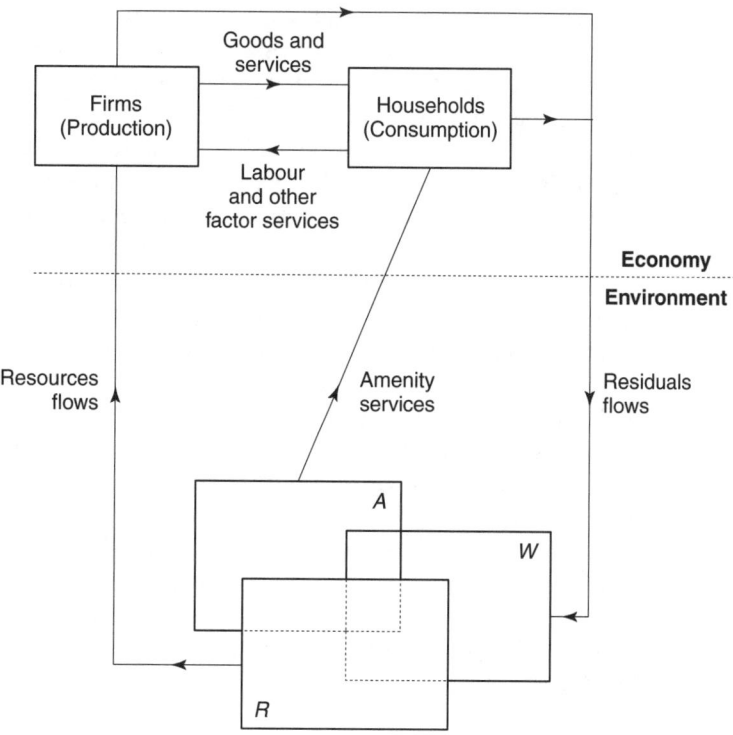

Figure 1.1 Environment and the macroeconomy

watercourses. Similarly sewage, litter and other waste products result from many consumption activities. The key point here is that the natural environment is the ultimate dumping place or 'sink' for all these waste products or residuals.

We have now identified three economic functions of the environment: namely it functions as a direct source of consumer utility (A), as a resource supplier (R) and as a waste receptor and assimilator (W). Moreover these functions interact with other parts of the economic system and also with each other. This latter point is the reason for showing the three boxes A, R and W as overlapping each other in Figure 1.1. For example, a waterway may provide amenity services (A) to anglers and sailors, as well as aesthetic beauty to onlookers. At the same time it may also provide water resources (R) to firms situated alongside the waterway which can be used for power, for cleaning, as a coolant or as a direct input into production. Both consumers and producers may then discharge effluent and other waste products (W) into the waterways as a consequence of using this natural resource.

All three functions may readily coexist at certain levels of interaction. However, excessive levels of effluent and waste discharge could overextend the ability of the waterway to assimilate waste, thereby destroying the amenity and resource functions of the waterway. In other words, the three economic functions of the natural environment constantly interact with each other, as well as with the economic (circular flow) system as a whole. Chapters 3 and 4 look at ways of providing economic incentives or regulations which might bring about optimum levels of interaction between each function and within the economic system as a whole.

By bringing the environment into our modelling of the economy we are essentially challenging the traditional view that the environment and the economy can be treated as separate entities. Everything that happens in the economy has a potential environmental impact. For example, excessive price support for agricultural products under the Common Agricultural Policy (CAP) of the European Union (EU) will encourage overproduction of agricultural produce. Land which might otherwise be left in its natural state may then be brought into agricultural use, and increased yields may be sought by additional applications of fertilisers and pesticides. Hedgerows may be cut back to provide larger and more economical units of cultivation, and so on. In other words, most types of economic policy intervention will impact the environment directly or indirectly.

Equally, policies which seek to influence the environment will themselves impact the economic system. As we shall see in Chapters 6 and 7, attempts to reduce carbon dioxide (CO_2) emissions may influence the relative attractiveness of different types of energy, causing consumers to switch between coal, gas, electricity, nuclear power and other energy forms. There will be direct effects on output, employment and prices in these substitute industries and, via the multiplier, elsewhere in the economy. We must treat the traditional economic system and the environment as being dynamically interrelated.

So far the discussion on the environment and the economy has mainly involved macroeconomic (group) considerations. It may be useful at this stage to briefly review some **microeconomic** (individual) considerations, involving individual consumers and businesses.

The environment and the microeconomy

Our main concern here will be with the impact of environmental issues and concerns at the level of the individual consumer and business. In today's global economy a number of driving forces are arguably raising environmental concerns to the forefront of *corporate* policy debate.

Environmentally conscious consumers

Consumer awareness of environmental issues is creating a market for 'green products'. Patagonia, a California-based producer of recreational clothing, has developed a loyal base of high-income customers partly because its brand identity includes a commitment to conservation; a similar successful approach has been used by Body Shop. However, even when core activities and products have few direct environmental effects, consumer demand may be significantly influenced by the environmental implications of backward or forward linkages. For example, Shell petrol sales were adversely affected in 1996 when Greenpeace alleged that the proposed disposal of the Brent Spar oil platform (backward linkages) at sea posed a serious threat to the marine environment. Similarly, Asea Brown Boveri, a Swiss-based multinational, received extremely adverse publicity around the same time from environmental groups protesting at its alleged destruction of the Malaysian rainforest. Concern for their 'environmental footprint' is now widespread among multinational enterprises (MNEs) engaged in international business. Case Study 1.1 looks at BPAmoco's global rebranding initiative which was launched in 2000.

Reinhardt (1999) suggests that three key conditions are required for success with *environmental product differentiation*, i.e. segmenting the market so that consumers will pay higher prices for overtly 'environmentally friendly' products:

- First, the company must have identified a distinctive market segment consisting of consumers who really are willing to pay more for environmentally friendly products.
- Second, the branding/corporate image must clearly and credibly convey the environmental benefits related to the products.
- Third, the company must be able to protect itself from imitations for long enough to profit from its 'investment' in the previous two conditions.

Environmentally- and cost-conscious producers

Individual producers are increasingly aware that adherence to high environmental standards need not be at the expense of their cost base. In other words, they can be environmentally friendly at the same time as reducing (rather than raising) their cost base. For example, between 1975 and 1996 the multinational 3M reduced its waste released to the environment by 1.4 billion pounds in weight and at the same time saved over $750 m. in costs. Similarly, between 1992 and 1998 the multinational S.C. Johnson reduced its waste output by 420 million pounds in weight while saving over $125 m.

Rank Xerox even adopted an 'Environmental Leadership Programme' in 1990 in an attempt both to regain market share lost in the 1980s and to restore profit margins. This programme included waste reduction efforts, product 'return' schemes (when existing products are overtaken by technologically superior alternatives) and design-for-environment initiatives. Substantial cost savings were reported (several hundred million dollars between 1990 and 1995) together with revenue increases, and by the mid-1990s Xerox executives were hailing the programme as a major success.

Environmentally- and credit-risk-conscious producers

Individual businesses, especially MNEs, are increasingly aware that failure to manage environmental risk factors effectively can lead to adverse publicity, lost revenue and profit and perhaps even more seriously a reduction in their official credit rating, making it more difficult and costly (e.g. higher interest rates) to finance future investment plants.

Environmentally- conscious governments

Individual businesses have a further reason for considering the environmental impacts of their activities, namely the scrutiny of host governments. Where production of a product causes environmental damage, it is likely that this will result in the imposition of taxes or regulations by government.

CASE STUDY 1.1

Global rebranding of BP

In recent times the image of oil-based products has hardly been positive. As a fossil fuel it has been linked to CO_2 emissions and therefore to problems such as global warming and the emission of other hazardous substances. It is factors such as these which have led BP, the company which started the Middle East oil boom in the early twentieth century, to state in July 2000 that its name in future would signify 'beyond petroleum' rather than British Petroleum. Chief Executive Sir John Browne plans to spend £100 m. over the next 12 months reinforcing this image with a new logo, a make-over for its petrol stations and a media advertising blitz. The new logo has been named the Helios mark after the Greek sun god and is meant to signify dynamic energy from oil to gas and solar, said Sir John.

The official reason for this rebranding from its headquarters at Britannica House is that it reflects the growing interest in cleaner, more environmentally friendly fuels such as natural gas and solar power. Since the recent takeover of Amoco, BP has certainly become a major gas producer and a world leader in the development of solar power, even though the amount of money being spent is insignificant compared to its oil exploration. However, some believe that Sir John also has ambitions outside of the energy field, and that the new logo will aptly cover a growing product portfolio such as an office cleaning company or a supermarket chain as much as a hydrocarbon group. In fact a supermarket chain is on the way because BP has plans to open up retail outlets at all its major petrol stations as part of ambitions to increase retail revenues by 10 per cent. BP Connect stores will feature in-store e-kiosks where customers can check weather and traffic conditions, use touch-screen monitors to order food, call up directions, receive sports and news coverage, etc. Even solar panel energy is planned for these petrol stations.

Probably the most important reason, however, is an acceptance that the traditional image of the oil company has become a negative one in the hearts and minds of the consumer. Petrol prices are high and are meeting consumer resistance, and there is also a growing demand throughout the business sector for a social and ethical dimension in all that is done.

Further, the oil companies are aware that one petrol is the same as any other, making it almost impossible to build brand loyalty, as indicated by the fact that BP was 58th in a recent survey by consultant Interbrand on globally recognised product names.

Such rebranding is good business practice, and is being done by every truly successful brand around the world, says Robert Jones, a director at consultant Wolff Olins. Brands such as Starbucks, Disney or Virgin are despised by a few but liked by millions. In a market filled with coffee bars, Starbucks stands for sociability as well as beverages. Disney stands for much more than cartoons and theme parks. It stands for fun – while Sir Richard Branson's Virgin is nothing if not youthful and irreverent. It can sell anything its founder comes up with – records, airlines, financial services, mobile phones and even energy.

So BP is not mistaken in spending all that cash on rebranding, but it does raise the question of whether the message is correct. Saying BP stands for 'beyond petroleum' points people in an interesting direction but does not explain what BP now stands for, says Mr Jones. The challenge over the next few years will be to fine-tune the message so that consumers understand what idea they are buying into – and having been presented with a new standard delivering on that, consumers do not like to be let down. Nike is seen as a brand that represents more than shoes; it represents winning. Allegations that it was using low-cost labour from poor countries damaged the company's name.

BP is engaged is some of the most politically sensitive countries in the world, such as Colombia, where it has been accused by charities of not doing enough to halt human rights abuses, and Nigeria where it has also been criticised for supporting a military government and for damaging the environment of local peoples. Plans to drill in environmentally sensitive areas such as the Arctic have also led to its annual general meetings being log-jammed by protests from green-fingered shareholders. But BP has so far managed to walk the tightrope between making spectacular financial gains and being seen by the wider community as a company that cares for both customers and employees. Although it has made large numbers of redundancies after taking over first Amoco, then Arco and then Burmack Castrol, it has done so by awarding generous financial packages.

Sir John stresses that the bright new green and yellow logo is as much geared to inspiring people inside the organisation as outside. He has raised expectations that must be met.

> **Questions**
>
> **1** Why has BP undertaken such global rebranding?
>
> **2** Comment on the prospects for the success of this strategy.

● ● ● ● Ethical considerations

Ethical standards are generally regarded as those ways of acting or being, that are deemed acceptable by some reference group at a particular time and place. These standards can be implicit to the group or explicit, as in the case of a 'code of practice'. The objective of making such standards explicit usually involves an attempt to avoid an excess of self-interest that might mitigate against the 'good of all'. Of course, the key question is, what is the good of all? Before relating ethics to the particular context of the environment it may be useful to review some basic ethical perspectives.

Social contract theory

Thomas Hobbes suggested that human beings tacitly agree to laws and regulations on their behaviour so that they can live in harmony and achieve their own ends in relation to others. Donaldson and Dunfee (1999) take this argument further in their **integrated social contract theory,** suggesting that there are basic moral minima (or 'hypernorms') and other norms that govern all social relationships on the *macro level*. Figure 1.2 shows a global model of the integrated social contract theory (ISCT).

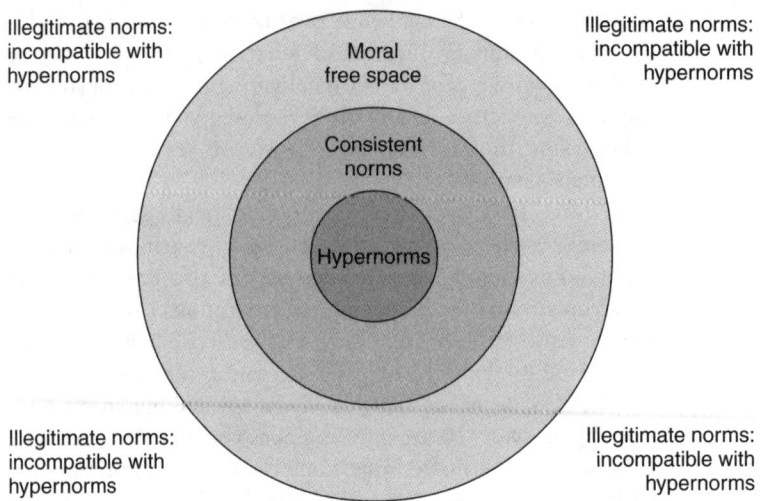

Illegitimate norms: incompatible with hypernorms

Moral free space

Illegitimate norms: incompatible with hypernorms

Consistent norms

Hypernorms

Illegitimate norms: incompatible with hypernorms

Illegitimate norms: incompatible with hypernorms

Figure 1.2 Global norms in the integrated social contract theory (ISCT)

- *Hypernorms* – these moral minima include, for example, fundamental human rights or basic prescriptions common to most major religions. The values they represent are, by definition, acceptable to all cultures and organisations.
- *Consistent norms* – these values are more culturally specific than those at the centre, but are consistent both with hypernorms and other legitimate norms. The ethical codes and vision value statements of companies would fall within this circle.
- *Moral-free space* – as one moves away from the centre of the circle one finds norms that are inconsistent with at least some of the other legitimate norms existing in other cultures. Such norms often reflect strongly held cultural beliefs, whether at the national, corporate or occupational level.
- *Illegitimate norms* – these are norms that are incompatible with hypernorms. When values or practices reach a point where they transgress permissible limits (as specified, say, by fundamental human rights) they fall outside the circle and into the 'incompatible' zone. Exposing workers to unreasonable levels of carcinogens (e.g. asbestos) for example is an expression of a value falling outside the circle.

This ISCT model has proved helpful for evaluating ethical behaviour involving the environment. Respect for the environment and the concern to pass on to future generations a sustainable environment are moral minima which feature widely across cultures and religions. In this sense some environmental perspectives can arguably be regarded as 'hypernorms'.

Where governmental, business or individual values and practices clearly contravene these 'hypernorms', then we may have little difficulty in designating them as 'illegitimate norms' from an ethical standpoint. A willingness to emit toxic substances into the environment beyond recognised safety thresholds might be regarded as one such example, as might commercial exploitation leading directly to the extinction of a particular species or habitat.

What is much more difficult to categorise from an ethical perspective are values and practices which can be located in the 'consistent norms' or 'moral free space' sectors of Figure 1.2. For example, some extra logging or mining may be consistent with what many would regard as the fundamental human right to employment, thereby enhancing human dignity and giving the opportunity to look after one's family. Yet such logging or mining may degrade the current environment in various ways and risk rendering it unsustainable. In this sense we are in 'moral free space', faced with deciding between actions which simultaneously support some legitimate norms but conflict with other legitimate norms.

Ethics versus economics

An interesting issue is whether ethical and economic considerations must invariably conflict. Case Study 1.2 would seem to suggest otherwise.

CASE STUDY 1.2

Ethics and profits

It has long been argued that environmental concerns and profits are inversely related: the more you have of one, the less you have of the other. Since 3rd July 2000, pension funds in the UK have had the opportunity of testing this theory. This is because from that date onwards pension funds have, by law, had to disclose whether or not they will take into account the environmental, ethical and social impacts of their investments. 'Socially responsible investing' (SRI) businesses are a group of businesses which advocated these principles for many years prior to 3rd July 2000 but, until recently, had been able to exert little effective control over the £800 bn of investments directly under the control of the UK pensions funds.

All this may now be about to change. An environmental consultancy, ERM, surveyed the UK's top 25 pension funds in 2000 and reported that 21 of these were planning to incorporate SRI principles into their future operations. For example, one major company involved in pension fund management, Schroders, planned to investigate the environmental practices of those larger companies in which it held (or was considering holding) shares which were members of the FTSE 350. It then intended to go on to investigate the environmental practices of smaller and medium-sized enterprises in which it had an interest.

The conventional wisdom has long been that the more environmentally aware the stance of a company, the lower the returns to shareholders. SRI companies deny this and point to their share portfolio outperforming the market average. John Gummer, a former environment minister, is now MD at Storebrand Principle Fund, an SRI member in pension fund management. He argues that environmental liabilities of a company will rapidly translate into financial liabilities. While admitting that the first duty-of-care to trustees of pension funds is to the financial interests of pensioners, he strongly believes that there need be no long-run trade-off between profits and environmental concerns.

The case of the Co-operative Bank usefully illustrates some of these points. In 2001 the Co-op Bank sought to put a value on the costs and benefits of its ethical stance over the past year. It argued that its support for ethical policies in areas such as renewable energy and the arms trade gave it an extra profit of £16 m. in 2000 (around 16 per cent of all pre-tax profits) even after taking into account the extra £2.5 m. of net costs incurred. The list below itemises some of the cost outlays and cost savings related to its ethical policies in 2000, identified in the bank's fourth annual *Partnership Report*.

Ethics tally

Extra costs	(£000s)
Income lost through turning down unacceptable business	1,696
Ethical audit	144
Staff salaries and overheads	370
Best practice, e.g. environmentally safe air conditioning	792
Community investment	2,520
Electricity from renewable sources	41
Replacing PVC in plastic cards	15
Recycling	36
Environmentally sound paper	52
Cost savings	(£000s)
Energy saved	112
Waste reduction	7
Reuse of furniture	7
Lower paper use	2,901
Net cost (before profit from extra business)	£2,587,000

On the revenue side, the bank stresses the benefit from having ethics as an important element of its brand image. Its marketing and finance specialists have estimated that ethical values can be linked to substantial revenue growth responsible for between 15 per cent and 18 per cent of the £96 m. pre-tax profit declared in 2000. Mori (the poll experts) conducted research for the Co-op Bank and concluded that over 25 per cent of its current account customers cited ethics or the environment as the main reason for banking with the Co-op.

Source: www.co-operativebank.co.uk/ethics

Questions

1 Why is it suggested that the more environmentally conscious firms might actually be more profitable than those which pay little heed to the environment?

2 To what extent do you agree with the statement of Paul Monahan, the partnership development manager of the Co-op Bank, that: 'People often claim that ethical business is good business, but nobody has provided hard numbers before.'

3 What implications might this study have for corporate business objectives?

Ethics and the stock exchange

Attempts are now being made to incorporate ethical considerations into formal stock exchange indices in the UK and other financial markets.

Table 1.1 The FTSE 4 Good Index (Aug. 20, 2001)   `FT`

Top 10 companies included	Market capitalisation (£bn)	10 largest European companies excluded	Market capitalisation (£bn)
BP (UK)	219.4	Total Fina Elf (France)	121.1
GlaxoSmithKline (UK)	206.6	Novartis (Switzerland)	116.6
Vodafone (UK)	177.6	Nestlé (Switzerland)	99.0
Royal Dutch Petroleum (Netherlands)	145.8	Vivendi Universal (France)	72.4
HSBC (UK)	130.6	Aventis (France)	70.3
Nokia (Finland)	125.5	Royal Bank of Scotland (UK)	70.2
AstraZeneca (UK)	97.2	Telefonica (Spain)	64.7
Shell (UK)	96.6	Roche (Switzerland)	59.1
ING (Netherlands)	75.5	ENI (Italy)	57.3
UBS (Switzerland)	74.9	Siemens (Germany)	55.4

FTSE 4 Good Index

A new *FTSE 4 Good Index* was launched in July 2001, using social and ethical criteria to rank corporate performance. All companies in three sectors were excluded, namely tobacco, weapons and nuclear power (representing 10 per cent of all FTSE companies). Of the remaining companies, three criteria were applied for ranking purposes: environment, human rights and social issues. If a company 'fails' in any one of these criteria, it is again excluded. Of the 757 companies in the FTSE All-Share Index, only 288 companies have actually made it into the index. Table 1.1 indicates some 'winners' and 'losers' in this respect.

The FTSE itself has produced figures showing that if this new FTSE 4 Good Index had existed over the past five years, it would actively have outperformed the more conventional stock exchange indices. The same has been found to be true for the *Dow Jones Sustainability Group Index* in the USA. This is a similar ethical index introduced in the USA in 1999. When backdated to 1993 it was found to have outperformed the Dow Jones Global Index by 46 per cent.

● ● ● ● **Sociocultural considerations**

The response of individuals and groups to environmental issues and concerns may in part be influenced by a range of sociocultural considerations. As human beings we are social animals, and it is from a constant interaction with one another that we learn acceptable ways of being, of behaving, of thinking and of acting. In our day-to-day lives we learn how to act in different circumstances, modelling our behaviour on those around us to build up a coherent set of preferences, beliefs, values and meanings that create our cultural context. At least two features help to distinguish culture from other attributes, such as opinion. The first and most important is that it is enduring and changes very little over time. The second is that it has a social context in that it is expressed as part of a community.

Geert Hofstede (1980) claimed to identify five key dimensions of culture, as indicated in Figure 1.3. It has been suggested that support for environmental initiatives may be closely correlated with these cultural dimensions. For example, national cultures which exhibit strong *collectivist* ('weak individualism') characteristics are more likely to support environmental initiatives which have long-term benefits for the 'group'. Similarly *femininity* ('weak masculinity') characteristics will tend to support environmental policies aimed at enhancing social value and quality of life, while *long-term outlook* characteristics will help support environmental policies which involve long periods of time before their benefits become apparent.

However, some have suggested that the linkages between culture and environment are a two-way process in that the environment may also play a part in the development of cultural characteristics. It has often been argued that harsh and 'unfriendly' climates and poor agricultural conditions can, over time and across generations, result in people who are hardworking, resilient, patient, tough and aggressive. Tayeb (2000) describes how this can happen using the example of the Aryan tribes who, thousands of years ago, migrated from Central Asia to India and

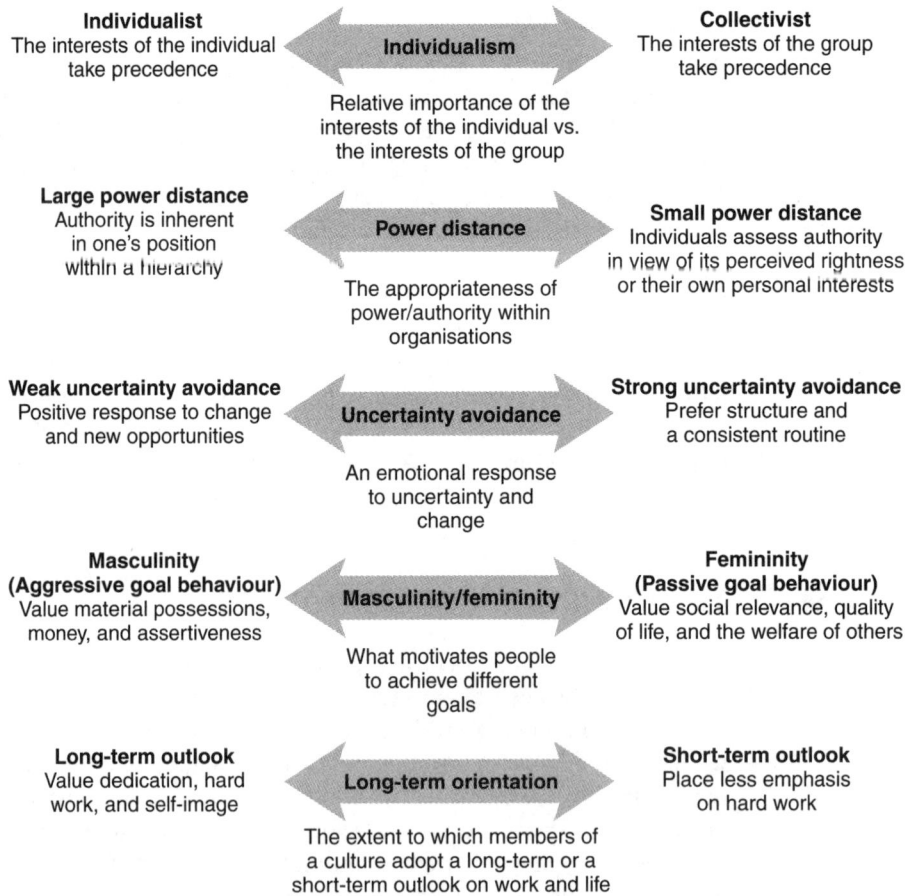

Figure 1.3 Hofstede's five dimensions of culture
Source: Adapted from Griffin and Pustay (1996)

Iran. Those who settled in India found a fertile land with plenty of water and rivers and a relatively mild climate. Those who settled in Iran faced harsh variable seasons, salt deserts and very few rivers. Tayeb suggests that it was hardly an accident that Hinduism and Buddhism took root in India, religions noted for their non-violence and passivity. By way of contrast, those from the same ethnic Aryan tribes who settled under the harsher ecological conditions of Iran became aggressive, fought other nations and built up the Persian Empire which ruled over a vast area for centuries.

Political and legal considerations

Many environmental issues involve geographical scale: for example, Chapter 6 looks at pollution on a local (e.g. national), regional (e.g. international: adjacent countries only) and global (e.g. international: worldwide) scale. Clearly policy responses may involve important considerations as to who has the political and legal jurisdiction over the relevant geographical areas. This can be of major importance when the particular tax/subsidy and other 'governmental' policy initiatives adopted may turn out to be critical factors in determining environmental outcomes.

Nation state

At the heart of governance is the notion of *sovereignty*, which implies the power to rule without constraint and which, for the last three centuries, has been associated with the nation state. We live in a world which is organised as a patchwork of nation states within which different peoples live, with their own systems of government exerting authority over the affairs within their territory. Of course groupings within those territories may arise from time to time which seek a measure of independence from the central authorities, sometimes claiming nation statehood themselves.

It has been argued that one of the major effects of globalisation is to threaten the notion of the territorial nation state. In a global economic system, productive capital, finance and products flow across national boundaries in ever-increasing volumes and values, with the nation state seeming to be increasingly irrelevant as a 'barrier' to international events and influences. Governments often appear powerless to prevent stock market crashes or recessions in one part of the world having adverse effects on domestic output, employment, interest rates and so on. Attempts to lessen these adverse effects seem, to many citizens, increasingly to reside in **supranational bodies** such as the IMF, World Bank, EU, etc. This inability of nation states to meet the demands of their citizens without international co-operation is seen by many as evidence of the declining competence of states, arguably leading to a 'widening and weakening' of the individual nation state.

Supranational bodies

The increased emphasis on international co-operation has brought with it an enormous increase in the number and influence of intergovernmental and **non-governmental organisations** (NGOs) to such an extent that many writers now argue that national and international policy formulation have become inseparable. For example, whereas in 1909 only 176 international NGOs could be identified, by the year 2001 this number exceeded 30,000 and was still growing! The formerly mono- lithic national state, with its own independent and broadly coherent policy, is now conceived by many to be a fragmented coalition of bureaucratic agencies, each pursuing its own agenda with minimal central direction or control. State autonomy is thereby threatened in economic, financial and ecological areas.

We have already noted the breadth of the issues which might be subsumed under the 'environment' heading. That being so, a large number of supranational bodies are often involved in environmental policy-making and analysis, both directly and indirectly. Just a few of the more important ones are briefly reviewed below.

World Bank

The *World Bank* is, in effect, a grouping of three international institutions, namely the International Bank for Reconstruction and Development (IBRD), the International Development Association (IDA) and the International Finance Corporation (IFC).

International Bank for Reconstruction and Development

The origins of the World Bank lie in the formation of the IBRD in 1946. The IBRD sought to help countries raise the finance needed to reconstruct their war-damaged economies. This often took the form of guaranteeing loans that could then be obtained at lower interest rates than might otherwise have been possible.

International Development Association

In 1958 a second international institution was created to operate alongside the IBRD, namely the IDA. The main objective of the IDA was to provide development finance for low-income nations which had insufficient resources to pay interest on the IBRD loans.

International Finance Corporation

The third international institution in the World Bank group is the IFC established in 1959. Unlike the previous two bodies, the IFC concentrates on lending to *private* borrowers involved in development projects. Initially much of this lending was for specific infrastructure projects such as dams, power facilities, transport links, etc. More recently the focus of lending has shifted towards improving the efficiency and account- ability of the administrative and institutional structures in the recipient countries.

Since 1980 the World Bank has been involved in various types of *structural adjust- ment lending* (SAL) which accounts for over 20 per cent of World Bank lending. These SAL programmes are non-project related, rather they involve lending to sup- port specific programmes of policy which may involve elements of institutional change. These SAL programmes are generally directed towards improving the 'sup- ply side' of the borrowing countries, intending to initiate and fund changes which will ultimately raise productive efficiency in various sectors of their economies.

UN international institutions

Here we consider a number of institutions that operate under the auspices of the United Nations. The United Nations itself was established by Charter in 1945 and consists of 185 member states. The mission statement of the UN is to establish a world order based on peace, prosperity and freedom, and its most visible decision-making body is the UN General Assembly in which all members participate.

United Nations Conference on Trade, Aid and Development (UNCTAD)

The conference first met in 1964 and has met subsequently at three- or four-year intervals. All members of the UN are members of the conference which has a permanent executive and secretariat. UNCTAD seeks to give particular support to the less developed countries (LDCs) in their various trade disputes with the more developed economies. An important contribution of UNCTAD has been to support the introduction of the 'Generalised System of Preferences' (GSP) in 1971 which has helped give some of the exports of LDCs preferential access to the markets of the advanced industrialised economies.

United Nations Industrial Development Organisation (UNIDO)

This was established in 1966 to provide technical assistance for developing countries seeking to industrialise. It helps countries undertake industrial surveys, formulate industrial development strategies, conduct project appraisals and implement productivity and marketing strategies.

Organisation for Economic Co-operation and Development (OECD)

The OECD was established in 1971 as a grouping of the advanced industrialised economies. Its main objectives were to encourage high levels of economic growth and employment among its member states, together with a stable financial system. It also seeks to contribute to the economic development in non-member states (including LDCs) and to expand world trade on a multilateral basis.

Group of Seven/Eight

This refers to the seven major industrial countries within the OECD that meet at fairly regular intervals to consider global economic issues, especially those of a macroeconomic nature. The seven countries involved are Canada, France, Germany, Italy, Japan, the UK and the USA (the Russian Federation has been added to this number on an informal basis in recent times when G7 became G8). Sometimes agreements to co-ordinate macroeconomic policies (e.g. exchange rates) are issued as communiqués at the end of these meetings.

Environmental codes and regulations

A number of national and international codes and regulations have elements dealing with the environment. There are, in addition, some important environment-specific codes and regulations:

- *ISO 14001*. The International Organization for Standardization has developed ISO 14001 as a means of certifying companies which adopt certain minimum standards of environmental management.
- *Regional agreements*. Bilateral investment agreements between nations (e.g. the Bolivia–US bilateral investment treaty) often contain minimum environmental standards as do broader-based 'regional' treaties such as NAFTA (the North American Free Trade Agreement).
- *Multilateral agreements*. The OECD countries have moved towards accepting wide-ranging minimum environmental standards in the Multilateral Agreement on Investment (MAI) draft treaty, yet to be ratified. Various *protocols* have also been agreed between countries (e.g. Montreal, Kyoto) as to overall reductions in greenhouse gas emissions, etc. International agencies have been established to support sound environmental practices: e.g. the Forest Stewardship Council (see Case Study 1.3) certifies companies which adopt minimum standards for sustainable forestry.

The following case study on the Amazonian rainforest gives you the opportunity of applying some of the economic and non-economic considerations touched on in this chapter to a particular environmental issue.

CASE STUDY 1.3

Managing the rainforests

Empty fields, as far as the eye can see, line the highway for most of the 300 km (186 miles) from Belém, eastern Amazonia's main city, to the timber-cutting town of Paragominas. Once it was all forest, but since the 1970s most of the trees in a broad strip beside the road have been cut – not just to extract timber, but to clear pasture for cattle-raising, encouraged by subsidies and tax incentives. Now, though, most of the fields lie empty and are becoming overgrown with scrub. Cows are seen so infrequently that they might be imagined to be an endangered species.

The deforestation, mostly in the past 30 years, of 14 per cent of the Brazilian part of Amazonia (about two-thirds of the Amazon rainforest, the world's biggest) has been as much an economic as an environmental disaster. The usable timber would be ripped out of a stretch of forest and the rest would then be burned, because the land would often be worth more when cleared than it had been as untouched forest. This value, however, was due partly to excessive optimism over the region's agricultural potential, and partly to a set of economically perverse incentives provided by the government. When farming was actually tried, it was frequently found to be unprofitable. And many did not even bother to try. Some chopped down the trees, grabbed the grants and then abandoned the land. Others used the 'farms' they carved out of the jungle to disguise (highly taxed) profits on other businesses as farming profits (which used to be tax free). As a result, there are now about 165,000 km² of abandoned land in Brazilian Amazonia.

In recent years, the handouts and tax breaks that promoted deforestation have been reduced. As a result, good quality forested land can be worth as much as 40 per cent more than cleared land. A law passed in 1998 introduced stiff penalties for cutting trees without permission from *Ibama*, Brazil's environmental protection agency. Though deforestation seems to have slowed since the mid-1990s, new figures due shortly will show that last year's deforestation was little different from that in 1998 and 1999, when about 0.5 percent of the forest was chopped down in each year.

Besides the cleared forest that shows up on the satellite pictures, each year a further unmeasured amount (at least 10,000 km^2, according to a study carried out in 1999) has its most valuable trees ripped out and is then abandoned. The big holes in forest cover caused by this reckless extraction make the area drier and thus vulnerable to fires. And if the forest does grow back, it grows differently, with fewer species, and choked by thick creepers that Amazonians call *cipo*. Though most of the rainforest remains intact – in contrast to the gloomiest predictions of the 1980s, which predicted it would be almost gone by now – it continues to be hacked away at a rate that will see it wiped out within the next 200 years.

Fortunately, there are stronger grounds than ever for hoping that this will not happen. Belatedly, in parts of Amazonia such as Paragominas, where much local forest is either razed or damaged, timber firms are coming to see unharmed woodland as an asset that, properly managed, can yield a good income for ever. Their enthusiasm has been bolstered by studies showing that 'sustainable management' of forests, also known as 'reduced impact logging' (RIL) can be more profitable than the reckless conventional methods of timber extraction. One such study, conducted near Paragominas, found that RIL was 12 per cent cheaper than conventional logging.

In RIL schemes, the area to be exploited is divided into perhaps 30 blocks, one of which has timber extracted each year, before being left alone for 29 years. This is enough for the forest to regenerate successfully, because in addition to rotation, the schemes take care to leave the oldest specimens of the exploited species standing. As well as providing cover from the tropical sun, the spreading branches of these tall trees reseed the block with new specimens. In haphazard, conventional logging, such trees are usually hacked down and, because their trunks are hollow or damaged, then abandoned – a waste of time and money for the lumberjacks, as well as maiming the forest. RIL reduces the damage further by plotting the position of each block's valuable trees on a computer, which then works out the shortest set of access roads that needs to be carved out to remove the felled trees. Lumberjacks are also taught ways of felling trees that avoid damaging those around them.

With planning, the forest's animals, as well as its plants, can be preserved, according to Adalberto Verissimo of *Imazon*, a local environmental research group. Amazonia's top predator, barring man, is the jaguar. This species needs about 500 km^2 of forest to form a viable population of 50 cats. Though a typical managed forestry scheme is only about a fifth of this size, by ensuring that at least 'corridors' of forest are maintained between neighbouring schemes, the big cats and all the other animal species below them in the food chain can, it is hoped, survive reasonably well. It should, in other words, be possible for a stretch of forest to provide an endless supply of tropical hardwood but still suffer a minimal impact on its ecosystem.

Sustainable forestry of this sort has been talked about in Brazil since at least the 1980s, but started taking off only in the mid-1990s. Across the country, including areas outside Amazonia, there are now thought to be 10,000 km^2 of forest under sustainable management. Foreign consumers of tropical hardwoods – furniture makers and sellers, for instance – are increasingly asking for timber that has been independently certified as coming from well-run RIL schemes, so that they can promise their environment-conscious customers that they are not contributing to the destruction of the rainforest.

The Rosa Group, a big timber firm in Paragominas, started using RIL in 1998, and is now applying for certification by the *Forest Stewardship Council* (FSC), an international agency that sets standards for sustainable forestry. Antonio Rosa, the firm's boss, sees certification as key to his plan to expand its exports to Europe and North America. Foreign buyers, he says, seem prepared to pay extra for certified timber, making it even more attractive.

But most timber felled in Amazonia is used in Brazil, so the growth of sustainable forestry – and the decline of reckless chopping – will depend on how quickly Brazilian consumers switch to demanding certified timber. There are signs that this is starting to happen. In 2000, 40 Brazilian firms, including Tok & Stok, a big furniture retailer, formed a 'buyers' group' to co-ordinate their purchases of certified wood, and jointly pledged to stop using uncertified timber by 2005. By creating a growing market for certified timber, it is hoped, supply will grow too. Imazon is conducting what it believes is the first ever study of who distributes and buys timber in Brazil, to suggest ways of accelerating the switch to sustainable forestry.

Since much of the rainforest is still untouched and unclaimed, and thus public property according to Brazil's constitution, the federal and state governments could accelerate the move to sustainability by declaring it all a national park and then licensing timber firms to run RIL schemes in selected parts of it. A study by Mr Verissimo and others for the environment ministry concluded that just 10 per cent of the remaining forest, managed sustainably, could meet all the existing demand for tropical hardwood. Much of the rest might then be declared untouchable.

In practice, policing such a huge preservation area against illegal logging would be an immense task. A national park that existed only on paper would not be worthy of the name. And Ibama, whose job it would be to patrol this park, has a reputation for inefficiency and corruption. It seems to be improving, but slowly. Timber firms in Paragominas say the local branch that inspects them is now doing a reasonable job, but they complain of 'unfair competition' from surrounding regions where the agency is ineffective.

Some environmentalists say the answer is to take the job away from Ibama (whose broad remit includes dealing with everything from oil slicks to urban noise) and create a specialised body similar to America's Forestry Service. Raimundo Deusdara, an environment ministry official responsible for forest preservation, agrees that the idea is worth considering. In the meantime, he hopes that a new environment tax, to be introduced soon, will at least double Ibama's budget, and thus make it more effective.

Another hindrance to the effort to control illegal logging has been that, since Brazil lacks a central land register, it has been easy to steal publicly owned forest. Only now has the federal government launched a campaign to seize back the vast tracts of Amazonia that have been stolen over the years. A law creating a land register has been passed, and the government hopes the register will be compiled by 2003.

Combined with better land registration, improved satellite imaging should help to monitor, and thus prevent, deforestation. Brazil's space research agency, INPE, currently produces its deforestation figures annually, but the Chinese Brazilian CBERS satellite it uses scans Amazonia once every 26 days, so it is studying whether it could produce figures more frequently. Mato Grosso state, which includes a small slice of Amazonian forest, is already doing this on its own. A state laboratory is downloading satellite images and comparing them with a computerised land register to spot breaches of the often flouted national forest code, which allows landowners in Amazonia to deforest only 20 per cent of their property, and even then, only with permission.

In theory, real-time detection of deforestation could be done for all of Amazonia, according to Thelma Krug of INPE, especially after the launch, due in 2004, of a Brazilian satellite that will provide images every two hours. *Sivam*, Brazil's giant radar surveillance system for Amazonia, is now being brought into service. Though its main role is in defence, and to monitor the traffic in illegal drugs, it could also be used to detect loggers' activities. But collecting and processing such masses of data would be expensive. And, of course, it would only be worthwhile if there were an effective forest service which had enough wardens with boats, planes and helicopters to rush them to remote areas where illegal logging had been spotted.

Encouraging sustainable timber extraction and suppressing illegal logging, are only part of what must be done to stop the rainforest being degraded and destroyed. The other big threat is population pressure. Last year's census found that about 12 million people live in Amazonia, and that the population there is increasing by 3.7 per cent a year. So there is a growing need to find ways of making a living for people without despoiling the forest.

This was one of the objectives of the Pilot Programme to Conserve the Brazilian Rain Forest, set up in 1992, with the promise of $350 m. from the Group of Seven rich countries – hence its nickname, PPG7. All sorts of projects were created to help forest dwellers make a living from such things as collecting fruits and plants. But, as an independent review concluded last year, progress has been very slow. Much of the $88 m. spent so far has been swallowed up by bureaucracy, and many projects have not got beyond being experiments (though PPG7 does pay for Mato Grosso's satellite-based enforcement system, which has already resulted in the jailing of 50 landowners).

One reason for the poor results, the report concluded, is that the scheme has done little to involve the private sector in creating forest-friendly businesses. But, here and there, independently of the PPG7, this is beginning to happen. In the Ilha de Marajo, an island twice the size of Wales at the mouth of the Amazon, Muana Alimentos, a food processing company, is working with the local authorities to persuade the growing numbers of *ribeirinhos* (riverbank dwellers) to cultivate the *acai* palms that grow abundantly in the swampy land around their wooden huts. The company wants to expand the supply of the two products it sells: palm heart, the soft inner stem at the tree top, from which the fronds sprout, which is pickled and used in salads and pies; and the pulp of the *acai* fruit, which is served as a delicious sorbet on Brazil's smartest beaches.

Arriving in the settlement of Piria, Georges Schnyder, director of Muana Alimentos, accompanies a state official on a boat trip to try to interest the *ribeirinhos* in taking a short course in cultivating the trees to maximise yields of fruit and palm hearts. 'You could be earning 8,000 reais (about $4,000) a year from this plot', Mr Schnyder tells Raimundo and Rubens, a father and son who live near by. The two smile politely but disbelievingly – incredulous that what is a small fortune by local standards might be within their grasp. The company already owns and tends its own plots of land on the island, but Mr Schnyder says he would rather leave the cultivation and processing to the locals and stick to being a distributor.

Like the lumberjacks in Paragominas, Mr Schnyder is seeking the FSC's certificate of sustainability, seeing it as a way to add value to his products. Despite the PPG7's poor progress, Mr Schnyder believes such schemes to find sustainable livings for forest dwellers can be made to work. But, he grumbles, environmental groups could do more to help; they seem keener on sitting in their offices writing damning reports than on setting up local branches in forest villages to foster sustainable development by offering training and advice.

Politicians must change their ways too. Though many of the incentives that led to chopping have gone, some persist. Amazonia's state governors opposed the recent decision by Brazil's president, Fernando Henrique Cardoso, to abolish Sudam, a corruption-riddled Amazonian 'development' agency, whose handouts have sponsored much futile forest clearance.

The military dictators who ran Brazil from 1964 to 1985 were obsessed with populating and developing Amazonia, convinced that otherwise another power might seize it. Such paranoia has died down (though many Amazonians believe America is plotting to invade on the pretext of saving trees), but *Advance Brazil*, the government's 776 billion reais economic development plan, still assumes that Amazonia needs to be opened up with new roads and waterways. Yet a study published by William Laurence of the Smithsonian Tropical Research Institute, and his colleagues, in *Science* in January 2001, argued that such transport links, when built near forests in the past, triggered massive deforestation. Extrapolating from past patterns to forecast the effects of the proposed roads and highways, the study said, at worst, only 5 per cent of Amazonia might remain as pristine forest in 2020, with a further 24 per cent being lightly degraded and the rest badly damaged or gone.

There are good reasons for hoping that things will not turn out so badly. Brazil's growing fiscal prudence may mean not all of Advance Brazil advances. It may also lead to further cuts in the remaining incentives to chop trees. Past deforestation may not be a guide to the future, because it was mostly in the drier fringes of Amazonia rather than the really rainy rainforest, where agriculture would be even harder. The government has stopped settling landless peasants in forested areas, which until recently had been a smaller but significant cause of deforestation. And the reaction in Brazil and around the world to the *Science* paper helped, by forcing the government to submit Advance Brazil to an independent environmental impact assessment.

Dr Laurence agrees that things may not turn out as badly as the paper's bleakest prognostications. But, he argues, it is not so much Advance Brazil that threatens the forest as the thinking behind the project. It assumes that economic development depends on 'extensifying', i.e. extending the amount of land in economic use, rather than intensifying the use of land already exploited. Maybe so, says Raul Jungmann, Brazil's land reform minister, but the trouble is that extensifying is cheaper and simpler than intensifying. If richer countries want the Amazon rainforest saved (and, he correctly points out, they are lecturing Brazil on preserving its forests after destroying much of their own and that of their colonies), they could offer more technology and capital to intensify the return on Brazil's existing agricultural land.

Though economic development has often been depicted as the environment's enemy, the richer a country gets, the more its people tend to worry about environmental matters. It is encouraging that it was mainly Brazilian 'greens', not foreign ones, who successfully campaigned last year against a plot by the big landowners' lobby in Congress to weaken the forest code, and are mobilising against a similar attempt this year.

Brazil has already lost one tropical forest: the Mata Atlantica, which used to run all the way down the country's southern coast, but of which only 7 per cent now remains, and that divided into small fragments. It is too early to guarantee the survival of the bigger, more famous one in Amazonia. Much more needs to be done to stop it being eaten away by 0.5 per cent or so each year. But its chances are improving, especially now it is increasingly being seen as a valuable economic asset, something that could produce returns for ever.

Source: 'Managing the rainforests', *The Economist*, 12–18 May, 2001

Questions

1 Use the text to provide examples of each of the following environmental considerations:
   (a) economic (macroeconomic);
   (b) business (microeconomic);
   (c) ethical;
   (d) sociocultural;
   (e) political/legal.

2 Identify potential areas of conflict ('trade-off') between some of these environmental considerations.

3 What are the implications of this case study for policy formation directed towards environmental sustainability?

Now try the self-check questions for this chapter on the companion website
www.booksites.net/ison
You will also find up-to-date facts and case materials.

Key terms

Abiotic factors Refer to non-living environmental factors such as land, water, atmosphere, climate, sound, odours and tastes

Biotic factors Refer to living environmental factors such as fauna, flora, ecology, bacteria and viruses as well as a wide range of interactions of these factors with human beings

Ethical standards Those ways of acting or being that are deemed acceptable by some reference groups at a particular time and place

Integrated social contract theory (ISCT) An approach which seeks to identify the moral norms that govern social relationships at the macro level

Macroeconomic issues Involve economic aspects of the group or community

Microeconomic issues Involve economic aspects of the individual, for example as consumer or producer

Moral free space Where norms conflict with other equally 'legitimate' norms

Non-governmental organisations (NGOs) These are sometimes referred to as pressure groups and include a wide variety of interested parties and bodies outside government which are active in environmental and other issues

Opportunity cost The next best alternative forgone when making a decision on allocating scarce resources

Supranational bodies Institutions and agencies whose remit crosses national boundaries.

References and further reading

Bowers, J. (1997) *Sustainability and Environmental Economics,* Longman, Harlow, especially Chapter 1.

Donaldson, T. and Dunfee, T.W. (1999) 'When ethics travel: the promise and peril of global business ethics', *California Management Review,* **41**, 4.

Field, B.C. (1997) *Environmental Economics: An Introduction,* McGraw-Hill, Singapore, especially Chapters 1 and 2.

Gilpin, A. (2000) *Environmental Economics: A Critical Overview,* Wiley, Chichester, especially Chapters 1 and 2.

Griffin, R.W. and Pustay, M.W. (1996) *International Business: A Managerial Perspective,* Addison Wesley, Harlow.

Hofstede, G. (1980) *Culture's Consequences,* Sage.

Reinhardt, F.L. (1999) *Down to Earth: Applying Business Principles to Environmental Management,* Harvard Business School Press, Boston, Mass.

Tayeb, M. (2000) *International Business: Theories, Policies and Practices,* FT/Prentice Hall, Harlow, especially Chapters 4, 13 and 19.

Useful websites

www.co-operativebank.co.uk/ethics
www.earthchartersummits.org/history
Environment Agency
Environment: (EC DGXI)
World Health organisation
United Nations
Office for National Statistics (ONS)
ONS Statstore and Statbase
Central Office of Information
Eurostat
International Monetary Fund (IMF)
Organisation for Economic Co-operation and Development (OECD)
United Nations development Program (UNDP)
World Bank

2

Valuing the environment

This chapter reviews a number of approaches which seek to place a 'value' on environmental changes, whether 'favourable' (benefits) or 'unfavourable' (costs). Sometimes the market mechanism may help in terms of monetary valuations by yielding prices for products derived from environmental assets. However, these market prices may be distorted by various types of 'failure' in the market mechanism (e.g. monopolies or externalities), so that some adjustment may be needed to these prices. For example, 'shadow prices' may be used, i.e. market prices which are adjusted in order to reflect the valuation to *society* of a particular activity.

On other occasions there may be no market prices to adjust, in which case we may need to use questionnaires to derive *hypothetical* valuations of 'willingness to pay' for an environmental amenity or 'willingness to accept' compensation for an environmental loss. These expressed preference methods of valuation differ from revealed preference methods which seek to observe how consumers *actually* behave in the market place for products which are substitutes or complements to the activities for which no market prices exist.

The issue of time is particularly important for monetary valuation of environmental impacts which may take many years to materialise. We therefore pay close attention to the process of calculating the *present value* of a stream of future revenues or costs, using the technique of discounting.

Many of the techniques discussed in the chapter are applied to public sector projects with environmental implications using a cost–benefit analysis (CBA) approach. The principles and practices of this approach to monetary valuation are carefully reviewed. So too are techniques seeking to identify non-monetary environmental impacts under the broad heading of environmental impact analysis (EIA).

Monetary valuation of environmental impacts must sometimes take explicit account of the *risk factors* which apply in various situations. By applying probabilities to different possible outcomes of events we can calculate the 'expected values' of those events or of different 'scenarios' associated with those events. Such risk factors are particularly important when valuing environmental risks to life and health as well as when valuing environmental disasters.

The chapter concludes by reviewing attempts to value the environment in the context of the national accounts. Recent attempts have been made to identify an 'Index of Sustainable Economic Welfare' (ISEW) which more accurately reflects depreciation of environmental as well as physical capital assets.

●●●● Total economic value

In recent years there has been considerable discussion as to how to find the 'total economic value' (TEV) of an environmental asset. The following identity has been suggested:

Total economic value ≡ Use value + Option value + Existence value

- **Use value.** The idea here is that 'use value' reflects the practical uses to which an environmental asset is currently being put. For example, the tropical rainforests are used to provide arable land for crop cultivation or to rear cattle in various ranching activities. The forests are also a source of various products, such as timber, rubber, medicines, nuts, etc. In addition, the forests act as the 'lungs of the world', absorbing stores of CO_2 and releasing oxygen, as well as helping to prevent soil erosion and playing an important part in flood control. Market values, via the price mechanism, can help in estimating at least some of these 'use values' (see page 28).
- **Option value.** There are obvious difficulties in deriving reliable monetary estimates for all these aspects of the 'use value' of the rainforest. However, it is even more difficult to estimate 'option value', which refers to the value we place on the asset now as regards functions which might be exploited some time in the future. For example, how much are we willing to pay to preserve the rainforests in case they become a still more important source of herbal and other medicines? This is a type of insurance value, seeking to measure the willingness of individuals (or groups) to pay for an environmental asset now, given some probability function of the likelihood of the individuals (or groups) wishing to use that asset in various ways in the future.
- **Existence value.** This refers to the value we place on an environmental asset as it is today, independently of any current or future use we might make of that asset. This is an attempt to measure our willingness to pay for an environmental asset simply because we wish it to continue to exist in its present form. Many people subscribe to charities to preserve the rainforests, other natural habitats or wildlife even though they may never themselves see those habitats or species. Existence value may involve intergenerational motives, such as wishing to give one's children or grandchildren the opportunity to observe certain species or ecosystems (i.e. existence value may incorporate an element of 'bequest value').

Overall, many estimates are finding that the 'option' and 'existence' values of environmental assets often far exceed their 'use' value. For example, existence values for the Grand Canyon were found to outweigh use values by the startling ratio of 60 to 1 (Pearce, 1991). In similar vein, non-users of Prince William Sound, Alaska, devastated by the Exxon Valdez oil spill in 1989, placed an extremely high value on its existence value (O'Doherty, 1994). The amounts non-users were estimated (via interviews) as willing to pay to avoid the damage actually incurred came to $2.8 bn, i.e. $31 per US household. This approach whereby interviewees are asked about the value of a resource 'contingent' on its not being damaged, is often termed 'contingent valuation' (see page 32).

However, there is a major problem in deriving 'non-use' valuations (option + existence). For example, a study of the River Darent in Kent (Garrod and Willis, 1996) had estimated non-use values to be just under 90 per cent of the total benefit ascribed to proposed modifications to this river. In other words, 90 per cent of the willingness to pay for flow improvement was ascribed to individuals who did not visit the Darent at all. The Thames Water Company subsequently used the findings of this study of the River Darent to estimate £13.2 m. as the non-use value of the River Kennet. However, a subsequent legal review by a government inspector dramatically reduced those non-use value estimates by 98 per cent from £13.2 m. to only £0.3 m., highlighting the rather subjective and problematic issues involved in deriving non-use values. We return to some of these issues below.

Market prices and value

All three elements of 'total economic value' are difficult to assess, but at least the market can help to some extent with 'use value'. For example, where an (environmental) asset is expected to yield various products to which market prices are attached, then there will be actual revenues (price × quantity) in the current time period and expected revenues in future time periods. The present value of any future revenue stream can then be calculated. Such revenue streams may be projected for the products, whether goods or services, of an environmental asset and are often expressed in *net* values, i.e. after deducting the estimated variable costs of providing the respective outputs in each future time period.

The ideas of *present value* (PV) and *discounting* can help us estimate the return on environmental assets yielding monetary returns (e.g. 'use values') over future time periods. Environmental assets (or liabilities) often involve projected returns (or losses) which persist long into the future. Briefly reviewing PV and discounting in Box 2.1 will therefore be useful to many issues of valuation encountered in this and subsequent chapters.

BOX 2.1

Present value and discounting

Discounting is the process of reducing a future flow of expected monetary values to a *present value* equivalent. You should be familiar with the idea that the *discount factor* applied to a given future sum £A is such that:

$$\text{Present value (PV) of £A received in year } t = £A \times \frac{1}{(1 + i)^t}$$

where t = rate of discount (as a decimal)

i = number of years to expected return

$\dfrac{1}{(1 + i)^t}$ = discount factor

▶

So, for example, a sum of £1,000 received in five years' time when discounted at an annual rate of 10 per cent will be worth today:

$$PV = £1,000 \times \frac{1}{(1 + 0.10)^5}$$

$$= £1,000 \times 0.6209$$
$$= £620.90$$

In other words, under these conditions you would be indifferent between a sum of £1,000 in five years' time and a sum of £620.90 today.

Net present value (NPV) is found by subtracting the cost in today's terms (supply price) of the project from the present value of the expected future receipts, i.e.

NPV = Present value of future receipts − Initial cost of project

For a project yielding a stream of expected future returns in each of the next n years, we can write:

$$NPV = \sum_{t=1}^{n} \frac{R_t}{(1+i)^t} - C_0$$

where R_t = expected return in year t
n = number of years
$\sum_{t=1}^{n}$ = sum of the present discounted values of future returns over n years
i = annual rate of discount (as a decimal)
C_0 = initial cost of project (supply price)

Market mechanism

Figure 2.1(a) outlines the familiar market mechanism, with a unique 'equilibrium' price P_1 and quantity Q_1. Only at this price/quantity combination does the market 'clear', in the sense that all the product supplied is demanded by consumers.

A stylised version of the *market mechanism* in competitive conditions suggests that no other price/quantity solution is feasible:

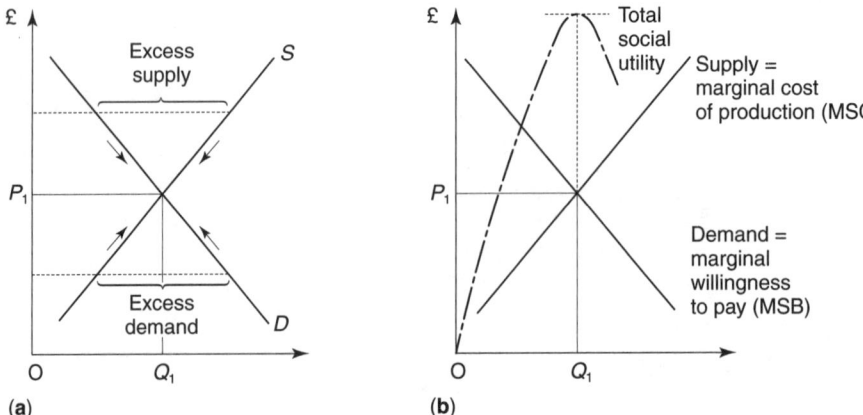

Figure 2.1 Role of the market mechanism: (a) 'clearing' the market; (b) maximising social utility via the market mechanism

- At prices above P_1, *excess supply* will induce producers to lower prices (to avoid carrying unsold stock), encouraging some consumers to demand more of this product and some producers to supply less. This adjustment mechanism will continue until equilibrium (balance) between buyers and sellers is reached at P_1/Q_1.
- At prices below P_1, *excess demand* provides opportunities for producers to raise prices (and therefore profit margins), encouraging some consumers to desist from buying this product and some producers to supply more (switching scarce productive resources into this product and away from the now less attractive alternatives). Again these adjustments will continue until equilibrium (balance) between buyers and sellers is reached at P_1/Q_1.

Perfect markets

Figure 2.1(b) represents an idealised world of competitive markets. Here price not only acts as a 'signal' to co-ordinate and harmonise thousands of independent decisions by producers and consumers in order to bring about a market equilibrium, it also acts as an appropriate measure of value. 'Appropriate' in the sense that the market price reflects the extra resource cost to society of producing the last unit of output of that product. Put another way, the market price reflects the *marginal social cost* (MSC) of production. The market price also reflects the consumers' (marginal) willingness to pay for the last unit of that product, which might be regarded as the *marginal social benefit* (MSB) of consumption.

The outcome of such a situation is believed by supporters of the market mechanism to be an allocation of resources which maximises social utility, with MSC = MSB. Each unit of output beyond Q_1 would reduce total social utility (MSB < MSC); each unit of output up to Q_1 would increase total social utility (MSB > MSC). Total social utility can only be a maximum at the equilibrium price P_1 and quantity Q_1.

However, such an outcome depends on a number of competitive market conditions being fulfilled, including the following:

(a) Large numbers of producers and consumers
(b) Market prices reflecting the full costs of production and consumption
(c) Perfect information in product and factor markets
(d) Ability of producers to exclude from consumption those unwilling to pay

In practice such an idealised economic system is wholly impractical. Instead we are faced with the real world situation of *market failure* in which one or more of these conditions are broken. As a result we often encounter situations in which 'inappropriate' prices are established which distort valuations or where no prices at all exist.

●●●● Market failure: valuation remedies

Using 'shadow prices'

Where market prices exist, it is at least feasible to obtain monetary valuations of future net revenues from an environmental asset. However, where one or more market failures occur, these prices may be deemed 'inappropriate' and in need of adjustment to more accurately reflect the true benefits and costs to society. Such adjustments give rise to **shadow prices**, i.e. prices which do not actually exist in the market place but which are assumed to exist for purposes of valuation. Box 2.2 illustrates the type of price adjustments which must be made when market failures occur.

As can be seen from Figure 2.2 in Box 2.2, the actual market price is too low (P) when compared to the 'appropriate' market price (P_S) corresponding to the best interests of society. Should government policy be unable to 'correct' this discrepancy (by tax or regulation) then, for valuation purposes, the product from this activity should be given a higher 'shadow price' of P_S and actual output Q compared to the actual market price of P and lower output Q_s.

BOX 2.2

Environmental impacts and 'shadow prices'

For the purposes of our analysis, we shall assume that two 'market failures' occur.

- One market failure involves an element of *monopoly power* in that the demand curve (D = AR) for the firm is negatively sloped instead of horizontal (perfectly elastic). Any extra output by the firm is significant in terms of industry output, so the firm must reduce its price in order to sell the extra output (rather than be able to sell all its output at the current market price). As a result the marginal revenue curve (MR) lies inside the demand curve (D = AR). Here we assume that the marginal revenue curve reflects both the marginal private benefit (MPB) of the firm and the marginal social benefit (MSB) of society.
- Another market failure involves an element of *externality* (see also Chapter 3, pages 59–61). In our analysis such an externality does not exist on the revenue (benefit) side (MPB = MSB) but does exist on the cost side (MSC > MPC). The suggestion here is that each extra unit of output produced by the firm adds more to the costs of society (MSC) than it does to the costs of the (private) firm (MPC).

If the production process results in environmental damage that the producer does not (at least initially) have to pay for, then *marginal social cost* (MSC) will be greater than *marginal private cost* (MPC). This is the case in Figure 2.2. The private cost *to the firm* of producing one more unit of output (MPC) is rising, due to extra labour, raw material or capital costs. However the cost *to society* of producing that extra unit of output (MSC) is rising by more than the cost to the firm (MSC > MPC). This is because of the environmental damage (e.g. emission of CO_2) caused by producing the last unit of output, which is a cost to society (e.g. ill health) even if not to the firm. The true cost to society of producing the last unit of output does include the cost to the firm (MPC) of using factor inputs (since these scarce factors are thereby *denied* to other firms). However, the true cost to society also includes any environmental damage caused by producing the last unit of output. We call any such damage the *marginal external cost* (MEC). We can therefore state that:

$$\text{Marginal social cost} = \text{Marginal private cost} + \text{Marginal external cost}$$
$$\text{MSC} \qquad = \qquad \text{MPC} \qquad + \qquad \text{MEC}$$

In Figure 2.2 a profit-maximising firm will equate MPC with MR, producing output OQ and selling this at price OP. However, from society's point of view the appropriate output is that which equates MSC with MR (which represents here both marginal private benefit and marginal social benefit), producing output OQ_S and selling this at price OP_S. Only at this output is total social utility a maximum.

▶

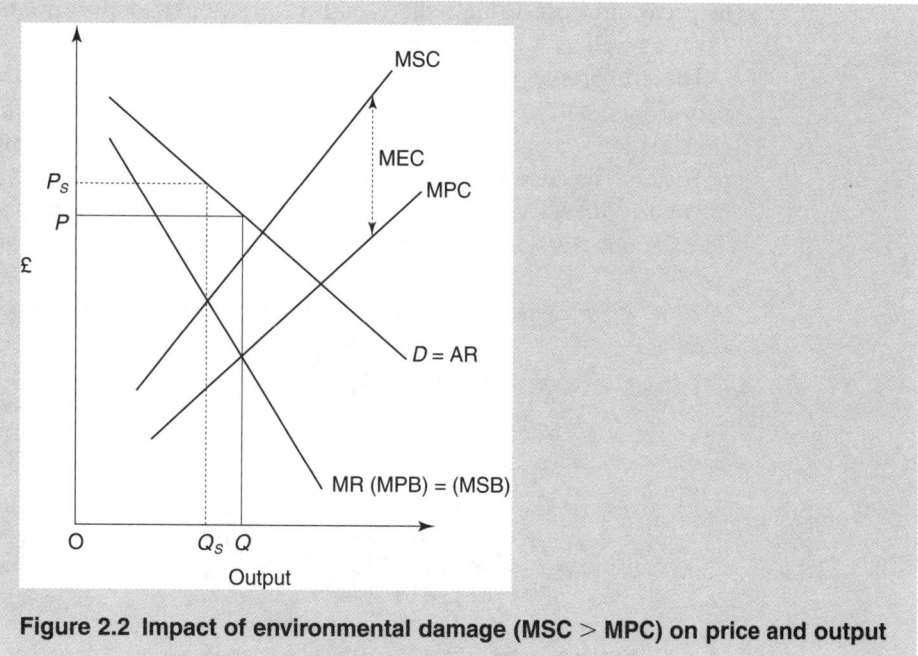

Figure 2.2 Impact of environmental damage (MSC > MPC) on price and output

Chapter 4 looks in more detail at the various policies available to governments for dealing with externalities. What is important to note here is that, left unadjusted, the market price shown in Figure 2.2 is inappropriate for valuation purposes. An adjusted ('shadow') price is therefore required.

In some cases, however, there may be no market price to adjust in order to derive a 'shadow price'. 'Expressed preference' and/or 'revealed preference' methods may then be used for valuation purposes.

Expressed preference methods

Where no market price exists individuals are often asked, using surveys or questionnaires, to express how much they would be *willing to pay* for some specified environmental improvement, such as improved water quality or the preservation of a threatened local amenity. In other words, an 'expressed preference' approach is taken to valuation. An example of the use of this approach is given in Case Study 2.1 (page 37) which uses survey evidence to estimate what individuals would be prepared to pay to reduce the risk of fatal and non-fatal accidents. A similar approach to valuation was used in Ukunda, Kenya, where residents were faced with a choice between three sources of water – door-to-door vendors, kiosks and wells – each requiring residents to pay different costs in money and time. Water from door-to-door vendors cost the most but required the least collection time. A study found that the villagers were willing to pay a substantial share of their incomes – about 8 per cent – in exchange for this greater convenience and for time saved. Such valuations can be helpful in seeking to make the case for extending reliable public water supply even to poorer communities. Questionnaires and surveys of willingness-to-pay have been widely used in the UK to evaluate the recreational benefits of environmental amenities. They can help capture 'use value' where market prices are inappropriate or do not even exist, as well as 'option' and 'existence' values.

These 'expressed preference' methods are sometimes referred to as 'contingent valuation' methods, since the users' 'willingness to pay' (WTP) is often sought for different situations 'contingent upon' some improvement in the (environmental) quality of provision. The same approach may involve asking individuals how much they are *willing to accept* (WTA) to avoid some specific environmental degradation. Box 2.3 outlines various types of contingent valuation approaches and some associated problems.

BOX 2.3

Types of contingent valuations

A number of methods may be used to derive 'willingness to pay' or 'willingness to accept' values for various situations (contingencies).

1 *Bidding games*: where individuals are simply asked how much they are willing to pay to bring about a particular environmental improvement (or willing to accept to avoid a particular environmental degradation). The 'option' and 'existence' values of an environmental characteristic can be assessed in this way.
2 *Convergent direct questioning*: where the individual is asked to respond to pre-existing 'low' values (above which they would certainly be willing to pay/below which they would certainly be unwilling to accept) and 'high' values (above which they would certainly be unwilling to pay/below which they would certainly be willing to accept). These extreme values are progressively narrowed (minimum raised, maximum reduced) until an 'equilibrium' value is attained.
3 *Trade-off games*: where each individual must rank various combinations of two items: one a sum of money, the other some environmental characteristic (e.g. clean water). For any *pair* of combinations, the individual must state a preference for one combination over the other, or state indifference between the two combinations. The marginal rate of substitution between money and a particular environmental characteristic can then be estimated at the point of indifference.
4 *Priority evaluation*: where each individual is given a hypothetical sum of money to spend on different combinations of everyday products and environmental characteristics with assumed 'prices' (which are allowed to vary between different combinations).

The budget limitation ensures that specific choices must be made, from which marginal valuations of environmental characteristics can be inferred.

Problems. Whatever the method chosen for contingent valuation, certain problems often occur.

● *'Free rider' problem*. Analysis shows that people often understate their WTP in questionnaires by between 10 and 30 per cent of the amount they actually do eventually pay. This suggests that in such questionnaires they may be attempting to 'free ride', i.e. understating their true WTP with the intention of restricting any actual payments, believing that the WTP of others will ensure the environmental amenity is provided.
● *Bias*. The values given for WTP depend to some extent on the ways in which the questions are framed:
  – *starting point bias*: the higher the initial value suggested for any starting bid, the higher the eventual WTP value declared;
  – *route bias*: the less realistic the route chosen for collecting the monies involved (e.g. charitable giving), the smaller the eventual WTP value declared;

▶

- *part–whole bias*: the less attention given in the questionnaire to reminding respondents of their budget constraints, the greater the WTP value declared for individual parts of an environmental 'package' relative to the whole;
- *WTP > WTA*: the 'willingness to pay' for a specific environmental benefit tends to exceed the 'willingness to accept' compensation values for giving up the same environmental asset.

Revealed preference methods

This approach seeks to avoid relying on the use of questionnaires or surveys to gain an impression of the *hypothetical* valuations placed by consumers on various environmental costs and benefits. Instead it seeks to use direct observation of the consumers' *actual* responses to various substitute or complementary goods and services to gain an estimate of value in a particular environmental situation. The focus here is on the 'revealed preferences' of the consumers as expressed in the market place, even if this expression is indirect in that it involves surrogate goods and services rather than the environmental amenity itself.

(a) Travel cost method (TCM)

Where no price is charged for entry to recreational sites, economists have searched for private market goods or services whose consumption is complementary to the consumption of the recreational good in question. One such private complementary good is the travel costs incurred by individuals to gain access to recreational sites. The 'price' paid to visit any site is uniquely determined for each visitor by calculating the travel costs from his/her location of origin. By observing people's willingness to pay for the private complementary good or service it is then possible to infer a price for the non-price environmental amenity.

In Figure 2.3 the demand curve D_{visits} shows the overall trend relationship between travel costs and visit rates for all the visitors interviewed. Using this infor-

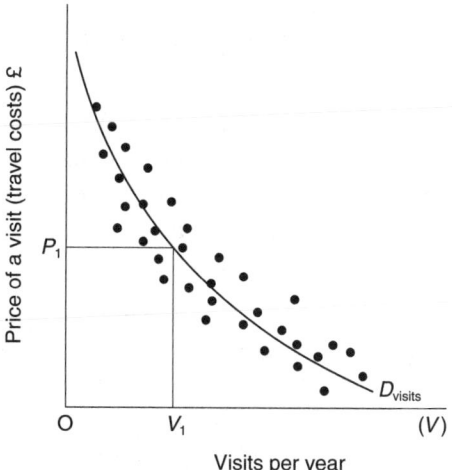

Figure 2.3 The relationship between the number of visits to a site and the price of the visit

mation we can estimate the average visitor's (V_1) total recreational value ($V_1 \times P_1$) for the site. Multiplying this by the total number of visitors per annum allows us to estimate the total annual recreational value of the site.

Problems. A number of problems occur when using the travel cost method for valuation:

- *Time costs.* Take, for example, travel costs estimated for car users. These are usually derived from the mileage travelled in visiting a site for different categories of vehicle, leading to estimates of petrol cost, vehicle depreciation, etc. However, the time 'costs' of the various occupants of the car in visiting the site may considerably outweigh these more direct travel costs. These are often omitted from TCM studies.
- *Apportionment.* If visitors go to more than one environmental amenity in a single day's journey, how do we apportion travel costs between the various sites?
- *Availability of rival amenities.* How do we take into account the fact that some visitors travel *x* miles to a particular site because no equivalent is within similar range of their initial location, but other visitors travel *x* miles to this site even when other equivalents are within similar range of their initial location?
- *Non-travelling visitors.* How do we value under TCM those who incur no travel costs to visit a site on their doorstep even when such visits are clearly valued by these individuals?

(b) Hedonic price method (HPM)

A further technique often used in deriving valuations where no prices exist, is the so-called 'hedonic price' method. This estimates the extent to which people are, for example, willing to pay a house price premium for the benefit of living within easy access of an environmental amenity. It could equally be used to estimate the house price discount resulting from living within easy access of a source of environmental concern.

House and other property prices are clearly determined by a number of independent variables. Some of these will involve variables related to the following:

- *Characteristics of the property*; number of rooms, whether detached, semi-detached or terraced, garage facilities available, etc.
- *Characteristics of the location*; number (and reputation) of schools, availability of shopping and recreational facilities, transport infrastructure, etc.
- *Characteristics of the environment*; proximity to favourable or unfavourable environmental factors.

Statistical techniques (such as multiple regression analysis) can be used to estimate the influence of these possible 'explanatory' (independent) variables on house and property prices. For example, a 'classic' statistical study of the impact of traffic noise in Washington, DC established an inverse relationship between house prices and the environmental factor 'noise pollution'; specifically each extra decibel of noise was statistically correlated with a 0.88 per cent fall in average house prices (Nelson, 1982).

Problems. A number of statistical problems are often encountered when using the hedonic price method for valuation:

- *Multicollinearity.* The variables designed as influencing house prices may themselves be correlated, so that it may be impossible to separate out the influence of the environmental variables. For example, if detached houses with larger numbers of rooms tend to be located in areas with least noise pollution, then it will be difficult to quantify the separate influences of these variables on house prices.
- *Identification problem.* House prices depend not only on demand-side factors (such as environmental quality), but also on supply-side factors, such as land availability for house building, government incentives to house builders, etc. Changes in house prices may then depend on variables which are outside our model and which are unrelated to environmental factors. In statistical terms, the demand curve for housing cannot clearly be 'identified'.

Non-demand curve valuations

Essentially both the expressed contingent and revealed preference methods are making use of demand curve analysis in placing monetary values on aspects of environmental quality. However, a number of valuation methods may be used which depart from this approach.

Replacement cost method

The focus here is on the cost of replacing or restoring a damaged asset. This cost estimate is then used as a measure of the 'benefit' from such replacement or restoration. For example, if it costs £1 m. to restore the façade of buildings damaged by air pollution, then this £1 m. cost is used as an estimate of the benefit of environmental improvement.

Preventative expenditure method

The focus here is on using the costs incurred in an attempt to prevent some potential environmental damage as a measure of 'benefit'. For example, the expenditure incurred by residents on double glazing to avoid 'noise pollution' from a new trunk road might be used as a proxy variable of the value placed by residents on noise abatement.

Delphi method

The focus here is on valuations derived from consulting a group of recognised experts. Each member of the group responds independently to questions as to the valuations that might be placed on various (environmental) contingencies in their area of expertise. The initial responses of the group are then summarised in graphical or tabular form, with each member given the opportunity to reevaluate their individual responses. The idea here is that through successive rounds of re-evaluation, a consensus valuation of the expert group may eventually emerge.

Cost–benefit analysis (CBA)

Under CBA, the techniques already discussed and others are used to assign monetary values to the gains and losses to different individuals and groups, often weighted according to some perception of the contribution of these individuals or groups to social utility (social welfare). It is for this reason that this approach is sometimes referred to as 'social' cost–benefit analysis. Some of the 'market failures' previously identified are taken into account, with some existing market prices adjusted (e.g. via weighting) and values attributed to some situations where no market prices currently exist. If the proposed reallocation of resources via new investment in some (environmental) project is evaluated as creating a monetary value that is greater to those who gain than the costs imposed on those who lose, then the project is potentially viable from society's perspective. In other words, if the net present value to society of a project is positive, then the project is at least worthy of consideration. Whether or not it will be undertaken may depend upon what restrictions, if any, apply to the level of resources (finance) available. If such resources are limited and must be rationed, then of course only those projects with the highest (positive) net present values to society may be selected.

Road transport

CBA was first used in a transport context in the UK during the 1960s to evaluate the M1 motorway. It led to the development of a computer-based technique called COBA used by the Department of Transport. This has been modified over the years, and is applied to inter-urban road schemes.

COBA acts as a benchmark, since it places monetary values on certain road user benefits, some of which are not readily available via the use of market prices and which may involve aspects of environmental quality. Unfortunately, from an environmental perspective, some environmental costs and benefits are excluded: noise and community severance and pollution are excluded mainly because of the difficulty in calculating them accurately. For example, it is difficult to determine what aspects of noise cause disutility. Is it loud, intermittent or persistent noise? Even if this could be determined, what monetary value should be put on the disutility? As well as excluding these environmental factors, no attempt is made to evaluate the direct costs and benefits of particular road projects to the regional or national economy, because these are also considered to be too difficult to estimate. The following analysis focuses on the ways in which monetary values are placed on those costs and benefits that are evaluated in COBA and representing similar models in the transport context.

CASE STUDY 2.1

Using CBA to value road improvements in the UK

Costs

When considering the COBA appraisal, the costs of any new road scheme can be divided into two distinct headings:

1 *The construction and preparation of roads.* A major component of cost is the construction work undertaken, involving earthworks, bridge building, noise abatement measures, and the acquisition of land, possibly through compulsory purchase. There is also the cost of public consultation and inquiry.

2 *Maintenance costs.* The construction of any new road will lead to changes in the costs of road maintenance. Such costs will be incurred on items such as lighting (which is not directly related to the traffic flow) and resurfacing (which is directly related to the traffic flow). Maintenance work itself subjects the road user to delays and thereby results in time, accident and vehicle operating costs incurred while the maintenance is under way.

Benefits

Road user benefits included in COBA cover journey time savings, accident cost savings and savings in vehicle operating costs.

Journey time savings

Forecasts have to be made as to the type of journey (e.g. for work or for leisure) and how many trips of each type are undertaken, so that an estimate of the time savings can be made. Such time savings are divided into working time and leisure time savings, and together they comprise the major benefit of new road schemes.

Working time savings are valued as a benefit to the employer, because it is assumed that they can be used in the production of a good or service. These savings are estimated by using the national average wage rate as a measure of the value of any unit of time saved. However, it is debatable whether small increments of time saved have real economic value when aggregated over a large number of vehicles. For example, it is quite obvious that one hour saved on a work journey can be of benefit in terms of the output that could have been produced in that time, but it is less clear how important a time saving of one minute would be. Also it is unclear, for example, whether a saving of one minute to 60 road users is equivalent to a time saving of one hour for one road user.

Non-working time savings are still more difficult to calculate because there is no economic market for leisure time. The way such leisure time savings are calculated is by observing actual travel behaviour and establishing individual preferences, as expressed through interviews and surveys. This technique involves asking individual travellers hypothetical questions in order to obtain information about what they would be prepared to pay in order to save time when undertaking journeys. On this basis the valuation of non-working (leisure) time is estimated to be 40 per cent of the value used for working time.

Accident cost savings

In the UK until quite recently, the *human capital approach* was used to place a monetary value on accidents. This approach placed a value on the gross contribution (in terms of lost output) that the victim of an accident would have made to the economy. It also included the direct cost in terms of damage to vehicles, plus the associated police and medical costs. An allowance, which was quite arbitrary, was also made for the pain, grief and suffering incurred by the victim.

Although the human capital approach is still used in a number of European countries, Britain now uses the *willingness to pay approach*. This approach assigns monetary values to fatal and non-fatal accidents. The values are based on research surveys that established what individuals would be prepared to pay to reduce the risk of fatal accidents and various types of non-fatal accidents. Basically, individuals are asked to place a value on safety. To this is added an allowance for things such as medical costs and vehicle damage. This new method of valuation has tended to place a higher value on accidents than the previous human capital approach. As a result the benefits from accident savings have increased on average from 15 per cent to 25 per cent of the total benefit of any COBA scheme.

By the late 1990s the average cost per casualty in the UK was £812,010 for a fatality, £92,570 for a serious casualty and £7,170 for a slight casualty. This gave an average valuation (the respective probabilities used as weights) for all casualties of £29,080.

Vehicle operating costs

Vehicle operating costs are a function of distance and speed, and comprise fuel, tyres, oil, maintenance and depreciation. Unlike the benefits of time savings and savings brought about by reduced accidents, overall vehicle operating costs as a result of a new road scheme can be either positive or negative.

Discounting

We have already considered aspects of discounting (Box 2.1). When undertaking a road scheme the majority of the costs will be incurred first, followed by a number of years of benefit, and this time profile must be taken into account when assessing a road investment scheme. However, because costs and benefits occur in different years it is necessary to express their values in terms of a particular year, i.e. the present value year. The technique of discounting is used to obtain the net present value (NPV) of a stream of future costs and benefits from a particular scheme, covering a 30-year period from the time the road is opened. The equation for the NPV can be shown as:

$$\text{NPV} = (B - C)_0 + \frac{(B - C)_1}{(1 + r)^1} + \frac{(B - C)_2}{(1 + r)^2} + ... + \frac{(B - C)_n}{(1 + r)^n}$$

In the equation, B refers to the benefits and C the costs (including the capital costs) of the particular road scheme. The subscripts $0,1,...n$ refer to the number of years over which the costs and benefits are said to occur (namely 30 years), and r is the discount rate (which is currently set by the Department of Transport at 8 per cent). The benefits (B) are assessed on a 'do-minimum and do-something' basis. The do-minimum scheme is the existing road network with only minor improvements, and the do-something scheme is the existing road network plus the new road being proposed. There will be user costs associated with each network, namely the time it takes to travel on the route, the number of accidents, and the operating costs of the vehicles. The difference between the user costs on the do-minimum and the do-something network is discounted to form the user benefit (*B*) of the new road scheme being proposed.

The costs (*C*) as stated above comprise the purchase of land, construction and maintenance costs. In terms of the equation, if the NPV is positive then it indicates that the scheme is economically justified. In order to compare projects that are of different sizes, it is necessary to divide the NPV by the capital costs, thus producing the NPV/*C* ratio, which can be used as a means of ranking projects. As stated in the UK government's *Expenditure Plans for Transport,* 'The average benefit:cost ratio of schemes in the national road programme, which have reached the stage of having a validated cost benefit assessment based on current traffic forecasts is 2.3:1.'

As noted previously, the major benefits of a new road scheme are the savings in terms of time and reduced accidents, and these are based on estimates of future traffic flows. It is important therefore to obtain figures on actual flows once a road scheme is in operation, in order to establish how successful the original Department of Transport forecasts have been.

> **Questions**
>
> **1** What modifications might you make on (a) the cost side and (b) the benefit side, if the environment is to be more fully represented in the COBA approach to road building by the Department of Transport?
>
> **2** Can you see any problems in implementing your suggestions?

CBA and large dam irrigation projects

Cost–benefit analysis has been extensively applied to the technical, financial and economic performances of large dams and irrigation projects. Performance indicators for large dam irrigation projects have typically included the following, to which monetary values of costs and benefits have then been applied:

- *Capital costs.* Large dams typically incur huge construction costs; over $6 bn for each of the three begun in 2001. The World Commission on Dams (WCD) has also suggested an average cost overrun of 56 per cent on initial estimates across the 81 large dam projects it surveyed (WCD, 2001). However much of this cost overrun has involved underestimates of future rates of inflation, so that the real economic costs of the materials and resources used have only actually risen by 21 per cent in terms of constant 1998 dollars.

- *Increased area of irrigation.* Many of the benefits to which monetary valuations have been applied, result from the projected increases in land under irrigation. About 20 per cent of the world's agricultural land is irrigated and irrigated agricultural land accounts for about 40 per cent of the world's agricultural production. In practice only around 70 per cent of the projected increase in area under irrigation has been achieved within five years of completion of the large dams. A study of 35 irrigation projects found actual cropped areas at between 60 per cent and 85 per cent of planned levels (WCD, 2001). This has generally reduced the actual output volumes for various crops well below those projected at the planning phase. However, values of crops have often fallen still further behind initial estimates. This has been linked to more rapid falls in the world prices of agricultural products than had been anticipated. For example in real terms, world prices for grains in 2001 are around half those existing in the 1950s.

- *Electricity generation.* This has been an important factor in the construction of many large dams. Hydropower currently provides 19 per cent of the world's electricity supply and is used in over 150 countries.
- *Flood protection.* Around 13 per cent of all large dams have a flood management function.
- *Social impacts.* The construction and operation of large dams have often had major impacts on human settlement patterns. Arguably, adverse population impacts include families directly displaced, host communities where families are resettled, river-based communities whose livelihood and access to resources are affected by altered river flows and ecosystems impacts, and so on.

In recent times decisions as to whether or not to proceed with major dam projects have depended largely on cost–benefit analyses, with 10 per cent rates of discount applied. Only those which have a positive NPV at this 'hurdle' rate of discount have tended to go ahead. Case Study 2.2 looks at the application of this approach to the Columbia Basin Project in the USA.

CASE STUDY 2.2

Using CBA to value the Columbia Basin Project

The Grand Coulee Dam was commissioned in 1941 as a 170 m high dam constructed on the Columbia River flowing between the USA and Canada. It involves a 270 m^2 reservoir which irrigates 276,000 ha of land and provides over 24,000 GWh per year of hydroelectric power. Some 6,000 people had to be resettled during its construction. At the time of its building, little attempt was made to justify the huge projected costs which in 1998 dollars, have been estimated at over $9 bn. However looking backwards, attempts have been made in recent years to identify and evaluate (*ex post*) the various costs and benefits of the dam. The WCD (2001) Case Study of the dam identified the following impacts:

- *Electricity production:* 24,050 GWh/yr supplied to industrial and agricultural sectors and to urban areas
- *Irrigation:* 276,700 ha, serving over 1,400 farms, yielding $637 m. per year (1998 $)
- *Tourism:* 3 million visitors per year, creating several thousand jobs to service 44 major tourist facilities, parks and recreation areas
- *Displacement:* over 6,000 indigenous people were physically displaced. In 1994 some $54 m. was awarded by the US courts to indigenous people for past losses. Ongoing compensation of $15 m. per year was awarded thereafter
- *Ecosystem:* high hydropower dams increase the gaseous content of water when it flows over the spillway, causing fish death (5–14 per cent of salmon stocks have been depleted via this effect along the Columbia River)

- *Cultural heritage*: ancestral homes and burial sites have been submerged by the dam waters
- *Construction*: some 10,000–15,000 workers were continuously employed during the construction period
- *Water diversion*: the 'opportunity cost' of water diverted in constructing the dam and in irrigating the Columbia Basin has been estimated at $39 m. per year

The building of the Grand Coulee Dam led directly to the major irrigation project in the Columbia basin in 1945, known thereafter as the Columbia Basin Project (CBP). This was never expected to cover its costs and was criticised by early opponents because it would not be economically profitable. Yet the WCD Case Study reports that a $2,150 per hectare increase in assessed land values has occurred for irrigated land within the project area. When applied to the 268,000 ha under cultivation, the capitalised increase in the value of the land would be $637 m. in 1998 dollars. Nevertheless even if the full value of this increase was due to the CBP alone, it is clear that it would not come close to the real cost of $3.6 bn (out of $9 bn overall for the Grand Coulee Dam) attributed to the CBD using 1998 dollars.

However, a better approach to assessing the project is to compare the *present value* of costs of the project with that of the benefits. The WCD Case Study in 1998 calculated the present value of CBP costs at $1.47 bn at a 10 per cent discount rate, well below the reported figure of $3.6 bn due to the long development period for implementing the irrigation projects and the effect of discounting. Whereas the costs can be reduced by this approach, the estimated value of benefits can be raised. For example, if two simple assumptions are adopted, much higher levels of benefit result. First, if all the average net production value of $500 per hectare per year as reported by a recent study of the CBP is now attributed to irrigation (i.e. as a return to irrigated water and not to improvements in other farming or capital inputs). Second, if these benefits are now considered to occur for all years since 1945 (the year of project start-up) and to all of the 268,000 ha. The resulting net present value of benefits now estimated as resulting from the CBP from 1945 to 2010 at a 10 per cent discount rate rises sharply to $1.32 bn. Note that the assumptions made are generous, given that in practice the actual acreage and gross value of production increased only gradually over time, and thus the actual magnitude of early economic benefits would have been considerably less than under these 'favourable' estimates.

As the benefits are less than the costs, the results still suggest that the CBP did not achieve a 10 per cent rate of return. Nevertheless this type of *ex-post* evaluation of projects via CBA provides a useful check on whether the assumptions under which decisions were actually made at the time have subsequently been supported by experience.

Questions

1 Using this retrospective CBA, what conclusions might be drawn?

2 Can you suggest how incorporating environmental aspects more explicitly into the (retrospective) CBA approach to the Columbia Basin Project might have influenced its results?

3 Does the use of a 'present value' approach have any significance for the analysis?

Criticisms of cost–benefit analysis

A number of criticisms have been levied against the growing use of CBA in terms of environmental project assessment:

- *Little attention to 'intrinsic value'.* By reflecting human preferences (as in 'willingness to pay') CBA is often criticised for paying too little attention to valuing nature and conservation for its own sake, independent of individual preferences. For example, Stevens *et al.* (1991) notes that 70 per cent or more of respondents agreed with the statement that 'all species of wildlife have a right to exist independent of any benefit or harm to people'. Similarly Fredman (1994) found that 70 per cent of Swedish respondents cited 'rights to existence' in their support for preserving the white-backed woodpecker, and Hanley and Milne (1996) reported some 99 per cent of respondents believing that wildlife and landscape have a right to exist. On the other hand, supporters of CBA suggest that these are merely 'warm glow' perspectives which tend to disappear when faced with real 'opportunity cost' issues. For example, the 99 per cent support for the existence of wildlife and landscape in the Hanley and Milne study shrank to 49 per cent when it was suggested that conservation costs money and jobs, and to 19 per cent when the cost was translated to be 25 per cent of the respondent's income.
- *Too many environmental issues are removed from consideration.* Case Studies 2.1 and 2.2 above certainly suggest a piecemeal approach to environmental considerations and the avoidance of environmental cost–benefit measurements where these are deemed 'too difficult'. However, attempts are being made to rectify this: for example, the UK Environment Agency has devised guidelines for using monetary values in assessing overtly environmental projects.
- *Many environmental standards are determined by non-CBA factors, e.g. threshold exposures.* Even here CBA is often used indirectly in devising target levels for exposure and in determining the time-paths for their achievement (see Chapter 3).
- *Political decisions often override the 'efficiency' considerations of CBA.* This is a widely reported criticism for many public sector projects with an environmental impact. As the World Commission on Dams has noted, 'In some cases, early political or institutional commitment to a project became overriding factors, leading subsequent economic analysis to justify a decision that had in fact already been taken' (WCD, 2001).
- *CBA often fails to embrace wider economic impacts.* For example, multiplier impacts on the wider economy (regional, national) are usually ignored. Broader goals such as employment creation and protection of competitive position are also often ignored.
- *CBA does not explicitly identify who gains and who loses from a project.* Data are invariably at the aggregate rather than the individual level, and redistributive issues between individuals (or groups) tend to be avoided.

Before moving on to a more detailed analysis of the values placed on illness, accident or injury in the context of environmental hazards, it may be useful to review the role of probability in such valuations (see Box 2.4).

BOX 2.4

Probability and valuation

Expected value

The expected value in an uncertain situation is a weighted average of the values associated with each possible outcome, the probabilities of each outcome being used as weights. For a situation in which there are two possible outcomes having values X_1 and X_2, with the probabilities of each outcome p_1 and p_2, respectively, then the expected value $E(X)$ is

$$E(X) = p_1X_1 + p_2X_2$$

For example, if there is a 60 per cent chance of damage valued at £1000 and a 40 per cent chance of damage valued at £5,000 from an environmental hazard then:

$$E(X) = 0.60 \, (£1,000) + 0.40 \, (£5,000)$$

i.e.

$$E(X) = £600 + £2,000 = £2,600$$

More generally, the expected monetary value (EMV) of a particular course of action over n possible outcomes can be defined as

$$EMV = \sum_{i=1}^{n} p_i X_i$$

where p_i = probability of ith outcome
X_i = value of ith outcome and
$$\sum_{i=1}^{n} p_i = 1$$

Scenarios

The probabilities assigned to an (environmental) outcome may be uncertain. In this case analysts may use scenarios, in each of which the probabilities of the various outcomes are assumed to lie in a particular direction, as with 'best case', 'medium case' and 'worst case' scenarios. For example, in the 'best case' scenario the probabilities of various unfavourable environmental outcomes are all assumed to lie in the lower ranges of those which are theoretically possible.

The value of environmental risks to life and health

Attempts to place a monetary value on environmental impacts often involve estimating any associated health effects (favourable or unfavourable) on the human population.

Much attention has been placed in recent years on attempts to value the benefits that individuals place on various risk reduction measures such as environmental improvements. These are often set against the costs of implementing such measures. Box 2.5 reviews the principles involved in placing a monetary value on increased exposure to environmental hazards.

BOX 2.5

Valuing increased exposure to environmental hazards

In terms of the labour market, attempts to place a monetary value on environmental risk have often made use of surveys involving questions such as 'What is the *wage premium* workers receive or require for exposing themselves to additional risk?' Of course any such premiums are the result of both labour supply decisions by individuals and labour demand decisions by firms.

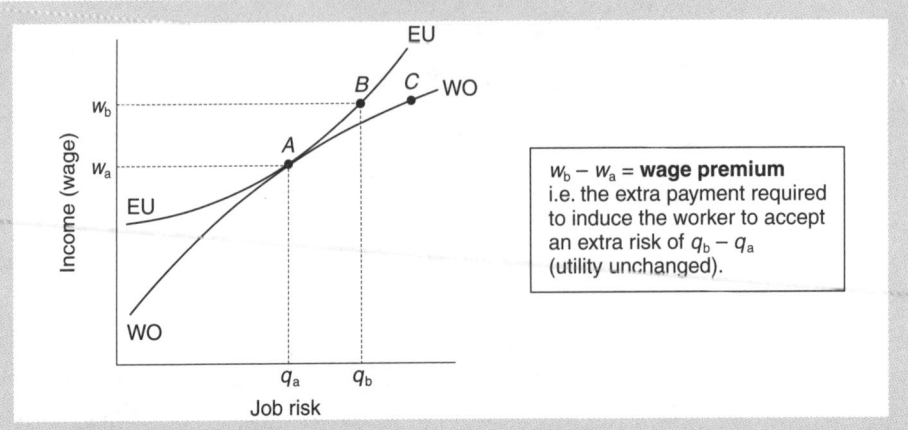

Figure 2.4 The employers' wage offer (WO) curve and the workers' expected utility (EU) curve

In Figure 2.4 we model labour supply decisions by individuals via an *expected utility curve* (EU). This reflects the different combinations of income (wage) and risk yielding a given level of utility. As drawn, the expected utility curve is convex to the horizontal axis, suggesting an element of 'risk aversion' (workers need to be paid progressively more to submit themselves to each extra unit of risk). Figure 2.4 also models labour demand decisions via a *wage offer curve* (WO). This reflects the different combinations of wage and risk yielding a given level of profit to the firm. To maintain the same level of profit, the firm must offer a lower wage rate to offset the additional cost of providing a safer (less risky) work environment. As drawn, the wage offer curve is concave to the horizontal axis, suggesting an increasingly higher cost of successive reductions in risk.

Workers will seek to select the available wage–risk combination from the wage-offer curve yielding the *maximum expected utility*, i.e. point A with job risk q_a and wage w_a.

In empirical attempts to evaluate the risk–money trade-off along EU, survey methods are frequently used. The worker's current wage rate (w_a) and assessed job risk (q_a) are, at least in principle, directly observable. Workers are then given information as to a specified additional risk to be incorporated into their job description (e.g. handling more toxic chemicals). They are then asked to assess the additional wage rate that they would require to remain on EU (i.e. the 'wage premium'). In terms of Figure 2.4 we are seeking to evaluate the additional wage rate ($w_b - w_a$) required to compensate for a specified increase in risk ($q_b - q_a$) associated with a move from A to B along a given expected utility curve (EU).

Survey evidence of the kind considered in Box 2.5 for many workers will clearly yield some kind of scatter diagram relating to additional income perceived by workers as being necessary to 'compensate them' (i.e. remain on EU) for a specified additional risk. A regression line (or curve) can then be fitted to the scatter diagram to derive an estimate of EU.

Of course some of the reasons for particular workers requiring more (or less) compensation than others for a given increase in risk may be due to their possessing differing individual characteristics. For example, older workers may be expected to place lower values on a given increase in job risk as they will be exposed to that risk for a shorter working life and, in any case, already face increased morbidity risks from other sources via the ageing process itself. Similarly,

Table 2.1 Hazards and actuarial risk

Source of risk	Annual fatality risk
Cigarette smoking (per smoker)	1/150
Cancer	1/300
Motor vehicle accident	1/5,000
Work accident (per worker)	1/10,000
Home accident	1/11,000
Poisoning	1/37,000
Fire	1/50,000
Aviation accident (passenger deaths/total population)	1/250,000

Source: Adapted from Viscusi (1993); the smoking risk estimates are averaged over the entire smoking population.

smokers and those already working in hazardous jobs have been found to place lower values on additional health risks. A multiple regression analysis can (with appropriate data sets) be used to relate the compensating wage increase to differences in these personal characteristics as well as to differences in job risk.

Valuing a life or an injury

Having identified the monetary value placed by workers on additional exposure to risk ('wage premium'), this information can then be used to estimate values of life or values of injury. The likely impacts of exposure to a particular hazard in terms of death or injury can be calculated in an actuarial sense, based on historical data (see Table 2.1). These probabilities can then be used, together with monetary estimates of the wage premium, to calculate the *implicit values* of life or injury.

Suppose, for example, that the wage premium for a worker is estimated at £1 for inducing him/her to accept the additional risk of, say, handling a toxic chemical (utility unchanged). Put another way, this *willingness to accept value* of £1 to compensate for the additional risk of handling the chemical can be equivalently expressed as a *willingness to pay value* of £1 for avoiding that risk. At least for small risk changes, willingness to accept (i.e. the wage premium) and willingness to pay values should be equal.

Valuing a life

Having estimated that the worker is willing to pay £1 for avoiding the risk of handling the toxic chemical, suppose the actuarial risk of death from handling that chemical is 1/5 million. It follows that since the worker is willing to pay £1 to reduce (by avoidance) the risk of death by 1/5 million, the implicit value of life is revealed as £5 million for that worker.

Table 2.2 presents some implicit value of life estimates for various fatal types of illness or injury after exposure to specified hazards. Clearly the implicit value of life estimates in Table 2.2 derived from various countries and approaches show some variation. Viscusi (1993) notes that for the USA, over a much wider range of estimates than those shown in the table, the majority fall in the $3 m. to $7 m. range. Of course, the value of life reflects the wage–risk trade-off

Table 2.2 Implicit value of life

Author (year)	Sample	Fatal risk variable	Mean risk	Implicit value of life ($m.)
Moore and Viscusi (1989)	Panel study of income dynamics	National Traumatic Occupational Fatality Survey	0.0001	7.8
Kniesner and Leeth (1991)	Two-digit mfg. Data, Japan	Industrial accident data, Japan	0.00003	7.6
	Two-digit mfg. Data, Australia, by state	Industrial accident data, Australia	0.0001	3.3
Douglas et al. (1991)	Authors' mail survey	Worker's assessed fatality risk at work	0.0009	1.6

Notes: All values are in December 1990 dollars; mfg. = manufacturing.
Source: As for Table 2.1.

relevant to the preferences of workers in a particular sample. Where the sample varies in terms of personal characteristics, such as age, smoking propensity, degree of risk already experienced in the current job, and indeed mean income, then we should expect some variability in the value-of-life estimates. Indeed when applying value-of-life analyses to samples of air travellers with higher mean incomes than their national counterparts, the value-of-life estimates in all countries tended to rise by upwards of 50 per cent. Clearly such variability warns us against too heavy a reliance on value-of-life estimates.

Costs against benefits

Having established estimates for the benefits of avoiding exposure to various hazards causing injury or death, it is clearly important to compare these with the costs of reducing such exposure. Policy prescription can then give highest priority to reducing or removing those hazards offering the greatest *net* benefits in the sense of benefits minus costs.

Information on costs, such as that presented in Table 2.3, can therefore play an important role in policy-making. The right-hand column is found by dividing the cost of reducing exposure to the hazard by a specified extent by the number of lives saved as a result.

Valuing an injury

So far we have looked at the value of life in the context of fatality. Sometimes an environmental hazard may lead to injury rather than death. In this case as well as using the approach outlined above, it may also be important to bring into the estimates the issue of treatment/non-treatment of any injuries involved.

This approach can lead to the types of estimates for the cost of saving one year of one person's life shown in Table 2.4. Some environmental policies are more cost-effective

Table 2.3 Risks of death in the USA: selected environmental hazards and their cost reduction

	Deaths per 1 million people exposed	Cost to avoid 1 death ($ m.)
Trihalomethane in drinking water	420	0.2
Radionuclides in uranium mines	6,300	3.4
Benzene fugitive emissions	1,470	3.4
Benzene occupational exposure	39,600	8.9
Asbestos occupational exposure	3,015	8.3
Arsenic/copper exposure	63,000	23.0
Acrylonitrile occupational exposure	42,300	51.5
Coke ovens occupational exposure	7,200	63.5
Hazardous waste land disposal	2	4,190.2
Municipal solid waste landfill standard	1	19,107.0
Hazardous waste: wood preservatives	< 1	5,700,000

Source: Adapted from Council on Environmental Quality (1991).

than others in achieving a given objective (here one extra year of life), and alternative (non-environmental) policies are sometimes the most cost-effective of all.

Quality adjusted life year (QALY) indicators

The idea here is that for individuals of specific ages a certain quality of life can be expected, as an average for such individuals. A *quality adjusted life year* (QALY) index score of 1 is then assigned to this expected life profile. Any deterioration in the expected quality of life from a given illness or injury will reduce the QALY

Table 2.4 Cost ($) of saving one year of one person's life: USA

	$
Passing laws to make seat-belt use mandatory	69
Sickle-cell anaemia screening for black newborns	240
Mammography for women aged 50	810
Pneumonia vaccination for people aged over 65	2,000
Giving advice on stopping smoking to people who smoke more than one packet a day	9,800
Putting men aged 30 on a low-cholesterol diet	19,000
Regular leisure-time physical activity, such as jogging for men aged 35	38,000
Making pedestrians and cyclists more visible	73,000
Installing air-bags (rather than manual lap belts) in cars	120,000
Installing arsenic emission control at glass-manufacturing plants	51,000,000
Setting radiation emission standards for nuclear power plants	180,000,000
Installing benzene emission control at rubber-tyre manufacturing plants	20,000,000,000

Source: Tengs *et al.* (1995), 'The Price of a Life', *Risk Analysis*, June.

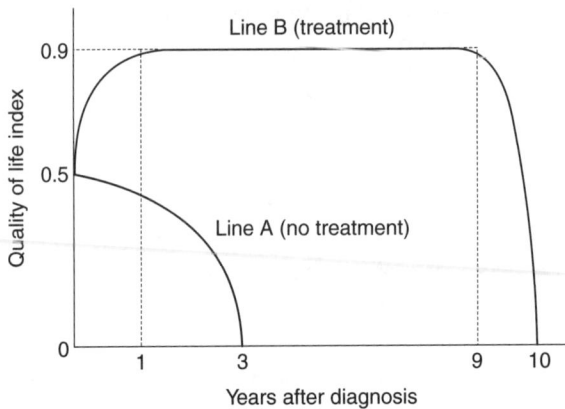

Figure 2.5 The QALY gains from treatment

index below 1 and towards zero. This approach is being used to develop models for each type of treatment and is illustrated in Figure 2.5.

Here a patient with a particular illness or injury has a 0.5 QALY score; in other words the particular illness or injury has halved the expected quality of life for a patient of that age. The patient, if untreated (line A), can expect to live for three more years with a progressive deterioration in his or her condition and therefore in the QALY index. On the other hand, if treated (line B), the patient can expect to recover to a 0.9 QALY within one year (i.e. 90 per cent of the expected quality of life), sustain that quality over a further eight years, then progressively deteriorate in the tenth year before dying.

The area between the axes and line B gives the number of QALYs from treatment. These QALYs from treatment can be compared with the number of QALYs from non-treatment (area between the axes and line A). The *difference* between the areas is the QALY gained from providing appropriate treatment for that person with that illness or injury.

Clearly a vast array of statistics are available to identify the likely prognosis and life pattern for those with certain types and severity of illness, which should help us identify both line B (treatment) and line A (no treatment). We can then compare the QALY gains from treatment (B − A) with the costs of such treatment. This will in turn enable us to calculate the 'cost per 1 QALY gained' for the different types of treatment. Such 'objective' data can help us make more informed decisions as to how scarce resources might be allocated.

In the UK, data have suggested a cost of £750 per QALY gained via hip replacements compared to £70,000 per QALY gained via brain surgery. An extra £1 m. could then yield either 1,333 QALYs if spent on hip replacement surgery, or 14 QALYs if spent on brain surgery. Of course there are many value judgements underlying such 'objective' measures, not least in assessing the comparative degrees of discomfort of particular illnesses and therefore the estimated pattern of decline in QALY.

Such analysis can also help in valuing environmental damages. For example, projected increases in specific types of illness and injury from an environmental hazard will reduce QALY scores, thereby implying a given expenditure to restore the status quo. Equally such analysis can help in valuing environmental improvements. For example, projected decreases in specific types of illness and injury from an environmental improvement will raise QALY scores, thereby implying the avoidance of a given expenditure which would otherwise be necessary to maintain the status quo.

Valuing environmental disasters

The degree of aversion we might have to a possible outcome can be built into a model by adjusting the probabilities. For example, suppose we have three possible outcomes for an environmental project: − £10 m. with a 20 per cent chance, + £10 m. with a 50 per cent chance and + £40 m. with a 30 per cent chance.

$$\textit{Expected monetary value (EMV)} = (0.2 \times - 10) + (0.5 \times 10) + (0.3 \times 40)$$
$$= -2 + 5 + 12$$
$$= + £15m.$$

However, if we are three times as averse to a loss as we are to a gain, then we can weight the probabilities accordingly. It might be more appropriate here to speak of expected utility:

$$\textit{Expected utility (EU)} = (0.2 \times [- 10 \times 3]) + (0.5 \times 10) + (0.3 \times 40)$$
$$= - 6 + 5 + 12$$
$$= + £11m.$$

We can see in Table 2.5 how such value judgements can be built into calculations to derive how much we are willing to pay to avoid a potential disaster.

Suppose, for argument's sake, we estimate the implicit value of life (v) as £4 m. In other words, society is willing to pay up to £4 m. to save a single life, whether in terms of prevention of illness, road accidents or whatever. Assume that the disaster in question has a one in a million chance of happening, so the frequency (f) of the event is 1/1 million. Further assume that the disaster might involve any one of three scenarios: 100 deaths, 500 deaths or 1,000 deaths, where N is the number of deaths.

Turner *et al.* (1994) point out that regulatory agencies use a variety of rules in viewing such disasters: for example the 'square rule', whereby in multiple deaths involving, say, 100 persons we should regard them as being equivalent to 100×100

Table 2.5 The value of a disaster

$f = 1/1,000,000$		
$N = 100$	$N = 500$	$N = 1,000$
$fN = 0.0001$	$fN = 0.0005$	$fN = 0.001$
$fN^2 = 0.01$	$fN^2 = 0.25$	$fN^2 = 1.0$
$300fN = 0.03$	$300fN = 0.15$	$300fN = 0.3$
$vfN = £400$	$vfN = £2,000$	$vfN = £4,000$
$vfN^2 = £40,000$	$vfN^2 = £1,000,000$	$vfN^2 = £4,000,000$
$v300fN = £120,000$	$v300fN = £600,000$	$v300fN = £1,200,000$

Source: Turner *et al.* (1994).

deaths in individual accidents. Another possibility is the '300 rule', whereby in a multiple death situation we weight each death as being equivalent to 300 deaths in individual accidents and so on.

The selection of the rule is crucial to assessing the amount that a government, agency or firm will be willing to pay for disaster aversion measures. As can be seen from Table 2.5, only £4,000 would be spent to cover a one in a million chance of 1,000 people dying in a single accident if no aversion factor is present, but £4 m. if the 'square rule' is used for the aversion factor and £1.2 m. if the '300 rule' is used.

● ● ● ● Environmental impact assessment (EIA)

Cost–benefit analysis (CBA) focuses on giving monetary valuations to a wide range of environmental and non-environmental impacts of a project. CBA is mainly used for public sector projects, with valuations applied from the perspective of society as a whole.

In contrast to CBA, environmental impact assessment (EIA) focuses exclusively on the environmental impacts, is applied to both public and private sector projects and often does not involve placing monetary valuations on environmental costs and benefits. An EU directive makes EIA compulsory for a range of planning applications.

EIA involves a critical appraisal by an independent source of how a proposed project is likely to affect the environment. The assessment is meant to assist the decision-making authority (local or national) and to include any adverse environmental effects on:

- the community (including buildings and places) or ecosystem
- the aesthetic, recreational, scientific or other uses of the locality
- species of fauna or flora
- long-term or cumulative impacts on the environment
- natural resources, waste disposal and overall sustainable development

In principle EIA is meant to apply to the entire process, from the inception of a proposal through to environmental auditing and post-project analysis. In practice EIAs have tended to improve the quality of proposals rather than to result in their abandonment. Case Study 2.3 looks at EIA in the context of constructing the new international airport in Hong Kong.

CASE STUDY 2.3

New international airport, Hong Kong

The international airport at Kai Tak, located on the eastern fringe of Kowloon, has been replaced by a new international airport with two independent runways at Chek Lap Kok to the west of Hong Kong. Land for the airport was formed by levelling the islands of Chek Lap Kok and Lam Chau, just off Lantau Island, and by using excavated material from marine borrow areas. The entire programme comprised 10 interlinked infrastructure projects, with a completion year of 1997. Apart from the airport itself, these projects included 1,669 ha of land reclamation, a harbour crossing and land tunnel, the longest road/rail suspension bridge in the world, a new town in Tung Chung, a 34 km airport railway and more than 30 km of expressway. The work was known as the Airport Core Programme, being one of the largest infrastructure programmes in the world. Moving the airport from its original location provided relief to the nearby 350,000 residents affected by severe aircraft noise and eased the congestion of air traffic.

The airport master plan study began in 1990, establishing a basic airport configuration. The configuration selected involved the dredging and disposal of more than 70 million m of marine mud and a requirement for over 150 million m of landfill. An early decision was made to retain a sea channel between the airport island and the coast of North Lantau. This enabled the natural coastline west of Tung Chung to be largely preserved, allowing also for tidal flushing of a potential area to the east of Chek Lap Kok.

An early EIA study of construction impacts identified a number of significant effects. About 70 dwellings would be adversely affected by noise from the construction programme on a 24-hour basis. The Hong Kong Executive Council granted exemption from the Noise Control Ordinances for the construction programme. However, this exemption was subject to conditions, including grants for the provision and installation of air conditioners in affected dwellings, thereby allowing windows and doors to be closed. In addition, a temporary 10 m earth berm was to be installed along the southern edge of the airport as a barrier to construction noise. Attention was also to be given to noise minimisation from the completed and operational airport. Aircraft noise impacts were predicted for various assumed aircraft fleet mixes using noise exposure forecast contours. It was concluded that by the year 2000 an acceptable level of noise would only be exceeded for a small number of dwellings at Sha Lo Wan on North Lantau, west of Tung Chung. These villagers were to be relocated, and all new noise-sensitive land uses were to be excluded from the airport vicinity.

Blasting, loading, transport and placement of landfill material were the primary sources of dust. Concrete/asphalt plants were also a source of pollutants. In order to control the amount of dust, permanent monitoring stations were set up.

The destruction of the two islands, along with their terrestrial and marine life, necessitated a number of compensatory conservation measures, among them the rescue, study and possible re-establishment of the rare Romer's tree frog.

The excavation works required stripping the existing vegetation, marine mud being disposed of by marine dumping. Potentially hazardous material and chemical wastes would require special measures. However, the EIA study confirmed that the airport island would have an insignificant effect on water quality, bulk and tidal regimes, subject to the preservation of a sea channel some 200 m wide, to assist tidal flushing.

Apart from incorporating environmental measures in the construction projects, the Hong Kong government forged links with the community to provide quick responses to their problems. An Environmental Project Office was created to provide a continuous overview of environmental effects, and to co-ordinate and monitor remedial action. The management of the airport development represented a further step in the implementation of EIA procedures, which became mandatory for all major public projects in 1997. The Hong Kong Environmental Impact Assessment Ordinance was enacted in January 1997, together with a Technical Memorandum on the EIA process.

The new international airport was officially opened in July 1998 by president Jiang Zemin.

Source: Gilpin (2000).

> **Questions**
>
> 1 Identify some of the beneficiaries and losers indicated by the EIA for the Hong Kong Airport.
>
> 2 What other factors might have been taken into account in appraising the environmental implications of this project?

Of course the EIA approach itself imposes various costs. *Direct costs* involving the assessment process itself typically comprise around 1 per cent of total project costs. *Indirect costs* involving 'delays' resulting from additional time required to complete various consultative procedures in the EIA may be more serious at around 10 per cent of total project costs. For example, co-ordination problems may occur between various environmental agencies, public pressure groups and government departments, resulting in time delays. These may be particularly lengthy when further unanticipated studies are required to clarify particular environmental impacts. For example, impact assessments may be required focusing on health, ecological or social aspects.

The EU directive on environmental impact assessment

Under the EU directive, environmental assessment has three stages:

1 Applicants for planning permission must submit an environmental statement to the planning authority. This statement identifies the potential direct and indirect effects on human beings, flora and fauna, soil, water, air climate and landscape; the interaction between these factors and the effects on material assets and cultural heritage; and the steps envisaged to mitigate or remedy these effects.
2 The planning authority must consult with various public bodies on the statement and also provide the public with an opportunity to express its opinion. To facilitate this a non-technical summary must be included with the statement. The environmental statement must be available to the public.
3 The planning authority must prepare an environmental assessment of the proposal that takes the consultations into account before taking a decision on the planning application.

An EIA is mandatory for a small number of major developments such as power stations and oil refineries, motorways and airports and for some projects that could have major environmental impacts, such as waste incinerators and toxic waste disposal facilities. EIA is also required for projects likely to have significant environmental effects because of their size, location or nature.

There is no requirement in the UK that such projects must also be subjected to CBA, although in practice this sometimes occurs. In this case the EIA is a useful complement to CBA.

Leitch guidelines

Historically these have been applied in the UK to the appraisal of trunk-road schemes. These 'guidelines' involve using a specific list of environmental factors when assessing the environmental consequences of such schemes. The assessment could then help inform those taking political judgements as to whether the environmental benefits outweigh the environmental costs of a given scheme. Although these 'guidelines' have been criticised for covering too restricted a set of environmental factors, they have some similarities with the EIA approach.

Cost-effectiveness analysis (CEA)

CEA seeks to find the *least-cost* method for achieving a given environmental objective. For example Table 4.2 (page 103) identifies the least-cost method available for achieving a 2 per cent per annum reduction in the projected CO_2 emissions for OECD countries. An obvious problem for CEA is that it is unable to compare approaches which seek to achieve different environmental objectives.

● ● ● ● Environmental accounting

We have seen how the growth of GDP may bring with it environmental costs. First, there may be costs of pollution to the health of a country's citizens, which might he given a monetary value (e.g. by estimating the additional number of working days lost). Second, there are resource costs involved in running down the stock of natural resources and therefore the country's capacity for future production. Attempts are being made to express such environmental factors in terms of the national accounts; for example, the World Bank estimated Mexico's net national product fell by almost 7 per cent in 1991 when an adjustment was made to take into account the depletion of oil, forests and groundwater associated with recent levels of recorded economic growth.

Rather more sophisticated attempts to capture environmental costs within a national accounting framework have been made by economists such as Jackson and Marks (1994) and with Ralls and Stymne (Jackson *et al.*, 1997). An **Index of Sustainable Economic Welfare (ISEW)** has been calculated for the USA and UK. Essentially, any increase in the GNP figure is adjusted to reflect the following environmental impacts which are often associated with rising GNP:

1 Monies spent correcting environmental damage (i.e. 'defensive' expenditures);
2 Decline in the stock of natural resources (i.e. environmental depreciation);
3 Pollution damage (i.e. monetary value of any environmental damage not corrected).

By failing to take these environmental impacts into account, the conventional GNP figure arguably does not give an accurate indication of sustainable economic welfare, i.e. the flow of goods and services that an economy can generate without reducing its future production capacity. Suppose we consider the expenditure method of calculating GNP. It could be argued that some of the growth in GNP is due to expenditures undertaken to mitigate (offset) the impact of environmental damage. For example, some double-glazing may be undertaken to reduce noise levels from increased traffic flow, and does not therefore reflect an increase in economic well-being, merely an attempt to retain the status quo. Such 'defensive expenditures' should be subtracted from the GNP figure (item 1 above). So too should be expenditures associated with a decline in the stock of natural resources. For example, the monetary value of minerals extracted from rock is included in GNP but nothing is subtracted to reflect the loss of unique mineral deposits. 'Environmental depreciation' of this kind should arguably be subtracted from the conventional GNP figure (item 2 above). Finally, some expenditures are incurred to overcome pollution damage which has not been corrected; for example, extra cost of bottled water when purchased because tap water is of poor quality. Additional expenditures of this kind should also be subtracted from the GNP figure, as should the monetary valuation of any environmental damage which has not been corrected (item 3 above).

We are then left with an Index of Sustainable Economic Welfare (ISEW) which subtracts rather more from GNP than the usual depreciation of physical capital:

ISEW = GNP minus depreciation of physical capital
             minus defensive expenditures
             minus depreciation of environmental capital
             minus monetary value of residual pollution

As we can see from Figure 2.6, the effect of such adjustments is quite startling. The UK GNP per capita (unadjusted) was 2.5 times greater in real terms in 1996 than it was in 1950 (Jackson *et al.* 1997). This corresponds to a 2.0 per cent average annual growth in real GNP, 1950–96. However, the adjustment outlined above for each year over the period gives an ISEW per head for the UK which is just 1.25 times higher in real terms than it was in 1950. This corresponds to a mere 0.5 per cent average annual growth in real ISEW, 1950–96. Such 'environmental account-ing' is suggesting an entirely different perspective on recorded changes in national economic welfare.

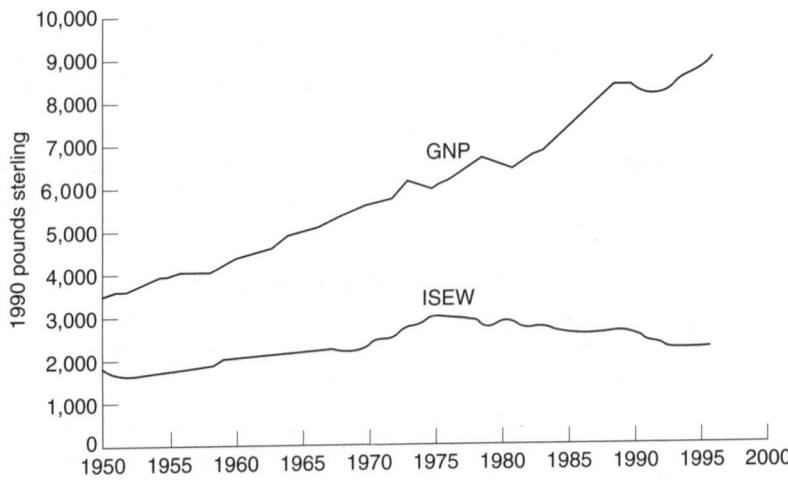

Figure 2.6 Real GNP and ISEW per capita, UK, 1950–96

Source: Adapted from Jackson *et al.* (1997)

> Now try the self-check questions for this chapter on the companion website
> **www.booksites.net/ison**
> You will also find up-to-date facts and case materials.

Key terms

Existence value Reflects the value placed on an environmental asset independently of any current or future use to which it might be put

Expected value In an uncertain situation, expected value is a weighted average of the values (pay-offs) associated with each possible outcome, with the probabilities of each outcome being used as weights

Expressed preference methods of valuation Use questionnaires or surveys to establish hypothetical 'willingness to pay' or 'willingness to accept'. Often used where no market prices exist

Externalities Occur where economic decisions create costs or benefits for people other than the decision takers

Hedonic price method Uses house price premiums (or discounts) to infer valuations of environmental assets (or liabilities)

Index of Sustainable Economic Welfare (ISEW) Adjustments to national income accounts to derive a GDP value which better reflects the environmental sustainability of that economy

Option value Reflects the value placed on an asset now as regards functions which might be exploited some time in the future

Public good A good (or service) that involves two key characteristics: non-excludability and non-exhaustibility. Non-excludability means that, once provided, it is difficult to exclude people from consuming the good/service

Revealed preference methods of valuation Use observed behaviour in markets for substitute products or complementary products to infer a value for an environmental activity

Risk An estimate of the chance of an event or series of events occurring

Shadow prices Market prices which have been adjusted to take account of the social costs and benefits associated with the activity

Use value Reflects the value placed by the market on the practical uses to which an environmental asset is currently being put

References and further reading

Bowers, J. (1997) *Sustainability and Environmental Economics*, Longman, Harlow, especially Chapters 10–12.

The Council on Environmental Quality (1991) *Environmental Quality: 21st Annual Report*, US Government Printing Office, Washington DC.

Field, B.C. (1997) *Environmental Economics: An Introduction*, McGraw-Hill, especially Chapters 6–8.

Fredman, P. (1994) *The Existence of Existence Value*, Arbetsrapport 202, Umea, Department of Forest Economics, Swedish University of Agricultural Sciences.

Garrod, G. and Willis, K. (1996) 'Estimating the benefits of environmental enhancement: a case study of the River Darent', *Journal of Environmental Planning and Management*, 39, pp. 189–203.

Gilpin, A. (2000) *Environmental Economics: A Critical Overview*, Wiley, especially Chapter 7.

Hanley, N. and Milne, J. (1996) *Ethical Beliefs and Behaviour in Contingent Valuation*, Discussion Papers in Ecological Economics, 96/1, Department of Economics, University of Stirling.

Jackson, T. and Marks, N. (1994) *Measuring Sustainable Economic Welfare – a Pilot Index: 1950–1990*, Stockholm Environment Institute.

Jackson, T., Marks, N., Ralls, J. and Stymne, S. (1997) *Sustainable Economic Welfare in the UK 1950–1996*, New Economics Foundation, London

Nelson, J.P. (1982) 'Highway noise and property valves: a survey of recent evidence', *Journal of Transport Economics and Policy*, XIC, pp. 37–52.

O'Doherty, R. (1994) 'Pricing environmental disasters', *Economic Review*, 12, p.1.

Pearce, D. (1991) 'Economics and the environment', *Economics*, XXVII, Pt.1, p. 113.

Royal Commission on Environmental Pollution (2000), 22nd Report, *Energy – The Changing Climate*, CM 4749.

Stevens, T., Echeverria, J., Glass, R., Hager, T. and More, T. (1991) 'Measuring the existence value of wildlife: what do DVM estimates really show?' *Land Economics*, 67, 4, pp. 390–400.

Turner, R.K., Pearce, D. and Bateman, I. (1994) *Environmental Economics*, FT/Prentice Hall, Harlow.

Viscusi, W. (1993) 'The Value of Risks to Life and Health', *Journal of Economic Literature*, XXXI, Dec.

World Commission on Dams (2001), *Dams and Development*, Earthscan, London.

Useful websites

Environment Agency
Environment: (EC DGXI)
World Health Organisation
United Nations
Office for National Statistics (ONS)
ONS Statstore and Statbase
Central Office of Information
Eurostat
International Monetary Fund (IMF)
Organisation for Economic Co-Operation and Development (OECD)
United Nations Development Program (UNDP)
World Bank

Setting the targets

The previous chapter looked at various ways of valuing the environment. We noted that in a 'perfect' market economy, the price mechanism could be relied upon to bring about an allocation of environmental resources which might be regarded as 'optimal' for both individuals and society as a whole. Unfortunately 'market failure' of one kind or another was seen to distort these valuations, suggesting that policy makers might have to intervene to adjust inappropriate market valuations or even to establish valuations where none currently exist.

This chapter looks in rather more detail at the types of market failure which often occur in the environmental context and the implications these may have for setting *policy targets*. Chapter 4 takes these issues further by considering the *policy instruments* which might be best suited to achieving the targets actually set.

Marginal analysis and target setting

You may be familiar with the role of *marginal analysis* in many aspects of management and business decision making. Particular attention is often paid by analysts to the last or 'marginal' unit, as though the actual decision takers were acutely aware of its importance. In practice this has rarely been shown to be the case, with firms and individuals typically more aware of 'average' levels of cost, revenue, satisfaction (utility) and so on. Nevertheless focus on the marginal unit of production or consumption has often helped policy makers determine the targets to which their policy instruments might be directed. Nor is this approach without some justification! For example, it can be shown that in order to maximise profits, the firm must equate marginal revenue (MR) with marginal (private) cost (MC). Even if it is entirely unaware of these marginal ideas and values, if experience, luck or good judgement are used by management to actually achieve profit maximisation, then they will be equating MR with MC even if they are entirely unaware of these concepts. This 'as if' approach is no different from, say, an expert snooker player who achieves a high break by potting many difficult balls involving complex calculations of angles of incidence and reflection which, at the time of each pot, are concepts which are hardly at the forefront of his or her attention!

We shall therefore make use of marginal analysis in assessing environmental targets despite readily admitting that most participants, whether firms, individuals or governments, have little if any conscious awareness of the marginal unit.

Marginal abatement and marginal damage cost curves

Pollution is considered in more detail in Chapter 6, but provides a useful context in which to discuss many aspects of target setting. This immediately brings into play the ideas of marginal abatement costs (MAC) and marginal damage costs (MDC).

Clearly, avoiding emitting a pollutant will impose costs on the firm or industry – we call these *abatement costs*. They might include, for example, the cost of installing expensive flue-desulphurisation plants in coal-burning power stations to reduce toxic emissions, etc. The **marginal abatement cost** (MAC) curve in Figure 3.1 represents the extra cost to the firm of *avoiding* emitting the last unit of pollutant. The MAC curve is shown as sloping upwards from right to left, suggesting that initial cuts in emissions of the pollutant can be achieved at little extra cost, but that it becomes increasingly costly at the margin to achieve progressively larger cuts in emissions of the pollutant.

However, where a pollutant is emitted it will impose damages, perhaps on those emitting the pollutant and perhaps on others – we call these *damage costs*. The **marginal damage cost** (MDC) curve in Figure 3.1 represents the extra damage to all individuals, firms, etc. from *emitting* the last unit of pollutant. The MDC curve is shown as sloping upwards from left to right after output Q_0. This suggests that the 'waste receptor' (sink) function of the environment is able to absorb up to Q_0 units of pollutant without damage, but that each unit of pollutant above Q_0 imposes increasing amounts of extra damage on the environment.

The socially optimum level of emission of pollutants is where marginal damage costs exactly equal marginal abatement costs for society, i.e. output Q_s in Figure 3.1. To emit one more unit of pollutants beyond Q_s would imply marginal damage costs from that unit greater than the marginal cost to society of abating that damage. In other words, it would cost society less to *avoid* emitting that extra unit of pollutant beyond Q_s than it would cost society to emit it. Society is clearly disadvantaged by any emissions in excess of Q_s. Equally, to emit one unit of pollu-

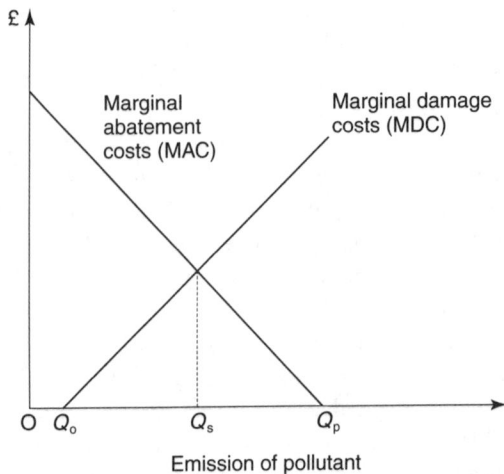

Figure 3.1 Using marginal abatement and damage costs to identify optimum emission of a pollutant

tant less than Q_s would imply marginal damage costs to society from one m
of pollutant which are less than the marginal cost to society of abating the da
from that unit. In other words, it would cost society less to *emit* that extra unit
pollutant up to Q_s than it would cost society to avoid emitting it. In this case society is disadvantaged by seeking to cut emissions below Q_s.

It is worth noting that the optimal target for society (Q_s) does not involve zero
pollution. The policy instruments we might use to achieve this target are considered
further in Chapter 4.

Externalities and target setting

So far we have used the term 'marginal damage cost' to refer to the impact of pollution emissions on the environment. Where those generating the pollution inflict
damage on the environment but are not held accountable (e.g. the environmental
damage does not appear in the firm's costs), then these 'marginal damage costs' are
better known as *marginal external costs.*

More generally, **externalities** occur when economic decisions create costs or benefits for people other than the decision taker; these are called external costs or external benefits. For example, a firm producing textiles may emit industrial effluent
polluting nearby rivers and causing a loss of amenity. The true cost to society is
then more than the (scarce) resources of labour and capital used up by the firm in
producing textiles. To these *private costs* of firm production, reflected by wage bill,
raw material costs, lease of premises, interest payments, etc., we must add any
external costs that do not appear in the firm's balance sheet but which have
resource implications for society, if we are to assess the true *social costs* of production. In terms of the widely used concept of marginal cost, we can say that:

Marginal social cost = Marginal private cost + Marginal external cost
$$\text{MSC} \quad = \quad \text{MPC} \quad + \quad \text{MEC}$$

Sometimes those who impose external costs in this way can be controlled by legislation (pollution controls such as Clean Air Acts with fines for breaches of minimum standards) or can be given incentives to reduce pollution through the tax
mechanism. On the other hand, firms creating social benefits may be rewarded by
the receipt of subsidies. If the industry is run in the public interest, it might be
expected that full account will be taken of any externalities, whether negative or
positive. For instance, it can be argued that railways reduce road usage, creating
external benefits by relieving urban congestion, pollution and traffic accidents. This
is one aspect of the case for subsiding railways so that they can continue to offer
some loss-making services. We return to possible policy prescriptions to take
account of externalities in Chapter 4 (pages 78–104).

You should also be familiar with the general idea that the presence of externalities may distort the signals conveyed by prices in a market economy. Although at
first sight it may seem a contradiction, when marginal social cost is higher than
marginal private cost (MSC > MPC) because of the existence of a positive
marginal external cost (MEC > 0), we use the term **negative externality**. This is the
situation shown in Figure 3.2, where we can see that the marginal social cost of

ction lies above the marginal private cost. In this case the firm that seeks to ...nise its private surplus (profit) will fail to maximise social surplus.

...e profit-maximising firm in Figure 3.2 will produce output OQ_1 at price OP_1 ... marginal private cost = marginal revenue (marginal private benefit) at this ...ut. Total profit can be regarded as total private surplus, and this is a maximum, ...n by area *JKL* in the diagram. To produce one extra unit beyond OQ_1 would ...ce total private surplus as the extra unit would incur a loss (MPC > MR); to produce one fewer unit than OQ_1 would also reduce this total private surplus, since that unit would have yielded a profit (MR > MPC) had it been produced. Unfortunately, this output Q_1 which maximises total private surplus (profit) is *not* the output that maximises total social surplus. This occurs where the marginal social benefit of production, MSB (here shown as being the same as MR), equals the marginal social cost of production, MSC. This occurs at output OQ_2 with total social surplus a maximum given by area *JMN*, using the same reasoning as before. Clearly this situation, if uncorrected, is one in which prices are conveying inappropriate signals to producers. They are leading to profit maximisers producing too much of the product and selling it at too low a price, as compared with the needs of society as a whole. Externalities of both a negative (adverse) and even positive (beneficial) type can have major impacts on resource allocation if left uncorrected.

You should be able to use Figure 3.2 to consider the implications of a **positive externality** (MSC < MPC) on firm output, as for example when a firm uses its scarce resources to support some type of environmental improvement. This time price signals, if uncorrected, are leading to profit maximisers producing too little of the product and selling it at too high a price, as compared with the needs of society as a whole. If marginal social costs (MSC′) were below marginal private costs in the diagram then the target output for society needs to be raised above OQ_1 if social surplus is to be a maximum.

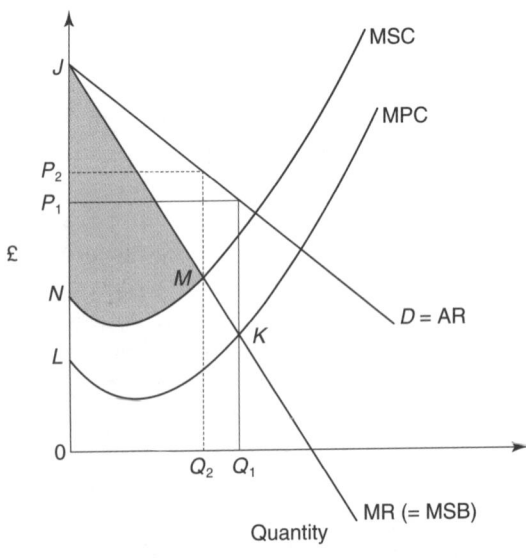

Figure 3.2 With negative externalities (MSC > MPC), the output Q_1 maximising private surplus (profit) differs from the output Q_2 maximising social surplus

CASE STUDY 3.1

Oil and cloud-forests do not mix

OCP Ecuador, a consortium led by an Argentine–Spanish oil giant, Repsol-YPF, and Canada's Alberta Energy, will build and operate the new $1.1 bn heavy crude oil pipeline that will run 500 km (310 miles) from Ecuador's oil-rich Amazon across the Andes to the export docks on the Pacific coast. The pipeline, already approved by the government, promises to double Ecuador's oil-transport capacity and boost GDP growth by 2.5 per cent a year until 2020. Unfortunately, it will also slice through one of the world's few cloud-forests still intact. For most of its length, the pipeline runs meekly parallel to the existing oil pipeline. But one 157 km section, known as the northern route, takes a new path through primary Andean cloud-forests in the Mindo-Nambillo reserve. The area supports over 450 species of birds, almost 5 per cent of the world's total, 46 of which are considered endangered. It also provides jobs in eco-tourism for over 70 per cent of the local population.

ENTRIX, the American company hired by OCP Ecuador to carry out the environmental study, says that, all things considered, the northern route was the best of the five studied. Environmentalists contend, however, that the company had decided on the northern route from the beginning, and failed to study the alternatives in sufficient depth. The risk of damage was highlighted last week when landslides ruptured Ecuador's state-owned transnational pipeline, spilling over 7,000 barrels of oil into the Andean forests east of Quito. Since 1998 this pipeline has burst 14 times, spilling a total of 145,000 barrels of oil.

Since the area is prone to landslides and earthquakes, accidents are inevitable, even if OCP Ecuador proceeds as carefully as it has promised. At the least, a corridor 7 m wide and 13.6 km long will have to be cleared through protected forest. Environmentalists say this must inevitably mean the building of access roads, and with the roads will come illegal colonisation and cattle grazing. Techint, an Argentine company that is part of the OCP consortium, has already been fined $13,800 by the environment ministry for felling trees in a federally protected forest.

With Ecuador's economy still struggling to recover from its worst period in over a century (GDP shrank by 7.4 per cent in 1999), environmental protection comes low on Ecuador's president, Gustavo Noboa's list. It was the energy ministry that had to bestow final approval on the environmental study, a clear conflict of interest. Days before the study was approved, Mr Noboa said the government liked the route and he would not let environmentalists delay things. 'I'm not going to let anyone screw with the country,' he said. 'I'll give them war.'

According to the government, the pipeline will provide 52,000 new jobs directly and indirectly while it is being built and will attract foreign investment of $2.6 bn over the next three years. In a country in desperate need of foreign direct investment and higher exports, and where 52 per cent of the population earn less than $2 a day, only the wildest environmentalists deny the need for the pipeline. They just wish it could go somewhere else.

Source: The Economist, 23 June 2001

● ● ● ● Public goods and target setting

Environmental assets and liabilities are often said to have 'public good' characteristics which will influence the targets set for their use. Before looking more closely at some specifically environmental examples it will be useful to consider 'public goods' in general.

A **public good** has two key characteristics:

- *Non-rivalry in consumption*, which means that consumption by one individual does not reduce the quantity available to others. In other words, if I consume an extra unit of a 'good' (which could be a service) so too can you. The value of the extra unit of that 'good' that you place on it can be added to the value that I place on it. As a result we can sum individual demand curves vertically (rather than horizontally) in deriving market or aggregate demand. For example, the provision of, say, a scenic view in a national park can benefit both you and others simultaneously. The overall willingness to pay for that view can therefore be identified by summing the valuation of each individual for that opportunity. Thus in Figure 3.3(a) we can identify the marginal social benefit (MSB) of an extra unit of the public good by summing the individual demand (WTP) curves corresponding to that unit vertically (MSB = $D_A + D_B$) rather than horizontally which would be the case if that extra unit only went to the highest bidder.
- *Non-exclusivity in consumption*, which means that it is impossible to exclude from consumption individuals who have not paid for the product. Defence is a classic example of a non-exclusive good. Once a nation has provided for its national defence, it would be extremely difficult if not impossible to exclude individual citizens from its benefits.

Pure public goods

Products (goods or services) that satisfy *both* these characteristics, such as defence, street lighting, lighthouses, are often called *pure public goods*. In this case we should have a situation similar to that shown in Figure 3.3(a) with two consumers for simplicity. Strictly speaking, the marginal social cost (MSC) of providing an extra unit of the pure public good to another consumer is zero. This follows from the non-rivalry characteristic: once provided for one person, someone else can also consume that unit at no extra cost and without reducing the first person's ability to consume that same unit. In this case we can regard the MSC curve as zero, coin-ciding with the horizontal axis.

The socially optimum solution is where MSB = MSC, i.e. output Q_s in Figure 3.3(a). In this extreme case we can see that the appropriate *target* is the output level demanded at zero price. Clearly private markets, driven by the profit motive, will have no incentive to be established under these conditions (zero price): hence the suggestion that these are public goods. Only if general tax receipts are used to fund such products will they be provided.

Mixed (quasi) public goods

The suggestion here is that a broader category of products (goods or services) will have elements of these characteristics, while not fully meeting the criteria for a pure public good. For example, many products may be *non-rival* in the sense that (at least up to the congestion point) extra people can consume that product without detracting from existing consumers' ability to benefit from it: e.g. use of a motor-way, a bridge or a scenic view.

However, the *non-exclusivity* condition may not apply, since it may be possible to exclude consumers from that product: e.g. tolls on motorways and bridges, or fen-cing (with admissions charges) around scenic views. So a market could be estab-lished for such a *mixed or quasi-public good*, with a non-zero price charged. Moreover, at least beyond the congestion point, the marginal social cost of provision is also non-zero, since extra cars cause existing users to slow down on roads and bridges, and extra people hinder the enjoyment of the scenic view. As a result MSB = MSC above the horizontal axis, implying a non-zero price at P' and *target* output of Q'_s.

In Figure 3.3(b) the socially optimum output (MSB = MSC) occurs at Q'_s with market price P'. This price might be composed of two parts (were price discrimi-nation possible in the market) equivalent to the individual valuation of each consumer of output Q'_s, namely P_A and P_B. Of course there is the practical

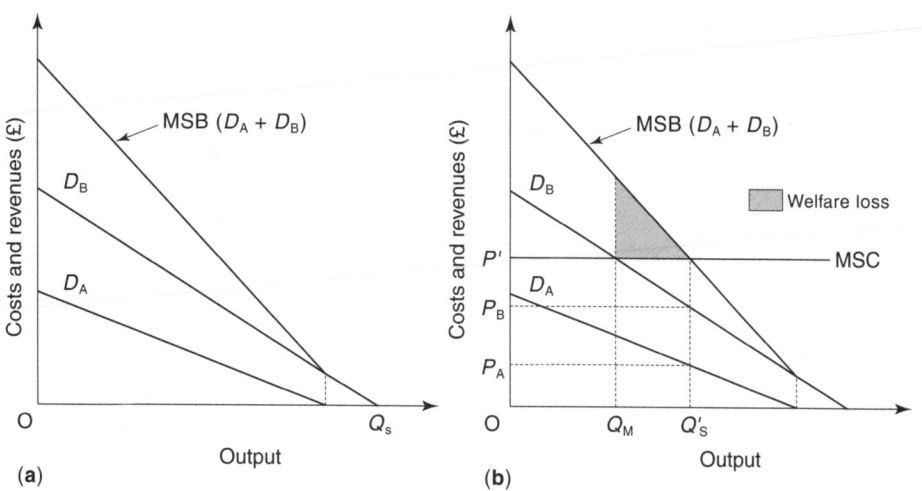

Figure 3.3 (a) Pure public goods and the socially optimum output; (b) Mixed public goods and the socially optimum output

problem of identifying what sum of money each person is really willing to pay for this output. If consumers want the product but understate their true preferences in the hope that they can 'free ride', then this social optimum output Q'_S may not occur. For example, if only consumer B reveals his true preference/willingness to pay market price P' in Figure 3.3(b) (perhaps via response to a questionnaire) then the market solution might be output Q_M, with the shaded area corresponding to the welfare loss resulting from the free rider problem.

This analysis highlights one of the problems with public goods: namely that everyone has an incentive to rely on their neighbours to provide them, rather than provide them themselves. A shipping company may desire lighthouses to guide its ships, as may other shipping companies. Unfortunately all may delay investment decisions, hoping that a rival builds the lighthouses, on which they can then 'free ride'. Eventually perhaps one company for whom the lighthouses have most value may relent and begin construction, but the level of provision may be less than optimal. This is because it is only the (vertical) sum of the marginal valuations of all consumers of the good that can help to determine the social optimum solution. If any consumer fails to express their true marginal valuation (i.e. attempts to free ride), then we have the suboptimal type of solution shown at Q_M in Figure 3.3(b).

Of course there are many combinations of characteristics that goods might possess: non-rival and non-exclusive (pure public good); rival and exclusive (pure private good); non-rival (up to congestion point) and exclusive (quasi public good) and so on. A more detailed classification of public goods is outlined in Figure 3.4.

CASE STUDY 3.2

Mixed public good: road transport congestion

Road transport is certainly not a 'pure' public good in that it is possible to charge for road use and to exclude non-paying users from a road, as in the case of erecting toll barriers at entrances to, or exits from, a motorway. Road transport therefore fails to meet the 'non-exclusivity' condition of the pure public good. It may even fail, at least in part, the 'non-rivalry' condition, especially when roads become congested. In this case it becomes more apparent that extra users of the road are imposing external congestion costs on other users.

Such external or *congestion costs* arise when the addition of more vehicles on to a road network reduces the speed of other vehicles and so increases the average time it takes to complete any particular journey. It is possible to gain some understanding of congestion by studying the relationship between speed and flow along a particular route. Figure 3.5 shows a *speed–flow curve* for the movement of vehicles along a particular road. It shows how motorists interact and impose delays and costs on each other.

In a free flow situation (around point *A*) there is little or no interaction between vehicles and therefore speeds (subject to the legal speed limit) are relatively high. However, as extra vehicles join the road, average speed is reduced; nevertheless an increased flow will still occur until point *B* is reached. The flow of vehicles depends upon the number of vehicles joining the road and the speed of the traffic. For the individual

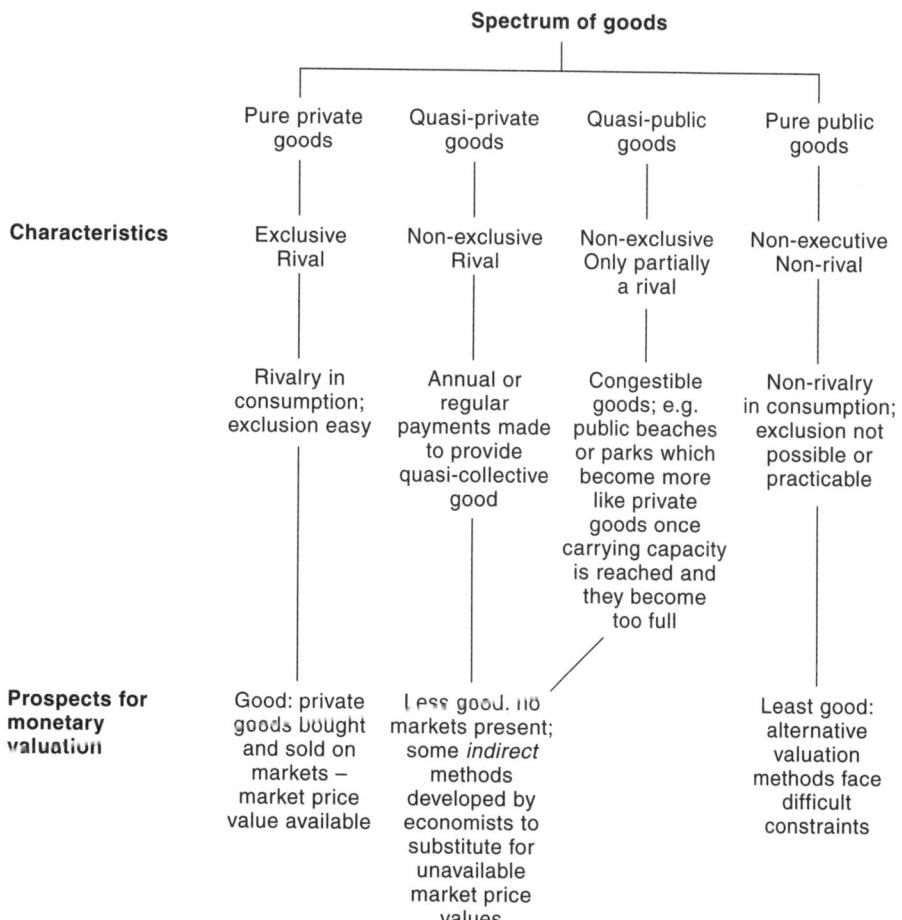

Figure 3.4 Spectrum of private and public goods
Source: Turner (1994)

user, maximum efficiency is where the speed is at its highest, i.e. point *A*. In terms of the system as a whole, however, the maximum efficiency is at point *B*, before the speed–flow curve turns back on itself. Once at point *B*, the road is said to have reached its *full capacity* at the maximum flow level. Motorists may continue to enter the road after *B* because they may lack perfect information, thus slowing down the whole flow. Point *C* may therefore be used to represent the speed–flow situation during a *peak period*. At this point the traffic is in a stop–start situation, perhaps where the traffic flow is subject to a bottleneck. This gives rise to high external (congestion) costs which the individual motorist is not taking into account. These costs on other road users will tend to increase the closer the road is to full capacity.

The costs of congestion

It is clear that a major strategy is needed to tackle the congestion problem, not only in urban areas but also on inter-urban routes. Congestion undermines competitiveness and hinders certain conurbations, particularly London, from attracting people and business. It also imposes a financial cost on the business community in terms of increased

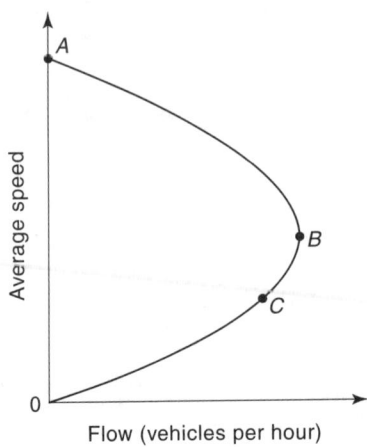

Figure 3.5 Speed–flow curve

commuter times and delays in the delivery of goods. One estimate calculated that congestion costs are over £3 bn per year in London and the six major English conurbations alone, and suggested that the total national congestion bill could be in the region of £10 bn per year. The Confederation of British Industry estimates that delays on the M25 cost £1 bn per year, and that London's inadequate transport system costs the nation around £15 bn per annum, almost two-thirds of which relates to London and the South-East. Specific businesses such as British Telecom and the Royal Mail (now Consignia) put the cost of congestion to themselves at £7.25 m. and £10.4 m. per annum, respectively. These costs were measured in terms of fleet inefficiency, lost drivers' time, and extra vehicle costs. According to the CBI, every British household has to spend at least £5 per week more than it needs to on goods and services in order to meet the costs to business of road and rail congestion. This is equal to 2p on the basic rate of income tax. The CBI estimate that if traffic delays could be reduced, thereby raising average speeds by 1.5 mph, then London's economy would be better off by £1 m. per day.

In 1997 the National Economic Research Associates (NERA) estimated the total cost of road congestion to road users to be £7 bn. This can be split into the cost to business (£2.5 bn) and the cost to private motorists, private van drivers and bus passengers (£4.5 bn). More recent estimates of congestion costs are even more substantial; for example, the RAC (2000) has estimated that congestion costs the motorist around £23 bn in time losses alone each year. This is approximately £800 per annum for every motorist in Britain irrespective of the extra fuel and wear and tear costs associated with congestion.

In terms of traffic speeds, the situation has worsened over the last 20 years. In central London, the morning and evening peak period travel speeds were 12.7 and 11.8 mph respectively in 1968–70, whereas by the late 1990s they had fallen to 10.0 and 10.2 mph respectively. Some indication of the causes of congestion is the dramatic rise in the number of licensed vehicles from just over 4 million to almost 28 million over the period 1950–2000. This sevenfold increase in road vehicles in 50 years has been mainly due to the increased use of private cars (rising from around 2.5 million in 1950 to over 22 million in 2000).

Questions

1 Review the case for imposing a charge on individual road users when congestion occurs on a particular road.

2 How might this affect the targets for the volume of road users on such roads?

3 Evaluate the impacts of road congestion on the wider economy.

Common property resources

Common property resources provide a useful illustration of the problems of target setting in the case of an environmental asset which possesses quasi public good characteristics. Box 3.1 looks at this issue in rather more detail.

BOX 3.1

Common property resources and public good characteristics

Common property resources are not, in fact, 'pure public goods' but rather 'quasi-public goods' in that only the first of these two key characteristics (or conditions) apply. The absence of property rights prevents exclusion, thereby fulfilling the 'non-exclusive' condition. However, there is some element of rivalry in that overfishing or overgrazing is technically possible, thereby violating the 'non-rival' condition.

The root problem is associated with that of the free rider. One co-owner may have little or no reason to consider the impacts of his action on other co-owners of the property rights. Even if conservation of the resource is regarded as desirable, he may hope to free ride by using the resource to the full himself while others voluntarily restrict their access. Alternatively, he may regard (given imperfect information) collective agreements to conserve as being unrealistic and/or unenforceable, thereby supporting any inclination he might already have to pursue his own self-interest, regardless of its impact on others. Any investment the individual might make in the common property resource (e.g. desisting from overuse; restocking fish supplies; reseeding grazing land) is discouraged by the fact that any returns on that investment cannot be wholly appropriated by that individual because of the absence of property rights.

Take the example of fishing in international waters. Each fisherman (trawler owner) fishes up to the point at which the marginal private benefit = marginal private cost. But since the high seas are a common property resource, the fisherman has no incentive to take into account the impact of his fishing on others. As a result the fisherman's marginal private cost (MPC) understates the true marginal social cost (MSC) of his activity. In the competitive market for fish (horizontal demand curve) shown in Figure 3.6 the outcome is likely to be overfishing. The profit-maximising solution (MPB = MPC) yields F_P fish per time period; the socially optimum solution (MSB = MSC) is only F_S fish per time period.

The main source of this particular market failure involves the institutional environment in which transactions take place. A simple remedy is therefore to change that institutional environment: e.g. let a single owner manage the resource. Again we would then be internalising the externality. The owner can now charge those using the resource for any costs they impose on the resource; here the excess of MSC over MPC. A Pigouvian-type charge (see Chapter 4) for using the resource (e.g. depleting fish stocks) would shift MPC vertically upwards to MSC, leading to the socially optimum fishing volume of F_S with a charge $a - b$ per fish (Figure 3.6).

▶

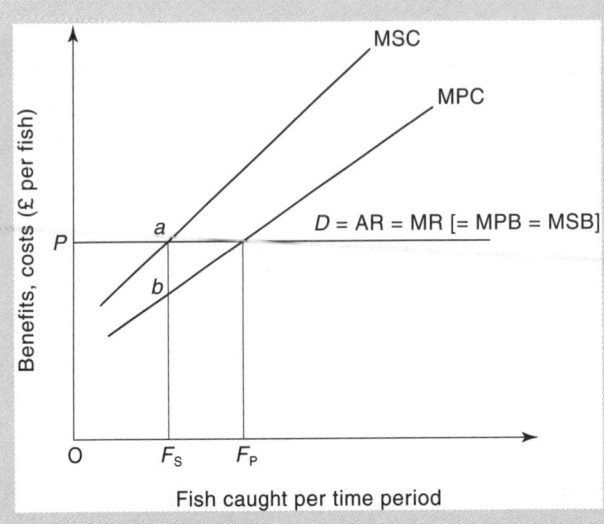

Figure 3.6 Overutilising a common property resource

Of course in practice many common property resources are huge, with single private ownership impractical. In this case public ownership or public regulation of private ownership may be more realistic.

Uncertainty and target setting

If we are to apply our analysis in practical ways we must seek to value both the marginal damage (external) cost and the marginal abatement cost curves. Again we are faced with the conceptual problem of placing a valuation on variables to which monetary values are at present only rarely attached, if at all. Another source of uncertainty lies in the fact that in a full cost–benefit analysis we must select a particular rate of discount (see Chapter 2, page 27) to be used in estimating present values, thereby enabling a comparison to be made between effects in the distant future and the costs of policies introduced today.

Uncertainty will therefore clearly be involved in any attempt to evaluate the costs and benefits of policy action or inaction. This can be shown by looking back at Figure 3.1. The target for reducing emissions of a pollutant from Q_p (with zero abatement costs) to the socially optimum level of Q_s will clearly be affected by such uncertainty. Analysts often use 'scenarios' of high, medium and low estimates for marginal damage and marginal abatement cost curves respectively. For instance, Nordhaus (1989–91) estimated a range of possible marginal damage cost curves for CO_2 emissions based on US data. His *high estimate* of marginal damage costs was calculated at $66.00 per tonne of CO_2, his *low estimate* at only $1.83 per tonne of CO_2. We can use the earlier Figure 3.1 to illustrate this analysis. In the high estimate case, the marginal damage cost curve (MDC) shifts vertically upwards, Q_s falls and the 'target' reduction in CO_2 emissions (i.e. Q_s–Q_p) increases. On this basis Nordhaus advocates reducing CO_2 emissions by 20 per cent. It is hardly surprising (in view of the valuation discrepancy noted above) that in his low estimate case, the marginal damage cost curve shifts vertically downwards in Figure 3.1, so that Q_s rises and the target reduction in CO_2 emissions (i.e. $Q_s - Q_p$) falls. On this basis Nordhaus only advocates reducing CO_2 emissions by about 3 per cent.

Prior to the Kyoto Conference on climate change in December 1997, the UK government's policy was to stabilise CO_2 emissions at their 1990 level by the year 2005. In practice this would have meant a reduction in CO_2 emissions in 2005 by between 20 per cent and 50 per cent, compared to their estimated uncontrolled levels by that date. This would have been rather higher than the restrictions advocated by Nordhaus, even in his 'high' cost scenario. Since Kyoto the targets have been raised still further. The UK government agreed to reduce emissions of a basket of the six main greenhouse gases (including CO_2) to 12.5 per cent below their 1990 levels by 2008–12. It has also set a self-imposed target for reducing CO_2 emissions to 20 per cent below their 1990 levels by 2010.

Health issues and target setting

Much of the discussion so far has involved target setting which reflects a *maximising* approach, whether for private surplus (profit) or, more usually, social surplus. The levels of output for environmentally related products and associated (output related) emissions of pollutants which maximised social surplus in particular then become the targets for national or international policy makers.

However, in many cases the focus for target setting in environmental policy areas may involve a variety of *non-maximising* approaches. In particular *dose–response* calculations have often been used to estimate threshold levels of exposure to various pollutants, above which there is deemed to be a theoretically significant risk to health. Target levels of outputs of environmentally related products are then established which, if met, will ensure that exposure to the various harmful substances remains below the recognised threshold levels.

In terms of Figure 3.7, output q_T corresponds to the output of an environmentally related product yielding an associated exposure to the output-related pollutant Q_T which corresponds to the current threshold recognised as 'safe'. In this case output q_T is above the social optimum output q_s. It would be pure coincidence if q_T and q_s were to coincide. It is often the case that the maximum level of output/exposure deemed to be safe becomes the target level of output/exposure. This is even more likely to be the case where total private surplus (profit) rises still further at levels of output in excess of q_T.

Political/legal considerations and target setting

Targets may be set nationally or internationally, depending on the nature of the environmental activities, their geographical scale and legal rights assigning jurisdiction over these activities. For example in Chapter 6 we note that where some nations pollute and other nations are damaged by that pollution, the existence of separate sovereign states means that there is no single authority able to impose environmental targets, monitor and enforce them. Settlement must therefore

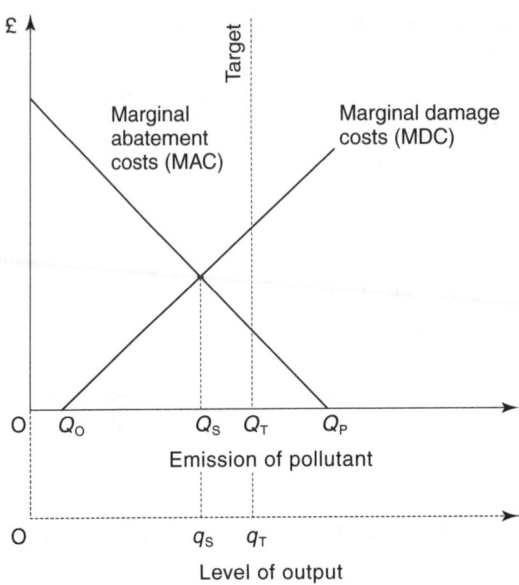

Figure 3.7 Using dose–response method to set the target level of output (q_T) and associated emission of pollutant (Q_t)

involve some type of international agreement involving the consent of the various parties. The relative political and economic strengths of the polluter and victim countries involved in such negotiations may ultimately determine the stringency of the particular environmental targets set and the degree to which these are monitored and enforced.

The Kyoto Protocol provides a useful example of political considerations influencing target setting. For example, the Kyoto Protocol only derives legal force when countries responsible for at least 55 per cent of the CO_2 emissions recorded in 1990 have ratified the treaty. At the time of writing the USA is refusing to ratify the Protocol, which means that the EU, the Russian Federation and Japan, which together contributed almost 50 per cent to 1990 CO_2 emissions, must ratify, together with one or more countries from Canada, Poland, Australia and the transition economies. Any or all of these countries are clearly in a politically strong bargaining position to influence the specific targets contained in the Protocol.

On the other hand, the political weakness of the developing countries has reduced their ability to shape the environmental agenda in their favour. For example, the developed economies are increasingly tying the availability of funds for development projects in the developing countries to their meeting specified environmental improvements.

Indeed political aspects would seem to have played an important part in the withdrawal of support by the Bush administration in the USA for the Kyoto Protocol. Well-established links to oil-related industries by the Republican Party have allegedly played a part in its reluctance to accept the 'challenging' Kyoto targets. The Kyoto Protocol calls for greenhouse gas (GHG) emissions expressed in CO_2 equivalents to be reduced in the period 2008–12 by some 5 per cent relative to their 1990 level. The reduction for the more industrialised OECD countries overall is to be around 7 per cent. These targets are tighter than they seem because of the growth of emissions that would normally occur in the meantime: relative to this 'business as usual' scenario, the targets imply reductions that may amount to some 30 per cent by 2012. For the USA the Kyoto target was to reduce CO_2 equivalent emissions of greenhouse gases by 7 per cent by 2008–12 on 1990 levels when in 1999 it was already emitting over 7 per cent *in excess* of 1990 levels. Such a dramatic reduction over the relatively few years remaining could clearly only be achieved by substantial switches away from petroleum and other fossil fuels induced by regulations discriminating against oil or significant tax increases on oil-based products or activities.

The following case study provides some useful insights into political influence on the targets set for the nuclear industry.

CASE STUDY 3.3

Does nuclear power have a future?

In May 2001, the Bush administration unveiled an energy policy that strongly supports nuclear power. This may revive a flagging industry, but the doubts remain as strong as ever. The gently rolling farmlands of central Pennsylvania do not prepare the casual visitor for what lies outside Middletown. Farmers tend cows and corn, diners serve simple food, and the occasional Amish buggy saunters by. But suddenly, there on the horizon, loom the cooling towers of the nuclear plant at Three Mile Island. The words still send a shiver down the spine. It was here, early in the morning of 28th March 1979, that a reactor started to overheat. A combination of mechanical failure and human error sent the temperature in the reactor core soaring, threatening a blast that would have released huge quantities of lethal radiation. With the lives of perhaps half a million people at stake, politicians and scientists argued over what to do. In the end, disaster was averted; but the world did not forget.

For a while, it seemed that the accident at Three Mile Island (TMI) had killed off nuclear power. No new plants have been built in the United States since then. In Europe, too, people began to have second thoughts. TMI led directly to a referendum in Sweden in 1980 that demanded an end to nuclear power. In 1986, an even worse accident, at Chernobyl in the Soviet Union, seemed to put the nail in the coffin of nuclear power in Europe. A number of countries, following Sweden's lead, campaigned for a ban. In Germany, the greens succeeded: the government has just agreed to end reprocessing of nuclear fuel by mid-2005. Moreover, Germany and Belgium have decided to ban new nuclear plants, although existing ones may serve out their useful lives. Even pro-nuclear France seemed to lose its enthusiasm for new plants.

For a while, Asia remained a bright spot for the nuclear industry. But the Asian financial crisis of 1998 cooled that enthusiasm. In recent months the new government in Taiwan, once a big fan of nuclear power, has tried to reverse course. In Japan, an accident soured public opinion: shoddy management practices at an experimental fuel-reprocessing plant in Tokaimura led in September 1999 to the deaths of two workers after they were exposed to radiation over 10,000 times the level considered safe. The Japanese government quietly scaled back its plans for 20 new plants.

The industry also hurt itself. In 1999, it emerged that British Nuclear Fuels (BNFL) had falsified records relating to shipments of nuclear fuel to Japan, sparking outrage in both countries. The firm had also understated the cost of nuclear clean-ups in Britain by some $13 bn. Clumsiness with deadly stuff, and now mendacity; in one way or another, nuclear power seemed to spell nothing but trouble.

Yet some did not lose faith, and are even looking at nuclear power in a new way. South Africa's Eskom is working with BNFL and Exelon, America's biggest nuclear energy firm, to build a reactor using new 'pebble-bed' technology. In Finland, a power company is now requesting permission to build a €2.5 bn ($2.2 bn) nuclear plant. Robin Jeffrey, the new chairman-designate of British Energy, Britain's largest nuclear operator, also sees a bright future for his industry. 'The mood is buoyant,' he says. 'Utilities with a nuclear portfolio are seen to be attractive places to put your money.' In fact, he has just completed a deal to take over the operation and maintenance of several reactors in Canada. Through AmerGen, a joint venture with Exelon, British Energy already manages a number of plants in the United States.

May 2001 produced the biggest boost of all for nuclear power: a strong endorsement from the Bush administration. On 17th May, a cabinet level task force unveiled a new energy policy that firmly supports the nuclear option. Vice President Dick Cheney, the head of the task force, argues forcefully not only for giving existing nuclear plants a new lease of life, but also for building more: 'We'd like to see an increase in the percentage of our electricity generated from nuclear power.'

What explains this burst of enthusiasm? The short answer is the arrival, at long last, of market forces in the electricity business. After decades of being run as monopolies, either by the state or the private sector, the electricity industry is being deregulated the world over. As a result of this, and of the current high price of fossil fuels, existing nuclear plants look attractive, and are beginning to be run as proper businesses by serious managers.

This is best seen in America, which deregulated its wholesale markets for power in 1996. The result of deregulation was a painful squeeze on America's dozens of nuclear plants, many of which were run as one-off investments by local utilities. That is rapidly changing, however, thanks to the flurry of deals that have led to mega mergers (like the one that created Exelon), joint ventures (like AmerGen), and other sorts of management coalitions. Nearly 30 GW, about a quarter of the country's nuclear capacity, has already been affected by this consolidation. In the near future, today's 50 nuclear utilities will probably be reduced to a dozen.

The advantages of such consolidation are many. Plant managers can benefit from economies of scale and can apply best practices more widely. As a result, plants are running at higher capacity utilisation rates and making better use of their fuel. Plant operators have also tried to expand capacity by upgrading their steam generators and turbines. Last winter, America's nuclear plants cranked out power at an operating cost of just 1.8 cents per kilowatt (kW)-hour; coal plants produced it for 2.1 cents per kW-hour, while those using natural gas (the price of which soared last winter) did no better than 3.5 cents.

Such improvements, argue nuclear fans, make a clear case for extending the licences of existing nuclear power plants beyond their original limit of 40 years or so. In America, for example, a number of these permits will start expiring in 2006, and nearly all will have gone by 2030. The story is similar in Europe and elsewhere. The fans are surely correct. Plants have been able to achieve such low operating costs because they are better managed and more efficient, and that, in turn, is linked to improved operational safety. When plants are safe, people do not mind living near them. Two plants have already received approvals from America's Nuclear Regulatory Commission (NRC) for another 20 years of operation. More will follow.

Tomorrow, the advocates say, nuclear power will be even cheaper. They point to promising new designs (such as pebble-bed technology) and argue that power plants are on the way that are safer and more cost-effective than today's. The industry is also mature now, they say; both companies and regulators know how to avoid the costly bureaucratic quagmire that followed the TMI accident. In future, new plants will be 'cheaper than coal'.

Maybe, maybe not. The new designs for nuclear plants are undoubtedly improvements. Technical experts agree that they are probably inherently safer, as they use 'passive' safety features that make a TMI-style meltdown virtually impossible. The NRC has already given its blessing to three advanced designs. However, critics argue that some new designs 'put all the safety eggs in the prevention basket', while short-changing systems that might limit an accident if one occurred.

Even if they do prove safer, the new designs may not necessarily be cheaper. By the reckoning of the International Atomic Energy Agency (IAEA), which has just produced a new analysis of the economics of nuclear power, the capital cost for today's nuclear designs runs at about \$2,000 per kW, against about \$1,200 per kW for coal and just \$500 per kW for a combined-cycle gas plant. History also suggests that not everything goes as planned when turning clever paper designs into real-life nuclear plants. What is more, the debts of any new plants, unlike the debts of existing plants, will not be written off. In fact, the true cost of power from today's plants is at least double the apparent figure, argues Florentin Krause, an American economist, once debt write-offs, government subsidies and externalities are accounted for.

The industry's advocates point to other benefits: security of supply, environmental benefits and so on. In some countries and in some circumstances, such arguments might have merit. But, taken together, do they make nuclear energy a special case that justifies subsidies or other forms of government intervention?

The energy security arguments vary, but mostly involve reduced reliance on fossil fuels, less vulnerability to an OPEC embargo, or a smaller bill for imported fuel. Whatever the political soundness of such arguments, an analysis done in 1998 by several agencies affiliated with the OECD is quite clear about the relative costs and benefits: 'For many countries, the additional energy security obtained from investing in non-fossil-fuelled generation options is likely to be worth less than the cost of obtaining that security.'

On environmental grounds, too, nuclear power does not emerge a clear winner. It is true that nuclear energy does not produce CO_2, the chief culprit behind man-made global warming. That, say fans like Mr Cheney, means that the world 'ought to' build more such plants. But handing out public money to the nuclear power industry (through production or investment tax credits, for example) is an inefficient way for governments to discourage global warming.

The better way would be through some sort of carbon tax, which would penalise fossil fuels but not any fuel free of carbon emissions, whether nuclear power or renewables. The IAEA's boffins have analysed how much of a boost nuclear power could get from a carbon tax, and the answer is quite a lot – possibly enough to compete with coal. Assume that the carbon tax falls between \$25 and \$85 per tonne of carbon, the level many experts think may be needed if industrialised countries are serious about the emissions targets agreed on in 1997 at Kyoto (some would set it higher still). The IAEA thinks that the highest of those taxes would boost the competitiveness of nuclear electricity against coal by 2 cents per kW-hour, and against natural gas by 1 cent. At the low end, nuclear gains an advantage of half a cent and a quarter-cent respectively.

But nuclear energy, even if boosted by a carbon tax, also carries grave environmental liabilities. Radiation is a threat to human health at every stage of the process, from uranium mining to plant operation (even in those new ultra-safe plants) to waste disposal. And waste disposal, despite decades of research and politicking, remains a farce. No country has yet built a 'permanent' waste-disposal site. The United States hopes to have one finished at Yucca Mountain, in the Nevada desert, in a decade's time; the European countries are a decade behind that. Even if these geological storage sites are completed, they are not the final answer. Nuclear waste may remain deadly for 100,000 years. To bury it in a big hole in the ground, and pray that some future generation may discover how to make it safe is simply passing the buck.

Lastly, when costing nuclear power, it is essential to remember the scope, scale and subtlety of the subsidies it has received. The IAEA analysis of nuclear economics shows that various OECD governments subsidise the industry's fuel supply services, waste disposal, fuel reprocessing and R&D. They also limit the liability of plants in case of accident, and help them clean up afterwards. Antony Troggartt, an industrial expert who has advised Greeenpeace, points to export loans and guarantees as another unfair boost.

How much does all this add up to? The IAEA's otherwise comprehensive analysis falls strangely silent on this topic, doubtless for political reasons. Reliable, comprehensive and up-to-date global figures from neutral analysts are scarce. Estimates by nuclear analysts are scarce. Estimates by nuclear opponents typically carry too many zeros to fit on this page. They are about as rigorous and credible as those put forth by the industry, which usually maintains the outrageous fiction that it no longer receives any subsidies at all.

Liability insurance is a good example of this. The American industry's official position is that there is no subsidy involved in the Price-Anderson Act, by which Congress limits the civilian nuclear industry's liability for nuclear catastrophes to less than $10 bn (a small fraction of what a Chernobyl-scale disaster would cost in America). Since there is no subsidy involved, why not let the Act lapse when it comes up for renewal next year? Mr Cheney's response is revealing: 'It needs to be renewed...(if not), nobody's going to invest in nuclear power plants.'

One concrete figure gives an idea of how enormous the overall subsidy pie might be. According to official figures, OECD governments poured $159 bn in today's money into nuclear research between 1974 and 1998. Some of that breathtaking sum is a sunk cost from the early days of the industry, but not all: governments still shell out about half their energy R&D budgets on this mature industry.

Source: The Economist, 19–25 May 2001

Questions

1 Identify some of the key political factors suggested as being involved in setting targets for the nuclear industry.

2 How might the nuclear industry's targets be different in the absence of these political factors?

3 What *environmental* benefits and costs might be attributed to nuclear energy? What *non-environmental* benefits and costs might be taken into account in target setting for this industry?

Economic 'welfare' and target setting

Before leaving the issue of target setting it may be useful to review some ideas which frequently arise when considering 'optimal targets'. Any target that is *suboptimal* can sometimes be expressed using the idea of 'deadweight loss'. This refers to the loss of economic welfare which is thought to result from pursuing (or achieving) the wrong target. *Economic welfare* is defined here in terms of two important concepts, namely:

Economic welfare = Consumer surplus + Producer surplus

where *consumer surplus* is the amount consumers are willing to pay over and above the amount they *need* to pay (as indicated by the market price), and *producer surplus* is the amount producers receive (in terms of the market price) over and above the amount they *need* for them to be willing to supply the product.

In Figure 3.8, the *optimal target* is price P_1 and quantity Q_1, with consumers surplus DvP_1 and producer surplus P_1vS. Total economic welfare is a maximum and is the sum of these two areas. Suppose now that the wrong target has been set, namely price P_2 and associated output Q_2. This will result in a *loss of economic welfare*. The reduction in output from Q_1 to Q_2 means a loss of area B in consumer surplus and loss of area C in producer surplus. However, the higher price results in a gain of area A in producer surplus which exactly offsets the loss of area A in consumer surplus. This means that the net welfare change is negative, i.e. there is a 'deadweight' loss of area B + area C.

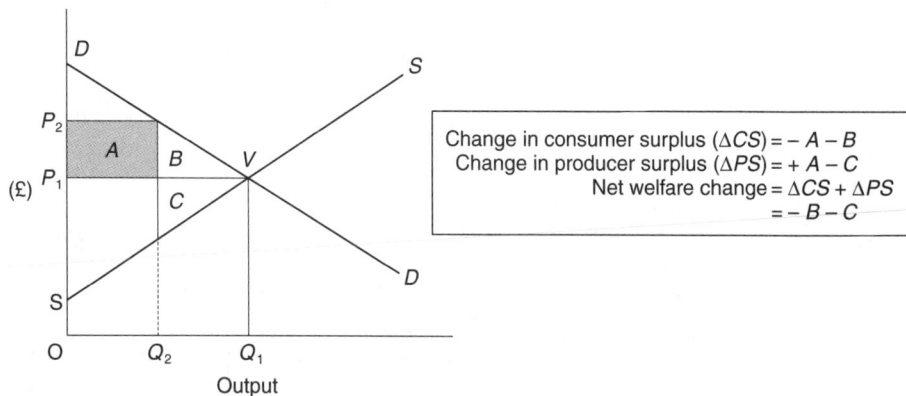

Figure 3.8 Welfare loss ('deadweight loss') from setting the wrong target (namely price P_2 and quantity Q_2 instead of price P_1 and quantity Q_1)

Now try the self-check questions for this chapter on the companion website
www.booksites.net/ison
You will also find up-to-date facts and case materials.

Key terms

Externalities Occur when decisions create costs or benefits for people other than the decision taker

Marginal abatement cost (MAC) The extra cost to the firm of avoiding emitting the last unit of pollutant

Marginal damage cost (MDC) The extra damage from emitting the last unit of pollutant; sometimes called marginal external cost (MEC)

Marginal social cost (MSC) The additional private cost and additional external cost involved in producing an extra unit of output (MSC = MPC + MEC)

Negative externality Where the marginal social cost exceeds the marginal private cost

Positive externality Where the marginal social cost is less than the marginal private cost (or where marginal social benefit exceeds the marginal private benefit)

Public good 'Pure' public good has two key characteristics. *Non-rivalry in consumption* so that the extra unit of output can be consumed by many (not just by one). *Non-exclusivity in consumption* so that it is impossible to exclude non-payers from consuming the output provided. 'Mixed' public goods have some of these characteristics but not all.

References and further reading

Bowers, J. (1997) *Sustainability and Environmental Economics*, Longman, Harlow, especially Chapter 3.

Field, B.C. (1997) *Environmental Economics: An Introduction*, McGraw-Hill, especially Chapters 4 and 5.

Gilpin, A. (2000) *Environmental Economics: A Critical Overview*, Wiley, especially Chapters 5 and 6.

Ison, S. (2001) 'Transport', in *Applied Economics* (9th edition), ed. Griffiths, A. and Wall, S., FT/Prentice Hall, Harlow.

National Economic Research Associates (NERA) (1997) *The Costs of Road Congestion in Great Britain*, NERA Briefing paper.

Nordhaus, W. (1991) 'To slow or not to slow: the economics of the greenhouse effect', *The Economic Review*, 10, 1.

RAC (2000), *Report on Motoring 2000*, 12th edition, London.

Royal Commission on Environmental Pollution (2000), 22nd Report, *Energy – The Changing Climate*, Cm 4749

Turner, R., Pearce, D. and Bateman, I. (1994) *Environmental Economics*, FT/Prentice Hall, Harlow.

Useful websites

Environment Agency
Environment: (EC DGXI)
World Health Organisation
United Nations

Office for National Statistics (ONS)
ONS Statstore and Statbase
Central Office of Information
Eurostat
International Monetary Fund (IMF)
Organisation for Economic Co-Operation and Development (OECD)
World Bank
United Nations Development Program

Achieving the targets: policy instruments

In free-market or mixed economies the *market* is often seen as an efficient method of allocating scarce resources, with the price mechanism acting as a 'signal' to both consumers and producers. This chapter begins by examining various ways in which the market can be used to provide incentives to either firms or consumers in order to bring about a socially optimum use of environmental assets or restriction of environmental liabilities. The chapter then moves on to discuss a number of *non-market* ('command and control') mechanisms which might be used to achieve the same outcomes. The strengths and weaknesses of these various policy instruments, both in principle and practice, are considered in some detail. The broad issue of 'pollution' provides a useful context for much of our discussion as to the relative merits of the various policy instruments, although 'pollution' as a topic in its own right is considered in more detail in Chapter 6.

For the purpose of this chapter we shall regard the use of bargaining, environmental taxes and tradable permits as essentially 'market-based' policy instruments. The use of regulations and standards will be regarded as essentially 'non-market-based' policy instruments.

● ● ● ● Bargaining and negotiation

The *bargaining solution* is based on the insights of Ronald Coase (1960) who argued that if *property rights* are assigned, then *bargains* may be struck which result in the optimum level of pollution being achieved. The idea here is that if we assign 'property rights' to the polluters giving them the 'right to pollute', or to the sufferers giving them the 'right not to be polluted', then bargains may be struck whereby pollution is curbed. For instance, if we assign these property rights to the polluters, then those who suffer may find it advantageous to compensate the polluter for agreeing not to pollute. The suggestion is that compensation will be offered by the sufferers as long as this is less than the value of the damage which would otherwise be inflicted upon them. Alternatively, if the property rights are assigned to the sufferers, who then have the 'right' not to be polluted, then the polluters may find it advantageous to offer the sufferers sums of money which would allow the polluters to continue polluting. The suggestion is that the polluters will offer compensation to the sufferers as long as this is less than the private benefits obtained by expanding output and thereby increasing pollution. Under either

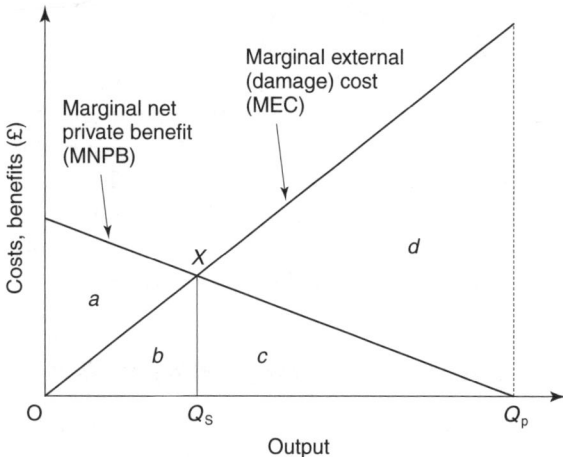

Figure 4.1 Finding a negotiated solution to the externality problem

situation, economists such as Coase have shown that clearly assigned property rights can lead to 'bargains' which bring about output solutions closer to the social optimum than would otherwise occur. In the view of Coase it is less important who has the property rights, polluters or sufferers of pollution, than that the property rights are assigned to someone.

Figure 4.1 captures many of the ideas already discussed. Here we consider product output, rather than pollutant emission, though it is assumed that the level of pollutant varies directly with product output. The marginal external (damage) cost (MEC) curve therefore slopes upward from left to right. At the same time the marginal net private benefit (MNPB) of each unit of output is assumed to vary inversely with product output and therefore slopes downwards from left to right. MNPB is essentially the marginal profit curve, representing the addition to net private benefit (revenue minus cost) received by the firm from selling the last unit of output.

If the pollution externality was not taken into account, then firms would produce up to output Q_p at which MNPB = 0. Only here would total net private benefit (i.e. total profit) be a maximum at $a + b + c$. However, the socially optimum level of output is Q_s, where MNPB = MEC. Each unit of output beyond Q_s adds more in damage (pollution) costs to society than it does to net private benefit, and is therefore socially inefficient to produce. Equally it would be socially inefficient to forsake producing any units up to Q_s, since each of these units adds more to net private benefit than to damage (pollution) costs for society. Note that in this analysis the social optimum does not imply zero damage (pollution). Rather it suggests that the benefits to society are greatest at output Q_s, with marginal damage costs being positive at $Q_s X$.

Property rights assigned to polluters

If **property rights** are assigned to the *firm that pollutes*, then those who suffer may be prepared to pay the polluter to reduce its scale of activity and therefore the level of pollution. In order to achieve the optimal level of pollution, Q_s, the sufferers may be willing to pay the polluter an amount up to a maximum of c plus d. This is an amount equal to the total damages incurred by the sufferer of the externality through the production of Q_s to Q_p. The polluter would, however, only be prepared to reduce its output from Q_p to Q_s for a sum not less than c, the total profit earned through the production of Q_s to Q_p. There is clearly scope for bargaining to take place between the two parties. The amount paid by the sufferers will thus be somewhere between c and 'c plus d' with the amount actually paid depending on the relative bargaining strengths of the two parties.

Property rights assigned to sufferers

If the property rights are assigned to the *sufferers* then a similar outcome may still result via bargaining. The starting point in this situation is the origin in Figure 4.1 since it is assumed that sufferers prefer zero pollution with zero damage. There is still, however, room for bargaining. Here the polluter will find it advantageous to produce the social optimum, Q_s, and compensate the sufferers of pollution with an amount equal to b, thus retaining an amount of total profit a. If the polluter produced an amount greater than Q_s the gains obtained in terms of profit would be less than the losses incurred in terms of compensation paid to the sufferers. When property rights are assigned to sufferers there is also scope for bargaining to take place and for a socially optimum solution Q_s to be achieved.

Income distribution and property rights

Whether the polluter compensates the sufferers or the sufferers pay the polluter, the socially optimum output Q_s is achievable. However, in terms of **equity** (fairness) the two outcomes are very different. When the polluter compensates the sufferer, then with solution Q_s the polluter gains a total profit of a and the sufferer compensation of b. When the sufferer pays the polluter, then with solution Q_s the polluter gains a total profit of at least $a + b + c$ (where c is the minimum payment by sufferers to the polluter *not* to produce $Q_s Q_p$); the sufferers no longer receive compensation of b and further have to pay a minimum of c to the polluter (as inducement *not* to produce $Q_s Q_p$). These are clearly very different income distributions associated with achieving the same allocation of resources. In this distributional context how property rights are assigned does matter!

Polluter pays principle (PPP)

In fact there is a long tradition of support for the **polluter pays principle** (see also Chapter 13, page 319). In addition to the equity argument, the reasons for this are that:

● Those affected by pollution often find it more difficult to organise themselves, not least because the sufferers may be large in number. Failure to organise will inhibit the offering of appropriate payments to polluters to induce the Q_s solution.

- Sufferers may not have sufficient funds to compensate polluters for the cost of reducing pollution. Again polluters may not then reduce their polluting output in line with the true social damage incurred.
- Individual sufferers may be reluctant to take the lead in terms of negotiations, preferring to let someone else take responsibility, thus taking a *free-ride*. The free-rider problem can be explored through the use of game theory (see Box 4.1).
- If polluters are aware of the fact that they will have to pay compensation in full to the sufferers of their emissions, then it could encourage research and development into more environmentally friendly technology.

BOX 4.1

Game theory and the free-rider problem

Assume there are two sufferers from the pollution emitted from a factory. The two sufferers, individuals A and B, each have a level of utility equal to 50 utils. Individuals A and B are thinking about involving themselves in negotiation with the factory polluter. In reaching their decision there are *four* scenarios:

- *Both individuals A and B decide not to negotiate with the polluter.* The outcome is that both continue to suffer and obtain a utility of 50 utils.
- *Both individuals A and B decide to negotiate with the polluter.* There is a cost in negotiating which is equal to 70 utils each. If they negotiate together however they are likely to obtain major concessions, which could be equal to 100 utils for each individual. In this situation both individuals A and B benefit by a further 30 utils, resulting in each having utility of 80 utils.
- *Individual A decides to negotiate while B free-rides.* In this situation the bargaining strength of the sufferers will be somewhat less and as such the gains from negotiation could be only 40 utils. In this situation the expected utility from negotiation for A would now be 20 utils (the original 50 utils plus the gain of 40 utils minus the cost of 70 utils). For individual B, however, the expected gain is 40 utils with no negotiation costs involved because of free-riding. Thus Bs expected utility is 90 utils.
- *Individual B decides to negotiate while A free-rides.* In this situation A's expected utility is 90 utils and B's 20 utils.

The information above can be presented in terms of a game theory pay-off matrix, as in the table below.

		Individual B			
		Negotiate		Free-ride	
Individual A	Negotiate	*80*	80	*20*	90
	Free-ride	*90*	20	*50*	50

Each individual has one of two options, either to negotiate or free-ride. The left side of each box (in italics) refers to individual A's outcomes (pay-offs) and the right side to individual B's outcomes (pay-offs). Taking a free ride might seem an attractive option for each individual, yielding the highest pay-off (90) in the belief that the other individual will indeed negotiate. However, if both decide to free-ride this essentially means both decide not to negotiate and the outcome is a less attractive pay-off (50). The situation is the same as in the prisoner's dilemma, which is also part of game theory (see Chapter 6, page 158).

- If each selects the best outcome for itself independent of the reaction of the other, then each will choose to free-ride, believing it can achieve a pay-off of 90 utils. This is the ▶

so-called 'dominant strategy' for the game, but in fact the outcome from following this strategy is only 50 utils each. Had each individual sought to negotiate rather than free-ride, then each would have been better off with 80 utils apiece. If sufferers are more likely to attempt to free-ride in this way, then giving them the property rights by making the polluter pay may be the best way of ensuring that the socially optimum bargaining outcome is achieved.

The above are arguments in favour of giving property rights to the sufferers when seeking a bargaining solution. A similar viewpoint can also be supported by a number of arguments against giving the property rights to the polluters.

- If the sufferers have to compensate polluters for reducing their emission levels it may encourage other polluting firms to relocate to the area, being keen to take advantage of the pay-outs. It may also act as a spur for new firms in these industries to enter the market, thus adding to the pollution problem.
- If the sufferers are imperfectly informed about the polluters' actual situation, then negotiations are more likely to break down than in the opposite case. Although it may seem administratively simpler to assign property rights to a small number of polluters, the bargaining prices may not lead to a successful outcome. For example, take a situation in which there is one polluter, who has been given the right to pollute, and one sufferer. Suppose projected profit from production beyond Q_s is £500,000 to the polluter, while the benefit in terms of less pollution by restricting production to Q_s is worth £800,000 to the sufferer. In such a situation there is the basis for bargaining and ultimately an agreement in which the sufferer compensates the polluter by an amount greater than £500,000 but less than £800,000. However, the fact that the extra production beyond Q_s is worth a further £500,000 in profit will be information which is known only to the polluter. The sufferer may be of the opinion that the polluter will be prepared to reduce its output to Q_s for an amount equal to, say, £400,000 and may in fact make what it believes to be a generous offer of £450,000. This offer is likely to be turned down by the polluter as unsatisfactory, with negotiations broken off. Yet if both sides had been privy to *perfect information*, an agreement satisfactory to both parties could have been reached.

The success of the bargaining solution depends in part on the numbers involved, although even with only two parties an agreement is by no means automatic. If there are a large number of sufferers and polluters then organising the two sides could be costly, inhibiting any negotiation. For these and other reasons governments may resort to alternative market-based methods of dealing with pollution, most notably environmental taxes and tradable permits.

Environmental taxes

An *environmental tax* is a tax on a product or service which is detrimental to the environment, or a tax on a factor input used to produce that product or service. An environmental tax will increase the private costs of producing goods or services which impose negative 'externalities' on society. A tax which exactly equals the value of the marginal external (damage) costs imposed is often called a **Pigouvian tax**.

In terms of Figure 4.2, left to his/her own devices the producer will maximise total net private benefit (total profit) at a level of activity Q_p with total profit OcQ_p. Output Q_p is well above the socially optimum output Q_s. However, if a tax of t (a Pigouvian tax) is imposed on the polluter it has the effect of shifting the MNPB curve vertically downwards by the amount of the tax (and therefore to the left), thus giving MNPB − t. The tax would be paid on each unit of pollution and the polluter would now maximise total net private benefit at a level of activity equal to Q_s, earning total profit O_aQ_s and paying an overall level of tax equal to area $OaeQ_s$. If the firm produced an amount greater than Q_s then it would pay more in tax on the extra units sold than it would receive in profit (MNPB). The tax would be exactly equal to the marginal external (damage) cost (MEC) at the optimum level of economic activity Q_s. As already noted, such a tax, which charges polluters the exact amount of damage they impose on the environment, is called a 'Pigouvian tax'. Using environmental taxes in this way is often said to be a policy of 'internalising' the externality. In other words, the firm itself now has the incentive to take the externality into account in its own decision making.

A move towards environmental taxes is in line with the 'polluter pays' principle adopted by the OECD in 1972 and discussed in the previous section. This principle states that 'the polluter should bear the cost of measures to reduce pollution decided upon by public authorities to ensure that the environment is in an 'acceptable state'. The idea behind adopting this principle across member states was to avoid the distortions in comparative advantages and trade flows which could arise if countries tackled environmental problems in widely different ways.

Slightly less than 2 per cent of UK total tax revenue is currently yielded by explicitly environmental taxes, although if general taxes on energy are also included in a looser definition of 'environmentally related' taxes, then this figure rises to some 8.5 per cent of UK total tax revenue. There are problems, however, with using an environmental tax, not least in determining the tax rate which will equate MNPB with the MEC.

Some further advantages and disadvantages of using environmental taxes are considered below.

Advantages

- With an environmental tax the producer has to pay a 'price' for the pollution it imposes on society. It follows that the polluter has a profit-based incentive to produce the optimum level of output, Q_s in Figure 4.2, since its own profits would now be maximised at MNPB = MEC, instead of producing the socially inefficient output Q_p which maximised its profits before the tax was imposed.
- One of the main advantages of environmental taxes (unlike regulations or standards) is that they allow firms the freedom to reduce their emissions in the best way they see fit, as opposed to a central agency dictating how such reductions should be achieved. We note below (page 103) that this may permit a given

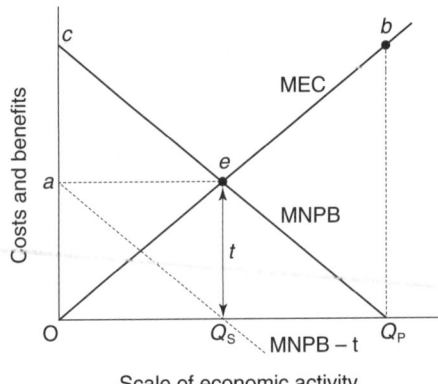

Figure 4.2 Using environmental taxes (*t*) to achieve the social optimum output (Q_s)

environmental outcome to be achieved at a lower cost (i.e. more efficiently) than by the alternative method of regulation.

- It could be argued that the polluter is penalised twice by the introduction of an environmental tax. First, if in Figure 4.2 tax *t* is imposed, the producer loses the profits which would have been earned by producing between Q_s and Q_p, measured by the area $Q_s e Q_p$. Second, when operating at the optimum output level Q_s, the producer must pay tax equal to area $OaeQ_s$.

- There are often political difficulties in introducing any new tax. For example, there may be resistance from industry, especially if there is a belief that the authorities could raise the tax rate even higher than the optimal tax *t*, in Figure 4.2 for purely revenue raising rather than 'efficiency' purposes. Even at the optimal tax rate *t*, tax revenue at $OaeQ_s$ exceeds the remaining total external costs of OeQ_s.

Disadvantages

- There are difficulties in determining the tax necessary to achieve the socially efficient level of output and pollution. In practice the aim may be to get as close as possible to the optimum tax. This may be a problem if the authorities have underestimated the true value of the MEC (see Box 4.2).

BOX 4.2

Difficulties if the optimum tax is underestimated

If the authorities have not established the optimal tax per unit, that is t_1, and have in fact set it too low at t_2, this may create a problem. If the marginal external cost is MEC_1 then setting too low a tax of t_2 per unit of pollution will result in the scale of economic activity Q_a, with the arginal external cost higher than it would be at the optimum level, that is *d* rather than *e*. On the other hand, if the marginal external cost is MEC_2, then the marginal external cost increases more sharply beyond *e*, rising to *c*, with too low a tax rate of t_2 which is substantially greater than the optimum level of *e*. It follows that any underestimate of the optimum tax rate may lead to substantially larger external (damage) costs. In a situation where ▶

the MEC curve rises sharply beyond the optimum point *e*, then a standard rather than a tax may be a more attractive option.

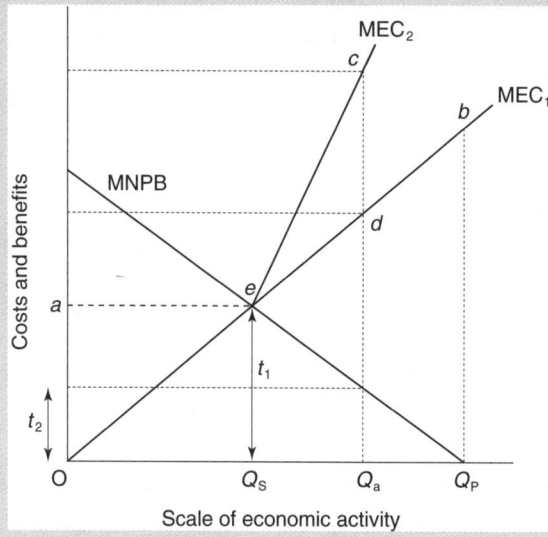

Figure 4.3 Underestimating the optimum tax rate

The carbon tax

We have noted the efficiency case for an environmental tax, and one which has received much attention is the so-called carbon tax. In fact, rather than seek to measure and tax carbon emissions, governments can simply impose a tax on the three fossil fuels – coal, oil and gas – in proportion to their carbon content. The proposed EU carbon tax was to be a tax on the carbon content of fossil fuels and a tax on all non-renewable forms of energy. Although intended to help the EU meet its commitment at the Rio Summit of 1992 to stabilise CO_2 emissions at 1990 levels by the end of the century, it has failed to be ratified. Nevertheless Germany, Italy, Austria, Norway, Sweden, Finland, Denmark and the Netherlands have some form of carbon tax (OECD, 1999), though the link with the carbon content of energy is usually weak. In any case, the carbon tax as initially proposed provides a useful study of a market-based policy instrument, in this case an environmental tax. The fossil fuels such as gas, coal and oil were to bear a tax made up of two components, one related to carbon content, the other to energy content. Other non-renewable energy forms (e.g. nuclear power) were to be subject to the energy part of the tax but not the carbon part. The idea was to combine the two parts in equal proportions, with half the tax related to the carbon content and half to the energy content, and to start the tax at

$3 per barrel of oil equivalent in 1993, moving in annual $1 increments to $10 per barrel of oil equivalent in the year 2000.

Higher private costs

A $10 tax per barrel of oil equivalent would have its main initial impact on industry and power stations making direct use of fossil fuels. Such users would have to pay 58 per cent more for hard coal, 45 per cent more for heavy fuel oil, and 34 per cent more for natural gas.

Higher prices for consumers

Higher producer costs would shift the supply curve upwards (and to the left), causing a rise in market prices. It has been estimated that the proposed carbon tax, when fully implemented, would raise the price of petrol by 6 per cent and the price of diesel fuels by 11 per cent. For domestic heating purposes, the tax would be equivalent to a 16 per cent increase in light fuel oil prices and a 14 per cent increase in natural gas prices.

Substitution effects

The tax on carbon emissions would cause some substitution within the fossil fuels. Coal has a higher carbon content than oil, which in turn has a higher carbon content than gas. A carbon tax would therefore penalise coal most. We have seen how the proposed carbon tax was expected to raise the prices of hard coal, fuel oil and natural gas by 58, 45 and 34 per cent respectively. There would also be substitution effects between fossil and non-fossil fuels. Alternative (and renewable) energy sources that do not emit carbon would now be relatively cheaper than fossil fuels for any given amount of energy provision. Wind, wave, solar and nuclear energy sources could all expect to benefit.

In practice these substitution effects were likely to be small. Various studies suggest that the price elasticities of demand for energy are low. For example, the UK price elasticity of demand for energy has been estimated (Rajah, 1992) at only (−) 0.1 per cent in the short run and (−) 0.3 per cent in the long run (after 10 years). This implies that there would need to be rather substantial carbon taxes in place in order to have a significant effect on carbon usage.

The greater use of renewable energy sources would contribute to a conservation effect. Even the carbon-emitting fossil fuels would benefit from this effect, as any wasteful use of such fuels now becomes more expensive.

Finally, a dynamic technological effect could be expected to result from a carbon tax that penalises carbon emissions pro rata. Any fossil fuels that could be burned in ways that emit less carbon per unit of energy would then pay less tax. This will give an incentive for research and development expenditure on carbon reduction technologies or into finding ways of taking gas from coal, instead of burning coal directly, and so on.

Income effects

Any tax will increase withdrawals from the circular flow of income and thereby depress levels of income and expenditure generally. The proposed carbon tax would, it was estimated, only marginally curb economic growth rates of the (then) 11 main EU countries – cutting them by only 0.9 per cent over the forecasting period to 2010. The inflationary impact of a tax rise would also depress real levels of income and expenditure. In the case of the proposed carbon tax, the additional price rises have been estimated as being 3 per cent over the period to 2010. These were again relatively modest, as was the fall in EU employment at around 0.8 per cent.

Equity effects

Fuel consumption takes a larger share of the expenditure of the poor than of the rich. A carbon tax would therefore be regressive. Some of the tax revenue raised from the tax would therefore be needed to offset some of the impacts on poorer households. However, in doing so, their consumption of carbon-releasing fuels might then increase.

Despite the efficiency advantages of a carbon tax, there are clearly practical problems involved in its implementation, although most of these could be overcome with careful forethought.

Questions

1 Briefly review:
  (a) the case for a carbon tax;
  (b) the case against a carbon tax.
2 Can you explain why the likely impacts of a carbon tax would cause different rates of price increase for different products?

More on environmental taxes

In a recent simulation by Cambridge Econometrics (Cowe, 1998), a 'package' of seven green taxes, including a carbon tax based on industrial and commercial energy use, was estimated as cutting CO_2 emissions by 13 per cent on 1990 levels by the year 2010. Rather encouragingly, this package of green taxes was estimated as raising a further £27 bn in tax revenue by 2010, which could be used to cut employers' national insurance by 3 per cent, leading to almost 400,000 extra jobs. Only a small (-0.2 per cent) deterioration was predicted for the balance of payments and for inflation (prices rising by 0.5 per cent) by 2010 and GDP was even predicted to have received a small boost ($+ 0.2$ per cent) by this package of green taxes. Such simulation studies are useful in that they 'model' impacts of tax measures throughout the economy, although one must carefully check the assumptions which underlie the equations used in computer models.

The climate change levy

In the 1999 UK Budget, the Chancellor, Gordon Brown, announced that a *climate change levy* (CCL) would be imposed on business use of energy from April 2001 (Blow, 1999). The intention being to base the levy (tax) on the energy content of different fuels for business use, while exempting fuels for private use. The CCL represents a further step in the evolution of government policy. The CCL is a tax applying to fossil fuel used by non-domestic (mainly commercial and industrial) users, applying at different rates to different fossil fuels. The rates are 0.42 p per kWh for electricity, 0.15 p per kWh for gas and 1.17 p per kilogram for coal. Fuel oils are not liable for CCL as they are already liable for separate duty.

The CCL is a revenue-neutral tax, meaning that the revenue produced by the tax will be recycled to companies so that for industry as a whole there will be no net increase in taxation. The revenues are recycled through a reduction of 0.3 per cent in employers' national insurance contributions, an increase in tax allowances for certain energy-saving investments by a company and payments from an energy-efficient fund for small and medium-sized companies. Certain large polluters are able to enter into negotiated voluntary agreement with the government to reduce energy consumption in exchange for a reduction (up to 80 per cent) of CCL. Note that the tax does not apply to domestic energy use, although households will bear some of the burden of this tax in so far as firms pass the tax forward.

Critics have suggested that a carbon tax which was based solely on CO_2 content would be preferable, since the energy content of fuel does not necessarily reflect its carbon content. However, an energy tax is believed to be simpler to administer, especially where it is applied (unlike CCL) at a uniform rate per kilowatt-hour for all 'primary' fuels (coal, gas, oil), rather than a more complex differential rate depending on their carbon content.

We have already touched on a number of strengths and weaknesses as regards using environmental taxes or standards in achieving specified targets. After reviewing environmental regulations and standards below, we compare and contrast taxes and standards in rather more detail (see pages 98–104).

● ● ● ● Tradable permits

As with an environmental tax, **tradable permits** are a market-based solution to the problem of negative externalities such as pollution. Whereas the use of an environmental tax option requires the authority to establish the tax rate and collect the tax revenue, a system of tradable permits operates in a more decentralised manner. It utilises the market-based approach but is based on interaction between the polluters themselves. With this policy option the polluter is issued with a number of permits to emit a specified amount of pollution, be it CO_2, sulphur dioxide or some other pollutant. The total number of permits issued places an upper limit on the total amount of emissions allowed, which can then be set within current guidelines as regards acceptable levels of emissions for that pollutant. Once issued, polluters can buy and sell the permits to each other, at a price agreed between the two parties. In other words the permits are *transferable*. Tradable permits essentially create a new type of property right, a 'permit' to pollute.

The market for permits can be illustrated by use of Figure 4.4. The horizontal axis represents the level of emissions and the number of tradable permits. In order to achieve the optimum level of pollution of Q_s, the agency responsible for permits must issue Q_s permits in total. This is then the effective supply curve of permits. The marginal abatement cost (MAC) curve can be viewed as the demand curve for permits in that it tells us how much it will cost the firm to abate (avoid) the last unit of pollution. At any given price of a permit, the firm will seek to abate the

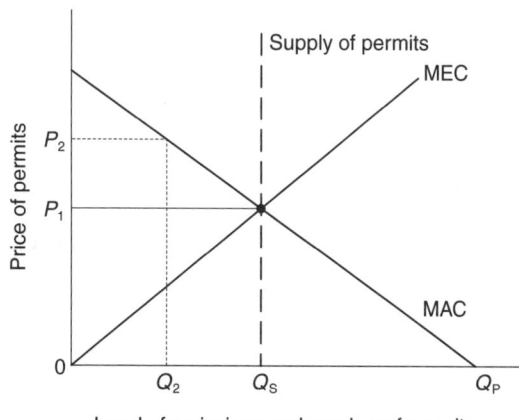

Figure 4.4 The market for tradable permits

quantity of emissions of the pollutant shown by the MAC curve. For example, at price OP_2 the (profit-maximising) firm will wish to abate Q_pQ_2 units of pollution (and emit OQ_2 units of pollution).

The suggestion here is that if the socially optimum number of permits Q_s is supplied, then the market for permits (supply and demand) will establish an equilibrium price (P_1) which will result in the appropriate level of pollution abatement (Q_sQ_p).

Of course, some initial total of permits must be agreed on, consistent with some recognised safety standard (e.g. the Kyoto targets) and then this total must be allocated among the nations according to some agreed formula. *Grandfathering* is one such formula, in which permits are distributed pro rata to those countries already emitting the pollutant, so that the largest polluter receives the greatest number of permits. As might be expected, there has been much disagreement as to the allocation mechanisms for permits, for example developing countries argue that 'grandfathering' disadvantages them unfairly.

The underlying principle of tradable permits is that those firms which can achieve a lower level of pollution can benefit by selling permits to those firms which at present find it either too difficult or too expensive to meet the standard set. This is outlined in Box 4.3.

BOX 4.3

The trade in permits

Suppose two power stations, A and B, both emit CO_2, but with different MACs, as illustrated in Figures 4.5(a) and (b). It can be seen that the MACs for power station A rise more quickly than for power station B as abatement increases and emissions are reduced. ▶

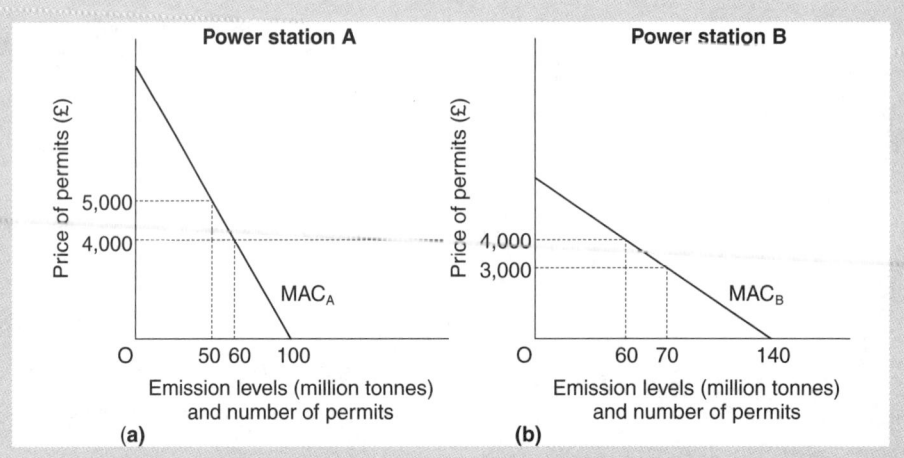

Figure 4.5 Differences in MACs as a basis for trading permits

With no controls on emission levels so that no abatement takes place, then total emissions of CO_2 are 240 million tonnes (t) per annum. Suppose, however, the authorities desire a reduction in emission levels of 50 per cent, so that 120 million t is the maximum emission level from the two power stations combined. This can be achieved by the issue of 120 million t tradable permits.

Suppose these permits are issued on the basis of past levels of emission (grandfathering). In this case power station A would receive 50 tradable permits and power station B 70. This being the case, A would have to reduce emissions to 50 and B to 70 (million t per annum) respectively.

If A were to reduce its emissions to 50 million t its MAC would then be £5,000 per tonne, thus if it could *buy* permits for less than £5,000 it would do so. If firm B were to reduce its emission to 70 million t, its MAC would be £3,000 per tonne. If B can *sell* its permits for a price greater than £3,000 per tonne it will do so, since the revenue earned from the sale would be greater than the extra cost of abatement incurred by reducing emission, whereas A will be willing to buy permits at prices between £3,000 and £5,000 per tonne. There is thus the basis for trade between the two power stations. The two power stations will continue to trade while their MACs are different. As can be seen in Figures 4.5(a) and (b) such trade can continue until their respective MACs are equalised at a price of £4,000, with 60 million t emitted by both power station A and power station B, with B selling 10 permits to A. The overall total of emissions, however, remain constant at 120 (million t).

Advantages and disadvantages of tradable permits

There are various advantages and disadvantages of the permit system for dealing with pollution.

Advantages

● Any new form of tax, such as an environmental tax, faces difficulties in terms of acceptability, not least since it is charging polluters for something that used to be done without charge. By using tradable permits, however, a new form of

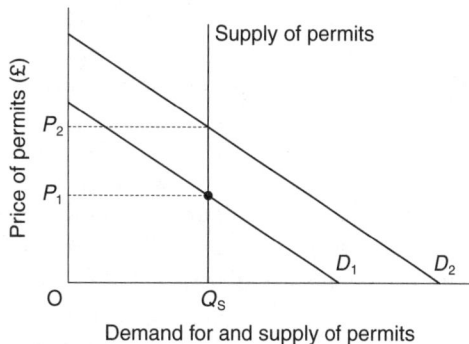

Figure 4.6 Increase in demand for permits

property right is issued which has a market value. This is likely to prove a more acceptable policy instrument to those directly involved.

- The price mechanism for tradable permits will help allocate the restricted supply of permits to those who most value them. In terms of Figure 4.6, new entrants into the industry would shift (increase) the demand curve for permits from D_1 to D_2. If there is no change in the supply of permits (Q_S) then the price of permits will increase from P_1 to P_2 and some existing holders of permits will be willing to sell them at this higher price. If the new entrants are willing to pay more than existing firms for the permits available, then they may be able to acquire them via the market mechanism.
- The supply of permits can be adjusted to meet changed conditions. For example, if the agency which has overall responsibility wishes to relax its control over pollution it can issue more permits, resulting in a shift in the supply curve to the right (increase). On the other hand, if the agency wishes to tighten its control over pollution it can buy back permits on the open market from polluters, thereby reducing the total in circulation.
- A potential advantage of tradable permits is their availability for purchase on the open market, increasing choice. For example, environmental groups may choose to buy permits as a way of reducing the overall level of pollution.
- Tradable permits can be viewed as cost-effective, providing incentives for polluters with low abatement costs to abate (avoid) pollution and sell the permits no longer required while providing incentives for polluters with higher abatement costs to purchase these permits rather than abate. A ready-made market exists for tradable permits with low-cost abaters selling to high-cost abaters, thereby reducing the total abatement cost of achieving a given target for pollution reduction.
- Tradable permits reduce the uncertainty which is often associated with an environmental tax. The agency can issue permits in line with current guidelines as to the maximum level of emissions which the environment can safely absorb. With environmental taxes, however, the tax set may be too low to achieve the socially optimum level of emissions.
- Inflation will reduce the real value of environmental taxes, so that they may have to be increased on a regular basis in order to maintain the required level of

pollution. However, inflationary pressures have no impact on the ability of tradable permits to achieve the target level of pollution. All that may result from such pressures is a tendency for permit prices to rise in line with inflation.

Disadvantages

- The market-based permit approach is based on limiting the number of permits in circulation. Since polluters will be keen to obtain as many permits as they can when the permits are first issued then an appropriate system of initial allocation is all-important. In Box 4.3 the allocation of permits was on the basis of current or recent past emission levels ('grandfathering'), with each power station receiving permits equalling 50 per cent of their emission levels. This can, however, create problems. Those firms which have been successful in reducing their emission levels will be penalised by being allocated fewer permits than those firms who have not reduced their emission levels. Indeed firms may even increase their emission levels if they believe that future permits will be allocated on the basis of past emission levels. An alternative to 'grandfathering' is to allocate permits equally to those emitting a particular pollutant. A difficulty with this approach is the fact that firms differ in the amount of pollution they currently emit. We can see from Case Study 4.2 that 'trading in emission permits may be doomed unless countries can agree on the rules of the game'.
- The permit system has been criticised on ethical grounds in that it gives the owner of a permit the right to pollute – a permit to emit pollutants.
- It is always likely that a few polluters may purchase all the available permits (cornering the market in permits) thus making it difficult for new firms, who also pollute, to enter the industry. The permit system could thus act as a 'barrier to entry' and be seen as anti-competitive.
- The administrative costs of a permit system could be excessive if there are a large number of polluters. For example, the agency may need to *monitor* transactions in permits to ensure that polluters are only emitting the amount of pollution that they are entitled to. It may then need to *enforce* any breaches of the regulations. These monitoring and implementation costs may be significant when permits are widely traded between a large number of parties.

Tradable permits and the Kyoto Protocol

The Kyoto agreements (see Chapter 7) have raised the profile of tradable permits as a policy instrument for dealing with global restrictions in emissions of CO_2. The suggestion is that the Kyoto targets could be better achieved if countries were able to trade CO_2 emissions permits between themselves. By allowing a market in permits to develop in which countries with higher abatement costs purchase permits from countries with lower abatement costs, it is suggested that there will be a move towards greater equality in marginal abatement costs and various efficiency gains, as outlined in Table 4.1. The target cuts in emission of greenhouse gases envisaged in the Kyoto Protocol are projected as having a less adverse effect on real national income in the various countries if these targets are met by using the tradable permit policy instrument.

Table 4.1 Costs of Kyoto in 2010, with and without tradable permits

	Change in real income (%)	
	Without tradable permits	*With tradable permits*
USA	−0.33	−0.40
Japan	−0.24	−0.19
European Union	−0.77	−0.33
Other OECD	−0.68	−0.64
OECD total	−0.48	−0.34

Source: Adapted from OECD (1999).

Some of the issues raised above are discussed in Case Study 4.2.

CASE STUDY 4.2

A bull market in hot air

From the *Financial Times*, November 1999 **FT**

At the launch of the 1997 Kyoto Protocol, the US vice-president, Al Gore extolled 'the magic of markets' as an instrument for tackling climate change. Across the world, this vision is being put to the test. In the last month, Canadian energy companies have struck two large deals in which they paid others to fulfil their commitment to cut greenhouse gas emissions. In one transaction, they paid Iowa farmers to refrain from tilling farmland, so retaining CO_2 in the soil.

In Australia, the Sydney Futures Exchange has joined forces with State Forests of New South Wales to launch the world's first exchange-traded market for 'carbon sequestration' credits. Buyers will be able to offset carbon emissions with credits generated by planting forests to absorb CO_2.

Meanwhile, in the UK, industry leaders have announced plans to introduce a UK-wide emissions trading scheme by April 2001. Businesses will be able to choose whether to meet emission reduction targets through their own efforts, or by buying surplus permits from elsewhere.

'I think what we are seeing is a convergence of capital and environmental markets', says Richard Sandor, a former senior Chicago Board of Trade official who now runs the specialist Environmental Financial Products company. He describes current schemes as 'unlike anything before'.

But the future is uncertain. Trading in emissions permits may be doomed unless countries can agree on the rules of the game. Although the Kyoto Protocol sketched out provisions for trading, there is little agreement over how an international trading scheme will work. Differences have emerged at the latest UN summit on the Kyoto Protocol in Bonn. Emissions trading puts the USA at loggerheads with the EU, and causes tension between developing countries and the industrialised world. It was recognised that unless these problems be resolved in the near future then the Kyoto Protocol could fall apart, which is in fact what has happened.

One contentious issue has been whether there should be limits on trading, an idea forcefully promoted by the EU, which wants countries to achieve half their Kyoto targets through domestic measures to cut energy consumption and to stimulate technological innovation. In contrast the USA has been implacably opposed to the imposition of constraints on the use of emissions trading. 'Limiting this ability would only make reducing greenhouse gases more expensive for everyone, with no gain to the environment', said the US special negotiator on climate change.

The USA cites its successful use of emissions trading to cut the sulphur dioxide emissions causing acid rain. Emissions have been reduced by 30 per cent more than required via emissions trading, and it claims that the cost of achieving these reductions was under half the level anticipated. The effectiveness of trading is endorsed by a recent study by the OECD (1999) which calculated that without emissions trading the impact of the Kyoto targets on the OECD countries would be comparable to doubling or tripling the price of oil from its 1995 level, whereas using trading could cut these projected costs by a third.

There is a snag. Part of the apparent gains from unfettered trading would come from higher overall emissions than would otherwise be the case. This is because much of the trading would probably involve Russia and the Ukraine. The ongoing contraction in the industrial base of these countries is expected in any case to reduce their emissions to well below the level required under the Kyoto Protocol by 2010. This will then put them in a position to sell spare credits – known as 'hot air' – and allow others to buy these to raise emissions.

Russia's potential windfall is expected to be worth $2 bn a year by 2010. Several developing and transition countries would also like to fix emissions targets at similarly undemanding levels. This appals some industrialised countries, particularly in Europe, which argue that it could undermine the objectives of the Kyoto Protocol by failing to curb the absolute total of greenhouse gas emissions significantly below what would otherwise have been the case in 2010.

The disagreement between diplomats at the UN talks contrasts with the enthusiasm of the private sector in wanting to get schemes going. The private sector is 'filling the vacuum', according to the head of greenhouse gas emissions trading at the United Nations Conference on Trade and Development (UNCTAD). The market pioneers have varying motives. Exchanges and brokers are promoting deals because they are keen to take a leading role in the development of what could become a huge new market. According to the Electric Power Research Institute, the total value of CO_2 permits alone could be worth $13,000 bn by 2050. The opportunities for trading permits and their derivatives could be immense.

For companies, the deals are partly designed to influence governments. By demonstrating the effectiveness of emissions trading, they hope to fend off the prospect of new regulations or taxes. They also want to hedge future liabilities that could emerge when they are forced to cut emissions. 'Not only does a global market for greenhouse gas emissions appear likely, but the potential rewards for smart players in the field are enormous', says Natsource, a New York-based over-the-counter broker of energy derivatives. Examples include the decision by BP Amoco, which has been experimenting with trading between some of its subsidiaries, to expand the scheme across the group in 2000. In another initiative, the European Association of Electricity Producers and Distributors and the International Energy Authority organised an internet simulation of greenhouse emissions trading.

National and international bodies are also getting involved. In Japan, the Ministry of International Trade and Industry has set up a company to monitor emissions trading.

The European Commission has proposed developing an internal trading system for greenhouse gas emissions that could be launched in 2005.

Meanwhile, UNCTAD has helped launch the International Emissions Trading Association. This association's members include the Australian Stock Exchange, the International Petroleum Exchange, Lloyds Register, Shell, BP Amoco, Statoil and Tokyo Electric Power. It is exploring ideas on how to create the global emissions market that the Kyoto Protocol implies should start by 2008.

There are many issues to be resolved before the goal can be achieved. In order to ensure a thriving market, the trading system would have to allow company-level emission permits to be traded internationally. Arguments over what counts as an emissions reduction must also be resolved. This means reaching a scientific consensus on the value of 'locking up' carbon in trees, crops and soils.

Crucial issues of compliance and verification also have to be sorted out. On the face of it, the issues that need to be resolved are overwhelming. Most companies and countries will be reluctant to invest time and effort in emissions trading unless there are clearer signals that the market will take off, yet there are signs that the fledgling emissions trading schemes being set up by pioneering countries and companies could take on a life of their own. UNCTAD is exploring the idea of setting up a network of bilateral agreements between interested countries that have emissions trading programmes. 'It is developing in parallel with the Kyoto Protocol', says Mr Joshua of UNCTAD. 'We need a multi-national agreement. But this is a step along the way.'

Even the most ardent advocates of emission trading acknowledge it can only be a partial answer to the problems of climate change. But by opening up markets, encouraging innovation and harnessing competition, it may do something to reduce the world's greenhouse gases.

Source: Adapted from the *Financial Times*, 4th November 1999

Questions

1 What is meant by 'hot air' in terms of tradable permits?

2 Outline the arguments for and against tradable permits advanced in the article.

Sulphur dioxide permits in the USA

Under the United States Clean Air Act legislation it is already possible to trade permits. The Tennessee Valley Authority, for example, has agreed to buy allowances to emit 10,000 t of sulphur dioxide, a key cause of acid rain, from privately owned Wisconsin Power and Light. Similarly, Duquesne Light of Pittsburgh has bought allowances from the same Wisconsin company to emit between 15,000 and 25,000 t of sulphur dioxide. Under the Clean Air Act, utilities had to cut emissions of sulphur dioxide in half by the year 2000, i.e. from a national total of 19 million t, and this outcome was more than met, as indicated in Case Study 4.2.

There are, arguably, at least two main benefits from this market in tradable permits in sulphur dioxide emissions:

● First, costs of production have been lower than they otherwise would have been in producing power consistent with the new overall environmental targets. This is because there has been a cost saving for those companies that would otherwise have had either to purchase expensive technology (e.g. 'scrubbers') to meet lower sulphur emission or to change capital equipment to deal with harder, lower-sulphur coal. This cost saving has, arguably, been achieved at no overall rise in projected levels of sulphur pollution since the 'cleaner' companies now had an incentive to more than meet the lower targets of sulphur emission, exchanging unneeded permits for cash in the market. In terms of our earlier analysis, these efficiency gains are the result of tradable permits enabling firms to equalise marginal abatement costs (see also Figure 4.5 (page 90), 4.9 (page 99) and Figure 4.10 (page 101)).

● Second, the market in tradable permits has helped to avoid other sources of environmental damage that would otherwise have occurred. For instance, the market has helped to avoid the hazards involved in transporting large amounts of hard, low-sulphur coal from the western states of the USA to the eastern states in which most of the soft, high-sulphur coal is produced, and in which most of the offending power utilities reside. It is now possible for the power utilities in the east to purchase permits from power utilities elsewhere, thereby avoiding the disruption of adapting capital equipment and working practices, as well as avoiding any environmental costs associated with bulk transport of cargo over long distances.

Many current environmental policies make use of regulations or standards, and it is to this non-market-based policy instrument that we now turn.

● ● ● ● Regulations and standards

Many current environmental policies make use of *regulations* establishing specified *standards*. For example, standards are set for air or water quality in the UK and many other countries and the polluter is then left free to decide on how best to achieve these minimum standards. A regulator is often appointed for these industries to monitor the environmental situation and to take action against any producers found to be in violation of the standards set.

In the UK, the Environmental Protection Act (1989) laid down minimum environmental standards for emissions from over 3,500 factories involved in chemical processes, waste incineration and oil refining. The factories have to meet the standards for all emissions, whether into air, water or on to land. Factory performance is monitored by a strengthened HM Inspectorate of Pollution, the costs of which are paid for by the factory owners themselves. The Act also provided for public access to information on the pollution created by firms. Regulations were also established on restricting the release of genetically engineered bacteria and viruses and a ban was imposed on most forms of straw and stubble burning from 1992 onwards. Stricter regulations were also imposed on waste disposal operations, with local authorities given a duty to keep public land clean. On-the-spot fines of up to £1,000 were instituted for persons dropping litter.

Regulations have also played an important part in the five 'Environmental Action Programmes' of the EU, which first began in 1973. For example, specific standards have been set for minimum acceptable levels of water quality for drinking and for bathing. As regards the latter, regular monitoring of coastal waters must take place, with as many as 19 separate tests undertaken throughout the tourist season.

Of course regulations may be part of an integrated environmental policy which also involves market-based incentives. We have already seen how the tradable permits system in the USA is working in tandem with the standards imposed by the USA Clean Air Act.

Operating a standards-based policy

A standard St_1 could be set as illustrated in Figure 4.7. This would achieve the optimum scale of economic activity Q_s and the optimum level of pollution associated with that output. As with an environmental tax, deriving the appropriate standard requires accurate information on MNPB and MEC. For example, with inaccurate information the standard might be set at St_2 which would require a scale of economic activity equal to Q_a. This is not an optimum position since the marginal benefits derived by the polluter Q_aX are greater than the marginal external costs Q_aY. In other words, the standard is too severe. Not only must the standard set be appropriate, the penalties imposed for breach of the standard must be at the right level. Even with the 'correct' standard St_1 in Figure 4.7, if the average penalty imposed by the courts for breach of that standard is only Pen_1, then the optimum scale of economic activity and pollution will not be achieved. In fact with a penalty of this value the polluter will be tempted to pollute up to Q_b since the penalty paid will be less than the profits received by the polluter as measured by the MNPB curve on each extra unit up to Q_b. The polluter will not produce in excess of Q_b since the penalty incurred would now be greater than the profit obtained from each extra unit of production.

Of course, it is always possible that the pollution will go entirely undetected and therefore no penalty will be imposed. In this case the polluter might be expected to pollute up to Q_p even with the 'correct' standard St_1. With the 'correct' standard of St_1 the penalty should be Pen_2 to achieve the optimal outcome Q_s and this penalty should be consistently enforced so that it is transparent to would-be transgressors.

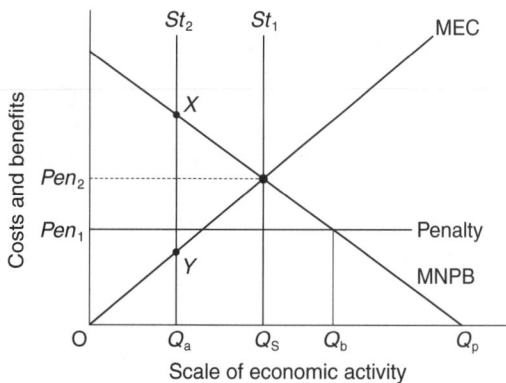

Figure 4.7 Setting a standard

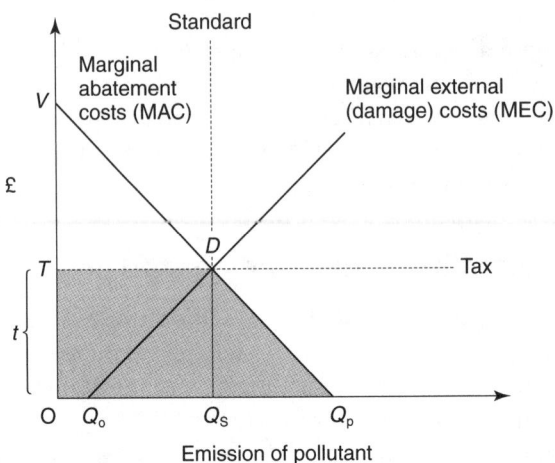

Figure 4.8 Standards versus taxes

Standards versus taxes

We can now turn to the issue of standards versus taxes in achieving an optimum level of pollution.

Firm perspective

From the point of view of the firm the use of standards might seem to be the more attractive option. We can see from Figure 4.8 that standards would be less costly for the firm to implement in achieving the social optimum, Q_s. This is because under the tax regime, the firm would pay $OTDQ_s$ to the government as tax revenue, and itself pay Q_sDQ_p in costs to abate pollution damage from Q_p to Q_s. Any unit of output beyond Q_s would of course, if produced, cause the firm to spend more in tax payment than in abatement cost. The shaded area $OTDQ_p$ represents the costs faced by the firm in achieving the social optimum level of emission, Q_s, under a tax regime. However, under a standards regime with emissions fixed at level Q_s the firm would only face abatement costs Q_sDQ_p.

Government perspective

From the point of view of government the use of tax might seem to be the more attractive option. For example, under the standards regime the government forfeits the $OTDQ_s$ of tax revenue available to it under the tax regime. A further complication that might make standards less attractive is the fact that the firms might fail to comply. Unless the penalty associated with breaking the standards was both sufficiently certain and sufficiently extensive, then the standards might not prove to be binding. For example, even if all offenders were caught, if the penalty actually imposed by the courts was less than OT, then the firm would have no incentive to cut pollutant emissions back to Q_s. In the earlier Figure 4.7, if the effective penalty line Pen_1, was below Pen_2 (the equivalent of OT in Figure 4.8), this situation would only provide incentives for firms to reduce emissions to Q_b rather than Q_s. It would cost less to pay penalties on emissions Q_s to Q_b than to pay abatement costs to avoid those penalties.

Standards are therefore only likely to be effective where there is a substantial probability of being caught for any breach, and an adequate deterrent payment. There is, of course, the further disadvantage to government of dependence on standards in having then to establish and fund a bureaucracy that will be required to set and monitor the standards regime.

Another argument governments may use in favour of a tax regime is that once a pollution standard has been set, a firm has no incentives to reduce pollution below this level. This is not the case with pollution taxes, which always provide an incentive for further reductions in emissions, as reducing the level of emissions reduces the amount of tax the firm is liable to pay. In this way, taxes may provide firms with greater incentives to invest in the research and development of new pollution abatement technologies or less pollution-intensive processes of production.

Governments may also favour a tax regime because of the higher resource costs they might expect to face in order to achieve the same result should they adopt a standards regime. We now explore this issue in rather more detail.

Standard setting with multiple firms

In practice policy makers may be faced with an alternative of setting a single tax or a single standard to be imposed on all firms. It is unlikely that a standards regime would be sufficiently well informed, or flexible enough, to impose a variable standard on each and every firm. Figure 4.9 indicates how an inflexible standards regime of this kind might achieve the same result as a tax regime, but at greater cost to the participating firms.

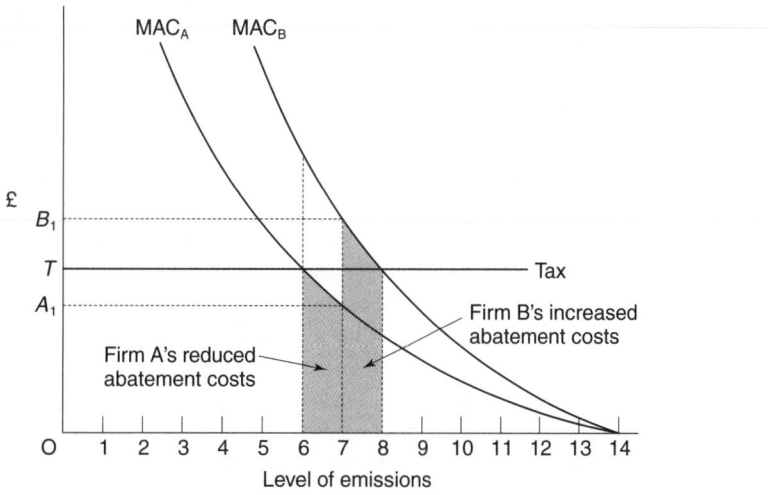

Figure 4.9 Extra cost of achieving a given level of emissions (14 units) via common standards on each firm as compared with a tax

In Figure 4.9, left to its own devices each firm will itself produce 14 units of pollutant, 28 in total. Suppose the government seeks 14 units of pollutant in total. This could be achieved either by the tax OT imposed on each firm or by restricting each firm to emitting 7 units of pollutant (we assume there to be inadequate information to apportion different levels of pollution emission to each firm). We can see that the tax regime would achieve the overall 14 units emission total by firm A producing 6 units and firm B producing 8 units, with each firm equating its respective marginal abatement costs to the tax rate, OT. However, if, under a standards regime, each firm were instructed to produce no more than 7 units of emission, then the shaded portions of Figure 4.9 indicate that firm B would incur increased abatement costs by having to reduce emissions from 8 to 7, whereas firm A would incur reduced abatement costs by no longer having to reduce emissions to 6 but only to 7. In our diagram, the increased abatement costs to B are greater than the reduced abatement costs to A. In other words, compared with the tax regime, our standards regime, in which a fixed standard is apportioned to each firm, is more costly in achieving a given result. The flatter the respective MAC curves, the smaller this cost differential will be.

Case Study 4.3 reviews the issue of standards versus taxes in the particular context of electricity generation.

Taxes versus standards: electricity generation

Whatever the targets set for reduced emissions, which policy instruments will be most effective in achieving those targets? The discussion by Ingham and Ulph (1991) is helpful in comparing market and non-market policy instruments. Many different methods are available for bringing about any given total reduction in CO_2 emissions. Users of fossil fuels might be induced to switch towards fuels that emit less CO_2 within a given total energy requirement. For instance oil and gas emit, respectively, about 80 per cent and 60 per cent as much CO_2 per unit of energy as coal. Alternatively, the total amount of energy used might be reduced in an attempt to cut CO_2 emissions.

Another issue is whether we seek to impose our target rate of reduction for CO_2 emissions on all sectors of the UK economy. Although difficult to be precise, the percentage of CO_2 emissions differ considerably by economic sector. In rank order for the UK (per cent): electricity generation (39), industry (24), transport (17), domestic (14).

Should we then ask for a uniform reduction of say, 25 per cent across all sectors? This is unlikely to be appropriate since marginal abatement cost curves are also likely to differ across sectors and, indeed, across countries. For instance, it has been estimated that to abate 14 per cent of the air pollution emitted by the textiles sector in the USA will cost $136 m. per annum. However to abate 14 per cent of the air pollution emitted by each of the machinery, electrical equipment and fabricated metals sectors respectively, will cost $572 m., $729 m. and $896 m. (World Bank 1992). As well as differing between industrial sectors within a country, abatement costs will also differ between

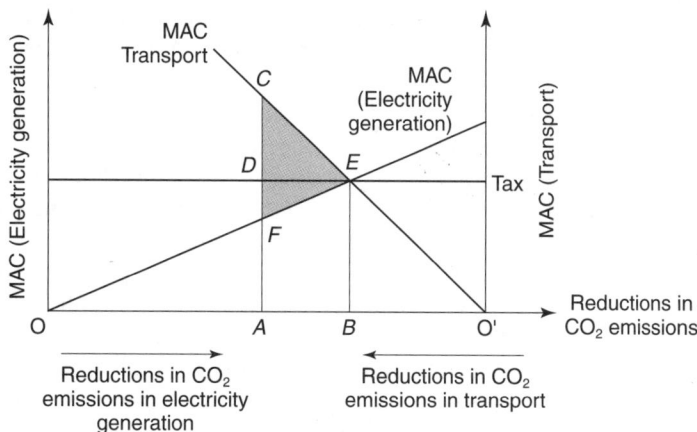

Figure 4.10 Finding the 'efficient' or 'least-cost' solution for reducing CO_2 emissions in a two-sector model

countries. For example, it has been estimated that a 10 per cent reduction in CO_2 emissions by 2010 (as compared to 1988 emission levels) will cost 400 euros per tonne of CO_2 abated in Italy, but only 200 euros per tonne abated in Denmark, and less than 20 euros per tonne abated in the UK, France, Germany and Belgium.

This point can be illustrated by taking just two sectors in the UK – say electricity generation and transport – and by assuming that they initially emit the same amount of CO_2. Following Ingham and Ulph (1991) suppose that the overall target for reducing CO_2 emissions is the distance O'O in Fig. 4.10. We must now decide how to allocate this total reduction in emissions between the two sectors. In Figure 4.10 we measure reductions in CO_2 emissions in electricity generation from left to right, and reductions in CO_2 emissions in transport from right to left. Point A, for example, would divide the total reduction in emissions into OA in electricity generation and $O'A$ in transport. A marginal abatement cost (MAC) curve is now calculated for each sector. In Figure 4.10 we draw the MAC curve for electricity generation as being lower and flatter than that for transport. This reflects the greater fuel-switching possibilities in electricity generation as compared to transport, both within fossil fuels and between fossil and non-fossil (solar, wave, wind) fuels. In other words, any marginal reduction in CO_2 emissions in electricity generation is likely to raise overall costs by less in electricity generation than in transport. In transport there are far fewer fuel-substitution possibilities; the major means of curbing CO_2 emission in transport are improved techniques for energy efficiency or a switch from private to public transport.

Given these different marginal abatement cost curves for each sector in Figure 4.10, how then should we allocate our reduction between the two sectors? Clearly we should seek a solution by which the given total reduction in emissions is achieved at the least total cost to society: we shall call this the *efficient* or *least-cost* solution. In Figure 4.10 this will be where marginal abatement costs are the same in both sectors, i.e. at point B in the diagram. We can explain this by supposing we were initially not at B, but at A in Figure 4.10, with equal reductions in the two sectors. At point A, marginal abatement costs in transport are AC but marginal abatement costs in electricity generation are only AF. So by abating CO_2 by one more tonne in electricity generation and one less tonne in transport, we would have the same total reduction in CO_2 emissions, but would have saved CF in costs. By moving from point A to the 'efficient' point B, we would save the area CFE in abatement costs.

It follows, therefore, that for any given target for total reduction in CO_2 emissions, 'efficiency' will only occur if the marginal cost of abatement is the same across all sectors of the economy (and indeed across all methods of abatement). Pollution control policies which seek to treat all sectors equally, even where marginal abatement costs differ widely between sectors, may fail to reach an 'efficient' solution.

We have previously seen that environmental policy instruments can be broadly classified into two types: market-based and non-market-based. Market-based policy instruments would include setting a tax on emissions of CO_2 or issuing a limited number of permits to emit CO_2 and then allowing a market to be set up in which those permits are traded. Non-market-based policy instruments would include regulations and directives. For example, in the UK, the non-fossil fuel obligation currently imposed on privatised electricity companies requires them to purchase a specified amount of electricity from non-fossil fuel sources.

We can use Figure 4.10 to examine the case for using a tax instrument (market-based) as compared to regulation (non-market-based). A tax of BE on CO_2 emissions would lead to the 'efficient' solution B. This is because polluters have a choice of paying the tax on their emissions of CO_2 or of taking steps to abate their emissions. They will have an incentive to abate as long as the marginal cost of abatement is lower than the tax. So electricity generating companies will have incentives to abate to OB, and transport companies to $O'B$, in Figure 4.10. Since every polluter faces the same tax, then they will end up with the same marginal abatement cost. Here 'prices', amended by tax, are conveying signals to producers in a way which helps coordinate their (profit-maximising) decisions in order to bring about an 'efficient' (least cost) solution.

The alternative policy of government regulations and directives (non-market-based instrument) in achieving the 'efficient' solution at B in Figure 4.10, would be much more complicated. The government would have to estimate the marginal abatement cost curve for each sector, given that such curves differ between sectors. It would then have to estimate the different percentage reductions required in each sector in order to equalise marginal abatement costs (the 'efficient' solution). It is hardly reasonable to suppose that the government could achieve such fine-tuning in order to reach 'efficient' solutions.

The market-based solution of tax has no administrative overhead. Producers are simply assumed to react to the signals of market prices (amended by taxes) in a way which maximises their own profits. Regulations, on the other hand, imply monitoring, supervision and other 'bureaucratic' procedures. Ingham and Ulph (1991) found that using a tax policy as compared with seeking an equal proportionate reduction in CO_2 emissions by regulations, resulted in total abatement costs being 20 per cent lower than they would have been under the alternative regulatory policy.

Questions

1 Why might a policy of asking all industrial sectors to cut emissions of CO_2 by 50 per cent be open to criticism?

2 What is the basis of the support for taxes rather than standards in this case study?

3 When might the use of standards be more attractive than the use of environmental taxes?

Least-cost solutions: taxes versus standards

Case Study 4.3 used the particular context of *electricity generation* when comparing standards with taxes as the least cost method for achieving a given target. The analysis favoured the environmental tax being used to equalise (differing) marginal abatement costs across the various sectors of electricity generation rather than a uniform standard involving an equal percentage cut in CO_2 emissions from each sector. More general support for the principle of using environmental taxes to equalise marginal abatement costs has also been given by some recent studies on curbing the growth in global emissions of CO_2. In seeking to curb growth in CO_2 emissions by a given target, namely 2% per annum relative to the 'business as usual' growth path, Table 4.2 indicates the cost of achieving that target via a *standard* in the form of an equal percentage cut in CO_2 emissions across all OECD countries as compared with an *environmental tax* which has the effect of equalising marginal abatement costs across the OECD countries.

Table 4.2 presents this comparison using three separate models over different time periods. The costs shown are expressed as a percentage of GDP. In column (2) these costs represent the equalisation of marginal abatement costs via an environmental tax, and are clearly projected as being lower under all three models than those in column (1), which represent equal percentage cuts in CO_2 emissions via a universally imposed standard. Under the OECD Green model the GDP loss in OECD countries would be reduced by more than a third, using the tax rather than the standard as policy instrument. OECD countries – which have high marginal abatement cost – would contribute only 22% of the total CO_2 abatement sought under the 'equalisation of marginal abatement costs' under a tax policy, but 32% under the equal percentage cut via a standards policy.

Who pays the environmental tax?

The case for environmental taxes is often made in terms of the polluter having to pay (via tax) for the damage caused. Of course where demand curves for the environmental product are *relatively inelastic*, as in Figure 4.11(a), then the producer is able to pass on the larger part of the tax *t* to the consumer in the form of higher

Table 4.2 Cost (% of GDP) of achieving a given target reduction in CO_2 emissions in OECD countries by alternative abatement strategies

WTB:	Edmonds-Reilly model (ERM)		OECD Green model		Manne-Richels Global model (MR)	
	(1)	*(2)*	*(1)*	*(2)*	*(1)*	*(2)*
2020	1.9	1.6	1.9	1.0	n.a.	n.a.
2050	3.7	3.3	2.6	1.9	n.a.	n.a.
2100	5.7	5.1	n.a.	n.a.	8.0	7.5

Source: Adapted from OECD (1999)

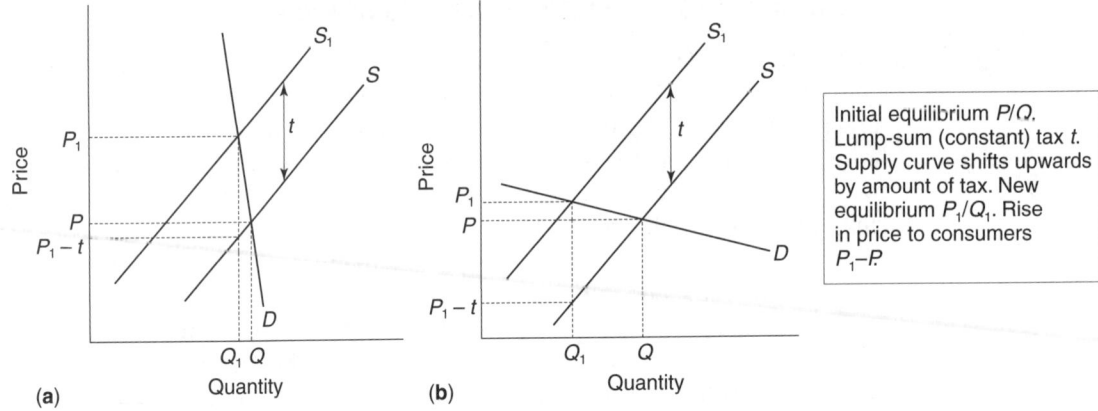

Figure 4.11 Impact of a lump-sum environmental tax (t) on the price paid by consumers: (a) relatively inelastic demand; (b) relatively elastic demand

prices. Where demand curves for the environmental product are *relatively elastic*, as in Figure 4.11(b), then the producer is less able to pass on the tax *t* to the consumer and instead the producer must absorb the larger part of the tax. Only in the latter situation of relatively elastic demand is the polluter actually paying for most of the environmental damage incurred.

It might therefore be argued that the case for taxes rather than standards is stronger on equity (fairness) grounds when the demand for the environmental product to be taxed is relatively elastic so that the polluter really does pay for much of the damage inflicted on others. On the other hand, the case for standards rather than taxes is arguably strongest (on equity grounds) when the demand for the environmental product to be taxed is relatively inelastic, so that the consumer rather than the polluter pays for much of the damage inflicted on others.

We have noted in this chapter that market-based policy instruments allow flexibility of individual responses, often resulting in the 'least-cost' method of pollution abatement being adopted. However, it should be pointed out that the method which reduces the total abatement cost of achieving a given environmental outcome is not necessarily the optimum solution from the point of view of society as a whole! What is arguably more important for society is that total damage costs be at a minimum as a result of some negative environmental externality, such as pollution. Chapter 6 (e.g. Case Study 6.1) looks at situations in which standards may have the edge over environmental taxes in this respect, using the particular example of water-based pollutants.

Now try the self-check questions for this chapter on the companion website
  www.booksites.net/ison
You will also find up-to-date facts and case materials.

Equity Fairness

Externalities Occur when decisions create costs or benefits for people other than the decision taker

Free-rider Where an individual or firm seeks an advantage by avoiding declaring a willingness to pay for a product

Marginal abatement cost (MAC) The extra cost to the firm of avoiding emitting the last unit of pollutant

Marginal damage cost (MDC) The extra damage from emitting the last unit of pollutant

Marginal social cost (MSC) The additional private cost and additional external cost involved in producing an extra unit of output (MSC = MPC + MEC)

Pigouvian tax A tax on the producer of an externality exactly equal to the net marginal damage (external cost) imposed

Polluter pays principle (PPP) That those imposing (external) costs on others should pay for the damage they cause

Property rights Legal rights assigned by law

Public good A good (or service) that involves two key characteristics: non-excludability and non-exhaustibility. Non-excludability means that, once provided, it is difficult to exclude people from consuming the good/service

Tradable permits Permits that give the holders the right to emit a specific volume of pollution. These permits can be traded on markets

References and further reading

Blow, L. (1999) 'Carbon taxes', *The Economist Review*, **17**, 2, Nov.

Bowers, J. (1997) *Sustainability and Environmental Economics*, Longman, Harlow, especially Chapters 4–6.

Coase, R. (1960) 'The Problem of Social Cost', *Journal of Law and Economics*, **III**, October.

Cowe, R. (1998) 'Green taxes come up against pain barrier', *Guardian*, 2nd February.

Field, B. C. (1997) *Environmental Economics: An Introduction*, McGraw-Hill, especially Chapters 5 and 6.

Gilpin, A. (2000) *Environmental Economics: A Critical Overview*, Wiley, especially Chapters 5 and 6.

Ingham, A. and Ulph, A. (1991) 'Economics of global warming', *The Economic Review*, **9**, 2.

OECD (1999) 'Policy challenges arising from climate change', *Economic Outlook*, **65**, June.

Rajah, N. (1992) 'The European carbon tax – a solution to global warming?', *The Economic Review*, **10**, 1.

Royal Commission on Environmental Pollution (2000) 22nd Report, *Energy – the Changing Climate*, Cm 4749.

Useful websites

Environment Agency
Environment: (EC DGXI)
World Health Organisation
United Nations
Office for National Statistics (ONS)
ONS Statstore and Statbase
Central Office of Information
Eurostat
International Monetary Fund (IMF)
Organisation for Economic Co-Operation and Development (OECD)
World Bank
United Nations Development Program
www.ipcc.ch (climate change)
www.unfccc.int (climate change)

Sustainable development

When was the last time you came across the use of the word 'sustainable'? There is a good chance that it was on the label of some consumer product or food packet or perhaps in a glossy company advertisement. 'Sustainable' and 'sustainability' are now key trigger words in the world of advertising for positive, emotive images associated with words such as 'green', 'wholesome', 'goodness', 'justice', 'environment', among others. They are used sophisticatedly to sell cars, nappies, holidays and even lifestyles. Sustainability sells – how has this come about and what exactly are we being encouraged to buy?

This chapter reviews the origins of the use and meaning of 'sustainable development' and its emerging policy implications. 'Rules' for achieving different versions of sustainability are explored (e.g. 'weak' and 'strong') and the important role of technological change reviewed. The more *anthropogenic* (human-related) perspective on sustainability is captured in the role of international institutions in supporting 'sustainable development' within a globalised economy. Chapter 12 takes some of these issues further with particular emphasis on the developing economies.

What is meant by 'sustainable development'?

According to Reid (1995), the origins of the modern uses of the words 'sustainable' and 'sustainability' can be traced back to the 1980 World Conservation Strategy published by the World Conservation Union (IUCN) which brought the phrase **'sustainable development'** to prominence. Yet the two individual words 'sustainable' and 'development' are not new, the former often being used in the context of endurance and maintenance whereas the latter has many more meanings, such as those with biological and evolutionary associations. According to the OECD, 'sustainable' is defined as 'capable of being maintained at a certain rate or level' whereas 'development' is defined as 'the economic advancement of a region or people, especially one which is currently under-developed'. The novel thing about the 1980 World Conservation Strategy was that it combined these two words together to form a new, as yet undefined concept.

While there are debates about which individual or group originally coined the sustainable development phrase, it was certainly not mentioned in the earlier Stockholm Declaration on the Human Environment in 1972. The Stockholm

Declaration is usually taken as a starting point for describing the rise of global environmental consciousness in the latter part of the 20th century, yet the Declaration does not explicitly deal with social and economic development. By the early 1970s, fears were already growing about globally unsustainable social and economic development with an influential academic report entitled *The Limits to Growth* published in 1972 (Meadows *et al.*, 1972). The report explored alternative futures as to what might happen as a result of a rapidly growing global human population, including impacts on food production, natural resources and environmental degradation in a finite world. *Limits to Growth* was widely received as a message of impending doom and concluded that sooner or later one or more of these interrelated systems would collapse. The report had a significant impact, partly because it reinforced the growing economic and political uncertainty and fuelled the general pessimism of the time. *Limits to Growth* was followed soon after by the onset of the first oil crisis in late 1973, which compounded fears about finite oil and other energy resources.

The modern understanding of the concept of '**sustainable development**' was perhaps most clearly articulated in 1987 through the publication of a United Nations report entitled *Our Common Future*. This was the final report of a process called the United Nations World Commission on Environment and Development (WCED). The report is also sometimes known as the Brundtland Report after the Norwegian Prime Minister Gro Harlem Brundtland, the then chair of the WCED. *Our Common Future* is famous for providing the following most widely cited definition of sustainable development. Sustainable development is 'development which meets the needs of the present without compromising the ability of future generations to meet their own needs' (WCED, 1987).

UN negotiations work on a consensual basis, with statements agreed among 180 countries tending to have been edited down to the lowest common denominator of international agreement. To increase the acceptability of a statement usually implies increasing its ambiguity – so that everyone can find their own meaning and interpretation in the text. The well-intentioned 'wooliness' of the above definition has been the subject of much academic and political debate. How do we define needs? And how exactly do we deal with the question of intergenerational equity?

The Brundtland Report was seen as a major step towards a more realistic discussion of environmental issues at the international level. However, it soon became patently clear to most observers that global environmental protection and sustainable development were not going to happen on their own. Fine and well-intentioned statements of values by governments were seen as being no substitute for international law. The Brundtland Commission's high-level and ambitious goals would, at the very least, need a strengthened and more coordinated international legal framework.

Two years on from the WCED report, preparations began in 1989 for a major international meeting on environment and development. The 'Earth Summit' or to give it its legal title, the UN Conference on Environment and Development (UNCED), was held in June 1992 in Rio de Janeiro in Brazil. Attended by over 30,000 governmental and non-governmental organisations from over 170 countries, the Earth Summit dramatically changed the international legal framework involving environmental issues. The origins of much of the politics of today's international negotiations on sustainable development stem from the so-called Rio Agreements of 1992 (Grubb, 1992). It is therefore important that we review the main outcomes of the 1992 Earth Summit in some detail.

1992 UN Conference on Environment and Development (UNCED): The Earth Summit

The purpose of the UNCED was to create an 'Earth Charter' – an environmental bill of rights delineating the principles for economic and environmental behaviour of peoples and nations. Altogether, Rio produced five significant agreements:

- The Rio Declaration
- Agenda 21
- The United Nations Framework Convention on Climate Change
- The Convention on Biological Diversity
- The Convention to combat Desertification

It also produced a Statement on Forest Principles. Of these the Rio Declaration is often seen as the highlight of the Earth Summit.

The Rio Declaration on Environment and Development

The *Rio Declaration on Environment and Development* aims to establish 'a new and equitable global partnership through the creation of new levels of cooperation among States, key sectors of societies and people' by '...working towards international agreements which respect the interests of all and protect the integrity of the global environmental and developmental system' (preamble to the Rio Declaration). The main themes of the Rio Declaration are outlined below. Although the actual text is much longer, this list gives a good idea of the vast range of issues covered.

Principle 1	Humans are centre of concerns for sustainable development.
Principle 2	Countries must not cause damage to the environment of other states.
Principle 3	Development must equitably meet developmental and environmental needs of present and future generations.
Principle 4	Environmental protection are an integral part of the development process.
Principle 5	Eradicating poverty an indispensable requirement for sustainable development.
Principle 6	The special situation and needs of (least) developing countries must be given special priority.
Principle 7	States have common but differentiated responsibilities to conserve, protect and restore the health and integrity of the Earth's ecosystem.
Principle 8	States should reduce and eliminate unsustainable patterns of production and consumption and promote appropriate demographic policies.
Principle 9	States should cooperate to strengthen endogenous capacity-building for sustainable development.

Principle 10	Need to improve access to environmental information, public awareness and participation.
Principle 11	States shall enact effective environmental legislation.
Principle 12	Open international economic system.
Principle 13	Liability and compensation for the victims of pollution and other environmental damage. Develop further international law regarding liability and compensation for adverse effects of environmental damage.
Principle 14	Discourage or prevent transfer to other states of any activities and substances that cause severe environmental degradation or are found to be harmful to human health.
Principle 15	The precautionary approach shall be widely applied by states. Where there are threats of serious or irreversible damage, lack of full scientific certainty shall not be used as a reason for postponing cost-effective measures to prevent environmental degradation.
Principle 16	Internalisation of environmental costs (i.e. polluter pays).
Principle 17	Environmental impact assessment.
Principle 18	States shall immediately notify other states of any natural disasters or other emergencies that are likely to produce sudden harmful effects on the environment of those states. Every effort shall be made by the international community to help states so afflicted.
Principle 19	Early consultation on possible trans-boundary environmental effects.
Principles 20–22	Women, the youth of the world and indigenous people.
Principle 23	People under oppression, domination and occupation shall be protected.
Principles 24–25	Warfare and peace.
Principle 26	Environmental disputes to be solved peacefully.
Principle 27	States and people shall cooperate in further development of international law in the field of sustainable development.

Source: Adapted from the Rio Declaration (1992).

The Rio Declaration contains many sensible principles and proclamations. However, a major weakness as an international treaty is its lack of any enforcement or compliance system. In legal terms, the Rio Declaration is what is called 'soft law'. Nevertheless, some of these principles are starting to play important roles in the development of future detailed legal frameworks around trade and environmental agreements.

Agenda 21 – Global Programme of Action on Sustainable Development

Agenda 21 was also agreed at the Earth Summit in Rio, its title chosen to emphasise the social, economic and political relevance of human development in the twenty-first century. The UN website explains that 'Agenda 21 is a comprehensive plan of action to be taken globally, nationally and locally by organizations of the United Nations System, Governments, and Major Groups in every area in which humans impact on the environment'. (www.un.org/esa/sustdev/agenda21.htm)

In fact Agenda 21 is an extremely ambitious and detailed action plan. Its 40 chapters are divided into 4 key sections:

- social and economic dimensions
- conservation and management of resources for development
- strengthening the role of major groups
- means of implementation

The texts of Agenda 21 actively employ many of the principles proclaimed in the Rio Declaration. The goals, targets and actions embodied in Agenda 21 cover the breadth of stakeholders, from international organisations, to national and local governments, from the private sector to NGOs and individuals. An international framework of declarations involving practically everyone doing everything is not, however, the sort of international agreement which lends itself to easy or practical implementation or measurement. But once again, the document reflected a global consensus and political commitment at the highest level as regards development and environment cooperation. But for all its fine words, as with the Rio Declaration, Agenda 21 has no legal teeth. There are few, if any, legal consequences for non-compliance of Agenda 21 or provisions for its enforcement.

Nevertheless most developed and developing countries have implemented various elements of the Agenda 21 programmes. Perhaps the most important impact of Agenda 21 has been at the local level where Agenda 21 officers have been able to try out practical ideas which seek to implement sustainable development on the ground.

Key conditions for sustainable development

It has already been noted that the Brundtland Commission defined 'sustainable development' (SD) as development that meets the needs of the present generation without compromising the ability of future generations to meet their own needs. This would seem to imply at least two key aspects be present if social and economic development is to be regarded as 'sustainable':

- *Intergenerational equity*: namely that the development process seeks to minimise any adverse impacts on future generations. These clearly include avoiding adverse environmental impacts such as excessive resource depletion today reducing the stock available for future use, or levels of pollutions emission and waste disposal today beyond the ability of the environment to absorb them, thereby imposing long-term damage.
- *Intra-generational equity*: namely that the development process seeks to minimise tendencies towards excessive income and wealth inequalities within and between nations and groups of nations at any point in time.

Attempts have been made to operationalise these aspects of sustainable development still further. For example, various 'rules' have been devised to reflect views as to what might constitute 'weak' and 'strong' sustainability practices.

Weak sustainability (WS)

Under WS practical efforts will be made to fully compensate those adversely affected by development:

- *Future generations:* e.g. depletion of scarce resources 'compensated' by income transfers to future generations or by technological developments increasing the efficiency of future resource use (less resource requirements per unit of output). Significant attempts will be made under WS to 'decouple' adverse environmental effects from economic growth. Support will also be given to the 'constant capital' rule, namely that this generation must pass on to future generations an *aggregate capital stock* no smaller in value than the one it inherited. Less environmental capital (e.g. fewer natural resources) can be passed on so long as it is replaced by an equivalent value of physical capital (e.g. buildings and infrastructure) since physical capital is seen under this 'rule' as a credible substitute for environmental capital. Attempts will be made to capture environmental impacts within the macroeconomic accounts so that the 'constant capital' rule can be monitored (e.g. the Index of Sustainable Economic Welfare considered in Chapter 2, page 53).
- *Current generations:* e.g. the poor and those disadvantaged by development must be compensated by various support programmes and other policy measures. Higher priority must be given under WS to attempts to tackle poverty both at home and abroad (e.g. debt relief for developing countries).

Strong sustainability (SS)

Under SS attempts will also be made to compensate those adversely affected by development. However, under SS that compensation must be explicitly 'environmental':

- *Future generations:* e.g. the 'constant capital rule' no longer applies. Any loss of environmental capital in this generation must be offset by the addition of an equivalent 'value' of environmental capital to future generations (e.g. deforestation must be fully offset by an equivalent 'value' of tree planting). Physical capital is seen under SS as a highly imperfect substitute for environmental capital. The focus is on the conservation and preservation of ecosystems, landscapes and other 'natural' features.
- *Current generations:* e.g. although there is still concern under SS for support for individuals disadvantaged by development, the focus shifts from individual valuations and concerns to the *collective* value ascribed to ecosystems and other environmental assets.

Turner *et al.* (1994) captures some of the features of WS and SS in Figure 5.1. A distinction is also made between very weak sustainability (VWS) and very strong sustainability (VSS) perspectives. Some alternative terminology is also presented (e.g. 'Deep ecology', 'Cornucopian') which is often used to describe different environmental perspectives on sustainable development.

The exact definitions given to WS and SS and their variants are clearly a matter of some debate. Box 5.1 considers a number of more precise definitions when examining the issue of sustainable development in the context of the developing economies.

'Cornucopian'	'Accommodating'	'Communalist'	'Deep Ecology'	
Resource exploitative, growth-orientated position	Resource conservationist and 'managerial' position	Resource preservationist position	Extreme preservationist position	**Green labels**
Anti-green economy, unfettered free markets	Green economy. Green markets guided by economic incentive instruments (Eis) (e.g. pollution charges)	Deep green economy, steady-state economy regulated by macroenvironmental standards and supplemented by Eis	Very deep green economy, heavily regulated to minimise 'resource-take'	**Type of economy**
Primary economic policy objective, maximise economic growth (max gross national product [GNP])	Modified economic growth (adjusted green accounting to measure GNP)	Zero economic growth; zero population growth	Reduced scale of economy and population	**Management strategies**
Taken as axiomatic that unfettered free markets in conjunction with technical progress will ensure infinite substitution possibilities capable of mitigating all 'scarcity/limits' constraints (environmental sources and sinks)	Decoupling important but infinite substitution rejected. Sustainability rules: constant capital rule. Therefore some scale changes	Decoupling plus no increase in scale. 'Systems' perspective – 'health' of whole ecosystem very important; Gaia hypothesis and implications	Scale reduction imperative; at the extreme for some there is a literal interpretation of Gaia as a personalised agent to which moral obligations are owed	
Support for traditional ethical reasoning: rights and interests of contemporary individual humans; instrumental value (i.e. of recognised value to humans) in nature	Extension of ethical reasoning: 'caring for others' motive – intragenerational and intergenerational equality (i.e. contemporary poor and future people); instrumental value in nature	Further extension of ethical reasoning: interests of the collective take precedence over those of the individual; primary value of ecosystems and secondary value of component functions and services	Acceptance of bioethics (i.e. moral rights/interests conferred on all non-human species and even the abiotic parts of the environment); intrinsic value in nature (i.e. valuable in its own right regardless of human experience)	**Ethics**
Very weak sustainability	**Weak sustainability**	**Strong sustainability**	**Very strong sustainability**	**Sustainability labels**

Figure 5.1 Perspectives on sustainability

BOX 5.1

Sustainable development: a technical approach

Following Pearce (1998), Figure 5.2 uses *well-being per capita* on the vertical axis and *time* on the horizontal axis, where time is split into three generations of people. Pearce suggests that an economy that develops along a path like *A* is pursuing *sustainable development*, securing increases in well-being that last over future generations. Even an economy developing along path *B* is 'sustainable' because later generations are no worse off than the first one: well-being is 'non-declining'. However, the economy on path *C* is not sustainable, because per capita well-being grows, then declines for succeeding generations.

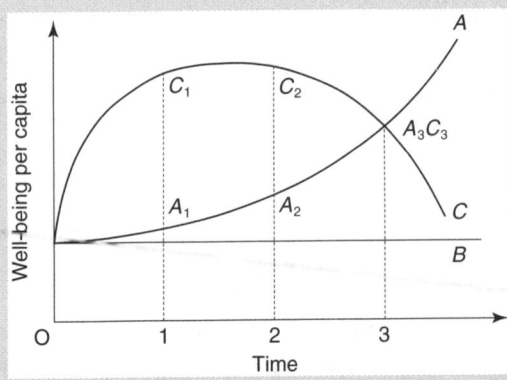

Figure 5.2 Sustainable and non-sustainable development paths

Note that sustainable development is not necessarily 'optimal' in that path C ($C_1 + C_2 + C_3$) yields a total well-being in excess of path A ($A_1 + A_2 + A_3$).

Sustainability 'rules'
Whatever the concept of 'well-being' applied (GDP or 'quality of life' indices – see Chapter 8, page 213) the condition for sustainable development is that each generation should leave the next generation a stock of capital assets no less than the stock it 'inherits'. The next generation will then have the capacity to generate the same (or more) 'well-being' as the previous generation.

At least four types of capital asset are often identified:

1 *Man-made capital* (K_M) – factories, machines, roads, computers, etc.
2 *Human capital* (K_H) – knowledge, skills embodied in people.
3 *Natural capital* (K_N) – the stock of environmental assets that provide natural resources to sustain life, to use in production, to help in the assimilation of wastes and provide amenity attractions.
4 *Social capital* (K_S) – values and relationships which give a particular society its sense of identity.

- **Weak sustainability rule**. The total stock of capital ($K_M + K_H + K_N + K_S$) should not fall, though individual elements within it can vary.
- **Strong sustainability rule**. Each element within the total stock of capital should not fall.

Sustainable development is a key issue for both developed and developing countries. However, it is clearly the developing countries which will have the greatest problems in conforming to *either* of these sustainability rules. This is especially true if these capital rules are expressed per capita, given the current and projected rapid population growth for the developing countries (see Chapter 12). Of course the 'weak sustainability rule' gives more scope for the developing economies, in that it permits environmental degradation (fall in K_N) to be offset by gains elsewhere. For example, a fall in K_N (per capita) via, say, deforestation in Amazonia, can, at least in principle, be offset by investing the monies received in education and training, giving an offsetting rise in K_H (per capita).

The extent to which such offsets are feasible depends on how easily one form of capital can be *substituted* for another form in terms of its contribution to 'well-being'. If K_M, K_H or K_S (per capita) can more than offset a decline in K_N (per capita) then achieving 'weak sustainability' for both developed and developing economies will at least be more plausible. It is in this context that many are placing their hopes for sustainable development on further advances in technological capabilities, thereby raising output per unit input of these various types of capital asset.

Measuring sustainable development

It has often been pointed out that an implication for fulfilling the 'weak sustainability rule' is that the total savings of a nation must be greater than the total depreciation of its capital assets $(K_M + K_H + K_N + K_S)$. Only then can the nation replenish its capital assets so that they are at least as extensive at the end of the time period as they were at the beginning.

> **The general savings rule**: for development to be sustainable (weak form), total savings must at least cover depreciation of the four types of capital.

Estimates (if imperfect) of savings by nations are available from the national accounts as are also estimates of man-made capital depreciation (K_M). Environmental economists have also made progress in developing indicators of natural capital depreciation (K_N). This involves the environmental 'negatives' of depletion of natural resources (e.g. oil, timber) and of waste-receiving capabilities (e.g. via pollution) and the environmental 'pluses' of new discoveries of natural resources and growth of renewable resources.

Progress has been made in developing indicators of human capital depreciation (K_H), which tends of course to be substantial and positive in sign in the poorer developing economies, but via increased education, training and improvements in the quality of life to be negative in sign in the developed economies, implying *appreciation* of K_H. Indicators for social capital depreciation (K_S) remain somewhat elusive.

A dilemma facing the developing economies and particularly the poorer LDC grouping, is that, expressed as a percentage of GNP, savings are often insufficient to more than offset any (net) depreciation estimated for the other four capital assets combined. The richer countries would certainly seem to be sustainable in terms of the 'general savings rule' and in a context of 'weak sustainability'. Problems clearly exist elsewhere, as in much of Africa and in the Middle East where assets appear to be depreciating faster than they are being replaced.

Technical change and sustainability

Technical change is not usually included in national savings ratios, although many would argue that it is a factor to be added to general savings. Pearce (1998) suggests a rich economy such as the USA would gain an extra three percentage points on its 'genuine savings' measure by adding on technological change. The number is likely to be far less, perhaps zero in many developing economies. However, a major debate is currently under way on the extent to which technological change might become a major factor in supporting sustainable development in the low-income, developing economies.

Figure 5.3 indicates how technological change can play a key role in development, in terms of our earlier analysis enhancing human capital (K_H), man-made capital (K_M), social capital (K_S) and arguably even natural capital (K_N). The *Human Development Report* of the United Nations (2001) emphasises the benefits of technology for developing economies, producing drought-tolerant plant varieties for farming in uncertain climates, more efficient industrial processing, vaccines for

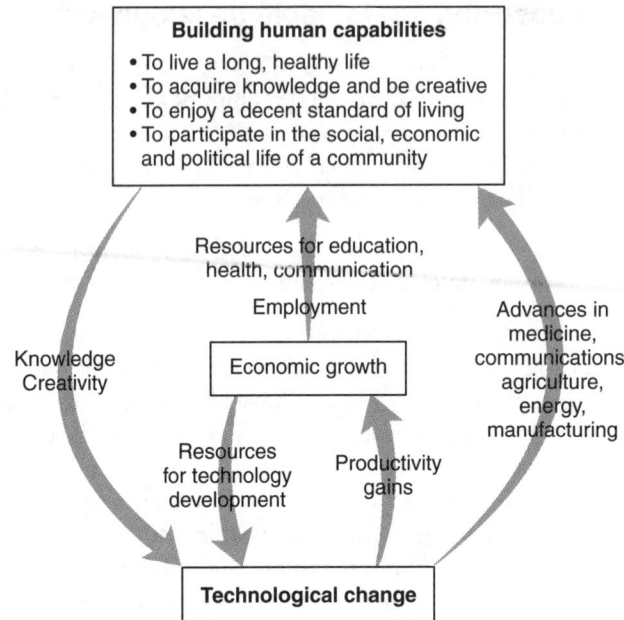

Figure 5.3 Links between technology and human development
Source: Human Development Report (2001)

infectious diseases, clean energy sources for domestic and industrial uses. In these ways new technologies support economic growth through productivity gains in agriculture, industry and service activities and by supporting a healthier, more highly educated and skilled workforce.

We return to the issues of sustainable development in the specific context of the developing economies in Chapter 12 (page 283). Here we continue to chart the increasing importance given to aspects of 'human capital' and 'social capital' in the contemporary debate on sustainable development.

Globalisation and sustainable development

The debate about sustainable development has moved on significantly from Rio and must now be seen in the context of globalisation and its various implications for world trade, standards of living and global inequalities. Over a decade on from the Earth Summit, the world seems to have become an even smaller place. Cheaper air travel, lower freight costs, e-mail, the internet, global financial markets, and the so-called 'CNN-effect' of 24-hour rolling global news reporting are all characteristics of what is often described as '**globalisation**'. Events in one place can have significant and immediate impacts across the world, with the global impacts of the terrorist events of 11th September 2001 vividly illustrating the point. The rapid acceleration in the rates of flow of people, finance, information, technology, culture and ideas are all-important features of globalisation.

The world seems to have become a still more socially, economically and politically interconnected and interdependent place. The news is dominated by international institutions, organisations, intergovernmental negotiations and international business.

Globalisation – characteristics

Globalisation is much talked about in the media, and has been approached from the perspective of at least four academic disciplines, within each of which it tends to take on different characteristics:

- *Economists* focus on the growth of international trade and the increase in international capital flows.
- *Political scientists* view globalisation as a process that leads to the undermining of the nation state and the emergence of new forms of governance.
- *Sociologists* view globalisation in terms of the rise of a global culture and the domination of the media by global companies.
- *International relations experts* tend to focus on the emergence of global conflicts and global institutions.

Certainly the world is seen as becoming increasingly interconnected as the result of economic, political, sociological and cultural forces. A one-dimensional view of globalisation, which thinks purely in terms of market forces, is likely to result in only a partial picture at best. 'Globalisation is a complex process which is not necessarily teleological in character – that is to say, it is not necessarily an inexorable historical process with an end in sight. Rather, it is characterised by a set of mutually opposing tendencies' (Giddens, 1990).

In fact McGrew (1992) has tried to identify a number of these opposing tendencies:

- *Universalisation versus particularisation.* While globalisation may tend to make many aspects of modern social life universal (e.g. assembly line production, fast food restaurants, consumer fashions), it can also help to point out the differences between what happens in particular places and what happens elsewhere. This focus on differences can foster the resurgence of regional and national identities.
- *Homogenisation versus differentiation.* While globalisation may result in an essential homogeneity ('sameness') in product, process and institutions (e.g. city life, organisational offices and bureaucracies), it may also mean that the general must be assimilated within the local. For example, human rights are interpreted in different ways across the globe, the practice of specific religions such as Christianity or Buddhism may take on different forms in different places, and so on.
- *Integration versus fragmentation.* Globalisation creates new forms of global, regional and transnational communities which unite (integrate) people across territorial boundaries (e.g. the MNE, international trade unions). However, it also has the potential to divide and fragment communities (e.g. labour becoming divided along sectoral, local, national and ethnic lines).

Some argue that globalisation is a long-standing phenomenon and not really anything new, pointing out that world trade and investment as a proportion of world GDP are little different today from what they were a century ago and that international borders were as open at that time as they are today with just as many people migrating abroad.

However, those who believe that globalisation really is a new phenomenon tend to agree that at least three key elements are commonly involved:

- *Shrinking space.* The lives of all individuals are increasingly interconnected by events worldwide. This is not only a matter of fact but one which people increasingly perceive to be the case, recognising that their jobs, income levels, health and living environment depend on factors outside national and local boundaries.
- *Shrinking time.* With the rapid developments in communication and information technologies, events occurring in one place have almost instantaneous (real-time) impacts worldwide. A fall in share prices in Wall Street can have almost immediate consequences for share prices in London, Frankfurt or Tokyo.
- *Disappearing borders.* The nation state and its associated borders seem increasingly irrelevant as 'barriers' to international events and influences. Decisions taken by regional trading blocs (e.g. EU, NAFTA) and supranational bodies (e.g. IMF, World Trade Organisation) increasingly override national policy-making in economic and business affairs as well as in other areas such as law enforcement and human rights.

Box 5.2 attempts to capture some of the features which currently underpin the use of the term 'globalisation' as being something different from what has gone before.

BOX 5.2

Globalisation and its characteristics

New markets
- Growing global markets in services – banking, insurance, transport.
- New financial markets – deregulated, globally linked, working around the clock, with action at a distance in real time, with new instruments such as derivatives.
- Deregulation of anti-trust laws and growth of mergers and acquisitions.
- Global consumer markets with global brands.

New actors
- Multinational corporations integrating their production and marketing, dominating world production.
- The World Trade Organisation – the first multilateral organisation with authority to force national governments to comply with trade rules.
- A growing international network of non-governmental organisations (NGOs).
- Regional blocs proliferating and gaining importance – European Union, Association of South-East Asian Nations, Mercosur, North American Free Trade Association, Southern African Development Community, among many others.
- More policy co-ordination groups – G-7, G-8, OECD, IMF, World Bank.

▶

New rules and norms
- Market economic policies spreading around the world, with greater privatisation and liberalisation than in earlier decades.
- Widespread adoption of democracy as the choice of political regime.
- Human rights conventions and instruments building up in both coverage and number of signatories – and growing awareness among people around the world.
- Consensus goals and action agenda for development.
- Conventions and agreements on the global environment – biodiversity, ozone layer, disposal of hazardous wastes, desertification, climate change.
- Multilateral agreements in trade, taking on such new agendas as environmental and social conditions.
- New multilateral agreements – for services, intellectual property, communications – more binding on national governments than any previous agreements.
- The (proposed) Multilateral Agreement on Investment.

New (faster and cheaper) tools of communication
- Internet and electronic communications linking many people simultaneously.
- Cellular phones.
- Fax machines.
- Faster and cheaper transport by air, rail, sea and road.
- Computer-aided design and manufacture.

Source: Adapted from *Human Development Report* (1999)

Globalisation – north and south

As we have seen, the term 'globalisation', like sustainable development, is not well defined. There is a vast array of conceptions of globalisation. Interpretations range from statements of value to descriptions of how current systems are working. Northern and Southern perspectives on globalisation often differ markedly. Some Northern perspectives have framed it as liberalisation, creating a climate of trust, enhancing wealth creation, whereas Southern perspectives often emphasise marginalisation, exploitation, divisiveness and the exercise of power, viewing neo-liberal economic polices as destructive of livelihoods, communities, cultures and natural resources.

Many supporters of globalisation are aware of its shortcomings and unintended side effects, and argue that the challenge is finding rules and institutions to preserve the advantages of globalisation while taking account of these problems. Hence the search for 'globalisation with a human face', which can embrace concerns for ethics, equity, inclusion, human security, sustainability and development.

The rise of 'anti-capitalist' protest

Meetings of various international finance, trade, political and economic forums which were once routine, have become the focus of unprecedented protest and attendant media coverage. Since the Seattle meeting in November 1999, a wave of other protests has crashed around the world including Bolivia, Ecuador, Washington, Paris, Prague, Nice, Quebec, Gothenburg and Genoa.

Seattle represented a turning point in what some now describe as the 'anti-globalisation movement'. Though one account of events in Seattle maintained that people both outside and inside were confused about what they wanted, it captured the attention of the world's media and brought the issues surrounding globalisation on to screens and into people's homes. International economic and political meetings now invariably focus on the major themes of trade, debt relief and globalisation. Although hard to understand, this new 'movement' is now given much attention in the media.

Is the anti-capitalist movement merely the focus of today's privileged, excluded or bored OECD youth – an anarchist travelling circus? Such explanations are too simplistic. The coalitions of stakeholders taking to the streets appear to be unlikely alliances of disparate groups transcending age-groups and economic and social classifications, including trade unionists, representatives of NGOs, shareholder activists and students. Although the movement certainly contains anti-globalisation and anti-capitalist elements, it appears to be united over the central issue of political, economic and social exclusion. All these groups have experienced the transfer of power from government to big corporations, the acceleration of inequalities within and between countries as a result of current economic policies and political ideologies, and the sense that society is itself being shaped and defined by big corporations. In rising up and dissenting against a sense of dispossession, the anti-globalisation movement is in effect creating a society for those who feel excluded (Peake, 2001).

Sustainable development, open economies and trade

A key issue already touched on is whether globalisation helps contribute to raising global standards of living, enhancing human and social capital in both North and South and therefore contributing to sustainable development, or whether its impacts are quite the opposite. This debate has largely crystallised around perspectives as to the role and impacts of international institutions such as the World Trade Organisation, World Bank, IMF and so on. We have already noted that the anti-capitalist protestors regard these roles as inimical to sustainable development. But is this really so? We now address this key issue in rather more depth, with the particular emphasis on whether an 'open' world trading regime supports or hinders sustainable development.

Trade and the WTO

The World Trade Organisation (WTO) is a powerful institution of international global governance whose rules and procedures are having a profound impact on global economic, social and political development. Agreeing trade rules that work for the benefit of the many and not the few will be about reaching agreement on the ultimate purposes and goals of trade liberalisation itself. Box 5.3 looks in more detail at the role of the WTO.

BOX 5.3

WTO and GATT

General Agreement on Tariffs and Trade (GATT)

The General Agreement on Tariffs and Trade (GATT) was signed in 1947 by 23 industrialised nations that included the UK, USA, Canada, France and the Benelux countries. The objectives of GATT were to reduce tariffs and other barriers to trade in the belief that freer trade would raise living standards in all participating countries. Since 1947 there have been seven 'rounds' of trade negotiations with the average tariff in the industrialised nations falling from 40 per cent in 1947 to below 5 per cent in 1995 when the GATT was replaced by the WTO. Supporters of the role of GATT point to facts such as the volume of world trade rising by 1,500 per cent and world output by 600 per cent over the years of its existence.

World Trade Organisation (WTO)

The WTO replaced GATT in 1995 and now has 135 members, rising to 136 with China's recent entry and with another 30 in the queue to join. WTO members in total account for more than 90 per cent of the value of world trade. The objectives of the WTO are essentially the same as GATT's, namely to reduce tariffs and other barriers to trade and to eliminate discrimination in trade. In this way it aims to contribute to rising living standards and a fuller use of world resources. Trade disputes between member states now come under the auspices of the WTO which has been given more powers than GATT to enforce compliance, using a streamlined disputes procedure with provision for appeals and binding arbitration. Whereas under GATT any single member (including the one violating GATT rules) could block a ruling of unfair trade, the findings of the WTO's disputes panels cannot be blocked by a veto of a member state. Countries found to be in violation of a WTO principle must remove the cause of that violation or pay compensation to the injured parties. If the offending party fails to comply with a WTO ruling then the WTO can sanction certain types of retaliation by the aggrieved party.

Since its creation in January 1995, more than 200 cases have been brought before the WTO against only 200 cases brought before GATT in the 47 years of its existence. More than half of these have involved the USA and EU, while around one-quarter have involved developing countries. The WTO also seeks to provide a forum for further multilateral trade negotiations.

Both the GATT and its successor the WTO have sought to implement a number of principles:

- *Non-discrimination.* The benefits of any trading advantage agreed between two nations (i.e. in bilateral negotiations) must be extended to *all* nations (i.e. become multilateral). This is sometimes referred to as the 'most-favoured nation' clause.
- *Progressive reduction in tariff and non-tariff barriers.* Certain exceptions, however, are permitted in specific circumstances. For example, Article 18 allows for the protection of 'infant industries' by the newly industrialising countries, whereas Article 19 permits any country to abstain from a general tariff cut in situations where rising imports might seriously damage domestic production. Similarly Articles 21–25 allow protection to continue where 'strategic interests' are involved, such as national security.
- *Solving trade disputes through consultation rather than retaliation.* Again certain exceptions are permitted. For example, Article 6 permits retaliatory sanctions to be applied if 'dumping' can be proven, i.e. the sale of products at artificially low prices (e.g. below cost). Countries in dispute are expected to negotiate bilaterally, but if these negotiations break down a WTO-appointed working party or panel can investigate the issue and make recommendations. Should any one of the parties refuse to accept this outcome, then the WTO can impose fines and/or sanction certain types of retaliation by the aggrieved party. ▶

The WTO has inherited 28 separate accords agreed under the final round of GATT negotiations (the Uruguay round). These accords sought to extend fair trade rules from industrial products to agricultural products, services, textiles, intellectual property rights and investment.

Trade liberalisation has certainly met many of its own objectives, with various trade rounds having resulted in a tenfold reduction in border tariffs on industrial products from 50 per cent in 1947 to around 5 per cent in 2001. However, many believe that it is the multinational corporations and the North in general that have benefited most from these trade freedoms. Nevertheless some, even from the South, argue that the WTO is needed to protect developing countries, and that it is a broadly successful institution of global governance to be reformed and improved, but not abandoned. Others stress that the WTO goes much too far, pointing out that it forces domestic laws to conform to trade law; in 10 out of 11 WTO cases between 1995 and 2001, national government regulation has been struck down. In essence some see the WTO as a mechanism for putting trade rules above every other kind of law, in the interests of its most powerful members. For example, Southern governments argue that the focus tends to be on Southern rather than Northern non-compliance! Case Study 5.1 looks at different perspectives on some recent WTO rulings involving 'dumping'.

CASE STUDY 5.1

WTO puts the brakes on anti-dumping bandwagon

To proponents, who include steadily more governments worldwide, anti-dumping policy is a legitimate defence against unfair foreign competition. To critics, it is a dangerous weapon that enables countries to flout liberalisation commitments by arbitrarily restricting imports.

In March 2001 the WTO handed critics a potentially far-reaching victory. The WTO's appellate body found that some of the arcane methodology used by the EU to determine whether imports are being dumped on its market violated WTO rules.

Many trade lawyers expect the decision – in a case brought by India over EU measures against bedlinen imports – to constrain Brussels' use of anti-dumping and limit the punitive duties imposed on offending imports.

Some expect the consequences also to affect the USA, which employs similar methodology to the EU and has recently been a more active user of anti-dumping measures, notably against steel imports.

'This decision has a broad application. It tells you how the appellate body will rule in these matters. I suspect it will lead to WTO cases being brought against the US', said David Palmeter, a partner in Powell Goldstein, a Washington law firm.

Although the first of its kind against the EU, the ruling reflects the WTO disputes adjudicators' growing readiness to take members to task over their anti-dumping practices. In doing so, they brave the wrath of powerful domestic political and business lobbies that firmly support tough enforcement of national laws. The adjudicators have already ruled against Washington's anti-dumping practices in cases involving steel and D-ram chips, and an independent arbitrator last week told the USA to amend its 1916 dumping law.

But Mr Palmeter says the latest ruling is the most significant yet, because it affects techniques central to most cases. The appellate body decided that the EU violated WTO rules on three counts in calculating 'dumping margins' – the amount by which it estimated exporters were selling products below cost or more cheaply than on home markets. The calculations, used to measure exporters' costs and profits and compare them with competitors', are key to finding that products are dumped and to setting the level of duties. Critics say the procedures are so elastic that they can be used to find that almost any product is dumped, harming producers in importing countries.

The WTO ruling is expected to impose more rigorous disciplines. 'It will lead to lower anti-dumping margins and, to some extent, lower levels of duties', said Jacques Bourgeois of the Brussels office of Akin Gump, a US law firm.

The EU Commission, which has promised to implement the ruling, has long insisted its procedures meet WTO rules, which were tightened in the Uruguay round. It has been supported by the European Court of Justice, which has rejected all but two of the more than 20 complaints by companies against Brussels' handling of dumping cases.

Mr Bourgeois said the changes in EU practices required by the WTO meant Brussels was less likely to win so easily. That could lead aggrieved companies to bring more court cases challenging past measures. The ruling places another brake on the EU's anti-dumping bandwagon, which is already slowing, partly because liberal-minded member states have grown more resistant to Commission dumping findings.

After peaking in 1999 the number of new investigations has fallen sharply, and the Commission last year ended many outstanding cases. Staff in its anti-dumping unit, which doubled in the mid-1990s, has been cut back, and some of those left are said to be underemployed.

The EU has also increasingly challenged in the WTO other countries' dumping laws, notably those of the USA. The Commission said it planned to ensure the practices of other countries, including the USA and India, also complied with last week's ruling.

Ironically, the fastest-growing users are now developing countries, notably Mexico and some other Latin American states, which have long complained bitterly of rich countries' excessive use of anti-dumping measures to restrict their exports.

Some observers think many poorer nations will be reluctant to seize on the latest WTO ruling as a precedent, for fear of provoking challenges to their own practices. However, a number of WTO members, including Egypt, Hong Kong and Japan, as well as India, continue to contest the use of anti-dumping measures against their exports. They are likely to find a powerful ally in China, the biggest target of anti-dumping cases, once it joins the organisation.

Source: Financial Times, 6th March 2001

Questions

1 How does the WTO ruling affect 'dumping'?

2 What arguments might be made on environmental grounds for and against this ruling?

While any country has a chance of winning a case at the WTO, not all can impose effective sanctions. For example, a small developing country can win a WTO ruling but, even with WTO permission, would hardly benefit from imposing retaliatory sanctions on a large, advanced industrialised country. In contrast, developing countries fear the impact of trade sanctions imposed by the more powerful WTO members who have won a WTO ruling against them.

The influence of multinational companies on devising the current trade rules at the WTO arouses strong emotions. Many would like to see an end to a system in which trade rules are set after discussions between government trade representatives and the government relations representatives of multinational companies. Trade rules are widely held to have been set to the advantage of the business community, restricting the capacities of national governments to make their own trade-related decisions. Such cross-border and internally invasive intervention has been an important source of public disenchantment with the WTO and similar bodies.

The anti-capitalist protests have significantly changed the dynamic of the trade negotiations. The conventional wisdom that 'trade is good for the poor, it makes people richer – and hence improves the environment' is now being openly challenged. While more trade may very well benefit higher-income groups in many countries, in some cases it would seem to have had negative effects on low-income groups in both developed and developing countries. For example, the sustained decline in commodity prices to their lowest levels in the post-war period has further eroded the incomes of the poor in many developing countries. However, Case Study 5.2 suggests why many believe that the reform, not the abandonment, of institutions such as the WTO may be in the ultimate interests of the world's poor. In other words, the essential maintenance of an 'open' world trading system with institutional support to prevent its worst excesses.

CASE STUDY 5.2

Anti-capitalist protests and sustainability

In recent years many groups have demonstrated against globalisation and world trade patterns at Seattle, Geneva, Prague, Gothenburg and elsewhere. Yet the question remains, do world institutions such as the IMF, World Bank, WTO, EU, etc. help or hinder those in the developing economies?

The cause of the protestors is not reform of these institutions. Their aims are bigger than that. They claim to 'value human and ecological dignity over corporate profits and trickle-down economics'. They oppose the WTO, the Bank and the Fund because they are 'the chief instruments used by political and corporate elites to create today's unjust, destructive global economic order'.

The question they raise is not the role of specific international institutions in today's liberal global economy. It is whether there should be such an economy at all. The answer is that there must be, for the reason advanced by Larry Summers, the US Treasury secretary under President Clinton: 'Quite simply, rapid, market-led growth is the most potent weapon against poverty that mankind has ever known.'

The only alternative to growth must be redistribution from the rich of the world. In 2000, according to the World Bank, average world income per head was $5,150 (*World Development Report*, 2002). The 885 million inhabitants of high-income countries had average real incomes per head of $27,510, while the 3.5 billion people in the low-income countries had average incomes of only $420 and in the lower-middle-income countries of only $1,140.

With such global redistribution ruled out, only events within individual developing countries can eliminate mass poverty. Here the evidence is clear for two propositions: first, sustained growth raises the real incomes of the poor; second, intelligent exploitation of opportunities in the world economy contributes mightily to growth. On the first of these, an unpublished paper by two World Bank economists, David Dollar and Aart Kraay[1], provides what appears to be incontestable evidence. Using a sample of 80 countries over four decades, and defining the poor as those in the bottom fifth of the income distribution, they reach four conclusions.

First, the incomes of the poor tend to rise in the same proportion as those of the population as a whole. Second, the effect of growth on the incomes of the poor is the same as in rich countries; third, the incomes of the poor do not fall disproportionately during economic crises; and, finally, the relationship between poverty reduction and growth has not changed in the era of globalisation.

None of this should be controversial. We know that the bulk of the world's destitute live in the world's poorest countries: more than two-thirds of those living on less than a dollar a day live in South Asia and sub-Saharan Africa. We know, too, that the biggest reductions in mass poverty have occurred where there has been the fastest growth: in East Asia.

The paper by Mr Dollar and Mr Kraay also indicates that the policies economists would recommend for improving growth performance also help the poor. High inflation is bad for overall growth and particularly harmful to the poor; and an effective rule of law is good both for average incomes and the poor. None of this should be seen as mere 'trickle-down' economics: macroeconomic stability and honest law enforcement directly benefit many of the poorest people. It would be ludicrous to suggest otherwise.

Turn then to the second proposition: the role of increased openness to trade. The paper by Mr Dollar and Mr Kraay concludes that this raises average incomes. They also conclude, contrary to much of the conventional wisdom, that there is no relationship between increased openness to trade and rising inequality. Trade raises average incomes and the incomes of the poor in roughly equal proportions.

That open economies tend to grow faster than closed ones is, as a joint IMF and World Bank staff report to this weekend's meeting of the Development Committee notes, consistent with a range of empirical studies.[2] To take just one example, Sebastian Edwards of the University of California at Los Angeles concludes in a study of 93 countries that there is a close link between openness and rates of productivity growth. The latter is the most important determinant of long-term growth.[3]

The conclusions are straightforward. Rightly or wrongly, the world is not going to embark on a redistribution of incomes from the rich countries to the poor ones that would be sufficient, in itself, to transform the lot of the destitute. Even the campaigners propose no such thing. But the countries where most of the poorest live are evidently too poor to achieve the needed redistribution themselves: one cannot get far with redistributing nothing.

Happily, it is clear that the poor benefit from growth. Happily, too, growth itself is helped along by just the policies many of the demonstrators oppose: by macroeconomic stability, and by openness to trade. So the activists are not just wrong. Hoping to help, they intend to remove the only effective medicine for mass poverty.

This does not mean that the WTO, World Bank and IMF are beyond improvement; that global governance needs no reform; that securing faster growth is easier; or that faster growth is all one should try to achieve to reduce poverty. There is room for debate on all these points.

On the central question, however, there is none. What the world will witness in the anti-capitalist protests are people who intend, in effect, to kick the ladder of market-driven economic growth down behind them. Some – notably the trade unions – do so out of self-interest. Others are well-intentioned but foolish; they want to protect the poor from the process that delivered their own remarkable prosperity. They will inflict great harm, in the belief that they are doing good. This happened repeatedly in the twentieth century. It must not do so again in the twenty-first.

Notes:
[1] 'Growth is good for the poor', March 2000.
[2] 'Trade development and poverty reduction', (www.worldbank.org/devcom)
[3] 'Openness, productivity and growth: what do we really know?' National Bureau of Economic Research, 1997 (www.nber.org)

Questions

1 Briefly outline the criticisms of the WTO, IMF and World Bank.

2 What arguments can be made in support of these international institutions?

World Summit on Sustainable Development (WSSD)

The UN General Assembly called for a 10-year review of progress since Rio 'to reinvigorate the global commitment to sustainable development'. The World Summit on Sustainable Development (WSSD or Rio + 10), held in Johannesburg in 2002, was also seen as an opportunity to underscore the special needs and circumstances of the least developed countries (LDCs), over two-thirds of which are in Africa. The backdrop is one of ever-increasing uncertainty. When and where will the next civil war begin? What about debt burdens, unfair trading systems, conflicts over food, water, land, equity, famine – and lack of access to basic human needs? The task of the WWSD was to translate the goals of the 1987 Brundtland Report for sustainable development into reality given the limited progress in implementing the commitments made in Rio.

The Malmö 2000 Ministerial Declaration had previously declared there to be 'an alarming discrepancy between commitments and action' on achieving sustainable development. The gap between rhetoric and reality was further elaborated in the conclusions of the Malmö Declaration which declared that 'At the dawn of this new century, we have at our disposal the human and material resources to achieve sustainable development, not as an abstract concept but as a concrete reality.'

There is little doubt that relations between the so-called 'North' and 'South' are at their most fragile for some time. The issue of finance is particularly emotive. While the global economy has boomed, overseas development aid has declined from 0.4 per cent of OECD GNP in 1992 to 0.2 per cent in 2001. Developing countries no longer trust developed countries to live up to their internationally agreed commitments.

The WSSD for the first time sought to address sustainable development in its entirety, i.e. the economic, developmental, environmental *and* social dimensions simultaneously. The last 10 years have taught us that dealing with one or other item in isolation simply distorts and perpetuates many of the underlying problems. The agenda for the WSSD Summit of 2002 in Johannesburg was devised using a bottom-up, stakeholder-driven approach. The challenges identified include the following:

- Forging a more constructive global alliance between North and South, between governments, civil society and NGOs;
- Enhancing international environmental governance – including the implementation and monitoring of legally binding commitments (taking into account the circumstances of developing countries);
- Operationalising the concept of 'common but differentiated responsibility', together with other important principles contained in the Rio Declaration;
- Strengthening the role of the North in ensuring an enabling environment for the sustainable development of the South;
- Agreeing new development goals based on the social, economic and environmental requirements for sustainable development;
- Bringing a new impetus against global poverty and to increase ODA to the agreed international 0.7 per cent target;
- Accelerating the diffusion and transfer of environmentally sound technologies in support of sustainable development;
- Effectively developing and implementing national sustainable development strategies;
- Integrating the trade and sustainable development agendas – and how in practice this could be effectively achieved (e.g. integrating sustainable development into trade or vice versa?);
- Facilitating the private sector in a greater engagement with issues around sustainable development;
- Engaging the new economy's contribution to sustainable development – e.g. harnessing the contributions of information and biotechnologies;
- Implementing the precautionary principle/approach in relation to science and technology – for example, should risk assessments of sustainable development frameworks, programmes and projects be enhanced?

International development targets

Today's political orientations towards development are firmly centred on the use of international development targets (IDTs). This approach is usefully illustrated by the *UN Millennium Declaration* which included a commitment to a set of millennium development goals, broken down into targets (see Box 5.4).

BOX 5.4

The UN millennium development goals (MDGs)

Goals and targets	*Indicators*
Goal 1 Eradicate extreme poverty and hunger	
Target 1 Halve, between 1990 and 2015, the proportion of people whose income is less than one dollar a day	1. Proportion of population below $1 per day 2. Poverty gap ratio (incidence x depth of poverty) 3. Share of poorest quintile in national consumption
Target 2 Halve, between 1990 and 2015, the proportion of people who suffer from hunger	4. Prevalence of underweight children (under five years of age) 5. Proportions of population below minimum level of dietary energy consumption
Goal 2 Achieve universal primary education	
Target 3 Ensure that, by 2015, children everywhere, boys and girls alike, will be able to complete a full course of primary schooling	6. Net enrolment ratio in primary education 7. Proportion of pupils starting grade 1 who reach grade 5 8. Literacy rate of 15–24-year-olds
Goal 3 Promote gender equality and empower women	
Target 4 Eliminate gender disparity in primary and secondary education, preferably by 2005, and to all levels of education no later than 2015	9. Ratio of girls to boys in primary, secondary and tertiary education 10. Ratio of literate females to males of 15–24-year-olds 11. Share of women in wage employment in the non-agricultural sector 12. Proportion of seats held by women in national parliament
Goal 4 Reduce child mortality	
Target 5 Reduce by two-thirds, between 1990 and 2015, the under-five mortality rate	13. Under-five mortality rate 14. Infant mortality rate 15. Proportion of 1-year-old children immunised against measles
Goal 5 Improve maternal health	
Target 6 Reduce by three-quarters, between 1990 and 2015, the maternal mortality ratio	16. Maternal mortality ratio 17. Proportion of births attended by skilled health personnel
Goal 6 Combat HIV/AIDS, malaria and other diseases	
Target 7 Have halted by 2015 and begun to reverse the spread of HIV/AIDS	18. HIV prevalence among 15–24-year-old pregnant women 19. Contraceptive prevalence rate 20. Number of children orphaned by HIV/AIDS
Target 8 Have halted by 2015 and begun to reverse the incidence of malaria and other major diseases	21. Prevalence and death rates associated with malaria 22. Proportion of population in malaria-risk areas using effective malaria prevention and treatment measures 23. Prevalence and death rates associated with tuberculosis 24. Proportion of tuberculosis cases detected and cured under directly observed treatment short course
Goal 7 Ensure environmental sustainability	
Target 9 Integrate the principles of sustainable development into country policies and programmes and reverse the loss of environmental resources	25. Proportion of land area covered by forest 26. Land area protected to maintain biological diversity 27. GDP per unit of energy use (as proxy for energy efficiency) 28. Carbon dioxide emissions (per capita) (Plus two figures of global atmospheric pollution: ozone depletion and the accumulation of global warming gases)

►

Target 10 Halve by 2015 the proportion of people without sustainable access to safe drinking water

Target 11 By 2020 to have achieved a significant improvement in the lives of at least 100 million slum dwellers

29. Proportion of population with sustainable access to an improved water source
30. Proportion of people with access to improved sanitation
31. Proportion of people with access to secure tenure (urban/rural disaggregation of several of the above indicators may be relevant for monitoring improvement in the lives of slum dwellers)

Goal 8 Develop a global partnership for development

(Some of the indicators listed below will be monitored separately for the LDCs, Africa, landlocked countries and small island developing states)

Official development assistance

Target 12 Develop further an open, rule-based, predictable, non-discriminatory trading and financial system (includes a commitment to good governance, development and poverty reduction – both nationally and internationally)

32. Net ODA as percentage of OECD/DAC donors' gross national income (targets of 0.7% in total and 0.15% for LDCs)
33. Proportion of ODA to basic social services (basic education, primary health care, nutrition, safe water and sanitation

Target 13 Address the special needs of the LDCs (includes: tariff and quota free access for LDCs' exports; enhanced programme of debt relief for HIPCs (Heavily Indebted Poor Countries) and cancellation of official bilateral debt; and more generous ODA for countries committed to poverty reduction)

34. Proportion of ODA that is untied
35. Proportion of ODA for environment in small island developing states
36. Proportion of ODA for transport sector in landlocked countries

Market access

Target 14 Address the special needs of landlocked countries and small island developing states (through the Programme of Action for the Sustainable Development of Small Island Developing States and the outcome of the twenty-second special session of the General Assembly)

37. Proportion of exports (by value and excluding arms) admitted free of duties and quotas
38. Average tariffs and quotas on agricultural products and textiles and clothing

Target 15 Deal comprehensively with the debt problems of developing countries through national and international measures in order to make debt sustainable in the long term

39. Domestic and export agricultural subsidies in OECD countries
40. Proportion of ODA provided to help build trade capacity

Debt sustainability

41. Proportion of official bilateral HIPC debt cancelled
42. Debt service as a percentage of exports of goods and services
43. Proportion of ODA provided as debt relief
44. Number of countries reaching HIPC decision and completion points

Target 16 In co-operation with developing countries, develop and implement strategies for decent and productive work for youth

45. Unemployment rate of 15–24-year-olds

▶

Target 17 In co-operation with pharmaceutical companies, provide access to affordable essential drugs in developing countries	46. Proportion of population with access to affordable essential drugs on a sustainable basis
Target 18 In co-operation with the private sector, make available the benefits of new technologies, especially information and communications	47. Telephone lines per 1,000 people 48. Personal computers per 1,000 people
	[Other Indicators to be decided]

Source: UN.

Despite growing recognition for these targets in their present form, international development targets are not new. Many previous summits have included targets. What does seem to be new, however, is the seriousness of tackling the issue of sustainable development on a broad front, bringing into play economic, social, political, environmental and technological elements in a comprehensive and integrative approach. Effectively monitoring and implementing these targets on a global scale will ultimately determine whether a more coherent approach in principle can result in more sustainable development in practice.

Beyond the WSSD: challenges and actions

- Critically assessing progress in an integrated manner – assessing environment, development and social objectives as well as human rights and respect for ethical values, cultural diversity and cultural knowledge;
- Persuading the minority of the world's population to cut down on their consumption so that poverty eradication does not lead to an overall increase in consumption and production; and
- Strengthening institutional capacities to deal with globalisation, poverty eradication, trade and sustainable development issues in a coherent and integrated manner.

> **Now try the self-check questions for this chapter on the companion website www.booksites.net/ison.**
>
> **You will also find up-to-date facts and case materials.**

Key terms

Globalisation No single definition can be complete, but involves the ideas of shrinking space, shrinking time and disappearing borders

Savings rule For development to be sustainable, total savings must at least cover all types of depreciation in any given time period

Strong sustainability (SS) Where each element within the total stock of capital should not fall between generations

Sustainable development No single definition can be complete, but involves the idea that any increase in well-being can last over future generations

Weak sustainability (WS) Where the total stock of capital should not fall between generations, though individual elements within it can vary

References and further reading

Bowers, J. (1997) *Sustainability and Environmental Economics*, Longman, Harlow, especially Chapters 13–15.

Field, B.C. (1997) *Environmental Economics: An Introduction*, McGraw-Hill, especially Chapter 5.

Giddens, A. (1990) *The Consequences of Modernity*, Polity Press.

Gilpin, A. (2000) *Environmental Economics: A Critical Overview*, Wiley, especially Chapter 4.

Grubb, M. (1992), The Earth Summit Agreements, Royal Institute of International Affairs, London.

Human Development Report (1999) *Globalization with a human face*, UN Development Programme, OUP.

Human Development Report (2001) *Making New Technologies Work for Human Development*, UN Development Programme, OUP.

McGrew, A. (1992) 'A global society' in S. Hau, D. Held and McGrew A. (eds), *Modernity and its Futures*, Open University Press, Milton Keynes.

Meadows, D.H., Meadows, D.L, Randers, J. and Behrens, W.W. (1972) *The Limits to Growth*. Potomac Associates, Washington D.C.

Open University (2002) 'Introduction to sustainability' in *U213 International Development: Challenges for a World in Transition*, Open University, Milton Keynes.

Peake, S. (2001) Globalisation and Sustainable Development: Deeper Issues behind the Johannesburg (R10 + 10) Agenda, *Report of Wilton Park Conference*, WP656.

Pearce, D. (1998) 'Sustainable development – taking stock of the future', *The Economic Review*, **16**, 1, Sept.

Reid, D. (1995) *Sustainable Development*, Earthscan, London.

Royal Commission on Environmental Pollution (2000), 22nd Report, *Energy – the Changing Climate*, Cm4749.

Rio Declaration (1992) *UN Framework Convention on Climate Change*, UN, New York.

Turner, R.K., Pearce, D. and Bateman, I. (1994) *Environmental Economics*, FT/Prentice Hall, Hemel Hempstead.

WCED (1987) *Our Common Future*, Oxford University Press, London.

World Development Report (2002) *Building Institutions for Markets*, The World Bank, OUP.

Useful websites

Text of Agenda 21: www.un.org/esa/sustdev/agenda21text.htm

UNEP's Global Environment Outlook 2000: www.unep.org/Geo2000/english/index.htm

World Bank summary of international law:
www4.worldbank.org/legal/legen_int/legen_IEC.html

Excellent review of international environmental law just post-Rio, written by an authority on the subject, Peter H. Sands: www.ejil.org/journal/Vol4/No3/art4.html

International Environmental Law Ombudsman: http://earthsummitwatch.org/ombud.html

OECD DAC's Working set of indicators of measuring development progress: www.oecd.org/dac/Indicators/htm/list.htm

International Development Goals Website: www.developmentgoals.org/

Environmental Treaties and Resource Indicators (ENTRI): sedac.ciesin.org/pidb/pidb-home.html

Greenpeace's Convention Resources Page from their Legal Department: www.greenpeace.org/~intlaw/othconf.html

Good links to Earth Summit Agreements: iisd.ca/rio15/earthsummit.htm

UN homepage for Agenda 21: www.un.org/esa/sustdev/agenda21text.htm

View the Earth Charter in several languages: www.earthcharter.org/

Report of Wilton Park Conference on R10 + 10: http://www.wiltonpark.org.uk/web/conferences/reportwrapper. asp? confref = WP656

Pollution and the environment

The issue of pollution and its environmental impacts appears in various guises throughout this book. However, in this chapter we pay particular attention to some specific aspects of the pollution debate. A more comprehensive definition of 'pollution' is attempted, together with a typology of various types of pollutants, using terms such as cumulative and non-cumulative, geographical scale, point and non-point source and continuous and episodic.

The focus then moves to a more detailed enquiry into the issues and policies involving water, air and land pollution respectively. In applying our analysis to these particular types of pollution, some of the 'target' materials of Chapter 3 and 'policy instruments' of Chapter 4 are taken further. For example, the issue of water-based pollution provides a useful context for further considering the relative merits of market and non-market environmental policy instruments. The same is true of the discussion on land-based pollution involving the use of landfill sites or recycling.

The theoretical issues involved in dealing with transboundary pollution at various levels of geographical scale are considered in some detail. A number of policy issues are reviewed, including the need for international bodies to monitor, enforce and arbitrate in the context of regional and global pollution. Some of these issues are taken further in Chapter 7 on climate change.

●●●● Defining pollution

When seeking to define **pollution** a useful reference point is the *ambient* quality of the environment. This refers to the environment in its 'natural state', i.e. before the intervention of humankind. Even in the 'natural state', environments such as forests produce or are exposed to varying quantities of substances that might be regarded today as pollutants. For example, background radiation, gases such as carbon dioxide (CO_2), chemicals such as nitrates, and so on.

The term 'pollution' is most commonly applied to situations in which man-made activities *reduce* the ambient quality of a particular environment. In this view the introduction of any substance or energy form that lowers the ambient quality of the environment (i.e. 'pollutant') can be regarded as 'pollution'.

Clearly 'pollution' is by no means a straightforward concept. However, Figure 6.1 provides a useful overview of the impacts of human activities on the land, air and

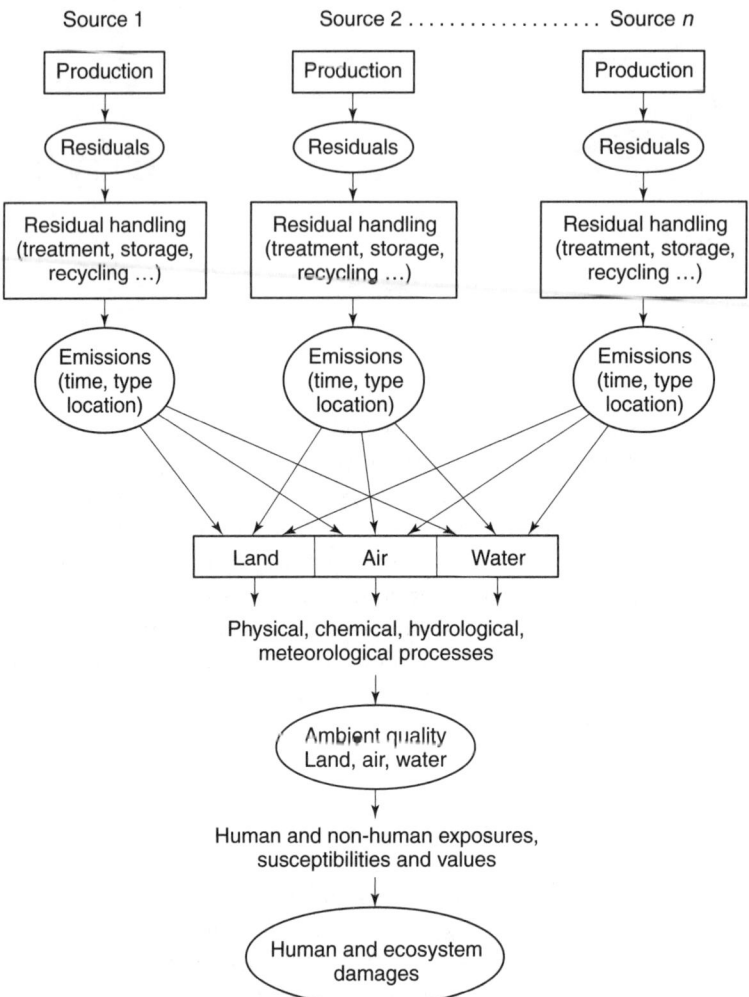

Figure 6.1 Sources of pollution and outcomes
Source: Field (1997).

water constituents of the natural environment, reducing the ambient quality of those constituents and thereby causing 'pollution' in the strict sense of environmental damages. The diagram suggests *n* different *sources* of human activities, each involving the conversion of factor inputs into outputs, some of which are consumed. *Residuals* refer to materials and substances left over after production or consumption, which must be 'handled' in some way (treated, stored, recycled, etc.). Some part of these residuals from production or consumption remain in the form of *emissions* into the environment and impact, directly or indirectly, on to the key constituents of the natural world, namely land, air and water (sometimes called the 'environmental medium'). The outcomes of these impacts are varying degrees of human and ecosystem damage.

●●●● Types of pollutants

The types of substances and energy forms which result in a lowering of the ambient quality of natural environments and which we therefore regard as pollutants, are many and various. The following typology indicates just some of the categories into which they might be placed.

Cumulative and non-cumulative pollutants

- **Cumulative pollutants** tend to be retained in the environment over time in roughly the same amounts as when first emitted. Radioactive wastes decay so slowly (e.g. the half-life of the carbon-14 isotope is 5,700 years) that they can be regarded as almost permanent. Most plastics and some chemicals are non-biodegradable (i.e. cannot be broken down by micro-organisms in the soil) and so are often placed in the category 'cumulative pollutants'.
- **Non-cumulative pollutants** tend to dissipate quickly after being emitted, for example noise. A few plastics and many chemicals are biodegradable and may therefore be placed in this category.

Of course many substances and energy sources fall somewhere in between these two extremes, such as organic wastes. Further, the category into which we place a substance/energy source may depend not on its own characteristics but on the *assimilative capacity* of a particular environmental medium. For example, at low levels of emission of organic waste or CO_2, the environmental media of water or the atmosphere can, respectively, usually assimilate these emissions with little or no long-term damage. If, however, 'threshold' levels of emissions are exceeded, then the assimilative capacity of the environmental media to absorb further emissions without damage is impaired. In this case what might initially have been regarded as a 'non-cumulative' pollutant may now be regarded as a 'cumulative' pollutant.

Global, regional and local pollutants

The geographical scale of the impact of the pollutant is sometimes used as a means of classification:

- **Global pollutants** are those which, while emitted from a local source, have potentially worldwide impacts. The impacts of CFC (chlorofluorocarbon) emissions on the ozone layer in the world's stratosphere is an example of a global pollutant (see Chapter 7, page 168).
- **Regional pollutants** are those which, while emitted from a local source, have impacts which extend geographically far beyond that source, though not worldwide. This can involve 'regions' within a country, but more usually 'regions' involving geographically adjacent countries. Oxides of sulphur and nitrogen emitted via the combustion of fossil fuels in particular localities have been held as responsible for 'acid rain' deposited by various types of precipitation (rain, snow or hail), which has degraded forests, lakes and buildings in geographically adjacent countries (see Box 6.1, page 141).

- **Local pollutants** are those which are emitted from a local source and which have impacts on a local scale. Pollutants such as noise and those which affect the visual appearance of the environment come within this category.

Point-source and non-point-source pollutants

- **Point-source pollutants** are those for which the actual point of discharge can readily be identified, e.g. sulphur dioxide emissions from power plants and organic wastes from sewage outflows.
- **Non-point-source pollutants** are those for which no well-defined point of discharge can be identified, such as 'runoff' of various agrochemicals used in large-scale farming into numerous streams and underground aquifers.

Continuous and episodic pollutants

- **Continuous pollutants** are those which follow some type of uninterrupted time profile, such as emissions from production units which are in operation for 24 hours, e.g. power plants and waste treatment plants.
- **Episodic pollutants** occur on a 'one-off', intermittent basis, e.g. oil or chemical spills.

●●●● Water pollution

Types of water pollutants

One method of categorising water pollutants is to focus on their chemical and physical properties:

- *Organic substances*: chemicals such as pesticides, oils, solvents, detergents; degradable wastes such as domestic sewage.
- *Inorganic substances*: chemicals such as toxic metals, acids, salts; plant nutrients such as nitrate and phosphorous compounds.
- *Energy forms*: radioactive wastes.
- *Infectious agents*: bacteria, viruses.

Another approach is to use the taxonomy of types of pollutants previously outlined (page 135):

- *Cumulative (persistent) water pollutants*. These remain for long periods, either because they are non-degradable or have extremely low rates of degradation. Numerous organic and inorganic chemicals fall into this category, often embodied in wastes and residuals from households and industries. Agricultural sources include fertilisers and soil runoff. Metal wastes from mining operations and radioactive wastes can also be included here.
- *Non-cumulative (degradable) water pollutants*. These are capable of changing their characteristics after emission when subjected to various biological, chemical and physical processes. Within this category particular attention is often paid

to the 'biochemical oxygen demand' (BOD) of the water pollutants (see below).

● *Point sources* of water pollutants include outfalls from factories and from domestic waste treatment plants whereas *non-point sources* include agricultural runoff of pesticides and fertilisers.

● *Continuous* water pollutants are often related to emissions from factories, sewage and water treatment plants. *Episodic* water pollutants involve accidents such as the introduction of aluminium sulphate into the Camelford water system in Comwall in 1989.

Biochemical oxygen demand (BOD)

This refers to the amount of oxygen required to decompose organic materials under specified conditions of temperature and time. Water resources with higher levels of dissolved oxygen (DO) are better able to degrade wastes via associated oxygen-using chemical processes. Clearly the lower the BOD levels of degradable water pollutants, the less of the oxygen content of the water resources is required. This is important since, during the chemical process degrading the wastes, the dissolved oxygen level of the water temporarily falls.

The DO profile in Figure 6.2 illustrates this so-called DO 'sag' over time (or distance) t to t_1 during the degradation process itself. However, once the water body has assimilated the degradable materials and their associated BOD load, natural aeration processes normally help the DO level of the water to recover.

Policy instruments and water pollution

The issue of market failure in the form of externalities (see Chapter 3, page 59) is an important aspect of the debate on how to deal with water pollution. For the discharge of untreated effluent into underground (aquifers) or surface (reservoirs, lakes, rivers) water sources will have an impact on individuals and firms who have themselves had no part in the discharge. Those abstracting (taking) water further downstream will find that purification costs are higher, while others using rivers or estuaries for recreational or leisure activities will also be

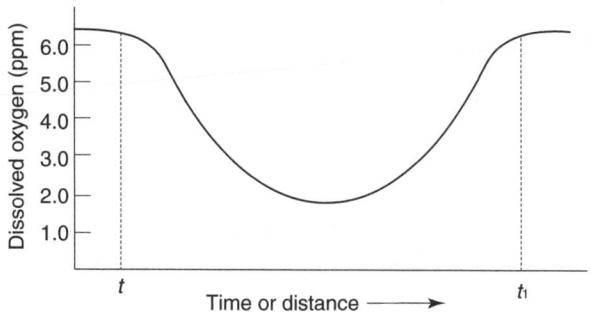

Figure 6.2 Dissolved oxygen profile in water after a BOD load has been introduced

adversely affected. The source of this water-based pollution is only likely to take these external costs into account if regulated or taxed.

In the UK, water pollution is mainly a local or regional issue, implying that the economic instruments discussed in Chapters 3 and 4 be applied flexibly, depending on the particular local circumstances:

- *Pigouvian tax rates* equivalent to the net marginal social damage when levied on effluents would need to vary across rivers, depending on the initial level of pollution of that river.
- *Tradable permits* schemes would need to be specific to particular rivers, lakes and estuaries – since abatement in one watercourse is not a perfect substitute for abatement in another.
- *Regulations* would need to take into account different local impacts, e.g. equivalent discharges may seriously damage one watercourse but not another which might have a higher rate of river flow and fewer abstractions of water or fewer leisure uses downstream.

The many instances of non-point source water pollutants further complicate the choice of policy instruments, making it extremely difficult to trace the causes of water pollution to individual sources.

Current UK policies

In the UK it is a criminal offence to pollute watercourses. However, industrial sources of effluent discharges can obtain 'consents' and 'authorisations' from the Environment Agency (EA) in England and Wales and the Scottish and Northern Ireland equivalents. These 'consents' will specify the conditions to be applied to these discharges, such as time, place, volume, temperature and composition. Maximum concentrations of specified substances are also part of many 'consents'. Such standards may be set by:

- the EA itself, reflecting its general approach of ensuring 'no deterioration' from current water quality;
- the EU via statutory legislation and various directives.

Although the EA levies a charge for 'consents', these are not based on marginal (abatement) cost principles (see Chapter 4, page 98). Rather the charges are fixed throughout the country and relate to 'maximum allowed discharges' rather than actual discharges. In other words, the charges for consents seek to recover the administrative costs of the EA in its monitoring and compliance work associated with the 'consents' system rather than varying with the pollution damage from the effluent. As a result the tariff per unit of discharge actually falls, since monitoring and compliance costs typically rise less than in proportion to volumes of discharge.

Case Study 6.1 follows Cowan (1998) in reviewing the case for using consents, taxes or tradable permits to achieve a specified volume of water discharges at the least environmental cost.

CASE STUDY 6.1

Tackling water-based pollution

The use of marginal abatement cost (MAC) curves is covered in Chapter 4 (page 98–102). Here we apply the analysis to finding the least-cost methods of controlling the pollution contained in water discharges.

Figure 6.3 shows MAC curves for two rivers, 1 and 2. It suggests that to abate (avoid) an extra unit of discharge (pollution) in river 1 costs more than to abate the same unit of discharge in river 2. A condition for least-cost abatement is that the marginal costs of abatement of different watercourses are equal.

Discharges in the absence of any abatement are, for simplicity, assumed to be the same and equal to D_0. Abatement is measured from D_0 leftwards, and the marginal costs of abatement are MAC_1 and MAC_2 for rivers 1 and 2 respectively.

Here we consider one non-market-based or regulatory system (consents) and two market-based systems (taxes and tradable permits):

- *Consent system.* This requires that discharges from each source do not exceed $\bar{D}$. The question is whether a tax system can achieve this same total abatement ($2\bar{D}$) at a lower cost.
- *Tax system.* Under a tax system, abatement will continue until the marginal cost of abating on each river equals the marginal benefit from abating (i.e. the tax *avoided* by abating each unit of discharge).

A tax at rate p causes the high-cost source, river 1, to increase its pollution beyond $\bar{D}$ to D_1, while the low-cost source, river 2, will reduce its discharges to D_2. If p is appropriately chosen, river 1's increase in pollution is exactly offset by river 2's reduction, i.e. $D_1 - \bar{D} = \bar{D} - D_2$. The saving in the total cost of abatement relative to the consent system is

$$A + B + C - D$$

which is positive since $\bar{D} - D_2 = D_1 - \bar{D}$.

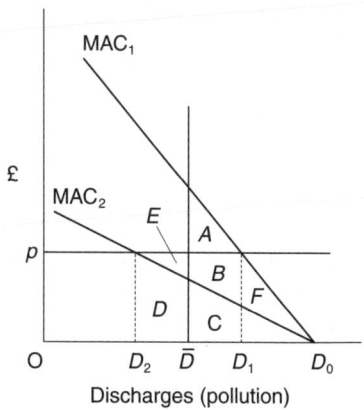

Figure 6.3 Tackling water-based pollution in two rivers

- *Permit system*. Here market forces determine the price of a permit. When the total number of permits is $2\overline{D}$ the market price will be p. This is the only price at which river 2 will have an incentive to sell exactly the same number of permits $(\overline{D} - D_2)$ as river 1 will wish to purchase $(D_1 - \overline{D})$. The outcome in terms of resource allocation would then yield the same efficiency gains as for the tax system.

Both types of market-based instrument (tax or permits) allow each source to use its own cost information and thus decentralise decisions about abatement levels. However, an economic instrument only provides a cost saving, for a given total pollution level, if marginal abatement cost functions differ. The more similar these functions are, the smaller the gains from using an economic instrument rather than a regulation ('consents').

In the water context the case for economic instruments rather than regulations ('consents') in tackling pollution should not be overstated:

- Sewage treatment works operated by one company that discharge into both rivers might have similar abatement cost functions.
- The regulator may be better able to discriminate between pollution sources than a regime of (uniform) taxes. For example, water-borne pollution is mostly of local concern. A river which has little amenity value, from which little water is abstracted (taken out) downstream and which has a stronger flow might be better able to bear the environmental burden of polluting discharges than another river. If this is the case for river 2, then a tax at a uniform rate p could *lower welfare* even though it reduces total abatement costs vis-à-vis 'consents'. This is because the tax regime raises discharges from river 1 ($\overline{D}$ to D_1) but reduces discharges from river 2 ($\overline{D}$ to D_2) where extra pollution could more easily be sustained by the environment.

Questions

1 What does the case study suggest about the least-cost methods for achieving a given level of reduction in water pollution?

2 Explain why the 'least-cost' method of avoiding water pollution is not necessarily the most environmentally appropriate.

3 What does this case study tell us about the environmental taxes versus standards debate?

Air pollution

Some 95 per cent of the planet's air occurs in the lower level of the Earth's atmosphere, i.e. the troposphere. In its ambient state, such surface air contains some 78 per cent nitrogen, 21 per cent oxygen, small amounts of other gases and water vapour. The remaining 5 per cent of the planet's air occurs in the upper level of the earth's atmosphere (i.e. the stratosphere), together with various trace gases such as ozone.

One method of categorising air pollutants is to focus on their chemical and physical properties:

- *Organic substances*: oxides of carbon, nitrogen and sulphur, volatile organic compounds.
- *Inorganic substances*: suspended particulate matter; lead, acids.
- *Energy forms*: radioactivity (some would add heat and noise).

Another method for categorising air pollutants is to focus on whether they are released directly into the air as gases or fine particles or are the indirect product of reactions in the atmosphere:

- *Primary pollutants* are produced directly and released into the air.
- *Secondary pollutants* are formed in the air from chemical reactions between primary pollutants.

Table 6.1 provides more detail on primary and secondary air pollutants.

Table 6.1 Primary and secondary air pollutants: sources and effects

Air pollutant	Source	Damaging effects
Primary pollutants		
Sulphur dioxide	Combustion of fossil fuels (mainly industry)	'Dieback' in trees, reduced crop plant growth
Nitrogen oxides	Combustion of fossil fuels (mainly vehicles)	'Dieback' in trees, reduced crop plant growth
Carbon monoxide	Combustion of fossil fuels (mainly vehicles)	Human respiratory diseases
Carbon dioxide	Combustion of fossil fuels	Global warming
Chlorofluorocarbons (CFCs)	Aerosol cans, refrigerators	Destruction of ozone layer
Particulate matter	Smoke (mainly from industry)	Human respiratory diseases, cancer
Radioactive substances	Nuclear tests, nuclear power stations	Increased mutation rates
Lead	Lead vehicle exhaust, from leaded petrol	Mental development in children impaired
Secondary pollutants		
Acid rain	Mixture of sulphuric and nitric acids, derived from sulphur dioxide and rainwater	Death of freshwater fish, corrosion of stone buildings
Ozone	Formed from chemical reaction with nitrogen oxides and UV light	'Dieback' in trees, reduced crop plant growth, skin cancer

Box 6.1 looks at one widely recognised type of secondary pollutant, namely acid rain, while Box 6.2 looks at another, namely ozone depletion.

BOX 6.1

Acid rain

Acidic oxides such as sulphur dioxide, sulphur trioxide and nitrogen dioxide are released into the atmosphere by the burning of fossil fuels. They combine with water in the atmosphere and react with sunlight and ozone to form a mist of acid droplets with a pH less than 7. If there is a lot of dust in the air, these acid droplets may also condense to produce an unpleasant smog, which attacks the conjuctiva of the eye and the alveolar epithelium of the lungs.

The major source of sulphur dioxide (SO_2) pollution is from the combustion of fossil fuels by cars, industry and power stations. The acid rain causes defoliation and death of coniferous trees, and runs off from the soil into lakes and rivers where it reduces the pH to a level which kills all fish and many other aquatic organisms.

Clean Air Acts now prohibit the burning of coal in open fires over much of Britain and many other countries, so urban smogs have largely disappeared. However, acid rain is still an important environmental issue in countries downwind of power stations in their own or other countries. For example, much of the SO_2 emitted from power stations in the UK is carried by prevailing winds to Scandinavian countries, where it falls as acid rain. Acid rain has been widely attributed to the cause of forest 'dieback' (large-scale death or poor growth of trees) in North America and in Europe and to the erosion and damage of many types of building. In terms of biodiversity, a number of species have been depleted or put at risk by acid rain: for example, a much higher rate of depletion of lichen species has been found to occur with increased exposure to acid rain.

Table 6.2 shows substantial reductions in gaseous emissions which contribute to acid rain over the past decade. In fact across all sources, an overall 40 per cent reduction in these acid precursors was achieved between 1991 and 1998 in the UK. The most significant reductions have taken place within the electricity, gas and water supply industries (56 per cent), and wholesale and retail sectors (44 per cent).

Regulations and standards have played a part in these reductions in the UK and other parts of Europe. For example, members of the United Nations Economic Council for Europe (UNECE) have been working together since 1979 to set targets for reducing emissions of long-range transboundary air pollution, including these acid rain precursors. The 1999 UNECE Gothenburg Protocol has set ceilings for emissions of sulphur dioxide, nitrogen oxides and other gaseous contributors to acid rain.

Table 6.2 Acid rain precursors[1] in the UK by source, 1991 and 1998 (thousand tonnes)

Source	1991	1998	Percentage change 1991–98
Electricity, gas and water supply	3,020	1,330	−56
Wholesale and retail trade	90	50	−44
Manufacturing and construction	980	630	−36
Domestic	640	440	−31
Agriculture, mining and quarrying	770	680	−12
Transport and communication	570	520	−9
Others[2]	250	160	−36
All sources	6,310	3,810	−40

[1] Acid rain precursor emissions include sulphur dioxide, nitrogen oxides and ammonia, expressed in thousand tonnes of sulphur dioxide equivalent.
[2] Includes public administration, financial intermediation, education, health and social work, and other services.
Source: *Social Trends* (2001).

BOX 6.2

Ozone depletion

Ozone (O_3) is concentrated at a ratio of 10 parts per million in the ozone layer of the stratosphere. Normally the layer lies between 25 and 35 km above the Earth's surface. It absorbs incoming ultraviolet radiation. Reducing this filter as ozone is depleted leads to the warming of the stratosphere, which plays a part in the so-called 'greenhouse effect'. There has been a recorded decline of 10 per cent in ozone over the northern hemisphere over the past decade, a decline some four times faster than had been predicted. There is also evidence of 'holes' in the ozone layer over the northern hemisphere.

The ozone layer is disturbed by chlorofluorocarbon gases (CFCs) because ultraviolet light causes the chlorine to destroy ozone molecules (1 chlorine molecule can destroy up to 100,000 ozone molecules). Though now banned in the advanced industrialised economies, CFCs have been used in aerosols, in plastic foams, refrigerants and in fire extinguishers.

As well as contributing to the greenhouse effect, by eroding the protective ozone layer in the upper atmosphere, CFCs have resulted in ultraviolet radiation increasing in intensity, producing higher rates of skin cancer, cataract-related illnesses and even crop failures as ultraviolet radiation destroys proteins and nucleic acids in plants.

The linkage between environment and economy can be usefully illustrated here. Ozone depletion and the associated increases in ultraviolet radiation are expected to cut by one-fifth the yields of vegetable crops such as peas, barley and oilseed rape over the next five years. These and other species of plants are highly sensitive to ultraviolet radiation and show a 1 per cent fall in yield for every 1 per cent reduction in the protective ozone layer. Plants exposed to higher levels of UV-B radiation are often smaller, less fertile in terms of reproduction, and have a lower oil and protein content (e.g. soya bean). Cereal crops such as wheat are also affected. With a 10 per cent reduction in the ozone layer already experienced over Europe in the past 10 years, the impact of reduced crop yields is expected to be seen in progressively higher food prices than would otherwise have been the case.

Another approach to air pollution is to use the taxonomy of types of pollutants previously outlined (page 135). For example, many airborne pollutants are emitted on a *continuous* basis, as in the case of CO_2 from fossil fuels used in power plants and factories in 24-hour operations. Other emissions are more *episodic*, as in the case of radioactive emissions from incidents such as Chernobyl.

Point source emissions can be traced to stationary sources (factories, offices) or to mobile sources (motor vehicles, planes). *Non-point source* emissions may be said to occur in processes such as 'respiration' (release of energy from the breakdown of food molecules in living cells) by which all organisms release CO_2 as a waste product.

The *geographical scale* of air pollutants may also be used for classification, with terms such as *local, transboundary* and *global* sometimes applied (see page 155).

The categories *cumulative* (persistent) and *non-cumulative* (degradable) are less easy to apply to air pollutants. For example, CFCs are gases which are capable of change (i.e. are arguably 'degradable') but in reacting with ozone in the stratosphere result in fewer molecules being available to absorb harmful ultraviolet radiation over long periods of time (i.e. have persistent effects).

Air pollution and health

Chapter 2 has reviewed various methods for valuing risks to life and health. Exposure to air pollution increases the risk of suffering various health effects, such as coughing, congestion, asthma, chronic bronchitis and even sudden death. In the UK, the Department of Health estimated that the premature death of between 12,000 and 24,000 vulnerable people may be brought forward by short-term exposure to air pollution each year (*Social Trends*, 2001).

Value of statistical life (VSL)

Attempts have been made to place monetary valuations on various health effects (see Chapter 2, page 43). For example, statistical studies have tended to place an estimate on the risk of accidental death of around £2m. (Markandya and Mason, 1999). However, this VSL figure is an average value of 'willingness to pay' (WTP) to avoid the effects of a variety of life-threatening hazards for a person with a 40-year life expectancy. The WTP to avoid the acute effects of *air pollution* has been estimated at £100,000 for those with a life expectancy of only 1 year and £9,600 for those with a life expectancy of only 5 weeks.

Value of life years lost (VLYL)

It has been suggested that these estimates based on VSL need to be adjusted further when dealing with air pollution:

- Risks are not so much of sudden death, as of a progressive deterioration in quality of life which may begin some considerable time after initial exposure.
- Risks associated with a given exposure to air pollution are often higher for older people (more prone to respiratory diseases) than for younger people.
- Those most affected by air pollution (the elderly) have a shorter expected lifespan and a lower quality of life than the 'average' member of the population.

There is another aspect in which the risks from air pollution differ from accidental mortality risk. Studies have shown that the value that people place on reducing *voluntary risk*, such as the risk that they accept by choosing certain actions such as driving a car, is lower than the value that they place on reducing *involuntary risk*. Air pollution is an example of involuntary risk since people cannot avoid being exposed to it. This is an argument for measuring the value of reducing the risks from air pollution explicitly, rather than inferring it from studies that value other types of risk.

The main environmental problems associated with air emissions are harm to human health, the acidification and eutrophication of water and soils (see page 192), and damage to natural ecosystems, cultural heritage and crops. These often involve transboundary effects, as pollutants in the air can travel a considerable distance away from their source and may give rise to particular problems in selecting appropriate policy instruments (see page 155).

Patterns and trends for UK air pollution

Table 6.3 shows the principal forms of UK air pollution to be sulphur dioxide, nitrogen oxide and carbon monoxide emissions, fine particles (especially those whose

Table 6.3 Percentages of the different types of air pollutant, by source

	Carbon dioxide	Carbon monoxide	Sulphur dioxide	Nitrogen oxides	Volatile organic compounds	PM_{10}
Road transport	21	73	1	46	27	24
Electricity	27	2	66	21	–	14
Domestic	16	5	3	4	2	16
Other	36	20	29	30	71	45

Source: *Social Trends* (2001).

diameter is smaller than 10 mm – indicated by PM_{10}) and ground-level ozone. The primary polluters today are the energy sector (particularly the production of electricity), road transport and domestic users. The production of electricity contributes around two-thirds of all sulphur dioxide emissions and over a quarter of CO_2 emissions. Although power stations tend to be located some distance away from major conurbations, they do contribute to regional atmospheric pollution. Road users produce almost three-quarters of all carbon monoxide, over two-fifths of all nitrogen oxides and a quarter of all PM_{10} emissions.

In general, there have been considerable air quality improvements in the UK over the past 30 years. Between 1971 and 2000 sulphur dioxide emissions fell by around three-quarters to 1.6 million t, PM_{10} emissions fell by three-fifths to around 0.2 million t, carbon monoxide emissions fell by over two-fifths to 4.8 million t and nitrogen oxide emissions fell by 29 per cent to 1.8 million t (Figure 6.4). These reductions are mainly due to a number of factors: EU legislation which requires reductions in sulphur dioxide and nitrogen oxide emissions from large combustion plants; a decline in heavy industries; a switch in power stations from coal to natural gas and nuclear; the move from coal fires to gas in the home; technical improvements for vehicles, such as cleaner fuels and catalytic converters. The importance of the latter can be gauged from the fact that although road traffic volumes in the UK

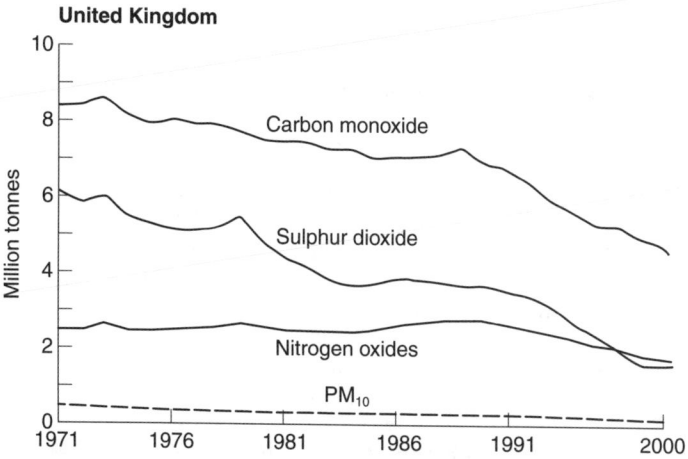

Figure 6.4 Air pollutants: emission of selected gases

increased by over 13 per cent in the period 1989–2000, many of the pollutants mentioned in Table 6.3 as being closely linked to road transport have fallen by over 40 per cent.

The new *Air Quality Strategy* published in January 2000 for England, Scotland, Wales and Northern Ireland sets out national air quality objectives over the next few years up to 2005 for sulphur dioxide, PM_{10}, carbon monoxide, ozone and nitrogen oxides, as well as lead, benzene and 1,3-butadiene.

Patterns and trends for EU air pollution

Trends for most local and regional air pollutants in the EU are encouraging. Mainly due to the impact of regulation (in other words, active public management of environmental resources), they have been declining (despite buoyant economic growth), and are predicted to do so for the EU in the foreseeable future (Table 6.4).

The first international treaty with strategies for reducing transboundary air pollution was the UNECE Convention on Long Range Transboundary Air Pollution (CLRTAP). Several CLRTAP Protocols are in force for the EU and its Member States, with the substances covered and the required reductions listed in Table 6.5. The Second Sulphur Protocol (UNECE, 1994) used, for the first time, the approach of setting emissions targets to reduce the extent to which critical deposition levels for national ecosystems were currently being exceeded ('gap closure'). This Protocol thus resulted in national emission reduction commitments that varied according to the sensitivity of different national ecosystems.

Table 6.5 summarises the main current and proposed targets for the EU. To help reach these targets, current European Community legislation aimed at reducing acidifying pollutants and ozone precursors includes a Directive on the reduction of emissions from large combustion plants together with various Directives on vehicle emissions, the quality of petrol and diesel fuels and the sulphur content of certain liquid fuels. A Directive on the Storage and Distribution of Petrol and the Solvents Directive on the reduction of emissions from the industrial use of organic solvents both aim to limit emissions of volatile organic compounds (VOCs).

Table 6.4 Pollution intensity of economic activity in the EU, 1990–2010 (1990 = 100)

Pollutant	1990	1995	2000	2005	2010
Sulphur	100 *(100)*	56.5 *(60.9)*	38.4 *(46.8)*	29.5 *(40.4)*	19.5 *(30.1)*
NO_2	100 *(100)*	87.7 *(90.5)*	66.3 *(77.3)*	48.4 *(63.9)*	35.1 *(51.9)*
Non-methane VOC	100 *(100)*	82.7 *(89.1)*	61.1 *(74.4)*	44.7 *(61.5)*	34.3 *(53.1)*
CO_2	100 *(100)*	90.2 *(97.6)*	–	–	67.8 *(105.6)*

Notes: Pollution intensity is expressed in kilotonnes of pollutant per billion (10^9) euro of GDP for the EU-15. The index in italics between brackets describes the trends in total emissions for EU-15, based on 1990 = 100.
Source: The EU Economy: 2000 Review, No. 71 (2000).

Table 6.5 Air pollution targets for the EU

Policy/pollutant	Base year	Target year	Reduction (%)
UNECE-CLRTAP			
Sulphur dioxide	1980	2000	62
Sulphur dioxide	1990	2010	75
Nitrogen oxides	1987	1994	Stabilisation
Nitrogen oxides	1990	2010	50
Non-methane VOCs	1987	1999	30
Non-methane VOCs	1990	2010	58
Ammonia	1990	2010	12
5EAP*			
Sulphur dioxide	1985	2000	35
Nitrogen oxide	1990	2000	30
Non-methane VOCs	1990	1999	30
NECD†			
Sulphur dioxide	1990	2010	78
Nitrogen oxides	1990	2010	55
Non-methane VOCs	1990	2010	62
Ammonia	1990	2010	21

Notes: Less restrictive targets for five designated EU countries as regards acidifying pollutants.
† Targets from the European Commission's 1999 proposal for a national emissions ceilings directive (NECD).

Policy instruments and air pollution

Closer consideration is given to various policy instruments directed towards reducing air pollution in Chapter 7 (climate change), Chapter 8 (natural resources and population) and Chapter 9 (transport). Here it may be useful to focus on the particular context of controlling emissions of CO_2 from burning fossil fuels. Two broad policy approaches have been identified in this respect (Royal Commission on Environmental Pollution, 2000):

● managing aspects of the global carbon cycle
● changing the ways in which energy is obtained and used

Managing aspects of the carbon cycle

The concentration of CO_2 in the atmosphere is the outcome of a natural cycle, namely the *carbon cycle*. Organic material, rocks and the ocean continuously *release* carbon into the atmosphere and continuously *reabsorb* it. For at least 10,000 years prior to industrialisation these rates were approximately in balance. As Chapter 7 notes, man-made intervention has now tipped this balance towards net release.

At least three sets of policy instruments suggest themselves here.

1 *Preventing the CO_2 produced when fossil fuels are burnt from reaching the atmosphere.* 'Cleaner technologies' may be deployed in this respect, such as capturing CO_2 from the mixture of flue gases leaving the power plant. 'End of pipe'

technologies of this kind are often expensive, increasing electricity generating costs by up to 80 per cent in the case of coal-burning power stations and up to 50 per cent in the case of gas power stations. Chemical absorption technologies using solvents are less expensive and progress is being made in developing membrane separation technologies.

An alternative method is to recover the CO_2 emitted and to dispose of it in the deep oceans. Unfortunately there are as yet unquantified risks of environmental damage to marine organisms and of the eventual return of CO_2 to the atmosphere.

2 *Increasing the amounts of CO_2 removed from the atmosphere by growing vegetation.* Some 30 per cent of the world's carbon is currently stored in forests and forest soils. It has been suggested that establishing new forests will help absorb some of the projected global increases in CO_2. However, it is only trees growing rapidly to maturity which make a significant contribution to the movement of carbon from the atmosphere into forests. An afforestation programme would have to be extensive and long-lasting to make a significant contribution to CO_2 absorption. For example, the Intergovernmental Panel on Climate Change (IPCC) in 1995 estimated that it would require a government-supported programme up to 2050 consisting of reduced deforestation and enhanced afforestation to absorb some 12–15 per cent of projected CO_2 emissions from burning fossil fuels over that period.

3 *Increasing the rate at which CO_2 is absorbed by the surface layer of the oceans and transferred to the deep ocean.* Historically there has been a net movement of carbon into the oceans, accounting for some 49 per cent of the extra CO_2 emitted since industrialisation began. Increasing the biological productivity of the surface layer of the oceans can further aid this process. For one-fifth of the oceans, especially the Southern Ocean, the amount of iron available is thought to be the main restriction on biological activity of the surface layer. Sprinkling iron on the ocean surface has been found to increase this productivity.

Changing the ways in which energy is obtained and used

Some of the policy instruments associated with this approach have been touched on elsewhere. At least three sets of policy instruments suggest themselves.

1 *Reductions in the use of energy.* The association between economic development and additional energy demand is considered in more detail in Chapter 12 (pages 284–95). Despite projections for still more rapid increases in energy demand as both global populations and worldwide standards of living rise, there is considerable scope for policy intervention to establish lower projected rates of growth if not absolute reductions in energy use. Pricing energy so that users take into account some of the external costs imposed would clearly help in this respect. Such a 'polluter pays' principle is embodied in the proposal for a carbon tax (Case Study 4.1). However estimates of *price elasticities of demand* for final energy consumption are rather low, suggesting that the carbon tax would have to be set at a high level to have a significant impact on demand. For example, the Energy Technology Support Unit (ETSU, 1999) reported that the carbon tax needed to bring about a 20 per cent reduction in CO_2 emissions in the UK

(compared to 1990 as base year) would need to be set at such a high level that it would cause a 72 per cent increase in domestic gas prices, a 23 per cent increase in domestic electricity prices, a 125 per cent increase in industrial gas prices and a 41 per cent increase in industrial electricity prices.

2 *Substituting lower carbon content fuels for higher carbon content fuels.* There is considerable potential for increasing the efficiency of energy use. This can involve the application of new technologies to the heating and cooling of buildings (see Chapter 10) and for transport propulsion in particular. It can also involve using new technologies to improve the efficiency rate for converting primary sources of energy (e.g. fossil fuels) into secondary sources (e.g. electricity) via power stations. For example, a new combined cycle gas turbine has an efficiency rating of 52 per cent in terms of converting primary energy into secondary energy as compared to only 40 per cent for coal-fired power-generating plants.

3 *Substitution of other energy sources for fossil fuels.* Case Study 8.2 (page 204) looks at this issue in the UK. Case Study 6.2 below looks at this issue from a broader geographical perspective.

CASE STUDY 6.2

The renaissance of renewable energy
From the *Financial Times*, January 2001

In autumn 2000, Robin Batchelor, a fund manager at Merrill Lynch, toured London, Switzerland and the Channel Islands to try to entice investors to a new fund for high-technology companies. The timing seemed poor, given the widespread disillusionment with internet and telecommunications businesses.

Yet the fund – which will invest in companies promoting novel energy technologies such as wind and solar power – was heavily oversubscribed, closing at £200m. 'People are realising the fantastically exciting potential of these companies,' says an animated Mr Batchelor.

Even a decade ago, alternative energy conjured up visions of idealists who wanted to change the world and few investors were interested. But the mood has now swung dramatically. Not only has the 2000 Californian energy crisis revealed the pitfalls of over-reliance on traditional fuels, but environmental concerns are growing over CO_2 emissions from fossil-fuel-burning power stations.

Renewed interest from politicians and consumers has given a huge boost to the 300 or so companies (two-thirds of them unquoted) whose main business is developing alternative energy solutions. Many have already been aided by government subsidies intended to increase the proportion – now less than 1 per cent – of the world's 3,300 GW electricity generating capacity that comes from alternative energy sources.

The EU wants a fifth of its power to come from 'renewable' sources by 2010. Some analysts believe that within 50 years half the world's electricity could come from non-fossil-fuel schemes, including well-established hydropower schemes but excluding nuclear energy.

A prime beneficiary of this trend has been Vestas, a Danish agricultural machinery maker that faced bankruptcy in 1986. The following year it refocused on wind energy and has not looked back; it has become the world's biggest maker of wind turbines, with a share price that rose 158 per cent in the past year, giving it a market capitalisation of $6bn (£4.1bn). The company is being helped by the 'fear and risk of climate change', says Johannes Poulsen, its managing director.

Of the various alternative energy fields, wind power is the most mature, with generation costs not far above conventional power stations. Global investment in wind power systems will total $27bn between 2000 and 2005, according to Dresdner Kleinwort Wasserstein, the investment bank. By 2020 world wind power generating capacity could total 400 GW, equivalent to 200 large power stations.

Germany, which is spending € 2bn (£1.3bn) a year to promote wind energy, has emerged as the world leader in the technology, with wind farms sprouting up around the country and the wind turbine business supporting an estimated 35,000 jobs. Mr Poulsen says the costs of producing power from the wind will continue to fall, thanks to engineering advances in components such as drives, gearboxes and generators.

Solar power too is becoming more economically viable. The cost of generating a single watt of electricity from a solar cell (a piece of silicon manufactured in a similar way to microchips) has fallen from $200 in 1980 to $3.50 in 2001, according to Peter Aschenbrenner, vice-president for sales at Denver-based Astropower, the world's fifth biggest maker of solar cells.

The four biggest companies in this field are all large enterprises – Germany's Siemens, Kyocera and Sharp of Japan and the UK's BP. However, many analysts expect 'pure play' solar companies such as Astropower, Energy Conversion Devices of the USA and Atlantis of Switzerland to do most to encourage the development of solar energy.

Astropower, which is quoted on Nasdaq, turns out solar cells using similar principles to making glass. Its shares have risen from $6 at its initial public offering three years ago to $37 yesterday. 'We are increasingly finding we can bypass utilities by selling our systems directly to consumers,' says Mr Aschenbrenner.

Another form of energy production attracting interest is fuel cells – devices that create electricity efficiently by mixing hydrogen (possibly from natural gas) and oxygen from the air. While General Electric, Siemens and Alstom, the world's three biggest makers of conventional power stations, are all keen on either developing or selling fuel cells, the pace in this sector is again being set by smaller companies, including Ballard of Canada and Plug Power and H-Power of the USA.

Frank Gibbard, chief executive of H-Power, who has signed a contract to provide 12,000 fuel-cell systems for rural cooperatives throughout the USA, concedes that fuel cells' manufacturing costs still need to fall by half, from $2,000/kW, before they are considered alternatives on cost grounds to conventional power sources. 'I think these cost reductions will come as companies gain experience with manufacturing and reliability in the field. No one is quite there yet but they could be in a year to 18 months', he says.

Most executives in 'new energy' companies agree that costs will fall further. Yet they are still eager for displays of support from large companies and governments. The most prominent move so far from a large industrial group came last year when ABB, the Swiss-Swedish engineering company, quit conventional power generation projects in favour of 'green' programmes such as wind power and high-efficiency gas-driven 'micro-turbines'.

Jeremy Leggett, a former Greenpeace scientist who is chief executive of Solar Century, a UK solar energy company, says government support is crucial in encouraging adoption of alternative energy sources. He argues that the government should give incentives to housebuilders to incorporate solar panels in new homes. Even in cloudy Britain, these can generate a lot of energy.

As for investors, they hope the ambitions of many of the new energy companies will be matched by reality. 'Right now we are a fly compared to the big companies (in energy)', says Frank Asbeck, chairman of Solar-world, a Bonn-based solar energy company with sales in 2000 of DM105 m. ($49 m.). That leaves plenty of room to grow, but as many internet companies now know, potential is not always enough.

Source: Financial Times, 30 January 2001.

Questions

1 What factors are increasing the prospects of renewable energy resources?

2 Identify some possible obstacles to these prospects.

Land-based pollution

This is mainly due to the disposal of human refuse and contamination by agricultural chemicals.

Disposal of human refuse

Humans produce millions of tonnes of waste each year, and this is usually buried in landfill sites or burned. Dumped refuse in landfill sites is a problem because it destroys natural habitats, is a breeding ground for disease and releases methane (a greenhouse gas), as the refuse decomposes. If buildings are eventually constructed on the landfill site there may be subsidence as pockets of methane gas escape, as well as the risk of explosion from concentrations of methane gas. Recycling is often seen as a useful policy instrument for reducing the amount of refuse requiring disposal.

Agricultural chemicals

Fertilisers, pesticides and herbicides are deliberately sprayed on to crops and the soil in many sectors of agricultural production. When it rains, they will be washed into rivers and eventually into the sea. Pesticides and herbicides are persistent – they remain active in the environment for long periods of time. Some aspects of land-based pollution associated with the intensification of agricultural practices are addressed elsewhere (Chapter 8, page 192, Chapter 11, page 261 and Chapter 12, page 304).

Case Study 6.3 analyses some of the principles and practices involved in issues of waste assimilation and recycling, with particular reference to the UK.

CASE STUDY 6.3

Waste assimilation and recycling

A Way with Waste was the title of a government publication in 2000 setting out a draft strategy for dealing with waste disposal in the UK over the next 20 years. Here we outline some features of the strategy and examine the economic issues that arise in assessing the management of waste.

It has been calculated that some 425 million t of waste (waste arisings) were created in the UK during the 1999 period. Of the total amount of waste created, most originated from agriculture (19 per cent), mining and quarrying (17 per cent), demolition and construction (17 per cent) and industrial (16 per cent) sources. Municipal waste from households accounted for only 6 per cent of the total waste generated, though even this small percentage accounted for 1.2 t of waste per household per year.

A Way with Waste is actually only concerned with waste arising from industrial, commercial and household sources since the remaining sources are already subject to specific regulation by government. In the case of households, the local authorities collect the waste, or waste is deposited by households at civic amenity sites. Table 6.6 shows how municipal waste is disposed of.

Landfill is the most popular method of disposal for waste from households and businesses. Businesses recycle about half their waste, with the remainder going to landfill. Landfill involves using holes in the ground, possible the result of past quarrying or mining activities, as a repository for the waste. Landfill has in the past been the most popular method of waste disposal, being relatively cheap. In the past decade or so, the climate of opinion has turned against the use of landfill because of the recognition that various externalities, such as pollution, are health risks that are associated with landfill sites. These externalities are the source of a great deal of local opposition to the opening of new landfill sites (the NIMBY – 'not in my back yard' – phenomenon).

Externalities occur when economic decisions create costs or benefits for people other than the decision takers. For example, landfill sites are operated by waste management companies, who, as profit maximisers, often ignore the external effects of their operations. Externalities are therefore a source of market failure.

The general argument is illustrated in Figure 6.5 where MC_p (marginal private cost) shows the cost to the site operator of increasing the volume of waste disposal at the site. Given the demand for landfill disposal (D), the level of waste disposal will be Q_1. This quantity is inefficient since it does not allow for the external costs of landfill. MC_s shows the marginal social cost of the landfill and is higher than the marginal private cost – the difference representing the marginal external cost. We assume here that we

Table 6.6 Disposal of municipal solid waste, 1998/99 (% of total)

Landfill	82
Incineration (with energy recovery)	6
Incineration (without energy recovery)	2
Recycled	10

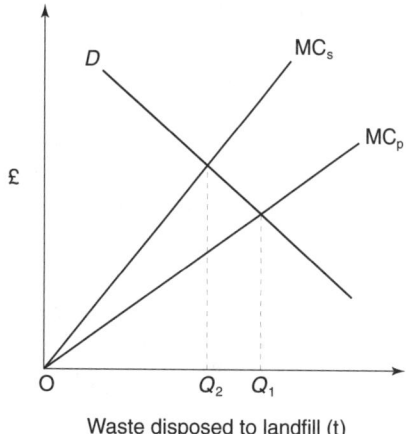

Figure 6.5 Private and social optima for waste disposal

can place a monetary value on these external costs. The social optimum amount of landfill disposal is Q_2 where MC_s equals D.

The argument above suggests the market will unduly favour landfill disposal since
the disposer's costs (as measured in MC_p) do not allow for the adverse environmental
externalities. Landfill disposal will therefore be inefficiently high, given the failure of the
market to include a value to cover the environmental costs. To correct this market
failure, economists usually favour the use of taxes on polluting activities as a means of
ensuring that the polluter takes account of the external effects of their operations. In
1996 the government introduced the *landfill tax* that imposed a tax on waste disposed
by businesses and authorities at landfill sites: the tax was £7 per tonne of active waste
and £2 per tonne of inactive waste (such as builders' rubbish). This has since been
increased to £10 per tonne for active waste, and will increase by £1 per tonne each year
from 1999 to 2004, at which date the operation of the tax will be reviewed.

The landfill tax has been called the UK's first green tax, in the sense that it was the
first tax to be introduced for explicitly environmental policy objectives. The aim of
the landfill tax is to 'internalise' the external costs associated with waste disposal to
landfill. The effect of the tax is to raise the *relative cost* of landfill, thereby creating an
incentive for firms to find alternative ways of handling their waste. The argument has
been that, in the past, landfill was too cheap since disposal costs did not include
externalities.

Alternatives to landfill

By raising the relative price of landfill, the government hopes that the landfill tax will
create an incentive for waste producers to seek alternative ways of handling their waste.
What are the alternatives? The immediate alternative is incineration of the waste, which
will significantly reduce the amount of solid waste to be disposed of. As may be seen in
Table 6.6, incineration with energy recovery is applied to only about 6 per cent of
waste. The main attraction of this option is the combination of incineration and energy
generation, since the heat that is produced by burning waste can be used in heating
schemes. Environmentally, this is beneficial in so far as the waste heat is a substitute for

electricity production by means of fossil fuels that create CO_2 and other gases. On the other hand, incineration transforms a solid waste disposal issue into an air pollution issue. To achieve the reductions in landfill disposal required by the EU Directive a substantial increase in the use of incineration would be required.

However, neither landfill nor incineration represents the government's preferred alternatives for waste disposal. Instead the government is aiming for greater recycling and reuse of waste products and a reduction in the quantity of waste produced.

'A way with waste'

The main general criterion that the government uses to assess the various alternatives available is the *best practical environmental option* (BPEO). This represents the option that provides the most benefits, or least damage, to the environment at an 'acceptable cost'.

When assessing the BPEO, the choice is guided by the *waste hierarchy*. This is a ranking of the different ways of handling waste from most preferred to least preferred. In rank order, the list is as follows: waste minimisation; reuse; recycle; waste disposal.

The preferred option is to minimise the quantity of waste that is produced in consumption or production of goods and services in the first place, thus eliminating the waste disposal issue altogether. Only if waste minimisation proves to be too expensive do we consider the next best option (reuse), i.e. if it is not possible to eliminate waste then the next best option is to seek to reuse the waste product (an obvious example is reuse of glass bottles). If reuse is too expensive, then we next consider recycling. At the bottom of the hierarchy is waste disposal, which should be considered only if all the previous options are considered too expensive.

The general idea behind the waste hierarchy is that of minimising the environmental impact of waste that is associated with economic activities. To mainstream economists, the choice of method for handling waste should be based on a calculation of the environmental costs associated with each option as well as the environmental benefits; thus the preferred option would be the one that gives the greatest excess of environmental benefits over environmental costs. The argument is illustrated in Figure 6.6, where we compare two options – landfill and recycling.

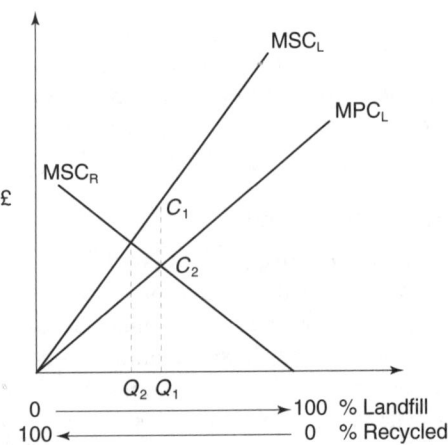

Figure 6.6 Options for waste disposal

MSC_L shows the marginal social cost of landfill disposal (with landfill measured from left to right in the diagram). MSC_R shows the marginal social cost of recycling (with recycling measured from right to left). The socially optimal level of recycling is Q_2 where the marginal social cost is the same for both landfill and recycling. The diagram also shows that if the private cost of landfill (MPC_L) is below the MSC_L unlike the situation for recycling, then left to the market mechanism the Q_1 solution will imply too much landfill and too little recycling. At Q_1 the marginal social cost of recycling (i.e. C_2) is less than the marginal social cost of landfill (i.e. C_1), suggesting that a switch from landfill to recycling would reduce the total cost to society of waste disposal.

The waste hierarchy is not directly constructed on economic principles. It considers the alternatives primarily in terms of their environmental impacts and does not directly incorporate a consideration of the economic costs of the alternatives. This is partially allowed for in so far as 'acceptable cost' is taken into account, but this is not the same as comparing the full economics of, say, landfill with recycling.

A second criterion suggested in *A Way with Waste* in determining the BPEO is the *proximity principle*. This asserts that waste should be disposed of as close to its source as possible. The rationale for this principle stems from two main factors. Firstly, that there are environmental impacts associated with the transportation of waste and thus it is desirable to minimise the extent to which waste is moved. Secondly, local disposal will require communities to recognise the environmental costs associated with their actions.

A Way with Waste is mainly concerned with establishing the general criteria to be used in formulating policy on waste disposal, and therefore it says little about actual policy initiatives to bring about the policy objectives. Therefore, it is left to the landfill tax to create new incentives for waste producers to minimise the environmental impact of waste. However, the landfill tax is levied on businesses and authorities and as such has no direct effect on the amount of recycling (rather than waste disposal) by households, because what they currently pay for waste disposal is part of their council tax and is not dependent on how much waste they generate. One of the central areas of debate will be how to introduce incentives for households to reduce the amount of waste they create.

Source: Swift (2000).

Questions

1 Explain why the landfill tax has received both support and criticism from environmentalists.

2 What are the strengths and weaknesses of the 'best practical environmental option' (BPEO) approach embodied in the policy document *A Way With Waste*?

●●●● Global and transboundary pollution policies

Where pollution crosses national boundaries, as is often the case, particular policy issues and instruments come into play. Bowers (1997) identifies three different types of transboundary pollution, namely unidirectional, regional reciprocal and global. We deal with each type in turn.

Unidirectional transboundary pollution

This exists where economic activity in one nation (or group of nations) imposes a negative externality on some other nation (or group of nations). It is sometimes referred to as 'upstream–downstream' pollution. The key point is that the negative externality is imposed in one direction only.

One polluter–one sufferer

We first consider the simplest form where one nation pollutes and one nation is damaged by that pollution. In the international context with separate sovereign countries, there is no single authority able to impose, monitor and enforce regulations ('command and control' instruments) as would be the case within the nation state. Settlement must therefore involve some type of international agreement involving the consent of both parties.

As noted in Chapter 3 (page 75), market imperfections such as negative externalities often generate a 'deadweight loss' in terms of economic welfare. The implication then is that 'correcting' the negative externality removes the 'deadweight loss', thereby increasing social surplus. This increase in social surplus then gives the potential for those who gain to more than compensate those who lose as a result of correcting the negative externality. Two exceptions to this 'rule' might usefully be noted here. First, in some cases of transboundary pollution the extra social costs from removing the pollution may actually exceed the social benefits from its removal. Second, even from an international (here two-country) perspective, different value systems may result in a situation where one country *perceives* itself to lose by more than the other country *perceives* itself to have gained, when more objective observers might have come to a different conclusion.

Here we initially disregard these possible exceptions and assume that the resource reallocation from removing the unidirectional pollution creates a 'net' social surplus which is then available for distribution.

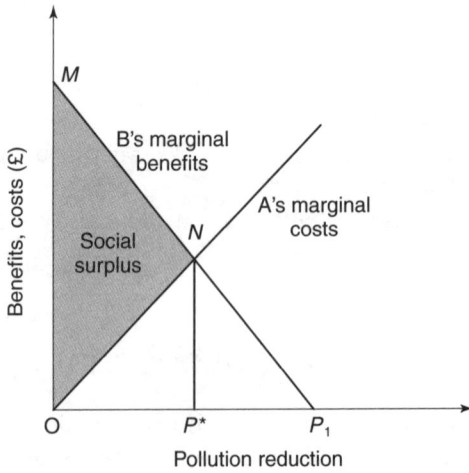

Figure 6.7 Unidirectional pollution: one polluter, one sufferer

In Figure 6.7 country A imposes pollution on country B. In the absence of any incentives, we assume that A will take no account of the negative externality imposed on B, giving zero pollution reduction (or abatement). However, should a mechanism exist whereby A takes B's situation into account with the overall objective being to *maximise their joint net benefit*, then the social optimum solution is pollution reduction P^*. Each unit of pollution reduction requires A to use some scarce resources in the 'clean-up', with the marginal cost of pollution reduction progressively rising as it becomes harder and harder to reduce pollution further. Each unit of pollution reduction yields benefits to the sufferer, B, with the marginal benefit of pollution reduction progressively falling as the effects spread out beyond the main beneficiaries. In this diagram the social optimum level of pollution reduction is OP^*, in that the *joint net benefit* is maximised at this level. Each unit of pollution reduction up to P^* increases B's marginal benefit by more than it increases A's marginal costs. Each unit of pollution reduction beyond P^* increases B's marginal benefit by less than it increases A's marginal costs.

In this case dealing effectively with transboundary pollution (i.e. P^* rather than zero pollution reduction) yields a positive social surplus which is available for distribution between the participants. If we treat this as a 'game' (see Box 6.3), then we have a *positive sum game* which can potentially benefit both 'players'. In other words, there is the potential for B to compensate A for pollution reduction initiatives, with both players better off than in the initial (zero) pollution reduction situation. Any part of the shaded social surplus areas in Figure 6.7 can be used by B to offer as a side payment (inducement) to make A better off in moving to pollution reduction level P^*. Note that at pollution reduction level P^*, from the total (sum of the marginal) benefit to B of $OMNP^*$, A must be offered ONP^* to cover its total (sum of the marginal) costs. To make A *better off* with this solution, more than ONP^* must be offered, i.e. some part of the social surplus OMN.

Of course reaching such a solution requires cooperation between the players of this 'game'. Some level of trust is then clearly implied, such as the belief by A that any compensation payments offered by B will actually be paid now and in the future. Should such trust be absent, then we move into various game-playing scenarios such as the 'prisoner's dilemma' (see Box 6.3) in which suboptimum outcomes for any 'game' may result. In terms of Figure 6.7, we will then fail to achieve pollution reduction level P^*.

The bargaining process between the interested parties may itself distort the final outcome, leading to a non-optimal solution (i.e. not P^*). For example, A may exaggerate its costs of pollution reduction and B may understate its benefits from pollution reduction. The use of independent agencies, such as NGOs, may help to bring more objectivity and rigour to the bargaining process.

Multiple polluters/sufferers

When more than two countries pollute and/or suffer negative externalities, the potential for non-optimal solutions increases still further. For example, if several 'downstream' countries suffer from a negative externality there is the possibility that one or more sufferers will attempt to 'free ride'.

The optimal level of pollution reduction when two countries, B and C, benefit from A's pollution reduction is now P_1^* in Figure 6.8(a). However, if C attempts to

Game analysis: prisoner's dilemma

Games in which strategies selected in isolation are likely to lead to all players being worse off are called prisoner's dilemma games. The original presentation of this approach is outlined here.

Two criminals have committed a major robbery and are arrested. However, the prosecuting authorities recognise that the evidence is inadequate to secure a conviction unless one or both criminals confess. The district attorney is willing to allow plea-bargaining such that if a conviction is secured by one person confessing, he will receive no punishment and the convicted criminal will receive a heavy sentence of 20 years. If both confess, the sentence of 10 years' imprisonment prescribed by law will apply. Of course, if neither confesses, they will each go free. Clearly each suspect has two strategies open to himself, with two counter-strategies available to his fellow suspect. The pay-off matrix for prisoners A and B is indicated in Table 6.7.

No confession by prisoner A can lead either to acquittal (if B does not confess) or 20 years' imprisonment (if B confesses). Confession by prisoner A can lead to acquittal (if B does not confess) or 10 years' imprisonment (if B also confesses). The possible pay-off for B is identical to that for A.

Table 6.7 Pay-off matrix (years' imprisonment): prisoner's dilemma

		Prisoner B's strategies			
		No confession		Confession	
		A	B	A	B
Prisoner A's strategies	No confession	0	0	20	0
	Confession	0	20	10	10

A *maxi–min* (best of the worst possible outcomes) approach by prisoner A will lead to A confessing and receiving 10 years' imprisonment. The same solution will apply to B, so both will confess and receive 10 years' imprisonment each. Clearly the uncertainty that might lead both players to select this suboptimal strategy could have been avoided by the sharing of information between the players or other forms of collusion.

free-ride on B by not declaring its benefits, then the solution may be P^* which is now suboptimal. Indeed in Figure 6.8(b) this attempt to free-ride may even lead to no pollution reduction whatsoever from A, when the social optimum level is P^*_2.

Regional reciprocal pollution

This exists when two or more countries simultaneously impose the negative externality of pollution and suffer from that pollution. Acid rain (see Box 6.1) is often cited as an example of regional reciprocal pollution when countries which burn

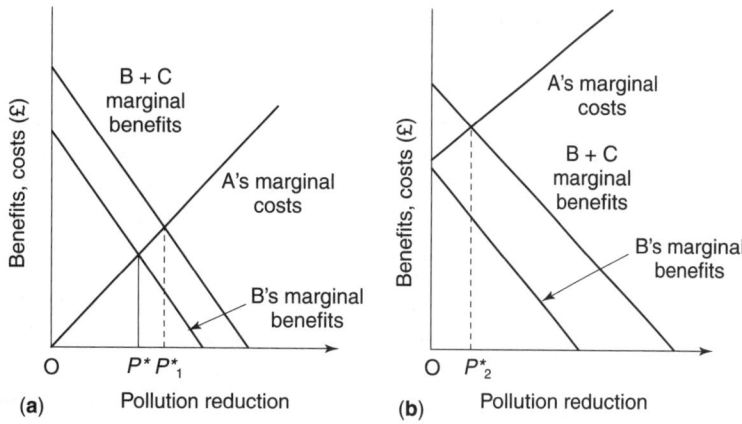

Figure 6.8 'Free rider' problem with multiple polluters/sufferers

fossil fuels and thereby emit sulphur dioxide, nitrogen oxides and hydrogen chloride, damage both their own environment via precipitation as well as that of other countries downwind.

Here each country has some interest in controlling its own pollution whether or not there is an agreement between nations. In Figure 6.9 A_{MB} is country A's marginal benefit to itself from pollution reduction and A_{MC} is country A's marginal cost of pollution reduction. Left to its own self-interest, country A maximises its own net benefit (social surplus) at LVO with a level of pollution reduction P_A.

However, all countries susceptible to this pollution in the region (R) benefit by A's pollution reduction. The marginal regional benefit (social surplus) from pollution reduction is given by R_{MB}. The maximum net benefit (social surplus) for the region as a whole is MWO, which implies a pollution reduction level by A

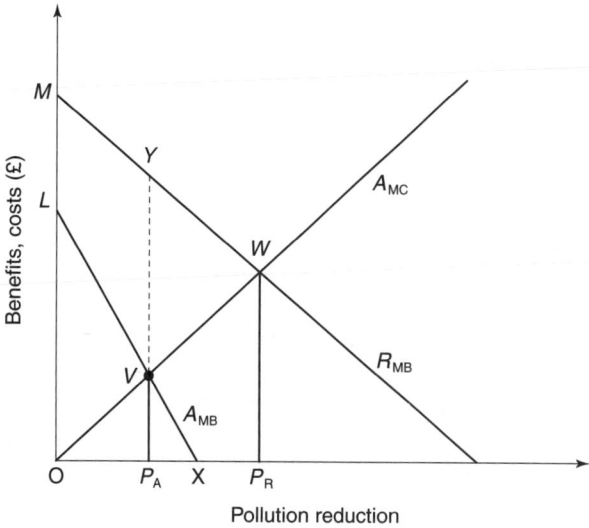

Figure 6.9 Regional reciprocal pollution and the need for negotiation

of P_R. The point here is that A will have no incentive to go beyond P_A which implies that the region as a whole is at point Y on its (regional) marginal benefit curve. Any further reduction in pollution by A beyond P_A only brings extra benefit to it up to X (area VXP_A) and even this is insufficient to cover its additional costs. In other words, there will need to be extensive compensation to A to induce it to curtail pollution to P_R, the optimum solution for the region as a whole.

This analysis suggests a number of things. With regional reciprocal externalities:

- All countries have *some* incentives to curb pollution on their own account. However, this non-cooperative (Nash) solution at P_A may not be sufficient for the best interest of the region as a whole.
- Co-operation may be necessary for each country to achieve the regional optimum for its pollution reduction. In this co-operative solution, compensation will be needed for those countries who gain little benefit themselves from any extra pollution reduction beyond their own self-interest but who thereby bring substantial benefits to others in the region (indicated in Figure 6.9 by the large gap between A_{MB} and R_{MB}).
- It will be particularly important to bring into a co-operative agreement any country which benefits little itself from pollution reduction but which imposes significant negative externalities on others.
- Co-operation may require some regional forum to bring the affected parties together and to arbitrate in situations of disagreements as to values of reciprocal costs and benefits. It may also need to implement a mechanism for transfers of income (compensation) between parties to the regional agreement.

Note that in this analysis the focus has been on the need for the *victim pays principle* (VPP) rather than the more conventional *polluter pays principle* (PPP). Unless those who suffer the most from pollution compensate those who benefit the least from pollution reduction, it may not be possible to reach and sustain a co-operative solution to the various 'games'.

Global pollution

Global pollution can be considered as a special case of regional reciprocal externalities, except that the 'region' in this case is the world. Damage to the ozone layer via emissions of CFCs, global warming via CO_2 emissions and loss of biodiversity are all, arguably, examples of global pollution.

The disparities between benefits of pollution reduction to individual countries and losses to the rest of the world are likely to be still more extensive in both size and number of countries in the context of global pollution. Still greater emphasis will then be placed on international bodies to implement, monitor and enforce co-operative agreements by which 'world' social surplus is maximised. This issue of appropriate international policy responses to global pollution in the context of climate change is considered more fully in Chapter 7.

> Now try the self-check questions for this chapter on the companion website
> **www.booksites.net/ison**
> You will also find up-to-date facts and case materials.

Key terms

Best practical environmental option (BPEO) The option that provides the most benefits or least damage to the environment at an 'acceptable cost'. Now used by the government to evaluate alternative waste disposal methods

Biochemical oxygen demand (BOD) The amount of oxygen required to decompose organic materials under specified conditions of temperature and time

Continuous pollutants Follow some type of uninterrupted time profile

Cumulative pollutants Those retained in the environment over time in roughly the same amount as when first emitted

Episodic pollutants Occur on a one-off, intermittent basis

Global pollutants While emitted from a local source have potentially worldwide impacts

Marginal abatement cost (MAC) The extra cost to the firm of avoiding emitting the last unit of pollutant

Non-cumulative (degradable) pollutants Tend to dissipate rapidly after being emitted

Point-source pollutants Where the actual point of discharge can be identified

Pollution Where man-made activities reduce the ambient (naturally occurring) quality of the environment

Proximity principle Whereby waste should be disposed of as close to its source as possible. To be taken into account under the BPEO

Waste hierarchy A ranking method by which alternative waste disposal methods are evaluated under BPEO

References and further reading

Bowers, J. (1997) *Sustainability and Environmental Economics*, Longman, Harlow, especially Chapters 4–9.

Cowan, S. (1998) 'Water Pollution and Abstraction and Economic Instruments', *Oxford Review of Economic Policy*, **14**, 4.

Energy Technology Support Unit (ETSU) (1999) *New and Renewable Energy: Prospects in the UK for the 21st Century – Supporting Analysis*, Harwell, UK.

EU Economy: 2000 Review, No. 71(2000).

Field, B.C. (1997) *Environmental Economics: An Introduction*, McGraw-Hill, especially Chapters 14–17.

Gilpin, A. (2000) *Environmental Economics: A Critical Overview*, Wiley, especially Chapter 8.

Markandya, A. and Mason, P. (1999) 'Air pollution and health', *The Economic Review*, 17, 2.

Royal Commission on Environmental Pollution (2000) 22nd Report, *Energy – the Changing Climate*, Cm 4749.

Social Trends (2001), Office for National Statistics.

Swift, S. (2000) Adapted and updated from 'A way with waste', *British Economy Survey*, 30, 1, Autumn.

UNECE (1994) Protocol to the convention on long-range transboundary air pollution on further reduction of sulphur emissions, UN Economic Commission on Europe, Geneva.

Useful websites

Environment Agency
OFWAT
Environment: (EC DGXI)
Food and Agricultural Organisation
Friends of the Earth
World Health Organisation
Agriculture: (EC DGVI)
Transport: (EC DGVII)
DETR
MAFF

7

Climate change and the environment

The global response to *climate change* could turn out to be the key event in shaping the course of worldwide social and economic development in the twenty-first century. If we manage to avoid even the most modest of predictions as to the potential welfare costs of climate change, we will have demonstrated a degree of technical, political and economic organisation and co-operation as yet unknown in the history of humanity on the planet. Fail, and we might reach a defining moment in our ability to devise, manage and control international institutions and technologies to meet human needs.

Climate change is a global environmental problem. Moreover, it is a truly three-dimensional environmental problem – from the bottom of the deepest ocean to the edge of space at the top of the atmosphere. It is also a problem of immense timescales. Some aspects of the Earth's climate system can take several hundred years to settle down once disturbed.

It may also be worth noting at the outset that there is a fundamental and important difference between air or water pollution and climate change as a pollution problem. Increased concentrations of traditional air or water pollutants tend to cause *direct effects* on living systems (e.g. asthma in humans and toxins in fish). However, increased concentrations of greenhouse gases implicated in climate change are not directly harmful to living systems (indeed they can be directly beneficial as in the case of CO_2-loving plants); instead it is the secondary or *indirect effects* of these increased concentrations that cause the damage (e.g. heat rays reflected back to the Earth via CO_2 in the atmosphere). This makes the link between pollutant and damage even more complex than in the case of air or water pollution.

Human activity is rapidly and significantly changing the nature of the Earth's climate, and this is happening at a rate above and beyond any previously experienced natural variation in climate. Scientists are virtually certain that recent observations of climate change are attributable to increased concentrations of the so-called **greenhouse gases**, which include CO_2, methane and nitrous oxide, together with a range of human-generated halocarbon compounds. These greenhouse gases have increased significantly over the last 150 years as the industrial and post-industrial revolutions have progressed. Despite technological change resulting in dramatic and continuous improvements in the efficiency of energy production from fossil fuels and the development of new forms of renewable energy, greenhouse gas emissions look set to continue to rise throughout this century (see Figure 7.2 and Chapters 6 and 8).

The dynamics of the Earth's **climate system** are complex and only partially understood. The most definitive scientific assessment of climate change to date is the **Intergovernmental Panel on Climate Change** (IPCC, 2001a). According to the IPCC, it is highly likely that the Earth's climate will continue to change rapidly and significantly over the next century – even if swift and successful action were taken to drastically reduce emissions from burning fossil fuels.

The international community began taking its first tentative steps towards developing a practical workable regime for combating climate change in 1994 with the entry into force of the **United Nations Framework Convention on Climate Change** (UNFCCC). Since then, the climate negotiations have concentrated on negotiating workable rules for the **Kyoto Protocol**. But important as these initial steps are, we are very much at the beginning of the story of how humans attempted to clean up an atmosphere they unintentionally swamped with greenhouse gases. How we deal with the problem of climate change over the course of the twenty-first century will, perhaps more than any other socio-economic or environmental issue, indicate the possibilities and constraints for policy intervention on the global scale.

The scientific basis of climate change

To understand climate change, we must first understand what we mean by 'climate'. We can begin to think more scientifically about climate by first thinking about the more simple idea of *weather*. Look outside. What is the weather like this minute? You can probably give a fairly detailed description in terms of temperature, rain, wind-strength, sunshine, cloud cover, perhaps even humidity. The different components that make up the weather are readily observable and easily understandable. Changes in the weather can have direct impacts on us, making us hot, wet, happy, tired or miserable. Weather frequently determines our day-to-day behaviour and mood.

Now think about the climate of your country. Looking out of the window does not help much in describing the climate because, unlike the weather, it is not possible to observe the climate directly. Instead you are probably thinking about your own climate in terms of it being generally warm, wet, windy, dry or sunny. In this sense 'climate' describes *average* weather conditions in a given place. Quantitatively this might involve the arithmetic mean (over a defined period) of the various elements of the weather (e.g. 20 mm rainfall per month, 4.2 hours of sunshine per July day, an average May wind speed of 1.2 m s^{-1} etc.). Climate can also be quantified as the *variability* of mean weather, including extremes – e.g. average lows of 5° C, average highs of 20° C in summer months, and so on.

But what if you were asked to describe the climate in your *region* of the world? Thinking about the climate over a region is still more complicated. Even across relatively small regions such as the 2,000 km or so between Edinburgh in Scotland and Marseille in the south of France, the climate varies dramatically and is dependent on factors such as latitude, height above sea level, coastal influences and local topography. As we define still larger geographical regions, the idea of an 'average' climate becomes even harder to conceive, as in the case of Europe as a whole. Comparing the climate differences between, say, Nordic and Mediterranean countries casts doubt on how meaningful a concept such as a 'European' climate might be! This is even more the case at a *global* scale. Again we must fall back on statistical data, this time involving global averages for the characteristics mentioned above and the variability in these characteristics around such averages.

The Earth's climate system

The climate system is driven by energy from the sun, with the average global temperature at the Earth's surface being particularly important in determining other climatic variables. For example, the 'greenhouse effect' is a term used to describe the way in which heat from the sun (i.e. solar radiation) entering the Earth's atmosphere is becoming increasingly 'trapped' by an accumulation of certain gases in the atmosphere. The build-up of certain gases is increasing the amount of long wave infra-red radiation reflected by the atmosphere towards the earth's surface. Slightly less thermal energy escapes into space and the atmosphere warms slightly.

Many of the main gases which make up the *atmosphere* each contributes to this greenhouse effect and hence are called 'greenhouse gases'. Water vapour (H_2O), carbon dioxide (CO_2), nitrous oxide (N_2O), methane (CH_4) and ozone (O_3) are the main greenhouse gases in the Earth's atmosphere.

The Earth's *climate system* consists of five main components (Figure 7.1):

- *atmosphere* (the envelope of gases surrounding the Earth)
- *hydrosphere* (oceans, seas, rivers, fresh waters, underground water)

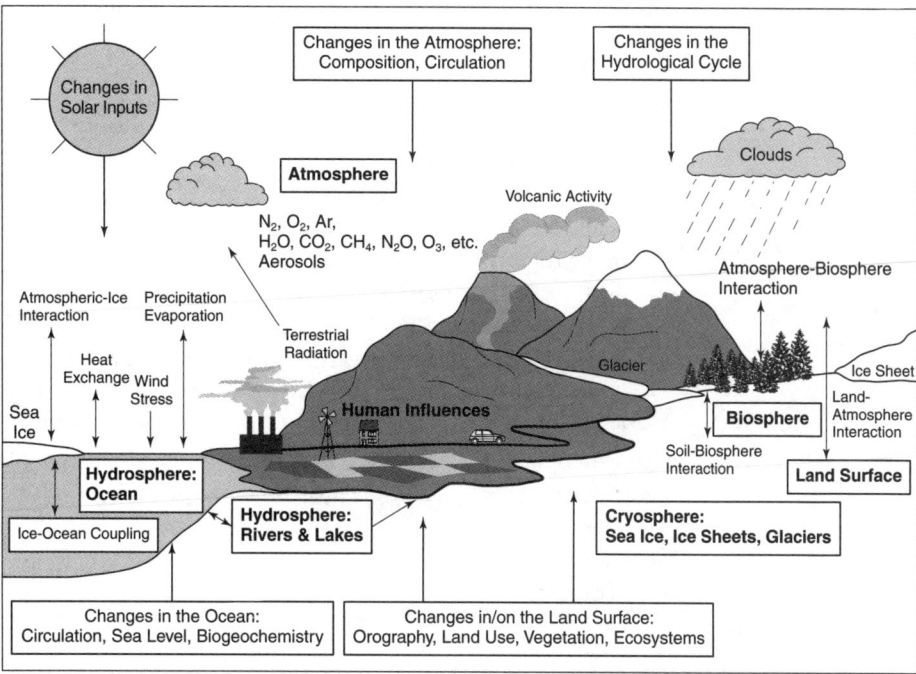

Figure 7.1 Schematic view of the components of the global climate system, their processes and interactions and some aspects that may change

Source: IPCC (2001a)

- *cryosphere* (snow, sea ice, ice sheets, glaciers and permafrost)
- *land surface* and
- *biosphere* (all ecosystems and living organisms)

Is the Earth's climate changing?

To most people, the idea of 'climate change' can sound very new, particularly as it is introduced in the context of debates about the environment, sustainable development and globalisation. It frequently sounds, or is made to sound, like a very modern threat to our ways of life on the planet. But to earth scientists (geologists, geophysicists, oceanographers, climatologists) climate change is old news. It is fundamental to understanding the history and functioning of the Earth as an integrated and dynamic system.

Viewed in terms of geological timescales, the Earth's climate is constantly changing. Over the last million years the Earth's climate has undergone numerous cycles of cooler and warmer periods, as in the case of the glacial and interglacial periods. Indeed rapid and significant climate change has been used as a popular theory to explain the extinction of dinosaurs! During the last ice age (around 20,000 years ago) there is evidence of abrupt temperature changes of as much as several degrees within a human lifetime. Imagine ice retreating from North Africa to the border of Scotland in a period of as little as 40 years!

There are two basic ways of measuring climate change.

1 Measurements can be taken *directly* using dedicated instruments. This 'instrumental record' consists of:
  - Direct measurements of surface temperature since the middle of the nineteenth century
  - Precipitation and wind measurements since around 1900
  - Sea level measurements dating back some 100 years (however most of the tide gauge record is over a shorter timescale)
  - Surface ocean observations made from ships going back 150 years (a network of dedicated buoys was established in the 1970s)
  - Subsurface ocean temperature measurements since the 1940s
  - Upper air observations since the 1940s (since 1958 using weather balloons)
  - Earth observation satellite measurements since 1979.
2 Measurements can also be taken *indirectly* using proxies from the palaeoclimatic record. This 'pre-instrumental proxy record' includes:
  - Trees
  - Corals
  - Sediments
  - Ice

Box 7.1 outlines some of these indicators of global climate change.

BOX 7.1

Some indicators of climate change

A variety of observations of different climate variables indicate a rapidly (in historical terms) warming planet. The IPCC's Third Assessment Report (2001a) identified the following indicators:

- Global average surface temperature has increased by 0.6 ° ± 0.2 °C since the late tenth century.
- The 1990s was the warmest decade in the instrumental record.
- Indications from the pre-instrumental proxy record suggests it is likely that the rate and duration of the warming of the twentieth century is faster and longer, respectively, than at any other time during the last 1,000 years.
- The pattern of changes in precipitation is mixed. In recent years (since around 1995) annual land precipitation has continued to increase in the middle and high latitudes of the northern hemisphere at a rate of around 0.5–1.0 per cent per decade, except over eastern Asia. Over the subtropics (10°N to 30°N) land surface rainfall has decreased on average at a rate of 0.3 per cent per decade.
- It is likely that total atmospheric water vapour has increased by several per cent per decade over many regions of the northern hemisphere.
- Cloud cover for the mid- and high-latitude continental regions of the northern hemisphere has increased by around 2 per cent since 1900.
- It is very likely that there has been a decrease of 10 per cent in the extent of snow cover since the 1960s. Northern hemisphere sea-ice extents are decreasing but there are no significant trends in the Antarctic sea-ice extent. There is likely to have been an approximate 40 per cent decline in Arctic sea-ice thickness in late summer to early autumn between the period 1958–76 and again during the 1990s with a substantially smaller decline in winter.
- Global mean sea level has risen in the range 1.0–2.0 mm per year over the twentieth century. Interestingly, the pre-instrumental proxy record reveals that since the last ice age (about 20,000 years ago) in some places the sea level is now 120 m higher than it was.
- Changes in atmospheric and oceanic circulation patterns are still being assessed. Since the mid-1970s, the El Niño Southern Oscillation has been more frequent, persistent and intense relative to its cool phase as compared with the previous 100 years.
- Analyses of extreme weather and climate events reveal: (a) pronounced increases in heavy and extreme precipitation events in the mid to high latitudes of the northern hemisphere; (b) no compelling evidence of changes in tropical and extra tropical storms; and (c) no long-term changes in severe local weather events (tornadoes, thunderstorm days and hail) in selected regions.

Source: IPCC (2001a)

Human influences and climate change

Long-term climate change happens because of two factors. Firstly, 'internal' changes in the interactions between different components of the climate system (the composition of the atmosphere, the oceans, etc.). Secondly, 'external' changes such as fluctuations in solar radiation and volcanic activity.

Table 7.1 The increase in key greenhouse gases since the industrial revolution

Concentration	Carbon dioxide (CO_2)	Methane (CH_4)	Nitrous oxide) (N_2O)	CFC_{11}	HFC_{23}	CF_4
1750 (pre-industrial)	280 ppm	700 ppb	270 ppb	Zero	Zero	40 ppt
1998	365 ppm	1745 ppb	314 ppb	268 ppt	14 ppt	80 ppt

Note: ppm = parts per million, ppb = parts per billion, ppt = parts per trillion.
Source: IPCC (2001a: Technical Summary, p. 38).

A variety of indicators suggest that the relatively rapid warming now taking place in the Earth's climate system is highly unusual in geological terms and that for the first time humans, rather than other internal or external factors, are responsible for a significant change in the Earth's climate. Moreover, there is every likelihood that more climate change is already 'in the pipeline', no matter what happens. A key element in this argument involves the factual recording of increased concentrations of the various greenhouse gases over the pre- and post-industrialisation time periods, as indicated in Table 7.1.

Just as it took many decades to conclusively prove the link between smoking and cancer, it is likely to take some time to conclusively prove the link between human activity and climate change. This is because scientists must first rule out other possible internal or external climate change factors. So while it is still not possible to say conclusively that human activity is causing climate change, the IPCC's Second Assessment Report concluded in 1995 that 'the balance of evidence suggests a discernible human influence on global climate'. The IPCC's most recent scientific assessment of climate change (Third Assessment Report) in 2001 concluded that 'most of the observed warming over the last 50 years is likely to have been due to the increases in greenhouse gas emissions'.

●●●● Predicting future climate change

By now you will have realised that detecting and attributing cause and effect to historic climate change is a complex task. Predicting *future* climate change is even more complex and uncertain. It involves, among other things, simulating the behaviour of the different components of the climate system (atmosphere, ocean, land surface, cryosphere and biosphere) under different scenarios of future levels of greenhouse gas emissions. The only way to do this is by using sophisticated and complex modelling techniques. The latest climate models, known as comprehensive *atmosphere–ocean general circulation models* (AOGCMs), exploit rapidly developing computing capabilities and incorporate submodels of the five main components of the climate system.

Future emissions are, however, highly uncertain and dependent on a diverse set of factors such as projections of population, the size and distribution of world incomes, technological evolution and diffusion, and so on. The IPCC have considered different possible combinations (or scenarios) of these driving factors together

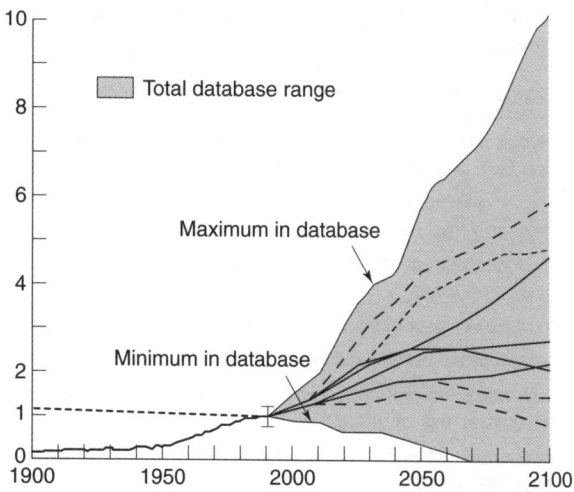

Figure 7.2 Global CO$_2$ emissions scenarios and database range (index, 1990 = 1)
Source: IPCC (2000)

with different future global emissions profiles. The main scenarios are shown by the lines in Figure 7.2. The overall conclusion is that emissions of CO$_2$ are likely to increase significantly in the future but then decline. The range of possible increase and timing of decline is highly uncertain and dependent on a number of factors, each of which has associated uncertainties.

Even if we had a crystal ball and could project greenhouse gas emissions clearly into the future, this would only marginally clarify predictions as to future climate change. In part this is because the sensitivity of the climate system to increasing greenhouse gas concentrations is itself uncertain. For a doubling of CO$_2$ concentrations our best estimate is for an increase in global mean surface temperatures of between 1.5 and 4.5°C.

Temperature and sea level are projected to rise under every scenario considered in the *Special Report on Emissions Scenarios* (IPCC, 2000):

- Globally averaged surface temperature is projected to increase by 1.4–5.8°C over the twenty-first century (a rate of temperature increase unprecedented during the last 10,000 years).
- Global mean sea level is projected to rise by 0.09–0.88 m over the twenty-first century.

Changes in other climate variables are also projected:

- Global average water vapour concentration and precipitation are projected to increase.
- Northern hemisphere snow cover and ice extent are projected to decrease further.
- Glaciers and ice-caps are projected to continue their widespread retreat during the twenty-first century.
- The Antarctic ice sheet is likely to grow (gain mass) because of greater precipitation, while the Greenland ice sheet is likely to lose mass (in this case the increase in runoff will exceed precipitation).

Table 7.2 Projected changes in the patterns of extreme events and their likeli-hoods

Changes in extreme event	Confidence of projection (over twenty-first century)
Higher maximum temperatures and more hot days over nearly all land areas	Very likely
Higher minimum temperatures, fewer cold days and frost days over nearly all land areas	Very likely
Reduced diurnal temperature range over most land areas	Very likely
Increase in heat index over land areas	Very likely, over most areas
Most intense precipitation events	Very likely, over many areas
Increased summer continental drying and associated risk of drought	Likely over most mid-latitude continental interiors (lack of consistent projections in other areas)
Increase in tropical cyclone peak wind intensities	Likely, over some areas
Increase in tropical cyclone mean and peak precipitation intensities	Likely, over some areas

Source: Extract from IPCC (2001a: Summary for Policymakers, p. 15, Table 1).

There is less confidence about how climate change might affect El Niño, monsoons and thermohaline circulation (e.g. the Gulf Stream). Projected changes in the pattern of extreme events are summarised in Table 7.2.

How certain are we about the science of climate change?

By now you may have gathered that the science behind climate change is broad and complex, involving many elements of the physical and earth sciences. The Earth as a system is unintentionally being used as a living laboratory of what happens when the atmosphere receives a sudden, significant and sustained injection of greenhouse gases caused by human activity. In the case of such a large, non-replicable and relatively (in human timescales) long experiment there are understandably large uncertainties in matching scientific theory with experimental practice.

Confidence interval estimates

The levels of uncertainty about previous climate change are expressed in the IPCC's reports using a *95 per cent confidence interval*. Below we list the ranges within which we can be 95 per cent confident that the following historic climate changes have occurred:

- Global average surface temperature has increased by 0.6 $\pm$ 0.2°C since the late nineteenth century.
- Precipitation in the northern hemisphere has increased by 0.5–1.0 per cent per decade over the last few years.
- Global mean sea level has risen in the range 1.0–2.0 mm per year in the twentieth century.

- There has been a 2–4 per cent increase in the frequency of heavy precipitation events in the latter part of the twentieth century in the northern hemisphere.

Codification of judgement estimates

Communication among the many hundreds of different kinds of scientists who worked together in small groups for the IPCC has evolved a system of *codification of judgement* as to the certainty/uncertainty associated with various aspects of climate science:

- *Virtually certain* (greater than 99 per cent chance the result is true)
- *Very likely* (90–99 per cent chance)
- *Likely* (66–90 per cent chance)
- *Medium likelihood* (33–66 per cent chance)
- *Unlikely* (10–33 per cent chance)
- *Very unlikely* (1–10 per cent chance)
- *Exceptionally unlikely* (less than 1 per cent chance)

We have already used this approach in Table 7.2.

Impacts of climate change

So the climate is changing at an unprecedented rate and humans are almost certainly the cause. How significant might this be for societies and their economies? What actual difference might this make to the lives and livelihoods of this and future generations?

Weather and climate are inextricably linked to many aspects of our economies and societies. In fact most economies are already very sensitive to weather and climate. Climate change could bring about significant impacts on the economy, both positive and negative. For example, increased CO_2 concentrations help plants photosynthesise and therefore speed their growth rates. In many existing agricultural areas, yields will rise. On the other hand, increased temperatures and reduced rainfall in drought areas will exacerbate already difficult agricultural conditions. Climate impacts are therefore varied and uncertain, and are likely to include both positive and negative environmental, ecological and socio-economic changes. However, it is generally assumed that the *net* outcome of climate change will be largely negative for human and non-human life on the planet.

The IPCC has introduced a categorisation of 'reasons for concern' about climate change. The impacts listed above can be viewed in terms of categories of different risks, including:

1 Risks to unique and threatened systems;
2 Risks from extreme climate events;
3 Risks or costs associated with the distribution of impacts;
4 Risk or costs associated with the size of aggregated impacts (measured econometrically);
5 Risks from future large-scale discontinuities.

Some countries are more vulnerable to the potential impacts of climate change than others. Often the most vulnerable are among the poorest, since these poor countries have less ability to *adapt* to climate change than richer ones (see Chapter 12).

Sectoral impacts of climate change

The potential impacts of climate change are typically categorised into a range of *sectors* listed below, together with some indicators of the generic types of impacts that are being observed or are envisaged. We should of course remember that not all of these impacts will manifest themselves in the same way in different regions (see Case Study 7.1).

- *Hydrology and water resources* – possible impacts include: relative increases/ decreases in flow of water in rivers depending on the region; a shift in peak streamflow from spring to winter in many areas where snowfall is a driver of the water balance; disappearance of many small glaciers; degrading of water quality by higher temperatures (but this could be offset in some cases by higher flows); increases in flood magnitude and frequencies in most regions; increased needs for irrigation.
- *Coastal zones* – possible impacts include: increasing flood-frequency probabilities and accelerated coastal erosion; inundation via rising water tables; saltwater intrusion and associated biological effects. Each of these in turn will have impacts on water resources, agriculture, human health, fisheries, tourism and human settlements.
- *Agriculture* – possible impacts include: changes in the location of optimal growing areas for particular crops, resulting in a shift in cropping zones; changes in size and type of crop yields; changes in the location and intensity of pests and diseases. Such impacts may in turn result in changes in farming practices, land use patterns, food security and import/export dependency. As well as microeconomic changes in production, farm income and rural employment, there may be associated macroeconomic changes in the structure of GDP.
- *Rangeland/livestock* – possible impacts include: changes in below-ground nutrient pools; in plant or forage quantity and quality; in plant adaptability or shifts in species; in livestock adaptability. Such impacts may in turn result in changes in food production and security, incomes, biodiversity and habitat impacts.
- *Human health* – possible impacts of climate change could include: increased heat-related mortality and morbidity; increase in photochemical and other forms of air pollution, with resulting increase in respiratory illness; increased mortality and morbidity as a result of increased frequency of floods, storms and other natural disasters; loss of habitable land, contamination of freshwater supplies, damage to public health infrastructure. Indirect health effects of climate change could include changes in the distribution and seasonal transmission of vector-borne diseases.
- *Energy* – possible impacts of climate change include energy consumption as well as production. Climate change will have impacts on the demand for air conditioning, space heating, water pumping, refrigeration and water heating. Hydroelectric energy production may be directly affected and, to a lesser extent, the thermal efficiencies of fossil fuel electricity generation. Energy production

facilities located on rivers or coastal zones may be at increased risk of flooding.

- *Forestry* – possible impacts include: shifts in the geographical area which can support forests; changes in the species composition of mixed-species forests; changes in the production of wood or non-timber forest products per unit area; changes in the type, location or intensity of pest and disease outbreaks and fires; changes in biodiversity via afforestation or deforestation as a result of land competition with agriculture.

- *Biodiversity* – possible impacts include species adapting to climate change in different ways. Those dependent on ecosystems that are now more fragmented will be more at risk of being unable to adapt at an appropriate rate; there could be strong negative impacts on migratory species as a result of shifts in the timing of seasonal events during the annual cycle; in some cases there will be an acceleration of existing problems of invasion by 'alien' species into natural ecosystems; negative impacts on arctic and alpine species as the extent of their native cold areas decline.

- *Fisheries* – possible impacts involve each of the three principal categories of fisheries – marine, coastal and estuaries – which may be affected by climate change in different ways. These include: potential loss of coastal wetlands and estuary habitats due to altered currents and sea levels; changes in the quality and/or availability of suitable habitats for different species; alteration of food webs; shifts in extent and locations of fishing grounds with associated socio-economic effects.

CASE STUDY 7.1

A world of extremes

If the predictions of the 2001 IPCC Report (IPCC, 2001b) by leading climate scientists proved correct, millions living in Britain and other northern climes would gain from milder winters and a longer growing season. There would also be more rapid rates of crop growth with higher concentrations of CO_2. However, further south, people would suffer the consequences of intense heatwaves that would kill many unused to extreme temperatures.

Insect pests would proliferate and there would be an increase in malaria; sunseekers would find the Mediterranean too hot for holidays in July and August.

According to the IPCC, the Earth is warming faster than at any time in the last 10,000 years and humans are causing the increase by burning fossil fuels, cutting down forests and making changes in agriculture. The changes predicted would cause coastal areas to be inundated and lead to major population changes. They would end the ski industry in Europe, cause the disappearance of many of the world's glaciers on which communities rely for regular summer water supplies, and have serious effects on agriculture.

The growing season for many of the stable crops in Africa would be cut too short for a reliable harvest because of excess heat and lack of moisture, and in Europe the Mediterranean fringe would be too dry for cereal crops. Many of the world's forests would die because of changes in water supply and the increasing heat. Night-time average temperatures would increasingly leave much larger areas frost-free, leading to increases in insect life. Heatwaves would increase over all northern land areas and droughts, already observed to be increasing in Africa and Asia, would become more severe. According to the report, nearly all land areas, including northern Europe, Asia and the United States, will warm far faster than average, possibly by as much as 8°C.

Climate models worked out by giant supercomputers have become far more reliable since the last report in 1995. This, combined with the climate changes observed over two decades, has convinced scientists that something very serious is happening and that it cannot be a natural process. There is far greater unanimity among the world's scientists over the issue than among politicians.

Recent floods in Britain and other parts of northern Europe are entirely consistent with climate change predictions. There has been an increase of 2 per cent in cloud cover but it is the rise in rainfall during heavier storms that has caused the floods. This is expected to get worse each decade.

A reduction in snow cover and in the area of sea ice in the Arctic has been seen since the late 1960s and is expected to accelerate. In the same period the remaining ice in the Arctic ice-cap has become 40 per cent less thick. A fall of two weeks in the annual duration of lake and river ice cover in mid and high latitudes of the northern hemisphere has already been observed.

A widespread retreat of mountain glaciers is expected to continue. Most of the sea level rise observed in the last century has been caused by the melting of glaciers in places such as the Alps and because of the thermal expansion of the oceans. So far the giant ice-caps on Greenland and Antarctica have been slow to react, but this will change.

Although the amount of sea level rise in the past decade has been slightly less than predicted in 1992, the report emphasises that the process will go on for thousands of years because of the time taken for the giant ice-caps of Greenland and Antarctica to react to increased temperatures.

Local warming over Greenland is likely to be one to three times the global average. If this warming were sustained, the complete melting of the Greenland ice-cap would result in a rise in sea level of about 7 m (23 ft), enough to drown all the major capitals of the world. A local warming of 5.5°C would be likely to result in a contribution from Greenland of 3 m to sea level rise over 1,000 years. If the west Antarctic ice sheet melted over the same period this would add another 3 m to sea level.

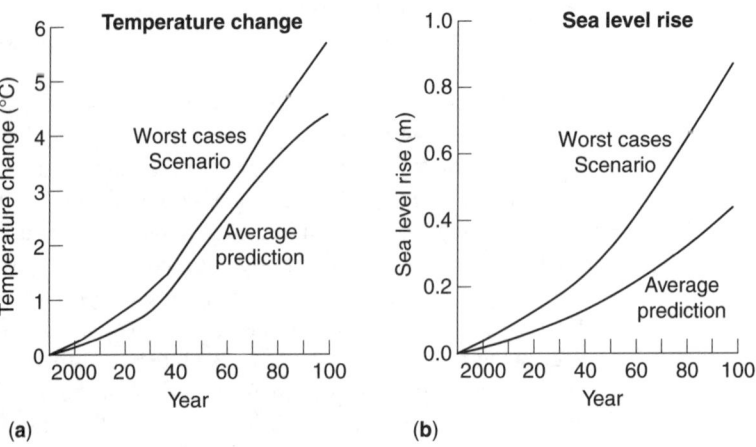

Figure 7.3 Temperature change: sea level rise
Source: IPCC (2001a)

One of the fears of scientists was that the flow of fresh water from the melting Greenland ice-cap would slow down or even halt the Gulf Stream, which warms Britain and the rest of Europe. The report says that while this may happen in the distant future, it is unlikely to have a serious effect this century.

The report suggests that the burning of fossil fuels is going to be 'the dominant influence' on climate in the next century. As the CO_2 in the atmosphere increases, the ability of plant life on land and in the oceans to soak it up decreases. In 1750 the concentrations of CO_2 in the atmosphere were 280 ppm (parts per million). By 2000 the figure had increased by 31 per cent. The report says the present CO_2 concentration has not been exceeded in the last 420,000 years and probably not for 20 million years. It is now going up at the rate of 4 per cent a decade and is expected to accelerate to reach 540–970 ppm by the end of the century. If it reaches the top of this range the temperature will rise up to 6°C, two degrees higher than predicted five years ago. The rate of warming is much higher than in the twentieth century and at any time in the last 10,000 years since the ice age ended.

Methane concentrations have risen by 151 per cent since 1750, partly due to fossil fuel burning, but also because of increases in rice culture and cattle, both of which generate methane from rotting vegetation. Landfill sites produce methane for the same reason but there are signs that these increases are levelling off.

Nitrous oxide, also a potent greenhouse gas, produced by industry, motor transport and agriculture, continues to increase and concentrations have not been exceeded in 1,000 years.

Other attempts by human beings to reduce pollution for other reasons are now known to increase global warming. The complex atmospheric changes that cause the hole in the ozone layer also allow heat to escape from the Earth. If the ozone hole is mended, as scientists predict it will be, then the Earth will heat up faster than it otherwise would.

Stopping acid rain and reducing the burning of forests will also allow more heat to reach the Earth. This will partly be offset by an increase in tiny droplets of water from storms and spray but the net effect will be a warmer Earth.

Questions

1 Give examples of some of the major benefits and costs from climate change.

2 How might the UK be affected by the climate change impacts deemed to be most likely?

●●●● Policy responses to climate change

National policy responses to the threat of climate change have been mainly driven by international developments and commitments. While the science behind greenhouse gases was being researched as early as the 1950s, climate change only became a major political issue in the late 1980s and early 1990s. By then politicians were finding it harder to ignore the growing body of science suggesting that emissions from fossil fuel burning could be contributing to a warming of the Earth. In fact some quickly saw political capital in acknowledging climate change. President George Bush (senior) and Prime Minister Margaret Thatcher both made important speeches on the topic of global warming in 1990. In March 1990 a meeting of world leaders from 24 countries called for the establishment of a new agency within the UN to combat global warming. Two years later, at the 1992 Earth Summit in Rio de Janeiro, world leaders signed up to the *United Nations Framework Convention on Climate Change* (UNFCCC) which came into force in 1994 (see Box 7.2).

BOX 7.2

United Nations Framework Convention on Climate Change (UNFCCC)

Over 170 countries have ratified the UNFCCC and are therefore parties to it. The UNFCCC is the central and overriding international agreement governing national and international efforts to combat global warming. However, beyond a good deal of promises and statements of value or intent, the Convention sets few measurable or binding goals.

The Convention consists of 26 articles. Here we briefly review some of the key articles.

Article 2: Objective – this is perhaps the most important article of the Convention:

'The ultimate objective of this Convention and any related legal instruments that the Conference of the Parties may adopt is to achieve... *stabilization of greenhouse gas concentrations in the atmosphere at a level that would prevent dangerous anthropogenic (human related) interference with the climate system. Such a level should be achieved within a time-frame sufficient to allow ecosystems to adapt naturally to climate change, to ensure that food production is not threatened and to enable economic development to proceed in a sustainable manner.'*

The ultimate goal of the Convention is therefore clear in the sense that it seeks to stabilize greenhouse gas concentrations when the current trend is for a rapid increase (and possibly accelerating increase) in concentrations of various gases. But look carefully at the italicised latter part of Article 2. Clearly it is a matter for expert or political judgement as to what constitutes 'dangerous' interference with the climate system. In addition there is a large amount of room for debate about what constitutes 'sustainable' economic development.

Article 3: Principles – the principles cover such things as equity; common but differentiated responsibilities; leadership; specific needs and special circumstances of developing country parties; the precautionary principle; the right to sustainable development; supportive and open international economic systems.

Article 4: Commitments – this article contains the real meat of the Convention. Much of the ongoing negotiations under the convention or the Kyoto Protocol revolve around different elements of this article. Some commitments concern all parties, others concern just developed country parties.

Article 4 commits *all* parties to:
- Publish inventories of greenhouse gas emissions
- Implement measures to mitigate and adapt to climate change
- Promote and cooperate in the development, application and diffusion including transfer of mitigation or adaptation technologies
- Promote sustainable management
- Cooperate in preparing for adaptation to the impacts of climate change
- Take care to minimise any adverse socio-economic or environmental effects that responding to climate change might have
- Promote and cooperate in relevant scientific research and technology

▶

● Promote and co-operate in education, training and public awareness

Article 4 commits *developed country* parties to:
● Adopt national policies to reduce greenhouse gas emissions and return these to earlier levels by the year 2000 (very few parties achieved this)
● Produce national communications periodically informing the Convention of progress
● Agree and use transparent methodologies for calculating greenhouse gas emissions
● Provide new and additional financial resources to meet the agreed full costs incurred by developing countries in meeting various commitments under the Convention (a sort of vague blank cheque)
● Assist particularly vulnerable parties in meeting the costs of adaptation
● Promote, facilitate and finance the transfer of, or access to, environmentally sound technologies to developing country parties

Special consideration is also given to *economies in transition*, to *developing countries*, and to other groups of vulnerable countries or systems (e.g. those dependent on fossil fuel exports).

Article 11: Financial Mechanism – a mechanism for the provision of financial resources on a grant or concessional basis through bilateral, regional and other multilateral channels. The **Global Environment Facility** is the largest and most important financial mechanism to date under the Convention.

All developed countries have now produced reports that outline national progress to date in implementing the Convention. But no sooner had the Convention entered into force in 1994 than negotiations began on a new and tougher agreement to supplement the UNFCCC. This time negotiators were trying to agree something with teeth – a *legally binding protocol* to the UNFCCC. Three years of detailed negotiations over quantified emission reduction objectives produced the *Kyoto Protocol* in December 1997.

BOX 7.3

Bringing the Kyoto Protocol into force

Legally binding promises made at international meetings by representative politicians and civil servants need to be brought home and ratified or accepted by national parliaments. When enough countries have deposited their 'instruments of ratification, acceptance, approval or accession' with the UN legal office in New York, an international UN agreement officially 'enters into force'. The conditions for entry into force of the Kyoto Protocol are when 55 per cent of all parties (developed and developing) have ratified, including enough developed or transition economy countries to represent at least 55 per cent of so-called Annex I 1990 CO_2 emissions.

The Kyoto Protocol will come into force 90 days after the date on which it receives the required number of ratifications. With the USA having declined to ratify in 2001, the EU, the Russian Federation and Japan must ratify, plus one or more others from either Canada, Poland, Australia or the countries with economies in transition, if the Protocol is to 'enter into force'.

The race to get Kyoto into force is on. In their *UN Millennium Declaration*, world leaders pledged to ratify in time to bring the Kyoto Protocol into force by the end of 2002. Many saw ▶

the World Summit on Sustainable Development in Johannesburg in 2002 as the political target to trigger the 90-day rule or better still to bring the Protocol into force.

The adoption of the Kyoto Protocol by the UNFCCC was significant. The main new elements that the Kyoto Protocol adds to the overall framework of international climate commitments include:

- Legally binding commitments by *developed* countries to collectively reduce their 1990 emission level of a basket of six greenhouse gases by 5 per cent by 2012.
- Individual commitments by *developed* countries to particular reduction targets.
- A compliance system with penalties for non-compliance.
- A so-called **'clean development mechanism'** (CDM). The CDM is a project-based approach to reducing greenhouse gas emissions in *developing* countries (see page 179). *Developed* countries that follow the right procedures and provide specific technologies can claim any estimated greenhouse gas reductions as a result of their involvement in a CDM project against their overall Kyoto Protocol emission reduction target.
- *Emissions trading* is allowed among developed countries and countries with economies in transition. Under the Protocol, emissions trading involves the registration and tracking of trades between eligible parties on a basic double-entry bookkeeping system.
- A previously existing mechanism called 'joint implementation' is also included, though it is expected that the CDM will be the main project-based mechanism used under the Protocol.

The most important aspect of the Kyoto Protocol is that it puts a negative economic value on greenhouse gas emissions and positive economic value on greenhouse gas reductions. It does this through the introduction of a global cap on emissions, individual national targets and a trading regime. Penalties will be incurred if countries fail to reduce their emissions below agreed targets to agreed timescales. This means that potential greenhouse gas reductions (where they can be certified) have a positive economic value in themselves. Estimates of the present value of carbon emissions abated (reduced) are in the range of $-$ \$5 to $+$ \$100 dollars per tonne of carbon, with a mean value around \$8.25 per tonne of carbon.

Greenhouse gas emissions trading and the Kyoto Protocol

If we assume that each developed country has accurately and transparently measured its current and historic greenhouse gas emissions in line with international guidelines (a heroic assumption given the uncertainties in measuring and monitoring some sources of greenhouse gas emissions), then at any point in time the aggregate sum of emissions from developed countries is known.

If developed country A cannot, in the current period, find emission reductions as cheaply at home as they are available at internationally traded prices, then it may purchase from another developed country (or country with an economy in transition) a certain amount of that country's emission entitlements. Emission entitlements (certified by permits) are then deducted from the recorded inventory for country A and added to the recorded inventory for country B, in a simple double-entry bookkeeping manner. For example, if country A has purchased 1,000 t of emission entitlements from country B, then A is deemed to have emitted 1,000 t less than the volume recorded and B 1,000 t more. In effect country A can emit 1,000 t more than its original target but country B must emit 1,000 t less than its original target.

National trading schemes can be far more complex and can involve the simultaneous trade in carbon, renewable and green energy certificates. The Kyoto Protocol, however, deals only with the simple double-entry bookkeeping system. Chapter 4 (page 88) looks more closely at the issue of tradable permits. Although the developing countries are excluded from the tradable permits mechanism under Kyoto, they feature prominently in the 'clean development mechanism'.

Clean development mechanism (CDM)

Suppose a *developed* country A sees an opportunity to help a developing country B reduce its greenhouse gas emissions by choosing a cleaner technology or by changing some practice or system. They may mutually agree to co-operate to reduce the greenhouse gases in B by upgrading its technology or changing some other aspect of its system. Developing country B gets the benefits of better technology (hopefully with all the attendant secondary economic benefits in terms of technology transfer and capacity building), while developed country A can claim the credit for the estimated greenhouse gas emissions *avoided* as a result of using the better technology. Everyone is happy – at least in theory.

However, the CDM is not without its critics. One key criticism of the CDM is that it may, paradoxically, in some cases act as a *perverse incentive* by actually increasing greenhouse gas emissions relative to what they might otherwise have been (the so-called 'baseline'). This could possibly arise if a developing country delayed installing or upgrading to cleaner technology in the hope that it could eventually find a CDM partner to share these costs. Another criticism is that the success of the CDM will have high transactions costs, being difficult to police and open to abuse by either party (or so-called 'designated entities').

The Kyoto Protocol is primarily a *mitigation* protocol – that is to say its main focus is on reducing emissions of greenhouse gases. Few of its provisions involve helping countries *adapt* to the impacts of climate change. However, adaptation is a key part of the UNFCCC itself; indeed Article 2 arguably implies that it is the ultimate objective of the whole Convention.

CASE STUDY 7.2

European Climate Change Policy (ECCP)

The European Commission's strategy to limit CO_2 emissions and improve energy efficiency began in 1991, since when the EU has implemented many climate-related initiatives.

The EU's long-term climate change strategy was consolidated into the European Climate Change Programme (ECCP) in June 2000. The goal of the ECCP is to ensure that the EU fulfils its obligations under the Kyoto Protocol. As new long-term targets to reduce greenhouse gas emissions are sequentially negotiated under the Kyoto Protocol (or other similar international agreements) throughout the twenty-first century, the role of the ECCP will become more strategic and possibly politicised.

It is likely that the 15 European member states will collectively meet their Kyoto target for the so-called *first commitment period*: the target involves an overall 8 per cent reduction in emissions by 2012 compared with 1990 emission levels. Indeed at the end of 1999 the EU was halfway to meeting this target, having achieved a 4 per cent reduction in the emissions of the six greenhouse gases regulated under the Protocol. The EU's 8 per cent reduction target is 336 million tonnes of CO_2 equivalent or approximately the annual amount of emissions generated in the UK.

Different EU member states have agreed among themselves to share the overall 8 per cent burden according to their effective abilities taking into account their different economic and national circumstances. Table 7.3 shows the different targets for each EU country, together with the trend over the period 1990–99.

Some countries appear to be doing much better at meeting their targets than others. Germany and the UK, for example, are well on the way to reaching their targets, but analysts suggest that this is in large part due to the well-established long-term decline in coal consumption and shift to gas-fired electricity generation in these countries, rather than the result of tough climate change policy measures. In fact many of the reductions achieved in Europe during the 1990s are one-off reductions as a result of changes in fuel supply and structural economic adjustments. Meeting future targets will cost more, be more hotly contested and will ultimately test the political and public willingness to act on the climate threat. Reducing greenhouse gas emissions in Europe involves a combination of national strategies as well as coordinated European actions. The nature of European energy markets, particularly for the networked gas and electricity sectors, means that future European climate actions are likely to have to rely on coordinated European strategies.

The EU 8 per cent reduction target is just the start. The ultimate goal of the UNFCCC is to stabilise greenhouse gas concentrations in the atmosphere at a 'safe level'. No one knows what a safe level of greenhouse gas concentrations is. Scientists are hurriedly building and refining complex models to try to predict more accurately what future climate impacts might be. Stabilisation at say 550 ppm (as against 385 ppm today) would require cuts of some 60–90 per cent in greenhouse gas emissions. The next round of greenhouse gas reduction targets is due to be agreed by 2005.

The overriding approach to planning for future emissions reductions is that of *cost-effectiveness*. The principle of cost-effectiveness (basically least cost) is a central pillar of current European environment policy and has been the basis of other environmental initiatives such as the European Auto Oil Programmes (see Chapter 13).

The ECCP has begun considering Europe's options for reducing greenhouse gas emissions in the long term. The programme has assessed various greenhouse gas reduction measures across different sectors taking into account cost-effectiveness, as well as time scales. Measures being considered include:

- EU framework for emissions trading
- Emission reductions achieved overseas through CDM projects
- Increasing use of combined heat and power technologies
- Further reductions from the switch from coal to gas-fired power generation
- Improving the efficiency of power generation
- Accelerating the growth of renewable energy technologies
- Reducing methane emissions from the oil and gas industries
- New legislative instruments such as energy efficiency and audit regulations

- Improved information
- Measures to reduce emissions in the industrial sector such as energy efficiency initiatives and eco-management and audit schemes (EMAS – see Chapter 13)
- Voluntary agreements to improve energy efficiency of end-use appliances such as light bulbs, white goods, vehicles.

Table 7.3 Greenhouse gas emission trends and Kyoto Protocol targets for 2008–12

	Change 1990–99[1] (%)	*Targets 2008–2012 under Kyoto Protocol and EU 'burden sharing' (%)*
Austria	+2.6	−13.0
Belgium	+2.8	−7.5
Denmark[2]	4(−4.6)	−21.0
Finland	−1.1	0.0
France	−0.2	0.0
Germany	−18.7	−21.0
Greece	+16.9	+25.0
Ireland	+22.9	+13.0
Italy	+4.4	−6.5
Luxembourg	−43.3	−28.0
Netherlands	+6.1	−6.0
Portugal	+22.4	+27.0
Spain	+23.2	+15.0
Sweden	+1.5	+4.0
United Kingdom	−14.0	−12.5
EU total	−4.0	−8.0

Notes:
[1]For the fluorinated gases some Member States have selected a base year other than 1990, as allowed for under the Protocol.
[2]For Denmark data that reflect adjustments for electricity trade (import and export) in 1990 are given in brackets. This methodology is used by Denmark to monitor progress towards its national target under the EU 'burden sharing' agreement. For the EU emissions total the non-adjusted Danish data have been used.

Source: European Commission.

Questions

1 Explain why Europe looks set to meet its 2012 Kyoto Protocol targets and why future targets might not be quite as easy (cheap) to achieve.

2 What options might be missing from the list of measures being considered under the ECCP?

●●●● The politics of global climate change

The international politics of climate change are, like several other international economic, social and environmental issues, frequently portrayed in terms of the 'North versus South' dimension – a euphemism for developed versus developing countries. Dividing the world up into these two basic camps offers a starting point (albeit a crude one) for understanding the politics behind climate change.

The texts of the UNFCCC and the Kyoto Protocol reinforce the North–South dynamic by placing different commitments upon *developed* countries (essentially the OECD countries), upon countries with economies in *transition* (former countries of the Russian Federation and other Eastern European countries) and upon *developing* countries.

In one way or another most of the politics of climate change can be explained around the framework of Article 3 of the UNFCCC Convention (see Box 7.2, under 'Principles'). Key elements include:

- equity
- common but differentiated responsibilities
- leadership
- specific needs and special circumstances of developing country parties
- the precautionary principle
- the right to sustainable development
- supportive and open international economic system

As a first approximation the politics can be reduced to two main issues:

1 How fast the *developed* countries should demonstrate progress in reducing their greenhouse gas emissions.

2 What special needs and specific circumstances of *developing* country parties need to be addressed.

Developed countries and reduced greenhouse gas emissions

The Convention makes it clear that the *developed countries* should take the lead in reducing greenhouse gas emissions. While all of them accepted the quantified emission reduction targets agreed for the OECD countries in 1992 and for Kyoto in 1997 (including the USA), very few developed countries have shown any real signs of reducing their greenhouse gas emissions in line with their Kyoto promises (Table 7.4). As the new millennium approached, statistics showed that of the OECD countries only the UK had made any demonstrable progress towards emission reductions (Germany's reduction relative to 1990 was largely a result of unification, rather than implemented climate actions). Even in the UK, much if not all of the reduction in greenhouse gas emissions has happened because of reasons other than implemented climate actions (e.g. the 'dash for gas' and long-term structural economic change away from energy-intensive manufacturing industry and towards services).

Developing countries have been highly critical of the failure to date of the OECD countries to meet their original 1992 promise of stabilising emissions at 1990 levels by the year 2000. The Kyoto targets are still higher but developed countries have been given more time to achieve these tougher targets.

Scientifically and from a global perspective each and every tonne of carbon (or other greenhouse gas) reduced, from whatever technology or process and wherever in the world, is equally important. Within the next decade total greenhouse gas emissions from non-OECD countries will for the first time be greater than those from OECD countries. The Kyoto Protocol therefore effectively covers deals accounting for less than half of the climate change problem. That fraction looks set

Table 7.4 Total greenhouse gas emissions, percentage change 1998 relative to 1990

Country	% change 1990–98
Latvia	− 68
Lithuania	− 54
Ukraine	− 51
Estonia	− 47
Bulgaria	− 46
Romania	− 38
Russian Federation	− 35
Slovakia	− 31
Poland	− 29
Luxembourg	− 24
Czech Republic	− 22
Hungary	− 18
Germany	− 16
United Kingdom	− 8
European Community	− 2
France	+ 1
Switzerland	+ 1
Finland	I 1
New Zealand	+ 2
Italy	+ 4
Iceland	+ 5
Sweden	+ 6
Austria	+ 6
Belgium	+ 7
Norway	+ 8
Netherlands	+ 8
Denmark	+ 9
Japan	+ 10
United States of America	+ 11
Canada	+ 13
Australia	+ 15
Portugal	+ 17
Greece	+ 18
Ireland	+ 19
Spain	+ 21
Monaco	+ 28

Source: UNFCCC official document reference FCCC/SBI/2000/INF.13: p. 6.

to fall still further over future time periods (see Chapter 12). Herein lies a major
political stumbling block in the negotiations. Developed countries – quite reasonably – point out that developing countries need also to honour their commitments
in the UNFCCC by reducing their future greenhouse gas emissions. Countries like

India and China recognise the scientific basis of this perspective, but argue that they have not yet had the same chance to develop economically using fossil fuels as the OECD nations have had throughout the industrial revolution.

The only way out of this dilemma would, in the foreseeable future, seem to be for OECD nations to accelerate the implementation of their national climate change action plans and for developing countries to start to talk about the sort of action they would be prepared to take to reduce their greenhouse gas emissions and on what timescale.

CASE STUDY 7.3

Climate change and the developing countries

'Special needs and specific circumstances' is a deliberately vague phrase, but is nonetheless a very important one in the climate negotiations. It was introduced in the language of the Convention and repeated in the Kyoto Protocol negotiations as a shorthand way of covering all the concerns held by the different developing countries about the impacts of climate change.

There are four very distinct types of climate change 'impacts' which concern developing countries:

● ongoing needs for sustainable economic development
● actual climate impacts (e.g. temperature rise, sea level rise, floods, droughts, disease)
● impacts on the economies of developing countries as a result of reducing their own greenhouse gas emissions
● impacts on developing economies brought about by the global shift away from burning fossil fuels

In theory most agree that the first priority of developing countries is poverty eradication and economic development. The problem comes in interpreting what kind of economic development. All sides emphasise the need for sustainable economic development, but beyond the rhetoric there is no shared vision of what exactly *sustainable* economic development means.

What has started to happen is that developed countries are paying more and particular attention to the environmental impacts of their ongoing development assistance programmes. For example, developed countries are increasingly putting environmental conditions on aid for development projects.

All countries, but particularly some of the poorest that are already the most vulnerable to climate variability, are concerned about the possible impacts of climate change. Many developing countries have received small amounts of bilateral and multilateral financial assistance to help them *assess* their vulnerability to climate change (typically in the order of $US100,000 per country). But however much money is spent on assessments, future uncertainties about the nature and extent of climate change mean that it is difficult for developing countries to decide on their priorities in terms of requests for assistance under the UNFCCC. Some countries, for various reasons, have not even conducted adequate vulnerability assessments.

In turn, developing countries frequently request assistance to help develop their capacities to adapt to actual or predicted climate change in their region. It will be some time yet before funding for actual adaptation projects (e.g. sea walls, new crops, dams) gets properly under way. This is a major source of frustration for developing countries and greatly affects the politics of climate change.

Developing countries want to eradicate poverty and develop economically. To do this they emphasise their need for advanced technologies and for building appropriate capacity infrastructure (training, education, institutional strengthening). However, developed countries (in particular the USA and Europe) emphasise the need for developing countries to create the right sort of 'enabling conditions' for their economies to grow. Some suggest that this is simply a way for the powerful OECD trading countries to try to gain access to developing country markets. Precisely how developed countries should help to build the developing countries economies is a major source of political argument.

Then there are the oil-exporting (and to a lesser extent coal-exporting) countries. OPEC countries wield considerable power in the climate negotiations. They consider the potential decline of the global petroleum industry as a 'climate impact' just as relevant to them, for example, as sea level rise is to small island states. In one sense, OPEC is just an extreme example of the political sensitivities that exist in most developed countries around solving climate change. Few developed countries have been open about their fears concerning the impact that taking actions to combat climate change might have on their domestic economies. To widespread international condemnation, President George W. Bush spoke openly in March 2001 about the negative impact he thought the Kyoto Protocol could have on the US economy.

During the recent Kyoto Protocol negotiations, other technical or methodological issues have become politicised. These include:

- the extent to which developed countries can use emissions trading or the CDM to meet their overall Kyoto targets (as opposed to reducing their own domestic levels of emissions)
- whether or not the greenhouse gases that are captured in forests and soils can be counted as reductions under the Protocol
- which energy technologies should be eligible under the rules of the CDM
- the nature and size of penalties for non-compliance with the Kyoto Protocol
- how exactly developed countries are going to meet their commitments on the transfer of technology under the convention
- the terms of compensation for the impacts of climate change or response measures, including insurance and technology transfer

Such issues are likely to dominate climate negotiations in the next few years.

Questions

1 How will climate change affect developing countries?

2 Why is it difficult for developing countries to prepare for the impacts of climate change?

3 Describe three concerns of developing countries in the climate negotiations.

● ● ● ● Integrated assessment modelling (IAM)

More than any other environmental problem encountered this century, climate change is requiring policy makers and other stakeholders in the policy process to make decisions in a context of extreme scientific complexity and uncertainty. Informed rational decision making about climate change demands an overview of all associated costs of response measures. These include the costs of reducing greenhouse gas emissions, the costs of adapting to impacts of climate change, as well as the costs of coping with climate damage. Future emissions of greenhouse gases depend on a host of uncertainties including projections for population, economic growth, structural change and technological evolution.

Integrated assessment modelling (IAM) involves the use of submodels to undertake four steps of analysis:

1 First, different scenarios about possible future emissions profiles of developed and developing countries must be generated. This step in turn requires energy–emissions–economy models to be used to explore the different possible plausible emissions pathways for different countries or regions.
2 Second, models of the interaction between the atmosphere, land surface, oceans and carbon cycle (and other greenhouse gas cycles) are then needed to translate the various emissions scenarios into various scenarios of concentrations in atmospheric greenhouse gas emissions.
3 Third, various scenarios of greenhouse gas concentrations must be translated into projections for global mean temperature changes and associated impacts on climate variables (sea level rise, precipitation, cloudiness, etc.).
4 Fourth, the social and economic impacts of such changes in climate variables must be assessed.

Any single stage of the above cascade of estimation and modelling is extremely complex. Already the various components of IAM have taken many thousands of person-years of effort. Nevertheless the uncertainties within integrated assessment models are likely to continue to be better understood and characterised. The use of such models is likely to be critical in developing comprehensive response strategies as an aid to decision making.

One explicitly rational cost–benefit approach is to characterise the problem as minimising the overall human welfare loss from climate change (Fankhauser, 1998). His model divides policy instruments into two broad types: *mitigation measures*, which reduce the amount of global warming occurring, and *adaptation measures*, which reduce the negative impacts of any given amount of global warming which does occur. The climate change welfare problem can then be expressed as finding the level of mitigation m and adaptation a which minimises the sum of the three cost elements: mitigation cost MC, adaptation cost AC and damage cost (D), i.e.

$$\text{minimize MC } (m) + \text{AC } (a) + \text{D } (m,a)$$

Mitigation and adaptation costs are likely to rise with the levels of mitigation and adaptation already achieved (see Chapter 3, page 58). However, damage costs are likely to decline as mitigation or adaptation costs increase. Hence at a global level, there are trade-offs between the costs of mitigation and/or adaptation and damage. A *global cost–benefit approach* to decision making about climate change could therefore involve comparing marginal mitigation and/or adaptation costs with the marginal benefits of avoiding damage. Chapter 3 (e.g. Figure 3.1) provides a simplified view of this approach.

In reality the international response to climate change has so far been focused on negotiating a *minimum acceptable rate of mitigation of greenhouse gas emissions*. For large contributors to current greenhouse gas emissions this makes sense. They will benefit from lower damage costs, and possibly from reduced costs associated with assisting vulnerable, less developed countries to pay for the costs of adaptation measures or climate damages. Interestingly, most countries in the world account for a relatively small proportion of total greenhouse gas emissions, many for a tiny fraction of a single per cent. From a small emitter perspective, the problem of climate change becomes one of finding the amount of adaptation that minimises the damage costs of a given amount of climate change. Essentially the interest of the small emitter is in optimising the amount of residual climate damage.

> **Now try the self-check questions for this chapter on the companion website www.booksites.net/ison**
> **You will also find up-to-date facts and case materials.**

Key terms

Clean development mechanism (CDM) A way in which a developed and a developing country can co-operate to reduce emissions and contribute to sustainable development (in the developed or 'recipient' country). The developed or 'donor' country receives credit for the emissions reduced as a result of the project

Climate Can be defined in a day-to-day sense as the 'average weather'. More scientifically it can be defined as statistical descriptions (means, variances, extremes) of variables such as temperature, precipitation, wind over a period of time

Climate system Consists of five major components: the atmosphere (the envelope of gases surrounding the Earth), the hydrosphere (oceans, seas, rivers, fresh waters, underground water), the cryosphere (snow, sea ice, ice sheets, glaciers and permafrost), the land surface and the biosphere (all ecosystems and living organisms)

Emissions trading In the context of the Kyoto Protocol, emissions trading refers to swapping, selling or trading between countries (only) the right to emit greenhouse gases without incurring penalties

Global Environment Facility (GEF) The central multilateral mechanism for assisting developed and developing countries with their commitments under the UNFCCC. Developed countries replenish GEF funds under the Convention on a regular basis. The money is spent on projects in developing countries (climate change is just a part of the GEF's work)

Greenhouse effect The temporary trapping (absorption and re-emission) of incoming heat energy from the sun in the Earth's atmosphere by various gases causing global warming

Greenhouse gases Component gases of the atmosphere that absorb and emit the infrared radiation emitted by the Earth. Water vapour (H_2O), carbon dioxide (CO_2), nitrous oxide (N_2O), methane (CH_4) and ozone (O_3) are the main greenhouse gases in the Earth's atmosphere

Integrated assessment modelling (IAM) The use of simulations and submodels to achieve an overall prediction as to the impacts of climate change

Intergovernmental Panel on Climate Change (IPCC) This is a large network of scientists from every region (and most countries) from around the world. The scientists are nominated by their governments and work together in small groups to produce state of the art assessments of the rapidly evolving science of climate change (in all its aspects including social)

Kyoto Protocol An agreement reached in the Japanese city of Kyoto in December 1997. It puts teeth into the international response to climate change. As a result not everyone is happy to move forward with the promises made in 1997. It will only come into force when enough countries have 'ratified' it.

United Nations Framework Convention on Climate Change (UNFCCC) The central and overarching international agreement setting out the basis for how countries should combat climate change

References and further reading

Bowers, J. (1997) *Sustainability and Environmental Economics*, Longman, Harlow, especially Chapter 17.

Fankhauser S. (1998) 'The cost of adapting to climate change', Working Paper 16, Global Environment Facility, Washington, DC.

Field, B. C. (1997) *Environmental Economics: An Introduction*, McGraw-Hill, especially Chapters 20–21.

Gilpin, A. (2000) *Environmental Economics: A Critical Overview*, Wiley, especially Chapter 9.

IPCC (2000) *Special Report on Emissions Scenarios*, Cambridge University Press, Cambridge.

IPCC (2001a) *Climate Change 2001: The Scientific Basis*. Contribution of Working Group I to the Third Assessment Report of the Intergovernmental Panel on Climate Change, Cambridge University Press, Cambridge.

IPCC (2001b) *Climate Change 2001: Impacts, Adaptation and Vulnerability*. Contribution of Working Group II to the Third Assessment Report of the Intergovernmental Panel on Climate Change, Cambridge University Press, Cambridge.

IPCC (2001c) *Climate Change 2001: Mitigation*. Contribution of Working Group III to the Third Assessment Report of the Intergovernmental Panel on Climate Change, Cambridge University Press, Cambridge.

Peake, S. (2001) 'Kyoto Lite', *ReFocus*, September, pp. 45–7.

Plambeck, E.L. and Hope, C. (1996) 'PAGE95: an updated valuation of the impacts of global warming', *Energy Policy*, **24**, 783–93.

Royal Commission on Environmental Pollution (2000), 22nd Report, *Energy – The Changing Climate*, Cm 4749.

UNEP (1998) *Handbook on Methods for Climate Change Impact Assessment and Adaptation Strategies* Version 2.0, October 1998 in association with the Institute of Environmental Studies, The Free University of Amsterdam.

Useful websites

www.ipcc.ch

www.unfccc.int

www.gefweb.org

Copy of UNEP Handbook: www.vu.nl/english/o_o/instituten/IVM/research/climate-change/Handbook.htm

Copy of Fankhauser, (1998): www.gefweb.org/Outreach/outreach-Publications /Working _paper16.pdf

Natural resources, population and the environment

Issues involving natural resources, population and the environment are touched on throughout the book, and in the particular context of pollution in Chapter 6 and the developing economies in Chapter 12. Nevertheless it may be useful to bring together in one chapter some of the key environmental facts and issues involving land, energy, mineral, water and human resources and to consider these within the framework of the various ecosystems. The term **'ecosystem'** is used here to refer to the community of species that interact with each other in the physical setting (*habitat*) in which they live.

This chapter pays particular attention to three important ecosystems, namely agricultural, forest and freshwater ecosystems, though others can readily be identified (e.g. coastal). At the present time the indicators most often used in assessing such ecosystems fall into one of three categories:

- *Pressures on ecosystems*, including overuse, degradation and population growth
- *Extent of ecosystems*, including physical size, shape, location and distribution
- *Output of ecosystems*, including crops, timber, medicines, minerals and fish

Of course, any indicators can at best provide only a partial picture of the 'health' of that ecosystem. For example, indicators as to output of an ecosystem tell us little or nothing about its underlying **carrying capacity**, i.e. the output level below which it can replenish itself and be self-sustaining.

We begin by taking a global perspective of each ecosystem before paying particular attention to some important issues involving ecosystem management, such as retaining biodiversity, using renewable resources wherever possible and recycling. Energy, mineral and human population resources are also considered. Chapter 12 applies many of the issues raised in this chapter to the particular problems faced by the developing economies.

A theme running throughout the chapter is that natural resources themselves, together with the ability of the environment to assimilate the various wastes derived from the use of these resources in production, may act as important 'limits to growth'. Economic activity can be viewed as being primarily concerned with the conversion of natural resources into products, which can themselves be regarded as embodied energy and materials. However, when products decay they become waste and it is the environment which must ultimately handle that waste. An increased output of products, via economic growth, will inevitably produce still more waste.

This in turn brings into focus the **first law of thermodynamics**. In this view, the Earth is a closed system in which a finite set of resources is available for current and future growth. In other words, the capacity of the economy to produce still more products is constrained or limited by the availability of natural resources. Even if resources are sufficient to permit growth, the extra production will simply 'drag through' more materials and energy embodied in products, which the environment must ultimately assimilate, since matter and energy cannot be destroyed. Wherever possible, materials must therefore be recycled, renewable energy sources must be used in preference to non-renewable sources, and waste emissions must be limited to the extent that the Earth can safely absorb these 'residuals'. This approach has led many economists to propose limiting our demand for goods and services in order to attain a level of economic growth that can be 'sustained' over future generations (see also Chapter 5).

Agricultural ecosystems (Agroecosystems)

Agriculture has been defined as involving 'areas where at least 30 percent of the land is used for crop land or for highly managed pasture' (PAGE, 2000). On this basis *agroecosystems* cover some 28 per cent of the land's surface (excluding Antarctica and Greenland). The Food and Agricultural Organisation (FAO) of the United Nations estimated in 2000 that agroecosystems accounted for $1,300 bn (i.e. $1.3 trillion) in value of output for food, feed and fibre, producing 95 per cent of all animal and plant protein and 99 per cent of the calories consumed by humans. Table 8.1 outlines these outputs and summarises some of the pressures on agroecosystems worldwide and their causes.

Table 8.1 Agroecosystems: goods and services, pressures and causes

Goods and services	Pressures	Causes of pressures
● Food crops	● Conversion of farmland to urban and industrial uses	● Population growth
● Fibre crops		● Increasing demand for food and industrial goods
● Crop genetic resources	● Water pollution from nutrient runoff and situation	
● Maintain limited watershed functions (infiltration, flow control, partial soil protection)	● Water scarcity from irrigation	● Urbanisation
	● Degradation of soil from erosion, shifting cultivation, or nutrient depletion	● Government policies subsidising agricultural inputs (water, research, transport) and irrigation
● Provide habitat for birds, pollinators, soil organisms important to agriculture	● Changing weather patterns	● Poverty and insecure tenure
● Build soil organic matter		● Climate change
● Sequester atmospheric carbon		
● Provide employment		

Some widely used indicators of agroecosystems are summarised below:

- Some 69 per cent of agroecosystems consist of land under permanent pasture and 31 per cent land used for crops.
- Food output has increased faster than global population growth. For example, food supplies per person are 24 per cent higher today than in 1961 and the real prices of food are 40 per cent lower.
- Food output must continue to grow to meet the needs of an extra 1.7 billion people over the next 20 years.
- Output per hectare has grown rapidly via 'intensification' of agriculture. Irrigated areas have increased, fallow time has decreased, the use of purchased inputs (pesticides, fertilisers, etc.) and new technologies have grown rapidly.
- Intensification has increased output per hectare, but at the cost of degradation. Over 66 per cent of agricultural land has been degraded in the past 50 years, with 40 per cent 'strongly' or 'very strongly' degraded. This has been the result of erosion, salinisation, compaction, nutrient depletion, biological degradation or pollution.

Two issues related to agroecosystems of particular environmental importance are intensification and biodiversity.

Intensification of agroecosystems

As population has grown, more marginal land less well suited to cultivation has been drawn into agriculture and existing agricultural land has been used more intensively. This whole process of **intensification** has often involved the increased application of inputs such as water, fertiliser and pesticides as well as labour and capital equipment. In some areas where population pressures have been strongest (e.g. Asia) almost all the cropland is harvested at least annually and sometimes two or three times a year. Land is now rarely left fallow to restore nutrients, as in more traditional farming practices, being replaced by the use of new varieties of rapid-growing seeds and the application of fertilisers. The result is often higher levels of soil salinisation (saltiness) via poorly managed irrigation systems, losses in soil fertility via overcultivation, compaction of soil by tractors or livestock and lowering of water tables via overpumping for irrigation.

Eutrophication is the nutrient enrichment of rivers, lakes and groundwater, mainly by nitrates and phosphates, both of which are widely present in artificial fertilisers applied to arable land. This problem is most acute in the developed countries and has resulted mainly from using increased amounts of fertilisers in order to raise agricultural productivity (e.g. output per hectare), especially in cereal production.

Nitrates are highly soluble and easily washed out of the soil profile into drainage water and groundwater. Although phosphate is less soluble, it readily attaches itself to soil particles which can also enter the drainage system. The excreta of farm animals is also rich in nitrates and phosphates.

The leaching of nitrates and phosphates into water systems has many adverse environmental impacts, resulting in declining amenity use and the need to treat water for domestic consumption. The World Health Organisation (WHO) and the EU have recommended that nitrate concentrations in drinking water should not exceed 50 mg 1^{-1} because of concerns linking nitrate intake to various cancers and other illnesses (e.g. 'blue baby' syndrome).

Policy remedies

Policies which may help avoid some of the problems from intensification include better management of agroecosystems (e.g. tree planting to reduce erosion), restrictions on fertiliser and pesticide use, regulating cultivation around local water sources, rehabilitating degraded soils, set-aside (land left fallow) and the adoption of new technologies. Removing some of the price incentives to over-production of agricultural produce under the Common Agricultural Policy of the EU is another key policy instrument. This is considered in more detail in Chapter 11 (page 262) together with providing incentives to support organic farming (page 267).

Biodiversity in agroecosystems

Biodiversity (or biological diversity) refers to the number, variety and variability of living organisms. Three levels of biodiversity are often identified:

- *Genetic diversity* involves the variety of genes within a species.
- *Species diversity* involves the variety of species within a habitat (e.g. rainforests) or a region.
- *Ecosystem diversity* involves the variety of ecosystems (communities of organisms) in a given place, which may be large in area (e.g. forest) or small in area (e.g. pond).

It is widely held that agricultural lands support far less biodiversity than the natural forests, grasslands and wetlands that they replace. This is especially true in areas of intensive agriculture. For example, in terms of genetic diversity more than 90 per cent of the world's calorific intake comes from just 30 crops, and only 120 crops are commercially viable (FAO, 2000). In addition, modern crop varieties are increasingly homogenous, developed from a progressively narrower gene pool selected to contain the more 'desirable' characteristics for that crop.

Benefits of biodiversity

Our earlier analysis of use, option and existence value (Chapter 2, page 26) can be applied here. Biological diversity adds value to a wide range of commercial activities:

- *Use value.* A study of 119 commercially useful plant-based drugs found that 74 per cent of these drugs were in prior use by indigenous communities (Swanson, 2001) and that many of these cannot be manufactured synthetically.
- *Option value.* Although we have noted that commercial cropping uses only a few plant species, several thousand plant species have been used as foodstuffs by humans and many more may, in the future, be found to be edible. Population pressures and global climate change result in shifting patterns of natural vegetation and enforce changes in agricultural systems. Retaining extensive plant genetic resources will allow a much more flexible response to such unpredictable future events. In these ways biodiversity provides 'insurance' against an unknown future.
- *Existence value.* This is independent of any current or future use of an environmental asset. For example, retaining biodiversity may involve the

intergenerational motive of giving one's children or grandchildren the opportunity to observe certain species or ecosystems.

Box 8.1 examines the alleged trade-off between biodiversity and economic development, with particular reference to agroecosystems.

Biodiversity and economic development

It is often claimed that economic development inevitably conflicts with biodiversity. For example, in economics it is widely recognised that the demand for any particular factor of production is derived from the demand for its product. It then follows that the demand for a given hectare of land is derived from the market price of the uses to which that land might be put. Suppose the hectare of land in its natural form is growing a diverse array of native grasses, excluding wheat, but that the market price of wheat is high and rising; it may then be that the hectare of land is converted to exclusively wheat production for commercial gain, with a consequent loss in biodiversity. This principle of specialisation constantly appears in attempts to achieve 'economies of scale' and often acts against the interests of biodiversity. For example, average costs often fall when farmers concentrate on the large-scale output of only a few crops, using specialised plant seeds, machinery and other supporting infrastructure. As has already been noted (page 193), over 90 per cent of the world's calorific intake results from just 30 crops, even though thousands of edible plants are potentially available.

Externality issue

The suggestion here is that the market signals may be such that the interests of individual farmers may be best served by less biodiversity than the nation might prefer, and the nation's many interests may be best served by less biodiversity than the global economy might prefer. This is the familiar externality problem, whereby markets fail to provide appropriate signals (via prices) to producers and consumers which would lead to optimal resource allocation.

Figure 8.1 considers both the private costs and benefits to the farmer of growing specialised crops on a given area of land and the social costs and benefits in terms of loss of biodiversity. The horizontal axis measures the amount of biological diversity, i.e. the amount of land devoted to growing diverse crops. The vertical axis shows how the marginal costs and marginal benefits of agricultural production vary with the amount of biological diversity. Three curves are shown in Figure 8.1:

- *Supply* (S) shows that the marginal private cost of agricultural production rises (via less specialisation) as the amount of biodiversity increases so that more land is devoted to growing diverse crops.
- *Private demand* (PD) shows that the *marginal private benefit* from agricultural production falls as the amount of biodiversity increases. Less land devoted to growing specialised crops implies the loss of revenues associated with such commercial farming.
- *Social demand* (SD) shows that the *marginal social benefits* (i.e. benefits to all members of the national or global economy) from any given amount of biodiversity outweigh the benefits to any individual farmer taking the decision on how to use this particular piece of land. In other words, the marginal benefit to society from a given amount of biodiversity on this piece of land is greater than the marginal benefit to the individual farmer. This is because the individual farmer does not take into account the benefits from biodiversity which accrue to all members of the (national or global) society.

Using Figure 8.1, how much biodiversity should there be? The answer depends on the perspective we adopt:

● *Private farmer.* Profit is maximised where the marginal cost of land use exactly equals the marginal private benefit from that land use. This gives the extent of biodiversity B_p.
● *Society.* Social return is maximised with a greater amount of biodiversity, namely B_S, where the marginal cost of land use exactly equals the marginal social benefit from that land use.

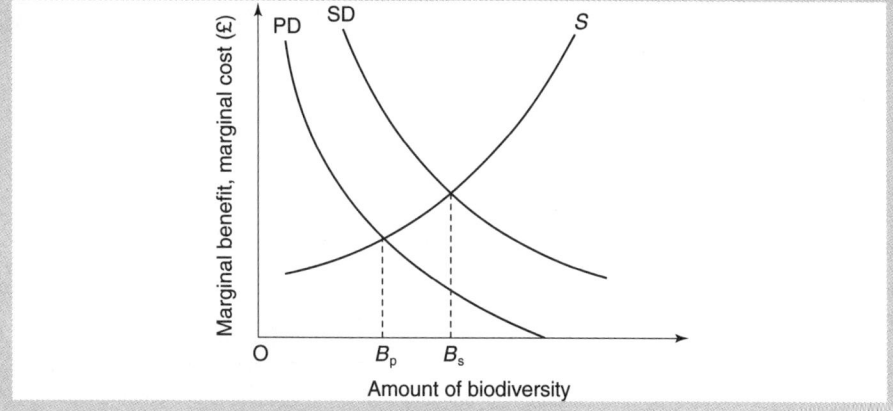

Figure 8.1 How much biodiversity is appropriate?

Policy remedies

As with other situations (e.g. pollution and climate change), the global perspective on biodiversity can arguably only be fully addressed via international co-operation. The United Nations Environment Programme (UNEP) introduced the Convention on Biological Diversity in 1993, with 168 country signatures, setting international standards for biodiversity conservation. More recently the UN Biosafety Protocol has been drawn up in an attempt to regulate attempts to modify the genetic structure of living organisms.

Environmental indicators and the agroecosystems

The OECD has begun to develop *agri-environmental indicators* (AEIs) to measure in a consistent fashion the environmental impacts of policies directed towards the agricultural and rural sectors of national economies. The indicators are being developed within what is called a 'driving force–state–response' (DSR) framework:

● The 'driving forces' are features of agricultural practice which can cause adverse changes in the state of the environment, such as the overuse of chemical inputs, for example. But they may also be beneficial, such as the water-storage capacity of farming systems which can reduce problems of soil erosion and flooding.
● The 'state' refers to the environmental conditions that arise from these driving

forces: their impact on, for example, soil, water, air, biodiversity, natural habitats, landscape and human health.

- The 'responses' refer to the reactions by farmers, consumers, the agri-food industry and government to perceived changes in the state of the environment. Such responses include, for example, the adoption by farmers of pest management practices that reduce the employment of pesticides; the voluntary adoption by the food industry of higher environmental standards; and the use by some governments of payments to farmers to promote environmental benefits in agriculture.

Table 8.2 outlines the agri-environmental indicators being developed in the OECD countries.

Table 8.2 Some agri-environmental indicators

Agri-environmental indicator (AEI)	Environmental features measured
Nutrients	The balance between inputs and outputs of nutrients, such as chemical fertilisers and manure, since (for example) excessive nutrients in the soil can pollute water
Pesticides	The environmental risks of pesticide use on water and soil quality, on wildlife and human health from spraying and the danger of contaminating food products
Water use	Water balances for both surface and groundwater resources so as to assess the efficiency of water use, particularly in irrigation
Land use and conservation	The effect of changes, such as the conversion of wetland for use as farmland, and the role of agriculture in reducing landslides, erosion and flooding
Soil quality	The impact on soil quality, in particular to reveal the risk of erosion
Water quality	The impact on surface and groundwater quality
Greenhouse gases	The contribution of agriculture to climate change through a net balance of the release and accumulation of such gases (expressed in CO_2 equivalents)
Biodiversity	The biodiversity of domesticated species used by agriculture, as well as the impact of agriculture on wild species
Wildlife habitats	Changes in habitat in agricultural areas (grassland, for example), the fragmentation of habitats, and length of contact zone between agricultural and non-agricultural land
Landscape	Changes in agricultural landscapes through, for example, establishing an inventory of physical features
Farm management	The impacts of farm management practices on nutrients, pests, soil, irrigation and the farm as a whole
Farm financial resources	The environmental impact of varying and different sources of financial resources for farms, so as, for instance, to be able to purchase new technologies
Sociocultural aspects	The impact of the sociocultural structure of rural communities on the environment, for example through changes in rural–urban population

● ● ● ● Forest ecosystems

Forests and woodlands have, throughout history, provided humans with shelter, food, fuel, medicines and building materials. In more recent times they have been a vital resource for new goods (such as pharmaceuticals, industrial raw materials and personal care products) and new services (such as recreation and tourism). Forests slow down soil erosion, filter pollutants (e.g. absorbing CO_2), regulate water discharge and act as a key repository for biodiversity.

Table 8.3 outlines the goods and services derived from forests and woodlands and summarises some of the pressures on forest ecosystems worldwide and their causes. Some widely used indicators for forest ecosystems are summarised below:

● Forests cover some 25 per cent of the world's land surface (excluding Greenland and Antarctica).
● Global forest cover has declined by at least 20 per cent since pre-agricultural times.
● Deforestation is continuing today. Forest areas have increased slightly in the high-income industrialised economies since 1980, but have declined by around 10 per cent in the low-income developing economies since 1980.
● Tropical deforestation is most rapid of all, with estimates of 130,000 km^2 per annum.

Table 8.3 Forest ecosystems: goods and services, pressures and causes

Goods and services	Pressures	Causes of pressures
● Timber	● Conversion or fragmentation resulting from agricultural or urban uses	● Population growth
● Fuel wood		● Increasing demand for timber, pulp and other fibre
● Drinking and irrigation water		
● Fodder	● Deforestation resulting in loss of biodiversity, release of stored carbon, air and water pollution	● Government subsidies for timber extraction and logging roads
● Non-timber products (vines, bamboos, leaves, etc.)		
● Food (honey, mushrooms, fruit and other edible plants, game)	● Acid rain from industrial pollution	● Poverty and insecure tenure
● Genetic resources	● Invasion of non-native species	
● Remove air pollutant, emit oxygen	● Overextraction of water for agricultural, urban and industrial uses	● Inadequate valuation of costs of industrial air pollution
● Cycle nutrients		
● Maintain array of watershed functions (infiltration, purification, flow control, soil stabilisation)		
● Maintain biodiversity		
● Sequester atmospheric carbon		
● Moderate weather extremes and impacts		
● Generate soil		
● Provide employment		
● Provide human and wildlife habitat		
● Provide for aesthetic enjoyment and recreation		

Case Study 1.3 has already considered some of the pressures leading to *deforestation* and the adverse environmental consequences which might follow. Here we focus on the more positive contribution to the environment of **afforestation**, not least to the 'sink' debate in pollution abatement (see Chapter 4, page 95).

Afforestation and the environment

As trees decay or are burned, CO_2 is released. As trees grow, they capture ('fix') CO_2. But afforestation reduces net emissions only as long as forests are growing. Once a forest is mature, the emissions from decay just offset the carbon fixing from new growth. If a forest is cut down and the wood used, its carbon will eventually be returned to the atmosphere. To offset emissions from the use of fossil fuels would require continual additions to the forest stock.

Temperate forests capture about 2.7 t of carbon per hectare a year for the first 80 years of their lives. In temperate areas about 400 million ha of growing forests would be required to capture 1 billion of the 3–4 billion t of carbon that accumulate in the atmosphere each year – more than the current forested area of the United States, which is about 300 million ha. In the tropics, where less carbon is captured per hectare, locking up 1 billion t of carbon a year would require about 600 million ha of growing forest, the equivalent of about 75 per cent of the area of the Amazon basin. Intensive forest management that reduced the rotation period could increase the rate of carbon capture per hectare, but only at substantial additional cost.

These calculations show that afforestation is no panacea for greenhouse warming. Nonetheless, afforestation projects that are justified on other environmental and economic grounds can also help to reduce net carbon emissions (see also Chapter 6, page 148).

Freshwater ecosystems

Rivers, lakes and wetlands provide less than 0.01 per cent of the world's available fresh water and occupy only around 1 per cent of the Earth's surface area. Nevertheless they provide a wide variety of goods and services valued at several thousand billion dollars per annum. Table 8.4 outlines these goods and services and summarises some of the pressures on freshwater ecosystems worldwide and their causes.

Some widely used indicators of freshwater ecosystems are summarised below:

- Around 50 per cent of the world's wetlands were lost in the twentieth century via conversion to agriculture and to urban developments.
- Dams have had the largest impact on freshwater ecosystems, with large dams increasing sevenfold in the past 50 years and now enclosing some 14 per cent of the world's runoff.
- Almost 60 per cent of the world's largest rivers are strongly or moderately fragmented by dams, diversions or canals.
- Over 1.5 billion people depend on groundwater as their sole source of drinking water.
- Some 8 million t of fish are caught annually from lakes, rivers and wetlands, a level of production widely regarded as unsustainable.

Table 8.4 Freshwater ecosystems: goods and services, pressures and causes

Goods and services	Pressures	Causes of pressures
• Drinking and irrigation water • Fish • Hydroelectricity • Genetic resources • Buffer water flow (control timing and volume) • Dilute and carry away wastes • Cycle nutrients • Maintain biodiversity • Provide aquatic habitat • Provide transportation corridor • Provide employment • Provide for aesthetic enjoyment and recreation	• Overextraction of water for agricultural, urban and industrial uses • Overexploitation of inland fisheries • Building dams for irrigation, hydropower and flood control • Water pollution from agricultural, urban and industrial uses • Invasion of non-native species	• Population growth • Widespread water scarcity and naturally uneven distribution of water resources • Government subsidies of water use • Inadequate valuation of costs of water pollution • Poverty and insecure tenure • Growing demand for hydropower

Case Study 8.1 looks at preserving water quality via the use of a 'natural' watershed protection plan for New York City as against constructing a water filtration plant.

CASE STUDY 8.1

New York City's watershed protection plan

To safeguard the city's drinking water, in 1997 New York City chose to launch an ambitious environmental protection plan, rather than build an expensive water filtration plant. By protecting its watershed the city would employ nature's ability to purify water while preserving open space and saving money. But as this widely heralded example of watershed protection is implemented, many question whether it will, in fact, deliver all that it promises.

For more than a century, New York City residents have enjoyed drinking water of such purity that it has been dubbed 'the champagne of tap water'. That water – about 1.3 billion gallons per day – flows from an upstate watershed that encompasses 1,970 square miles and three reservoir systems: the Croton, Catskill and Delaware. Until relatively recently, undisturbed soil, trees and wetlands provided natural filtration as the water travelled through the Catskill Mountains and the Hudson River Valley before reaching 9 million residences of the city and its suburbs. The only regular treatment needed was standard chlorination to control water-borne diseases such as cholera and typhoid.

But in the last several decades, development has brought increasing numbers of people and pollutants to the watershed, straining the land's buffering and filtering capacities. More than 30,000 on-site sewage treatment and disposal systems and 41 centralised wastewater treatment plants discharge wastewater into the upstate watersheds. Runoff from roads, dairy farms, lawns and golf courses contains fertilisers, herbicides, pesticides, motor oils and road salts.

The need to attend to the development-pressured upstate watershed became clear in 1990. The US Environmental Protection Agency (EPA) put New York City on notice: protect the source for the Catskill and Delaware reservoirs – the watershed, nature's own treatment plant – or construct and operate a water filtration system. Filtration would cost $3–$8 bn, according to various estimates, potentially doubling the average family residential water bill. By comparison, the City determined that the price tag for watershed protection would be just $1.5 bn, increasing the average water bill of a New York City resident by about 1–2 per cent, or $7 per year.

The EPA's warning was compelled by the 1989 Surface Water Treatment Rule, which requires that surface water supplies for public water systems be filtered unless stringent public health criteria are met and extensive watershed protection strategies minimise risks to the water supply. The rising levels of bacteria and nutrients in the watershed, plus the risks posed by antiquated sewage treatment plants and failing septic systems, put New York City's Catskill and Delaware supplies in danger of violating the rule. The Croton supplies east of the Hudson River were in bigger trouble already: because of that area's greater pollution pressures, filtration was mandated. Even though the Croton system supplies just 10 per cent of the City's water, compared to the 90 per cent that flows from the Delaware and Catskill systems, the cost to build and maintain that plant is still expected to be at least $700 m.

The cost savings from protecting the Delaware and Catskill supplies were clear, but crafting and implementing a major ecosystem protection plan is no small undertaking. Nationwide, less than 2 per cent of municipalities whose drinking water systems are supplied by surface water have demonstrated to the EPA that they can avoid filtration by instituting aggressive watershed protection programmes. The vast majority are far smaller than New York, less populated, and own substantially more of the critical watershed lands. When the protection agreement was rafted, New York city owned just 85,000 acres of the watershed, less than 7 per cent of the total critical area, including the land beneath the reservoirs; another 20 per cent was owned by the state.

With so little watershed land under its direct control, but millions of water users dependent on it, New York City needed to obtain the support of upstate landowners for open space conservation and stronger land user protection. But restrictions such as land acquisitions, limits on where roads and parking lots can be constructed, and strict standards for sewage treatment systems amounted to outsiders threatening local taxpayers' economic viability. Still, after years of contentious negotiations, city, state and federal officials, some environmentalists, and a coalition of upstate towns, villages, and counties forged a 1997 watershed management agreement that convinced the EPA to extend its filtration waiver until 2002.

Perhaps the most crucial element of the programme is the state's approval of New York City's plan to spend $250 m. to acquire and preserve land in the watershed, with priority given to water quality sensitive areas. A local consultation process helps protect the interests of watershed communities. Other plan elements include new watershed regulations, direct city investments in upgrades to wastewater treatment plants to minimise contamination, city funding of voluntary farmer efforts to reduce runoff, and payments to upstate communities to subsidise sound environmental development.

In addition to economic savings, the ecosystem protection programme offers some additional advantages that filtration cannot. It lowers health risks that are present even with filtration – for example, the risk that a sewage plant will malfunction or an incidence of the disinfectant-resistant pathogen *Cryptosporidium* will occur. Land acquisitions and development controls also mean more land for parks, recreation and wildlife habitats.

But whether this dramatic effort will prove to be a bargain remains to be seen. Among the unknowns are the effectiveness of voluntary pollution protection commitments by farmers, and still evolving knowledge of best management practices to control roadway, lawn, farm and other runoff. Environmental organisations are concerned that the negotiated settlement contains serious loopholes in the watershed rules and land-buying requirements. For example, the agreement provides no limits on the number of new sewage treatment plants that can be built in the City's cleanest reservoir basins.

Nor does the agreement specify an absolute acreage requirement that the City must purchase in the watershed, only that the City must solicit the purchase of 350,000 acres. The City projects that this approach could lead to its acquisition of about 120,000 acres, allowing it to increase its holdings to 17 per cent of the critical land area in the next 10 years. However, the City's solicitation efforts might yield far less land, since the plan relies on the co-operation of upstate residents – and even 17 per cent ownership gives the City limited watershed control. Another problem is that the plan sets criteria for types of land to be acquired but no assurance that the 'best' lands from the perspective of water quality will be purchased, since land is obtained on a willing buyer/seller basis. From the perspective of the Natural Resources Defense Council, the plan may allow too much development to take place on sensitive watershed lands and the scientific aspects of water management were given insufficient attention by negotiators under pressure to craft a politically acceptable plan. Other concerns include inadequate requirements for buffer zones of vegetation where discharge of pollutants, and development, cannot take place, and the agreement's failure to emphasise pollution prevention as much as pollution control.

Only years of extensive water quality monitoring will prove whether the watershed protection programme is sufficient to protect public health. At the moment, the water is still deemed safe to drink, but some still think filtration ultimately will be required.

Questions

1 Comment on the environmental benefits and costs of the watershed protection plan as against the use of a filtration plan.

2 What factors might ultimately determine whether the plan can be successfully implemented?

Other ecosystems can be identified and studied, such as coastal and grassland ecosystems. However, our attention now turns to assessing the natural resource situation as regards energy supplies, fossil and other fuels and mineral resources.

● ● ● ● Energy and mineral resources

Energy

Energy is the lifeblood of society because it drives all human activities. It is the means of providing heat, light and movement. All energy (except geothermal energy) is derived from the sun. During the twentieth century the rate of worldwide energy use increased almost tenfold, from around 1 trillion W in 1900 to over 10 trillion W in 2001. In terms of energy use per person, this corresponds to a fourfold rise from some 0.5 kW per person per year in 1900 to around 2.0 kW per person per year in 2001. The most rapid growth in energy demand has been for electricity supply and transport purposes, which now account for some 25 and 17 per cent of global final energy consumption. The association between economic development (e.g. rise in GNP per head) and increased demands for energy are explored further in Chapter 12 (pages 284–9).

Energy resources

The sources of energy supply to meet this growing demand have changed substantially over time. Whereas over 75 per cent of primary energy came from fossil fuels in 1930 (especially coal), that figure had risen to 90 per cent from fossil fuels in 2001. Table 8.5 breaks down the current sources of global primary energy supply.

Non-renewable energy resources are resources which have been built up over geological time and which take so long to form that they cannot be replaced in the foreseeable future. Using such resources is therefore a once-for-all activity involving 'opportunity cost', i.e. the sacrifice of an alternative use for these finite resources by this or future generations.

Of course new sources of minerals and fossil fuels may be discovered, especially when high prices induce more extensive exploration. High prices may also result in some known (existing) resources now becoming commercially viable. Demand

Table 8.5 Sources of global primary energy

Energy source	Share of global primary energy supply (%)
Oil	40
Solid fuels (including coal)	28
Gas	21
Nuclear	7
HEP	3
Other renewables	1

factors cannot therefore be separated entirely from the supply of non-renewable resources.

Fossil fuels come into this category, accounting for some 90 per cent of the global use of energy. Fossil fuels include oil, natural gas and coal. They also include peat, tar sands and oil shales.

Renewable energy resources may be used without any concern as to their depletion because they are continually available for use. Solar, wind and wave power are examples, as is hydroelectric power (HEP) generated by the force of falling water. Most HEP is generated in North America and Europe from dams constructed in the mountains. It is also possible to obtain HEP from multi-purpose schemes which are primarily designed to improve navigation on major rivers. Such barrages exist in the Rhine gorge and on the rivers Neckar, Main and Moselle in western Germany. In the developing world major barrages on rivers such as the Niger (Kanji), Volta (Akosombo) and Nile (Aswan) make a significant contribution to national energy needs. HEP is popular because it is cheaper than either oil- or coal-fired power. Tidal power barrages are another renewable energy resource but are few in number because of the high capital costs for their construction.

Box 8.2 outlines some of the terminology often used to describe the various types of energy.

BOX 8.2

Types of energy

- *Electromagnetic energy* is that derived from the sun, which has been stored in fossil fuels and which is received daily into the natural system.
- *Kinetic energy* is that lost as heat and friction by running water and waves.
- *Potential energy* is the energy stored in an object before it is released, e.g. before a wave breaks.
- *Nuclear energy* is a form of potential energy contained in the nucleus of an atom.
- *Geothermal energy* is contained in the Earth's interior and only usable when it comes near to the Earth's surface as geysers or hot springs.

Primary energy sources are the original sources of energy before conversion for human use. They are measured either in terms of their calorific value or in tonnes of coal equivalent. Coal, natural gas, oil, the sun, water, timber and peat are all primary energy sources.

Secondary energy sources are the sources of energy available after some form of conversion for human use. Electricity is the major secondary energy source and can be derived from thermal, oil, gas, HEP and nuclear power stations.

Energy and the environment

The impact of fossil fuels on greenhouse gas emissions and climate change has already been considered in Chapter 7. The use of fossil fuels has also contributed to other aspects of air pollution, with the emission of sulphur dioxide, nitrogen oxides, CO_2 and various particulates (see Chapter 6) damaging human health. For example, exposure in Britain over short periods to these emissions are estimated to have contributed to 24,000 deaths and 24,000 hospital admissions each year

(Department of Health, 1998). In addition, the deposition of acid sulphate and nitrate as 'acid rain' (see Chapter 6, page 141) has adversely affected lakes, forests and buildings thousands of kilometres from the source of the gaseous emissions.

Policy remedies

Two broad policy approaches have been suggested for combating these adverse environmental impacts of burning fossil fuels, particularly as regards emissions of CO_2:

- Managing aspects of the carbon cycle
- Changing the ways in which energy is obtained and used

These are considered in more detail in Chapter 6 (page 147). However, one particular aspect of the second of these policy approaches is considered here, namely the move towards renewable sources of energy. Case Study 8.2 looks at the potential in the UK for replacing non-renewable by renewable resources in the particular context of electricity production.

CASE STUDY 8.2

Potential of renewable resources in electricity generation

The Energy Technology Support Unit (ETSU) has tried to identify the amount of electricity that could be obtained from the 10 most significant *renewable sources* of energy in the UK and its cost. In 2001 the UK required some 41 GW of electricity.

- 'Accessible resource' refers to the amount of annual energy supply physically available from that renewable. To find 'accessible resource' we subtract from the 'feasible resource' those resources located in areas deemed environmentally unsuitable.
- 'Total cost-effective resource' refers to the annual rate at which electricity could be generated from that renewable at a cost of less than 7 p/kWh in 2025 (assuming a discount rate of 8 per cent).

'Resource-cost curves' were calculated for each renewable energy source to assess how much annual supply could be obtained from each renewable at a given date for a given cost. The middle column of Table 8.6 tells us the estimate (from these curves) for a cost of 7 p/kWh in 2025, i.e. for a cost that is currently deemed to be 'not excessive'. Of course diminishing returns is assumed to apply to each renewable, so that some part of this 'total cost-effective' resource could be provided for less than 7 p/kWh. The final column gives us the estimate for the cost below which at least 90 per cent of this 'total cost-effective' resource could be supplied in 2025.

Of course, estimates of the types shown in Table 8.6 are built on many assumptions, both as to supply conditions (e.g. technological change) and demand considerations. The latter is clearly implicit in any value regarded as 'not excessive' (e.g. 7 p/kWh in 2025). The following discussion of onshore wind power brings out some of the assumptions underlying Table 8.6.

Table 8.6 Renewable energy resources and electricity supply

Source	Accessible resource (annual average rate of supply, GW)	Total cost-effective resource (annual average rate of supply, GW)	Cost below which at least 90% of cost-effective resource available (p/kWh)
Non-carbon-based sources			
Onshore wind power	36	6.5	3.5
Offshore wind power	468	11.4	3.0
Photovoltaics	30	< 0.1	7.0
Small hydro	n/a	0.3	7.0
Alternative carbon-based sources			
Energy crops	n/a	3.7	4.0
Agricultural and forestry waste	n/a	2.4	5.0
Municipal solid waste	1.5	0.8	5.0
Landfill gas	n/a	0.9	3.0
Technologies being developed			
Wave power	95	3.7	4.0
Tidal stream	4.1	0.25	6.5

Source: Royal Commission on Environmental Pollution Report (2000).

Assessing the resource onshore wind power

ETSU first estimated the feasible *accessible resource* by modelling wind speeds; making assumptions about the characteristics of wind turbines (for example, their capacity and height); eliminating types of land cover deemed unsuitable for wind farms; and making assumptions about the placing of turbines. Areas of land designated at national level to protect the environment were then excluded in order to obtain the accessible resource; this was estimated to be capable of producing an average output of 36 GW (more than the average rate of UK electricity demand). The *maximum practicable resource*, however, is much less than that. Assumptions about the acceptable size and spacing of wind farms reduce considerably the resource regarded as being available; and limitations imposed by the UK electricity networks reduce it even further, to an average output of less than 1 GW. The resource regarded as being available in 2025 without excessive cost, is an average output of 6.5 GW (Table 8.6). The rate at which turbines could be manufactured and installed was evaluated, but would not be a constraint in the circumstances considered.

Questions

What effect on the estimate for *onshore wind power* in Table 8.6 might result from each of the following?

1 More rapid progress in developing efficient turbines for converting wind power into electricity.

2 Climate change forecasts suggesting progressively less windy conditions in the UK.

3 An increase in the assumed discount rate to 2025 from 8 to 15 per cent.

4 Increased consumer resistance to the environmental implications of using fossil fuels.

Mineral resources

Minerals are inorganic solid substances usually found in the ground. A distinction is sometimes made between *fuel minerals* and *non-fuel minerals*. We have already covered the former (e.g. fossil fuels).

Non-fuel minerals can be further subdivided into metals and industrial minerals:

● *Metals*: include *ores* such as iron, nickel and bauxite and precious metals such as silver.
● *Industrial minerals*: include *aggregates* such as crushed rock, sand and gravel, *fertiliser minerals* such as phosphate and potash, *cement* and *stone*. Minerals are exclusively *non-renewable* resources since any depletion of the existing stock cannot be replaced in the foreseeable future.

Minerals and the environment

Many of the environmental implications of mineral use relate to the processes of extraction and transportation, together with their implications for the landscape and pollution emissions. For example, the huge OK Tedi copper mine in Papua New Guinea is estimated to dump 80,000 t per day of untreated residuals into the OK Tedi River, destroying much of the river's aquatic wildlife and adversely affecting the subsistence agriculture and lifestyle of the local Wopkaimin people (Da Rosa and Lyon, 1998).

Conservation and recycling

To some extent we have already touched on the idea of conservation in our earlier discussion of biodiversity (page 193). More generally *conservation* refers to ensuring the continued availability of a non-renewable resource by making more efficient use of it. This can also bring into play the associated idea of *recycling*, which involves the reuse of non-renewable resources. The idea of *substitution* may also be involved, as in the switch from a non-renewable to a renewable resource (see Case Study 8.2) or from a scarce to a less scarce non-renewable resource.

Conservation

Useful examples of conservation can be found in attempts to use non-renewable energy sources more efficiently. For example, technological improvements have increased the efficiency of plants generating electricity from fossil fuels. Such efficiency gains are all the more important when we remember that some 25 per cent of global final energy consumption stems from electricity generation.

In the case of a coal-fired electricity generation plant, the average efficiency is around 40 per cent (where 'efficiency' is the ratio of useful energy output – here electricity – to thermal input in the form of chemical energy from burning the fuel). However, if the coal is first gasified, then it can be used in a combined cycle plant which has an average 'efficiency' of 42 per cent. By substituting the fossil fuel of gas for coal, electricity can be generated in a combined cycle gas turbine with an average 'efficiency' as high as 52 per cent (Royal Commission on Environmental Pollution, 2000).

Clearly there is considerable potential for increasing the efficiency of energy use and thereby conserving scarce fossil fuel resources by technological change, as is the case for many other types of non-renewable resource.

Case Study 8.3 suggests, however, that conservation is not always cost free! It looks at attempts by regulatory agencies in the USA to conserve the use of energy, given the shortages experienced there over the past few years. These have resulted in households and businesses in some parts of the USA such as California facing 'blackouts' as overstretched electricity suppliers have run out of power.

CASE STUDY 8.3

Aluminium smelting faces meltdown in north-west USA

From the *Financial Times*, April 2001

The Bonneville Power Administration (BPA), the US federal agency responsible for providing low-cost power to customers in the north-western USA, appears to be in danger of killing the US aluminium smelting industry it helped to create more than 60 years ago.

In April 2001, Steve Wright, the BPA's acting administrator, presented the region's smelters – which account for one-quarter of total North American smelting capacity – with an unpalatable choice. Either they agreed not to take power from the BPA for two years from October 2001, when their new contracts start, or they faced trebled or quadrupled power prices under the new contracts. Since the smelters would not be able to operate economically at such prices, either suggestion in effect means that the smelters will be out of business for two and a half years.

Mr Wright said the BPA did not intend to drive the smelters from their traditional base in the region – but analysts fear that this may be the result. The continuing power crisis on the US west coast has meant that over the past year, roughly 90 per cent of the 1.6 million t a year smelting capacity in the north-west has been closed down, on a 'temporary' basis. The rising cost of power on the free market – which has surged from $25 MWh to $300 – forced them to close some potlines. Moreover, the fact that the aluminium groups could make more money by reselling their low-cost BPA power than by using it to produce metal tempted them to close most of the remainder.

As the power crisis has tightened, the terms proposed by the BPA for the smelters' new five-year contracts have got steadily worse. In autumn 2000, the BPA said it would cut the quantity of power available to 1,500 MW – about half the smelters' total requirements – and increase the price by around a third. Then in January 2001 it said the price increase would be around 60 per cent overall, and possibly as much as 95 per cent in the first year of the new contracts. Now the agency is talking of price increases of about 200–300 per cent, which suggests rates of between $70 and $90/MWh. CRU, the independent analysts, has calculated that most smelters could not operate economically at above $40/MWh.

The north-west's power problems were triggered by the 2000 crisis in California, as shortages and ensuing high wholesale prices in the south sucked in power from other states. But they have been exacerbated by the unusually low levels of winter rain and snow in the region, which has left reservoir levels unusually low.

The BPA generates around 3,000 MW less power than the 11,000 MW its customers want to buy. It can either plug the gap by buying in the free-market power – thus raising the cost of its own – or persuade its customers to cut their demands.

Its strategy is to put the utilities, which supply individuals and small businesses, first. In April 2001, the agency asked the large utilities to cut usage by 5–10 per cent. The aluminium companies, however, are being asked to go off-line for two years, saving the whole of the 1,500 MW provisionally allotted to them. In effect, they are being told that power prices will be available, as long as they do not try to buy any.

The situation after October 2001 will be substantially worse for the smelters than it has been so far, because they will not be able to profit by reselling BPA power. From that time the BPA's proposed compensation amounts to little more than giving the aluminium companies enough money to pay their laid-off workers.

In the long term, the BPA's strategy is to wean the smelters off BPA power altogether and encourage them to build alternative power sources. Golden Northwest, which has two smelters in the area, recently agreed a $1.6 m. deal with the BPA under which the agency would build and operate a new gas-fired turbine plant. McCook Metals has acquired a smelter from Alcoa and shut it down while it makes it more energy-efficient and develops a new turbine energy plant with Enron.

Assuming that enough additional energy capacity is built, west coast power prices could ease by 2003. But analysts say that does not necessarily mean that aluminium companies will reopen all their idle capacity.

Source: Financial Times, 19th April 2001

Questions

1 Why is the BPA attempting to conserve energy supplies?

2 What policy instruments is the BPA adopting?

3 Comment on the benefits and costs of the BPA's conservation strategy.

Recycling

It was noted in our earlier discussion (page 191) of Newton's first law of thermodynamics that matter and energy cannot be created. It is therefore important to use only the minimum necessary amount of existing materials and energy to achieve any given output target. Recycling can help in this respect. For instance, if we recycle a tonne of crushed glass we can make a saving of around 25 per cent in terms of the oil and raw materials originally used to make that glass. Again, all metal production uses a lot of energy, particularly aluminium production. However, if we recycle aluminium, then we save 95 per cent of the energy that would otherwise be used to make the same amount of new aluminium. It is estimated that some 77 per cent by weight of the materials used in new car manufacture are now recycled in the UK. Steps have been taken to design items in a way that facilitates recycling; for example, BMW has designed cars for 90 per cent recyclability by weight.

The 'second law of thermodynamics' is also relevant to recycling in that it states that although energy can be turned from one form into another, in a series of energy changes it tends to become 'degraded' into less useful forms. Although it is impossible to achieve a 100 per cent return of waste products to the resource flow, recycling does allow *some* level of return to be achieved.

Types of recycling

Turner *et al.* (1994) identifies five types of *recycling flow* within an economic system, as can be seen in Figure 8.2. The numbers of the various recycled residual flows are indicated in the diagram.

1 *Home scrap flow*: here the recycled (secondary) materials stay within the reprocessing plant.
2 *Prompt scrap flow*: here some external intermediation is involved in collecting scrap materials from other processing plants and redirecting them back into basic processing activities.
3 *Commercial scrap flow*: here still more external intermediation is involved with specialist firms recycling packaging waste materials used extensively in retail/wholesale activities.
4 *Post-consumer scrap*: here recycling occurs from the extensive wastes of households and small businesses. Local authorities are often actively involved in providing facilities for collection of such wastes and their reclassification into potentially recyclable units, though specialist firms may undertake the actual recycling itself.
5 *Re-use*: here the relatively small number of items which can be reused (e.g. returnable bottles) are involved.

For each of the five residual flows, an **activity recycling rate** (ARR) can be established, where

$$\text{ARR} = \frac{\text{Tonnage recycled annually}}{\text{Annual tonnage availabe for recycling}}$$

Turner *et al.* suggest that four key factors will influence the activity recycling rates for each residuals flow.

- *Mass* (volume of recyclable materials)
- *Homogeneity* (consistency of recyclable materials, i.e. 'grade')
- *Contamination* (extent to which the recyclable materials are mixed with other materials)
- *Location* (number of points at which the materials are first discarded as waste)

The recorded ARRs are typically highest for residual flows (1) and (2) and to a lesser extent (3). We might usefully compare the likely ARRs for residual flows (1) 'home scrap' and (4) 'post-consumer scrap' on this basis. Residuals flow (1) is characterised by large mass, high degree of homogeneity, low contamination and often a single location. In contrast, residuals flow (4) is characterised by small mass, low degree of homogeneity, high contamination and multiple locations.

Clearly this analysis would suggest that the profitability of recycling activities is likely to be higher for residual flow (1), (2) and (3) than for residual flow (4). Put another way, there may be more need for intervention in the market by governments if ARRs are to be raised for residual flow (4). Should social cost/benefit analysts suggest that there are considerable net benefits from raising ARR in residual

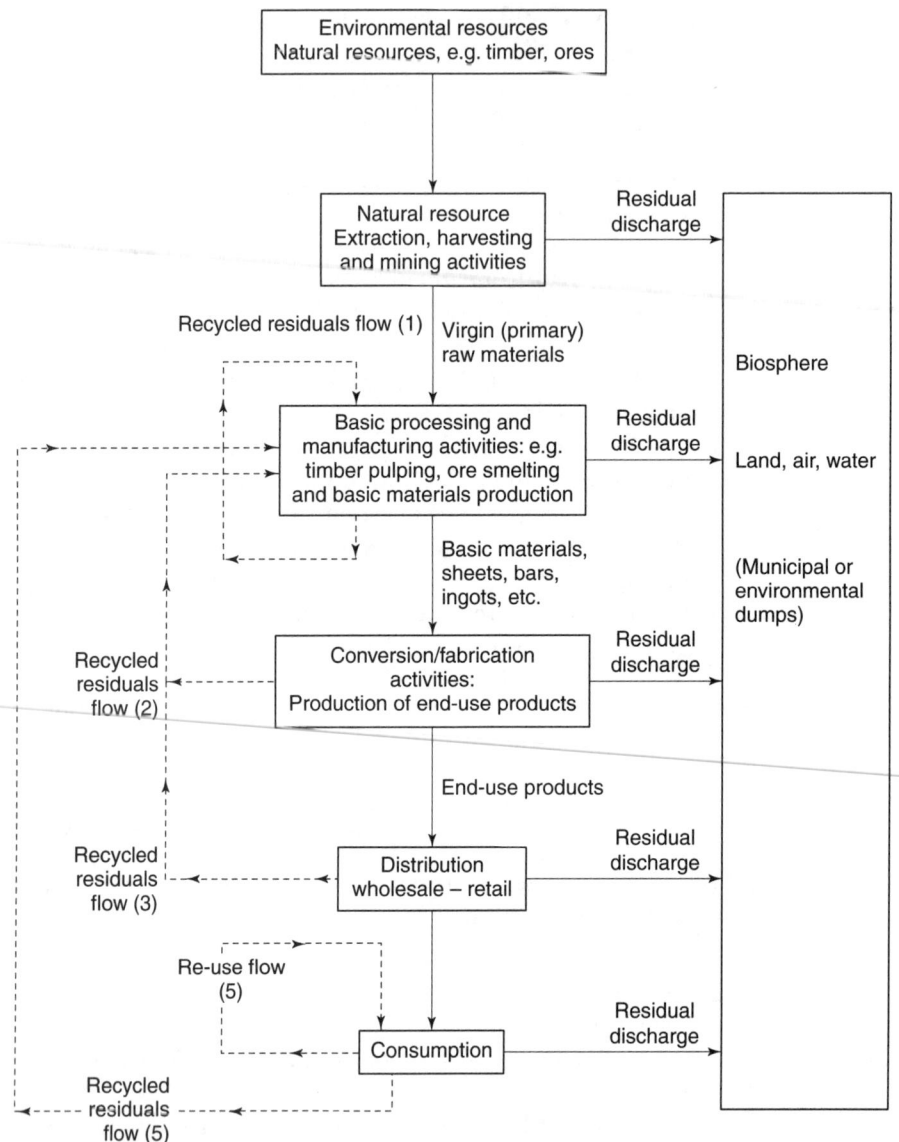

Figure 8.2 Recycling in a materials and residuals flow chart

flow (4), then appropriate interventionist policies will take on a higher environmental priority. Indeed recorded ARRs in residual flow (4) are often below 10 per cent which, given the huge volumes of this flow, would suggest considerable scope for additional recycling.

Of course market factors will play a part in the viability of all recycling activities. For example, the extent of any government subsidy needed to support intervention in residual flow (4) will depend on the market price available for the various recycled materials. Where residual flows are not recycled then they must be disposed of. Case Study 6.3 (page 152) considers different types of disposal mechanisms for solid wastes in the context of the recently established landfill tax.

●●●● Population and the environment

Each year the world population grows by some 80 million people, placing greater pressures on ecosystems and other resources. Although global fertility rates have fallen from 5.0 births per woman in the 1950s to around 2.7 in 2001, the population will continue to grow over the next 70 years or so. This is partly because of the large numbers (over 1.5 billion people) in the prime reproductive age of 15–29 years and the large numbers of young people still to join that cohort (1.9 billion people under 15 years) and partly because of the significant falls in the global mortality rate from around 20 deaths per year per thousand people in the 1950s to less than 10 today.

The world population is currently just over 6 billion people and is projected to peak at 9 billion around 2070, before falling back to 8.4 billion in 2100 (IIASA, 2001). Over the past 40 years the world population has more than doubled, so these projections point to a significant slowing in its rate of growth and even an absolute fall by the end of the century.

Despite continued projected falls in mortality rates and increases in life expectancies, falls in the birth rate are expected to more than offset these factors to give a stable, then declining world population after 2070. It is expected that, even in the developing economies (see Chapter 12), the continued rise in real income per head will reduce birth rates below the 2.1 children per woman required to keep a population stable, as has already happened in many high-income developed economies.

Some indicators of projected population changes include the following:

- World population is expected to peak at 9 billion in 2070, falling to 8.4 billion in 2100.
- North America (USA and Canada) will experience a continued growth of population from 314 million today to 404 million in 2100, mainly because of the tendency of first-generation immigrant families to have higher birth rates. Latin America will also grow from 515 million today to 934 million in 2100.
- Africa, despite disease, war and hunger, is expected to grow from 784 million today to 1.8 billion in 2100. Over one in five Africans will be over 60 in 2100, more than in the EU today.
- The China region (China, Hong Kong + five smaller neighbouring nations) will see its population fall from 1.4 billion today to 1.25 billion in 2100, mainly because of its education and one-child programme.
- India will replace China as the world's most populous nation by 2020.
- Europe (including Turkey and the former Soviet Union west of the Urals) will see its population fall from 817 million today to 607 million in 2100, declining from 13 per cent of the world's population to only 7 per cent over this period.
- Of today's world population, 10 per cent is over 60 years; this will rise to around 33 per cent in 2100.
- In 1950, Europeans outnumbered Africans by three to one; by 2100 Africans will outnumber Europeans by three to one.

Box 8.3 compares these population projections with those envisaged over 170 years ago by Thomas Malthus and by others in more recent times.

> **BOX 8.3**
>
> ### Population and natural resources
>
> Thomas Malthus (1766–1834) claimed that the human population would, left unchecked, grow exponentially (in a *geometric progression*). However, food production would grow only linearly (in an *arithmetic progression*), restricted by the need to bring new, less productive land into cultivation (an earlier forerunner of the theory of diminishing returns). Population would therefore double every 25 years and food production would be unable to keep pace. Periodic famines and high infant mortality, together with occasional wars, were seen by Malthus as the most likely 'checks' to population explosion. Malthus noted that even in nineteenth-century Britain, food production was already falling short of population growth, as evidenced by the high price of bread and increasing public expenditure on relief of the poor.
>
> A not dissimilar picture was portrayed by Dr Ehrlich in his best-selling book of 1968, *The Population Bomb*. He predicted that 'the battle to feed humanity is over. In the course of the 1970s the world will experience starvation of tragic proportions – hundreds of millions of people will starve to death.'
>
> As Bjørn Lomborg (2001) points out, these projections as to the inability of the world's resources to support an expanding population have proved far from the mark. According to the United Nations, agricultural production in the developing world has increased by 52 per cent per person since 1961. The daily food intake in poor countries has increased from 1,932 calories, barely enough for survival, in 1961 to over 2,650 calories in 1998 and is expected to rise to 3,020 by 2030. Likewise, the proportion of people in developing countries who are starving has dropped from 45 per cent in 1949 to 18 per cent today, and is expected to decline even further to 12 per cent in 2010 and just 6 per cent in 2030. Food, in other words, is becoming not scarcer but even more abundant. This is reflected in its price. Since 1800 food prices have decreased by more than 90 per cent and in 2000, according to the World Bank, food prices were lower than ever before.
>
> Both Malthus and Ehrlich failed to perceive that population growth has turned out to have an internal check: as people grow richer and healthier, they have smaller families. Indeed, the growth rate of the human population reached its peak of more than 2 per cent a year in the early 1960s. The rate of increase has been declining ever since. It is now 1.26 per cent and is expected to fall to 0.46 per cent in 2050. Both the United Nations and IIASA have estimated that most of the world's population growth will be over by 2100, with the population stabilising at just below 11 billion (UN) or around 9 billion (IIASA).
>
> Malthus and Ehrlich also failed to take account of developments in agricultural technology. These have squeezed more and more food out of each hectare of land. It is this application of technology and human ingenuity that has boosted food production, not merely in line with, but ahead of, population growth. It has also, incidentally, reduced the need to take new land into cultivation, thus reducing the pressure on biodiversity.

Optimum population

What exactly constitutes the 'optimum (best possible) population' depends on the perspective we adopt. Figure 8.3 reflects a commonly held view of the **optimum population,** namely that number which maximises output (GDP) per capita within the current technological and socio-economic constraints of the area. 'Overpopulation' then occurs where the resources are unable to sustain a population at the existing living standard without a reduction in that population. 'Underpopulation' occurs where an increase in population would result in the more effective use of resources which would raise living standards.

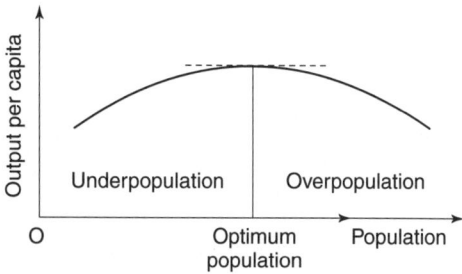

Figure 8.3 The relationship between population and output

This same idea is sometimes expressed in more ecological terms, namely *optimum carrying capacity*. Here the focus is on the ability of an area to support a population in such a way that the natural resources are fully utilised.

Whatever perspective is adopted, identifying optimum levels of population is fraught with difficulty:

- Values of outputs from different sectors of economic activities are often difficult to estimate (e.g. subsistence agriculture may have no market price).
- 'Quality of life' may not be fully reflected by economic indicators such as GDP per head.
- The resource base of geographical areas is constantly changing.
- The technical capabilities for utilising any resource base are constantly changing.

This type of debate brings into play the issue of **'sustainability'** (Chapters 7 and 12), this time in the particular context of population size. It could also be extended to involve broader indicators of standard of living than GDP per head. For example the optimum population might involve maximising the score for the Human Development Index, which includes socio-economic indicators such as life expectancy, educational attainment, etc. Chapter 12 on the developing economies gives a more detailed account of why such broader indicators may help give a more accurate picture of the true quality of life when making international comparisons (Chapter 12, page 299).

Human development index (HDI) classification

An interesting issue is whether the conventional GNP per capita figure can be merged with 'quality of life' indicators to give an overall index of economic well-being. A first step in this direction has in fact been made with the publication of the United Nations' *Human Development Index* (HDI). In Table 8.7 we present data for 17 countries, some developing and some developed. We also show the rank of these countries (out of 162 countries) in terms of real GNP per head using purchasing power parities (PPP$) and in terms of the HDI, which is a weighted average of three indicators:

- *Standard of living*, as measured by real GNP per capita (PPP$). Column 2 in Table 8.7.
- *Life expectancy at birth*, in years. Column 3 in Table 8.7.

- *Educational attainment*, as measured by a weighted average of adult literacy (two-thirds weight) and enrolment ratio (one-third weight). Columns 4 and 5 respectively in Table 8.7.

Each of these three indicators is then expressed in index form, with a scale set between a minimum value (index = 0) and a maximum value (index = 1) for each indicator:

- *Standard of living*: $100 real GNP per capita (PPP$) is the minimum value (index = 0) and $40,000 is the maximum value (index = 1).
- *Life expectancy at birth*: 25 years is the minimum value (index = 0) and 85 years is the maximum value (index = 1).
- *Educational attainment*: 0 per cent for both adult literacy and enrolment ratios are the minimum values used for calculating the weighted average (index = 0) and 100 per cent for both adult literacy and enrolment ratios are the maximum values used for calculating the weighted average (index = 1).

An index is then calculated for each of these three indicators, and the average of these three index numbers is then calculated, as shown for each country in column 6 of Table 8.7. This *average* of the three separate index numbers is the HDI.

Table 8.7 Rankings of countries by various indicators including HDI

	1 GNP per head ($) (1999)	2 Real GNP per head (PPP$) (1999)	3 Life expectancy at birth (years) (1999)	4 Adult literacy rate (%) (1999)	5 Enrolment ratio[1] (%) (1999)	6 Human Development Index (HDI) (1999)	7 Rank by real GNP per head (PPP$)	8 Rank by HDI
Mozambique	210	861	40	43	23	0.323	146	157
Ethiopia	100	628	44	37	27	0.321	158	158
Nigeria	300	853	52	63	45	0.455	147	136
Uganda	320	1,167	43	66	45	0.435	137	141
India	165	2,248	63	57	56	0.571	115	115
Indonesia	680	2,857	66	87	65	0.677	105	102
Philippines	1,050	3,805	69	95	82	0.749	91	70
Poland	3,900	8,450	73	100	84	0.828	49	38
Brazil	4,570	7,037	68	85	80	0.750	57	69
Uruguay	6,180	8,879	74	98	79	0.828	46	37
Greece	11,650	15,414	78	97	81	0.881	33	23
UK	21,400	22,043	78	99	100	0.923	19	14
Finland	24,110	23,096	77	99	100	0.925	15	10
Germany	25,850	23,742	78	99	94	0.921	14	17
USA	29,340	31,872	77	99	95	0.934	2	6
Japan	32,380	24,898	81	99	82	0.928	11	9
Switzerland	40,080	27,171	79	99	84	0.924	5	11

Note: [1]Percentage of population at Levels 1, 2 and 3 (combined) of OECD Literacy Survey.
Sources: Adapted from Human Development Report (2001); UN: World Development Report (2001); World Bank.

The closer to 1 is the value of the HDI, the closer the country is to achieving the maximum values defined for each of the three indicators.

From columns 7 and 8 of Table 8.7 we can see that the rankings of the countries (in order from 1 to 162) do vary with the type of indicator used. In other words, using a GNP per head indicator, even adjusted for purchasing power parities, gives a different ranking for countries than using the HDI which brings quality of life aspects into the equation.

The HDI, by bringing together both economic and quality of life indicators, suggests a greater degree of underdevelopment for some countries than is indicated by economic data alone. For example, Mozambique is 146th out of 162 countries when the real GNP per head data is used for ranking (column 7), but falls a further 11 places to 157th when the HDI is used for ranking (column 8). For Mozambique it would seem that the relatively disappointing enrolment ratio into education has helped depress the 'education' index which, together with a relatively low life expectancy, has given it a still lower ranking in terms of the overall HDI. On the other hand, the HDI suggests a smaller degree of underdevelopment for some countries than is indicated by economic data alone. For example, Uruguay is 46th out of 162 countries when the real GNP per head data is used for ranking (column 7), but rises by 11 places to 37th when the HDI is used for ranking (column 8). For Uruguay it would seem that the relatively high adult literacy ratio has helped increase the 'education' index which, together with encouraging life expectancy data, has raised the overall HDI.

Although only in their infancy, it may be that classifications of countries based on indices such as the HDI which bring together both economic and quality of life data, may give a more accurate picture of the level of development of the country and the relative well-being of its population.

> **Now try the self-check questions for this chapter or the companion website**
> **www.booksites.net/ison**
> **You will also find up-to-date facts and case materials.**

Key terms

Activity recycling rate (ARR) The proportion of the potentially recyclable total waste of a given type which is actually recycled

Afforestation Replenishing forests by new planting

Biodiversity The number, variety and variability of living organisms

Carrying capacity Output level below which an ecosystem can replenish itself and be self-sustaining. Sometimes expressed in terms of population level (see Chapter 12)

Ecosystem Community of species that interact with each other in the physical setting in which they live

Eutrophication Nutrient enrichment of rivers, lakes and groundwater, mainly by nitrates/phosphates in artificial fertilisers

First law of thermodynamics Finite, non-replenishable, set of resources available

Fossil fuels Oil, natural gas and coal; non-renewable energy resource

Intensification Often applied to agricultural practices which seek to increase output per unit area by increased application of herbicides, pesticides, fertilisers, etc.

Non-renewable energy Resources which are finite; includes the fossil fuels

Optimum population That number which maximises output per capita within the current technological and socio-economic constraints of the area

Renewable energy Resources which are continually available for use

References and further reading

Bowers, J. (1997) *Sustainability and Environmental Economics*, Longman, Harlow, especially Chapters 7–9 and 13–14.

Da Rosa, C. and Lyon, J. (1998) *Golden Dreams, Poisoned Streams: How Reckless Mining Pollutes America's Waters and How we can Stop it*, Mineral Policy Center, Washington, DC.

Department of Health (1998) Committee on the Medical Effects of Air Pollutants, *Quantification of the Effects of Air Pollution on Health in the UK*, The Stationery Office.

FAO (2000) Food and Agricultural Organisation databases available online at *http://apps.fao.org/*.

Field, B.C. (1997) *Environmental Economics: An Introduction*, McGraw-Hill, especially Chapter 2.

Gilpin, A. (2000) *Environmental Economics: A Critical Overview*, Wiley, especially Chapters 8 and 10.

Human Development Report (2001) *Making New Technologies Work for Human Development*, OUP.

IIASA (2001) 'International Institute for Applied Systems Analysis', Washington D.C.

Lomborg, B. (2000) 'The truth about the environment', *The Economist*, August 4–10.

Maddison, D. and Pearce, D. (1996) *Blueprint 5: The True Costs of Road Transport*, Earthscan Publications Ltd.

Newbery, D.M. (1995) 'Economic Effects of Transport', *Economic Journal*, 105, Sept.

PAGE (2000) 'Pilot Analysis of Global Ecosystems' in *World Resources 2000–2001: People and Ecosystems*, World Resources Institute, Washington DC.

Royal Commission on Environmental Pollution (2000) 22nd Report, *Energy – the Changing Climate*, Cm 4749.

Swanson, T. (2001) 'The economics of biodiversity', *Economic Review*, 18, 4.

Turner, R.K., Pearce, D. and Bateman, I. (1994) *Environmental Economics*, FT/Prentice Hall, Harlow.

World Development Report (2001) *Entering the 21st Century*, OUP.

Useful websites

Food and Agricultural Organisation
OPEC
World Bank
World Health Organisation
United Nations
Friends of the Earth

Jubilee 2000
Oxfam
European Bank for Reconstruction and Development (EBRD)
World Trade Organisation (WTO)
United Nations Development Program

See also:
UNICEF
MAFF

9

Transport and the environment

While there is no doubt that an efficient transport sector is important for economic growth and the quality of life, it is also the case that transport generates a number of serious environmental impacts not least in terms of air pollution and its effect on health, climate change and social aspects such as noise and accidents. The transport of passengers and freight can take a number of forms, most notably road, rail and air, and while there is increasing concern about the environmental effects of aviation (dealt with briefly in this chapter) it is road transport and the motor vehicle in particular which creates the most severe problems. This chapter will therefore concentrate on road transport, dealing with the changes in transport modes, their estimated environmental costs, the economic context for transport and the possible policy options available. The latter include a variety of market- and non-market-based policy instruments.

Changes in the mode of transport

In 1988 some 22,152,000 motor vehicles were licensed in Great Britain, but by 2000 the number had risen to over 27 million, an increase of over 20 per cent in little more than a decade. In addition there has been an increase of around 14 per cent in passenger kilometres travelled, made up predominantly by the private car. Table 9.1 gives a summary of passenger travel by mode over that period. As can be seen, the car dominates passenger transport in Great Britain, accounting for some 85 per cent of all travel and increasing by around 16 per cent between 1988 and 1999. Over the same period there has been a decline in bus and coach passenger kilometres, both in absolute and relative terms, and only a modest increase in rail travel.

Car domination is not just a British phenomenon. Table 9.2 compares Britain with various countries in terms of passenger kilometres travelled between 1988 and 1998. The table reveals that in all these countries the major mode of transport is the private road vehicle. It can be seen that even in Japan, where travel by rail is a major mode of transport, the car is still the most important.

Turning to freight transport, Table 9.3 gives the figures for billion tonne kilometres and the percentage by mode over the period 1988–99. The table reveals a 9.5 per cent increase in freight transported over that period, with road being the major form of freight transport. In fact, road transport had a 65 per cent share of all freight in 1999.

Table 9.1 Passenger transport by mode 1988–99 (billion passenger kilometres and percentages)

	Bus and coaches	%	Cars and vans	%	Motor cycles	%	Pedal cycles	%	All road	%	Rail	%	Air	%	All modes	%
						Road										
1988	46	7	536	84	6	1	5	1	594	93	41	6	5	1	640	100
1990	46	7	588	85	6	1	5	1	645	94	39	6	5	1	689	100
1992	43	6	583	86	5	1	5	1	636	94	38	6	5	1	679	100
1994	44	6	591	86	4	1	4	1	643	94	35	5	5	1	684	100
1996	44	6	606	86	4	1	4	1	658	94	38	5	6	1	703	100
1998	43	6	616	86	4	1	4	1	667	93	42	6	7	1	716	100
1999	45	6	621	85	5	1	4	1	675	93	46	6	7	1	728	100

Source: Adapted from DTLR Transport Statistics GB (2000).

Table 9.4 reveals a large increase in the number of miles travelled per person in terms of cars, vans and lorries between 1985 and 1999. In fact there has been a 41 per cent increase in terms of car-miles per person per year over the 24-year period. The car now accounts for 82 per cent of all mileage compared with 76 per cent in 1985.

Environmental impacts of transport growth

This growth in traffic has major environmental implications, including congestion, noise and air pollution. Road traffic congestion is considered in more detail below and in Case Study 3.2; air pollution, however, is more insidious and the costs to society not so easy to quantify.

Table 9.2 Passenger transport by national vehicles on national territory, 1988 and 1998 (billion passenger kilometres)

	Cars and taxis		Buses and coaches		Rail		Total of these modes	
	1988	1998	1988	1998	1988	1998	1988	1998
Great Britain	471.3	616.0	41.0	43.0	34.3	35.1	546.6	694.1
France	554.0	708.4	43.0	58.8	63.1	64.5	660.1	831.7
Germany	540.0	740.3	61.0	69.4	41.7	66.5	642.7	876.2
Italy	450.0	647.1	77.2	89.2	46.2	50.3	573.4	786.5
Netherlands	147.4	150.6	12.1	14.5	9.7	14.8	169.2	179.9
Spain	133.0	351.8	35.4	45.9	15.8	18.9	184.2	416.6
Sweden	83.6	95.0	9.0	9.5	6.3	7.1	98.9	111.6
Japan	500.0	780.0	103.0	93.0	355.0	364.0	938.0	1237.0
USA	4600.0	6085.0	195.6	233.0	20.0	21.0	4851.6	6339.0

Source: Adapted from DTLR Transport Statistics GB (2000).

Table 9.3 Freight transport by mode, 1988–99 (billion tonne kilometres and percentages)

	1988	1990	1992	1994	1996	1998	1999
All traffic							
Road	130.2	136.3	126.5	143.7	153.9	159.5	156.7
Rail	18.2	15.8	15.5	13.0	15.1	17.4	18.4
Water	59.3	55.7	54.9	52.2	55.3	57.2	53.0
Pipeline	11.1	11.1	11.0	12.0	11.6	11.2	11.6
All modes	218.8	218.9	207.9	220.9	235.9	245.3	239.7
Percentage of all traffic							
Road	60	62	61	65	65	65	65
Rail	8	7	7	6	6	7	8
Water	27	25	26	24	23	23	22
Pipeline	5	5	5	5	5	5	5
All modes	100	100	100	100	100	100	100

Source: Adapted from DTLR Transport Statistics GB (2000).

Road traffic and pollution

A variety of pollutants associated with road transport is shown in Table 9.5.

Table 9.5 indicates that road transport is a major polluter in terms of nitrogen oxide, carbon monoxide and black smoke. The decline in lead emissions is the result of the growth in the sale of unleaded petrol in the UK since 1986.

Nor is there any longer much doubt as to the serious impact of the negative externalities associated with air pollution and other non-congestion impacts from road transport, as Table 9.6 usefully indicates. This table excludes congestion costs and a number of other environmental costs, yet still calculates the environmental costs of

Table 9.4 Average distance travelled per person by mode of travel, 1985/86 and 1997/99

Mode	Miles per person per year		Percentage change
	1985/86	1997/99	1985/86 to 1997/99
Walking	244	191	– 22
Bicycle	44	40	– 10
Car	3796	5334	41
Van/lorry	228	227	– 1
Buses	406	347	– 14
Rail	292	332	14
Other vehicles	308	335	9
All modes	5317	6806	28
Percentage of mileage accounted for by car (including van/lorry)	76	82	

Source: Adapted from DTLR Transport Statistics GB (2000).

Table 9.5 Pollutant emissions from transport and other sources in the UK, 1988–98 (thousand tonnes)

	1988	1992	1996	1998	% of total in 1998
Nitrogen oxides					
Road transport	1,261	1,244	989	823	47
All transport	1,385	1,389	1,128	926	53
Non-transport	1,249	1,183	932	827	47
Carbon monoxide					
Road transport	4,819	4,487	3,313	3,491	73
All transport	4,859	4,532	3,357	3,519	74
Non-transport	2,032	1,739	1,288	1,239	26
Volatile organic compounds					
Road transport	1,149	1,103	832	747	38
All transport	1,187	1,142	874	783	40
Non-transport	1,453	1,347	1,237	1,175	60
Lead					
Road transport	3.1	1.7	0.9	0.6	57
Black smoke					
Road transport	184	217	198	153	55
All transport	187	221	202	157	57
Non-transport	332	255	136	120	43
Particulates					
Road transport	69	64	52	42	26
All transport	73	68	56	45	28
Non-transport	263	231	157	118	72

Source: Adapted from DTLR Transport Statistics GB (2000).

Table 9.6 Transport and environmental costs (£bn per annum in 1994 prices)

	Eighteenth Report	Newbery	Maddison and Pearce
Air pollution	2.0–5.2	2.8–7.4	19.7
Climate change	1.5–3.1	0.4	0.1
Noise and vibration	1.0–4.6	0.6	2.6–3.1
Total environmental costs	4.6–12.9	3.8–8.4	22.4–22.9
Road accidents	5.4	4.5–7.5	2.9–9.4
Quantified social and environmental costs other than congestion costs	10.0–18.3	8.3–15.9	25.3–32.3

Note: 'Eighteenth Report' refers to the Royal Commission on Environmental Pollution (1994). Details of the studies by Newbery (1990) and Maddison (1996) can be found at the end of the chapter.
Source: Adapted from Royal Commission on Environmental Pollution (1997).

road transport at between £8 bn and £32.3 bn per annum depending on which of the three studies is used and on whether the lower or upper estimates are selected in any given study. This is equivalent to between 1 and 4 per cent of UK GDP per annum. Even allowing for the uncertainty indicated by the differing estimates of each study and by the lower and upper ranges of the calculations, negative externalities of such magnitude have forced transport to the forefront of environmental debate.

The Royal Commission on Environmental Pollution (1994) set a range of targets for transport-related pollutants at specific future dates. For example, to limit emissions of CO_2 from surface transport in the year 2000 to the 1990 level, and in the year 2020 to more than 80 per cent of the 1990 level. To achieve such targets it proposed a range of policy instruments which included a blend of market-based and non-market-based instruments.

Road traffic and congestion

Figure 9.1 will be helpful in analysing the causes and consequences of traffic congestion. In Figure 9.1 it is assumed that there is a single road and the flow of traffic is measured along the horizontal axis. In undertaking a journey the motorist is likely to consider only his or her own *marginal private cost* (MPC). The MPC, which is assumed to increase with an increase in traffic flow, comprises the generalised costs of making a trip and includes the price of petrol, the wear and tear on the vehicle and travel time, which involves an opportunity cost to the motorist. There will, however, be costs incurred on *other road users*, which the individual motorist does not take into account. These will consist of such costs as congestion, air pollution and noise. If congestion is considered to be the only externality, then this can be shown as MPC + *congestion cost* in Figure 9.1. As the flow of traffic increases then so does the *divergence* between the MPC and the MPC + congestion

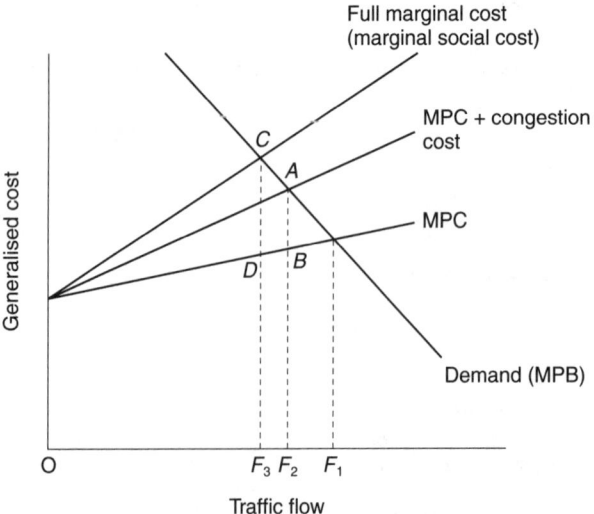

Figure 9.1 The equilibrium traffic flow

cost. The reason for this is that as additional drivers enter the road it imposes extra delays on every other road user.

Road users will equate their MPC with the *marginal private benefit* (MPB) obtained from making a trip, measured here by the demand curve. They will take no account of the congestion or other environmental costs they impose on the rest of society. There will thus be a flow of traffic equal to F_1. If congestion costs are added to the marginal private costs (MPC) then costs would be MPC + congestion cost, and the flow of traffic would fall to F_2. Thus at a flow of F_2, the private cost of making trips would be F_2B and the congestion cost would be AB. In other words, a tax or congestion charge of AB could be introduced to cover the real cost of congestion.

Case Study 3.2 looks at some of the evidence as to size of these congestion costs. In terms of the earlier studies outlined in Table 9.6 above, both Newbery and Maddison and Pearce valued the annual congestion costs of road transport at over £19bn in Great Britain (at constant 1994 prices).

Road traffic and all external costs

If, however, the other environmental implications of road transport (e.g. health impacts) are also considered, as illustrated in Figure 9.1, the *full marginal cost* (marginal social cost) would be much greater. The optimal traffic flow, if these environmental costs as well as congestion are taken into account, would be F_3, where the full marginal cost equals the MPB. Here the MPC would be F_3D and the overall congestion and environmental costs of CD would be covered by a road user charge (a road price) on the motorist of CD. Road user charging as a possible policy measure is discussed in more detail below.

●●●● Transport policies and policy instruments

In response to the growing problem of traffic and its environmental implications a number of policy options have been put forward. The taxonomy in Table 9.7 identifies a range of measures, which have been adopted or considered as a means of dealing with the problem. The table is categorised in terms of *market* and *non-market* (or command and control) based instruments. There tends to be a clear preference to use market-based instruments wherever feasible, as recognised by the Royal Commission (1994) which stated that 'Although economic instruments utilising the price mechanism are not a complete alternative to direct regulation, they tend to be more efficient.' However, it is also recognised that on occasions non-market-based instruments may be required.

In addition to structuring the table in terms of market and command and control policy instruments, the table also refers to *three* types of policy target, namely policies aimed at:

- dealing with vehicle emissions, such as measures aimed at making vehicle engines cleaner;
- reducing fuel use and increasing efficiency; and
- reducing the overall volume of road traffic.

Table 9.7 Taxonomy of policy instruments to control the environmental impact of motor vehicles

	Market-based instruments	*Command and control instruments*
Vehicle	• Differential vehicle tax (VED) • Graduated purchase tax on new vehicles	• Energy efficiency in car engines • Mandatory use of low-polluting vehicles – gas, electric
Fuel	• Fuel price increases • Differential fuel prices	• Fuel efficiency • Reducing speed limits
Traffic	• Parking charges • Workplace parking charges • Road user charging • Price of travel by public transport	• Car sharing • Making more use of alternative modes • Improvements in reliability/ frequency and quality of public transport – Comfort and speed – Bus lanes • Teleconferencing • Changing planning rules • Restraint on car use • Priorities for walking and cycling

●●●● Market-based policy instruments

Elasticities of demand and transport

The transport issue, like other policy issues involving prices, can only be understood by being familiar with the concept of elasticity. Box 9.1 briefly reviews these elasticity concepts which are then used later in the chapter.

BOX 9.1

Elasticity of demand and transport modes

Three types of elasticity of demand are relevant to the transport debate:

• *Price elasticity of demand* (PED). This measures the responsiveness of demand for a mode of transport to changes in its own price.

$$PED = \frac{\% \text{ change in quantity demanded of mode X}}{\% \text{ change in price of mode X}}$$

When this ratio is greater than 1 (ignoring the sign), we speak of a relatively elastic demand; when smaller than 1, a relatively inelastic demand.

- *Cross-elasticity of demand* (CED). This measures the responsiveness of demand for a mode of transport to changes in the price of some other mode of transport.

$$CED = \frac{\% \text{ change in quantity demanded of mode X}}{\% \text{ change in price of mode Y}}$$

Where X and Y are *substitutes* (mode), the sign of CED will be positive. A fall in the price of mode Y, the substitute, will decrease the quantity demanded of mode X $(-/- = +)$ Where X and Y are *complements in consumption* (fit together), the sign of CED will be negative. A fall in the price of Y, the complement, will increase the quantity demanded of X $(+/- = -)$.

- *Income elasticity of demand* (IED). This measures the responsiveness of demand for a mode of transport to changes in the real income of consumers.

$$IED = \frac{\% \text{ change in quantity demanded of mode X}}{\% \text{ change in real income}}$$

For transport modes with high (positive) values for IED, a rise in real income will shift the demand curve substantially to the right (increase), whereas a fall in real income will shift the demand curve substantially to the left. With a negative value for IED a rise in real income will cause demand to shift to the left (decrease).

Increasing fuel duties and vehicle excise duty (VED)

An increase in the price of petrol in real terms is one method of tackling the environmental costs of pollutants. An increase in the price of fuel is likely to result in a reduction in fuel consumption and the volume of traffic on UK roads. The Royal Commission Report on Environmental Pollution (1994) gave a number of advantages for the use of **fuel duty** as an economic instrument for influencing the decision about whether to undertake additional journeys, namely that:

- *The amount of tax paid varies with the environmental costs:* the amount of fuel duty used and paid is in the main proportional to the amount of CO_2 emitted, and (for any given vehicle) is closely reflected in the quantities of other substances emitted. Fuel consumption is substantially higher in congested urban traffic, and is therefore correlated to some degree with situations in which a vehicle is contributing to higher concentrations of pollutants, and where there is a higher exposure to the noise and vibration it is producing.
- *It is simple to administer:* it costs little to collect, is difficult to avoid or evade, and can easily be modified.
- *Road users have discretion about how to respond:* road users may respond either by reducing the number or length of their journeys or by reducing their use of fuel in other ways, such as switching to a smaller or more fuel-efficient vehicle or driving in a more fuel-efficient way.

Fuel duties and transport protests in the UK

- It is possible to vary the rate of fuel duty to provide an incentive to use environmentally less damaging forms of fuel, as in the case of the existing small differentials in favour of diesel and unleaded petrol.
- A fuel duty already exists.

Empirical studies have indicated that variations in fuel duty do indeed have an effect on road transport use. The Department of Transport has estimated that a 10 per cent increase in the price of fuel in real terms would lead to a fall in fuel use of up to 3 per cent, of which half would be the result of reduced vehicle use. The Royal Commission concluded that in order to meet the target of limiting CO_2 emissions from road transport to 1990 levels by this means alone, the price of fuel would need to double, relative to the price of other goods, by the year 2005. This would require an increase in fuel duty of some 9 per cent a year (in real terms) for 10 years.

In the March 1993 Budget the UK Chancellor of the Exchequer announced an increase in road fuel duty of 10 per cent, with projected increases in future Budgets of at least 3 per cent in real terms. Although the stated reason for this policy was environmental, directed towards reducing CO_2 emissions, it would also act as a disincentive to car ownership. The increase in fuel duty met with a certain amount of resistance, not least from road hauliers. Table 9.8 reveals that the duty on leaded and unleaded petrol increased by 4.25 and 3.79 pence per litre respectively as a result of the March 1999 Budget. This rise primarily affected car owners throughout the UK. By contrast, the price of diesel increased by 6.14 pence per litre, which represented an 11.6 per cent increase. This change adversely affected the road haulage industry since 99 per cent of their vehicles run on diesel. Overall, 85 per cent of the price of diesel is tax while 36 per cent of the total operating cost of road hauliers comprises the cost of fuel. Such issues were a key factor in the petrol blockades of September 2000 causing widespread disruption.

In terms of vehicle excise duty (VED), the March 1999 Budget increased the rate of duty for cars, taxis and vans by £5 to £155 per annum, but cars with engines up to 1,100 cc were eligible for a reduced rate of VED of £100. The Budget also stated that autumn 2000 would see the introduction of a graduated VED system for

Table 9.8 Changes to duties on road fuels, March 1999

	Changes in duty (%)	Effect of tax per litre (increase in pence)
Leaded petrol	7.35	4.25
Unleaded petrol	7.33	3.79
Higher octane unleaded petrol from 9 March 1999	7.33	4.20
Higher octane unleaded petrol from 1 October 1999	−5.96	−3.67
Diesel	11.60	6.14
Ultra-low sulphur diesel	9.82	4.96

Source: Economic and Fiscal Report and Financial Statement and Budget Report, March 1999.

cars first registered from that time, based primarily on CO_2 emissions. In terms of road hauliers, the VED for 40-tonne vehicles was increased by £2,000 to £5,750 per annum. The Freight Transport Association has estimated that the budgetary changes increased the operating cost of a 38-tonne vehicle travelling 75,000 miles per annum by £2,130, that is to £24,500 per annum.

One of the main reasons put forward for the higher increase in the tax on ordinary diesel, with a higher carbon content, was to meet the government's aim of protecting the environment by developing a tax policy focused on reducing the emission of greenhouse gases and improving local air quality. At the same time, the tax on ultra-low-sulphur diesel was increased by only 4.96 per cent since it has lower emission of particulates. The aim was to encourage a switch from diesel to this cleaner fuel and in line with the government's commitment to increase fuel duties by at least 6 per cent on average per annum in real terms. This was termed the *fuel escalator* but given the public resistance, it was withdrawn by the government in the 2000 Budget.

Table 9.9 illustrates the cost to UK hauliers in terms of fuel prices and VED as compared to other countries in Continental Europe. It can be seen, for example, that for a 40-tonne vehicle VED is over 10 times greater in the UK than it is in France and nearly 12 times greater than in Germany.

In terms of fuel prices, the price of diesel at the pumps is substantially higher in the UK than in Continental Europe. One of the main reasons for this is clearly the fuel duty.

Fuel duties and economic theory

Basic economic theory, as outlined above, can be used to explain what the UK government has tried to achieve in terms of its taxation policy with respect to transport. As illustrated in Figure 9.2, hauliers base their business decisions on their own *marginal private costs*, given by the MPC_1 curve. The reason for its positive slope, as stated previously, is because as the flow of traffic increases then the driver time taken to undertake journeys increases thereby raising private costs. The *full*

Table 9.9 Comparison of costs for selected European Countries

Countries	Average 1,000 litre tank of diesel (pump price)		Countries	VED rates for a 40-tonne vehicle (£)
	Ex. VAT (£)	Inc. VAT		
UK	636	746	UK	5750
Italy	402	480	Sweden	1909
Ireland	376	460	Germany	1856
France	370	447	Belgium	929
Netherlands	363	428	Italy	634
Germany	337	402	France	486
Spain	298	350	Greece	428
Greece	285	337	Portugal	308

Source: Road Haulage Association.

marginal cost curve includes the private costs plus the external environmental costs. If the hauliers took account of only their private costs, then given the demand curve in Figure 9.2, the flow of vehicles would be F_1 with a marginal private cost of C_1. The *optimum flow* (from society's viewpoint) is F_2 where the full marginal cost equals demand, at a cost of C_2. In theory, this optimum flow could be achieved by an increase in fuel duty. Since the marginal private cost curve includes the price of fuel, the effect of increasing fuel duty would be to push up the marginal private cost curve from MPC_1 to MPC_2. The optimum flow of F_2 would thus be achieved as a result of the increase in fuel duty. In this way increases in fuel duty could be used to cover the real cost of environmental pollution.

Obviously the success of a policy such as an increase in fuel duty and VED depends on the effect it has on road hauliers and motorists. Will they reduce the number of miles travelled or trips made? Will other modes of transport such as rail be used?

- In terms of an increase in VED it is a fee which allows a vehicle to be taken on to the road. It is a *fixed cost* in that it is a fee that does not vary with vehicle use. As such, the main disadvantage with this form of tax is that it bears no relation to the amount of mileage a vehicle travels. In fact, there is a danger that a high fixed charge could result in higher utilisation of the vehicle in order to 'spread the overhead costs'.
- In terms of an increase in fuel duty, there is the advantage of a direct relationship between the use made of the road network (with its environmental implications) and the amount of tax paid. The desired aim was illustrated in Figure 9.2, but whether it has the desired effect in practice is open to question. We have already noted the relatively price inelastic demand for fuel use in the UK which may result in little quantity adjustment in response to higher fuel taxes.

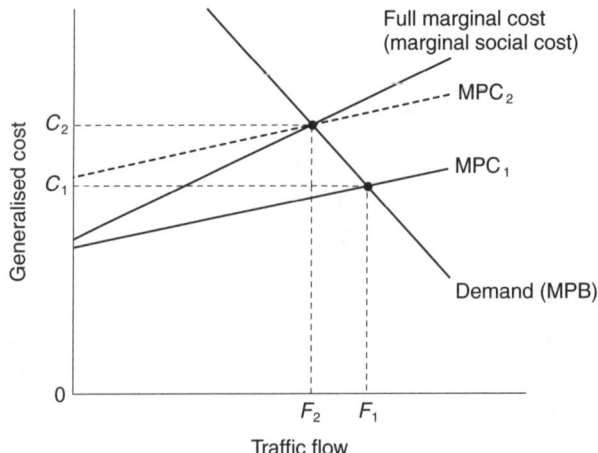

Figure 9.2 Motoring costs and traffic flow

Road user charging

Road user charging is gaining in popularity as a means of dealing with transport congestion and its associated environmental effects. Road user charging involves charging the motorist for road use. The growth in support for road user charging is primarily as a result of:

● *Growing concern with the level of congestion in urban areas throughout the world* and international doubts raised about road construction as a contemporary solution to the problem.

● *Growing concern about the effect of road transport on air pollution* and environmental degradation in towns and cities throughout the world.

● *The development of new technology* has greatly facilitated the adoption and implementation of efficient and effective demand management. The emergence of a new family of intelligent vehicle highway systems technologies has made road user charging in urban areas technically and economically feasible.

● *The increasingly stringent financial constraints under which authorities are operating* and thus a realisation of the revenue-raising qualities of urban road pricing. Drivers have been identified as a possible source of revenue to pay for the improvements from which they would benefit. In other words 'fiscal realities'.

In addition, Grieco and Jones (1994) argue that the culture of privatisation and the market philosophy has created pressure towards ensuring that the user and not the taxpayer provides the service. As such urban road pricing fits naturally into this 'economic logic'.

The term 'road user charging' requires clarification. The literature is awash with terms used to describe the imposition of a charge on moving traffic. Terms such as road-use pricing, congestion charging, congestion pricing, road user charging and congestion metering have all been used. It usually refers to setting the price equal to the marginal social cost of a trip so that, in economic terms, the congestion price ensures that only economically justified journeys are undertaken. Table 9.10 outlines five possible road user charging schemes involving various time periods, areas and means of charging. These five bases by which pricing could be levied were

---

Table 9.10 Five road user charging options

● *Congestion metering.* Charge, which reflects the congestion, caused by each driver. The charge would vary according to traffic conditions, both across the charged area and by time

● *Time-based charging.* A version of congestion metering, in which the charge is directly proportional to the time spent travelling within the charged area

● *Distance-based charging.* Drivers are charged directly for the distance travelled within the charged area

● *Point-based, or cordon, charging.* Drivers are charged when they pass a point, which forms part of a continuous boundary for a system of cells, or cordons encircling areas, or screenlines dividing an area or separating two areas. Charge levels can vary by the direction of travel

● *Supplementary licences.* Supplementary licences, for which a charge is levied, can be required to either enter an area (an entry permit) or to be within an area, during a specific period (an area licence). While electronic devices ('tags') could be used, the conventional concept is a paper-based licence, or 'sticker'

Source: The London Congestion Charging Research Programme (1995).

examined as part of the London Congestion Charging Research Programme (1995).

The UK has recognised the benefits to be derived from road user charging and in the *White Paper on the Future of Transport* (1998) stated that

> We will introduce legislation to allow local authorities to charge road users so as to reduce congestion, as part of a package of measures in a *local transport plan* that would include improving public transport. The use of the revenues to benefit transport serving the area where charges apply...will be critical to the success of such schemes.

The government has agreed that the revenue should be *ring fenced*, with the local authorities able to retain all the revenue generated for a period of 10 years from the implementation of a scheme, provided there are worthwhile transport-related projects to be funded. The Transport Bill includes powers to enable local authorities outside London, if they want to, to introduce road user charging and/or a workplace parking levy as part of their local transport plan. The mayor of London is currently minded to proceed with the option in the ROCOL Report (2000) of an area licensing system organised on the vehicle registration numbers with enforcement by digital cameras. The optimum road user charge would be *CD* in terms of Figure 9.1.

CASE STUDY 9.1

Charging the motorist

Until recently, the idea of charging for scarce road space was dismissed as political suicide, but some politicians have advocated road pricing and lived to tell the tale. Ken Livingstone, London's mayor, for instance, plans to introduce road pricing in the capital by 2003. Now a new study for the European Commission takes the argument further. Enticingly entitled *Revenues for Efficient Pricing*, it argues that current transport taxes should be replaced by charges to reflect the true marginal costs of different forms of transport – not only the additional cost of each journey, but also the costs of pollution, congestion and accidents. On this basis the London car driver and truck driver should be charged three times as much as at present for rush-hour journeys.

Marginal social-cost pricing, the economic jargon for this form of charging, would produce 50 per cent more revenue than current taxes on fuel and vehicles. It would also recover the full costs of transport infrastructure. The cost burden would shift from rail to road because the marginal cost of each additional car journey is greater than that of an additional rail journey. In London, for instance, motorists would have to spend up to three times as much as they do now for rush-hour journeys. Underground fares, by contrast, would fall by more than half.

Mr Livingstone's plans are modest, by comparison. He plans a £5 daily charge for drivers in part of inner London. This will have a modest impact on traffic. Rana Roy, author of the EC study, predicts that if the scheme were implemented, by 2005 road journeys in London would decline by 30 per cent while rail journeys would increase by 45 per cent.

The technology is not yet in place to introduce an efficient road-pricing system, but it is getting there. Microwave radio systems, allowing cars to communicate with roadside

charging units, are already in use in several European countries. Bus and lorry operators are using American global positioning satellites to track their vehicles on a minute-
to-minute basis. With digitised maps, such systems could calculate which vehicles used
what roads when, and charge them accordingly. The capital cost would be around £350
per vehicle; the operating cost, according to the EC, would be less than 3 per cent of
revenues.

Heavy goods vehicles are likely to be the first to use this technology. At present,
European lorries have to purchase a licence to travel on most European motorways. An
electronic charging system is emerging as its natural successor.

The political hurdles to introducing an efficient road-pricing system are greater than
the technological ones. Although there are big social gains implicit in this scheme (less
congestion, less pollution and fewer accidents) and big winners (public transport users,
mostly), there are also big losers. And as the government has learned, the motorists'
lobby is a formidable creature.

Questions

1 What is meant by 'marginal social-cost pricing'?

2 Outline the relative benefits and difficulties of introducing a road-pricing scheme.

Subsidising public transport

This approach is designed to shift the demand curve to the left in Figures 9.1 and
9.2, making travel by public transport more attractive relative to the private car.
Subsidisation can operate in one of two ways (Button, 1992). First, it can act as a
Pigouvian subsidy. In such a situation the generator of the negative externality is
given a subsidy, which can be viewed as a bribe, in order to reduce the scale of
activity, namely the traffic flow, to a level seen as being the social optimum. The
second method involves *subsidising modes of public transport*, which cause less
externalities than private transport. This is a policy which has been extensively
used in many European countries.

Subsidising public transport, such as a light rapid transit system (and also the
use of road user charging) can be analysed by the use of Figure 9.3, where the light
rapid transit system can be viewed as an alternative to the private car. A number
of assumptions are made, namely:

● The marginal cost of the light rapid transit system is assumed constant and the
fare charged is set equal to the marginal cost.

● The light rapid transit system is assumed to have no adverse effect on the environment so that there is no divergence between private and social cost. The private car, however, does cause externalities so that social costs exceed private
costs.

● The total number of trips is fixed at *OA*.

Given the assumptions and modal choice based on private costs, the initial split
between modes is given by point *M**.

At the margin, travellers are indifferent (in terms of *marginal private cost*)
between the two modes. Given this situation, the total number of trips by private

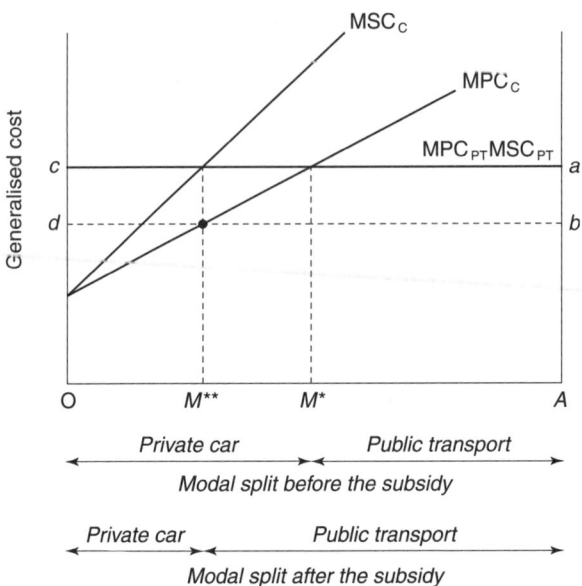

Figure 9.3 Subsidising public transport

car is OM^* whereas light rapid transit trips total AM^*. This cannot be viewed as the socially optimal mix since at M^* the marginal social cost of trip making by private car (MSC_C) outweighs the marginal social cost of public transport (MSC_{PT}), and a reallocation of trip making between the two modes would improve social welfare.

The optimal mix is M^{**} which involves less use of the private car and more of public transport. This could be achieved by the introduction of a subsidy on public transport equal to ab or a road user charging system of cd, as seen in Figure 9.3. The optimum position will be reached whether it is the taxpayer who subsidises public transport or the road user who pays the charge. The two strategies are very different, however, when considered in terms of *equity* (fairness). One approach (subsidy) is raising the real income of the (mainly lower income) groups using public transport. The other approach (road user charging) is reducing the real income of all motorists.

The case for a public transport subsidy rests heavily on the argument that the *cross-elasticity of demand* between private and public transport is non-zero and positive. In other words, a fall in the price of public transport should result in a decrease in demand for private transport. Empirical evidence would seem to suggest (Goodwin, 1992) that the cross-elasticity of demand is low. In fact Goodwin (1992), having surveyed 50 empirical studies, found that the overall average elasticity was negative at –0.41. This would even suggest that a fall in price of public transport *increases* the demand for private transport.

There are other limitations with subsidies:

● First, there is reason to suggest that higher subsidies lead to higher costs, with a significant proportion of the subsidies leaking into higher wages or into inefficient operations rather than being used for the benefit of passengers.

- Second, if there is latent demand for the use of road space, then a switch of travellers from car to public transport because of the subsidy (i.e. cheaper fares) will free up road space for those who previously did not make journeys. In other words, traffic would be generated as a result of the subsidy.

- Third, although subsidising fares may be of social importance in income distribution terms, it is quality of service (i.e. frequency, reliability, amenities) which is often of more importance to commuters.

Parking restrictions

One policy which has been extensively used in urban areas since the 1960s is parking restraints. The aim has been, through parking meters and restrictions on on-street parking, to limit the supply of parking spaces, so reducing the demand for urban routes. This policy, too, has limitations in that removing parking facilities from a road essentially increases the size of the road and may therefore encourage extra traffic flows. At the same time, parking restraints encourage illegal parking which may add to congestion. This is one of the main reasons for the introduction of wheel clamps in central London in 1986 and policies such as the tow-away scheme introduced in Cambridge in 1991, subsequently abandoned in 1996 given its unprofitability.

City councils have sought to use pricing policies at their car parks to encourage shopping and other short-stay motorists, while at the same time discouraging long-stay commuters. However, the success of this policy has been hindered to some extent by their lack of control over privately operated car parks and by high volumes of through traffic in most congested areas. Parking charges are also unable to discriminate between length of journey or route taken. Pricing policies could be used to encourage motorists to park at peripheral, out of town, car parks, which could be part of a park-and-ride scheme. Such schemes operate in Oxford, Cambridge and York.

By 2000 the lack of control over private parking had been addressed by the Transport Bill which gave local authorities not only the power to introduce road use charging, but also to levy a mandatory charge on workplace parking across all or part of their area. The levy would act as a licence fee, with the owners or occupiers of premises applying to the traffic authority for a licence stating the maximum number of vehicles that will be parked on their premises at any one time. A workplace parking charge per vehicle will then be multiplied by that maximum number. The aim is to 'reduce the amount of free workplace car parking available as a means of reducing car journeys and promoting greater use of alternative modes' (DETR, 1998b). It is hoped that the levy will act as an incentive for occupiers of property to reduce the total number of parking spaces, restricting the maximum number of vehicles for which a licence is sought. As with road user charging, there are a number of issues which need to be addressed. These include the need for complementary policies to be adopted, such as the introduction or strengthening of existing on-street parking outside the workplace to levels consistent with those applied to workplace parking.

These is also the problem of which premises or vehicles should be exempt, if any, and what the exact parking levy per vehicle should be in order to achieve the desired objective.

● ● ● ● Non-market-based (command and control) policy instruments

Catalytic converters

Catalytic converters have been fitted since 1992 to all new cars with petrol engines, in order to meet EU regulations. This should result in reduced emissions of nitrogen oxides, volatile organic compounds and carbon monoxide, 71 per cent of which was attributed to road transport in 1996. The converters, however, will only act as a temporary check on emissions, since the benefits of the converter will eventually be outweighed by the growth in traffic. A catalytic converter is fitted inside the exhaust and comprises a honeycomb of either ceramic or metal coated with platinum, palladium and rhodium, which convert the pollutants into less harmful forms. A limitation of the catalytic converter is that they only become effective after they have reached a certain temperature. Thus on shorter journeys it may be of little use. In addition the converter can only be used in cars that run on unleaded petrol.

Tighter government controls

- *The introduction of emission tests* for carbon monoxide as part of the MOT test and an increase in the *roadside enforcement programme* in order to catch the worst offenders in terms of emission levels, are both examples of tighter government controls.
- *Stricter enforcement of speed limits* would bring benefits of accident reductions. In this respect one option would be fitting cars with speed-limiting devices. Speed governors on cars would restrict the speed and with it reduce the carbon emissions by up to 1 million t.
- *Traffic calming measures* such as limiting access of vehicles to city centres and increased pedestrianisation are possible ways of reducing the environmental cost of vehicle exhaust emissions. It could be argued, however, that such physical control measures restrict vehicle access and result in longer journeys and therefore even more pollution. Other measures such as those used in Athens, where cars with odd and even registration number plates are allowed into the city on alternative days, might prove more difficult to implement in the UK.

The use of alternative fuels

As well as the options detailed above the utilisation of cleaner types of fuel is another means of attempting to deal with the problem, as suggested in Case Study 9.2.

CASE STUDY 9.2

Propulsion for transport

Energy demand for transport is not only very substantial, but has grown rapidly. Oil at present supplies 99 per cent of the energy used for transport in the UK, with almost all the rest provided by electricity.

Achieving a reduction in energy demand for transport over the next half-century will require both radical changes in technology and effective thoroughgoing implementation of integrated transport policies that will reduce the overall energy intensity of the transport system. This will involve reducing the need for mobility and making increasing use of modes that use less energy than private road transport.

Whatever degree of success is achieved in that direction, there will remain a very large demand for a readily portable energy source with a high energy density and power density suitable for propelling personal vehicles. It will be technically difficult to replace fossil fuels in that role, and for the time being it is likely to remain necessary to treat transport as the premium use for oil. The main emphasis in policy over the coming decades therefore must be on finding ways of using fossil fuels in transport that reduce the amounts of CO_2 emitted. There have been big improvements in the conversion efficiencies of internal combustion engines. In the case of personal vehicles, however, these have been offset hitherto by increases in the size and weight of vehicles and in their ancillary equipment.

Fuel cells using methanol offer another way of using fossil fuels in transport that both safeguards air quality and is more efficient, and is currently attracting great interest. The high power density and energy density of fuel cells make them suitable for use in transport, and a particular advantage over the internal combustion engine is that they achieve a high efficiency over a much wider range of power outputs. Thus, although a vehicle powered by a fuel cell using methanol emits CO_2, the emissions should be less than from an internal combustion engine. Whether there is an overall reduction in CO_2 emissions depends on how much energy has been used in producing methanol from fossil fuels and the source of that energy.

Electric batteries eliminate all emissions from vehicles. Despite extensive programmes of research and development on the use of batteries to propel vehicles, however, technological progress has so far been disappointing. They still have a relatively low energy density and power density and take a long time to recharge. A major breakthrough will be needed before battery-powered vehicles can offer a performance and range comparable to those offered by oil-engined vehicles, at reasonable cost. For this reason there is now much more interest in fuel cells as a method of propulsion for vehicles. The overall energy requirement for battery-powered vehicles, however, might be less than for vehicles powered by fuel cells using hydrogen because of smaller energy losses within the supply chain.

Liquid fuels for vehicles can be produced from crops. However, the production processes can be polluting and in some cases have a high-energy requirement. To produce biofuels on a large scale a large area of land is needed to grow the crops. It is unlikely that sufficient land could be found for this purpose in the UK, especially if (as seems a more promising approach) large areas of land are to be devoted to growing crops to provide energy in the form of heat. We do not therefore regard biologically produced fuels as a valid option for large-scale use in transport in the UK in the foreseeable future.

Source: Royal Commission on Environmental Pollution (2000).

Questions

1 Outline the various alternatives to fossil fuel detailed in this case study as a means of propulsion for transport.

2 What are the relative merits and drawbacks of these alternative fuels?

The environmental effects of aviation

While the environmental impact of aviation is small relative to road transport it is likely to be an area which will be of growing concern. The DETR's consultation document on the future of aviation spelt out six main areas of environmental impact, both global and local:

- The effect of aircraft emissions on climate change;
- Local air quality both from aircraft emissions at airports and from the infra-structure which serves the airport;
- Aircraft noise and the effect it has on individuals living near to or under the flight path of airports;
- Noise, emissions and congestion resulting from surface access provision to airports (most notably road transport);
- Both land take and urbanisation as a result of airport development;
- Contaminated land and waste.

As part of the consultation document it is stated that the government is particularly keen to develop the use of *economic (market-based) instruments* as a means of reducing the environmental effects of emissions from aviation, as part of the polluter pays principle. A number of possible economic instruments are considered, namely:

- *Taxation on aviation kerosene* seen as a way of placing environmental costs on the polluter and as such acting as an incentive to improve fuel efficiency, via technological advance. It is, however, recognised that the unilateral introduction of a tax on aviation fuel at an EU or national level would lead to a significant competitive disadvantage.
- *The introduction of tradable emissions permits* setting a cap or target on emissions and allowing airlines to buy or sell emissions permits. The whole idea of tradable permits is covered in more detail in Chapter 4.

In addition, the consultation document mentions *voluntary agreements* whereby the regulatory authorities and the aviation industry agree to reduce specific or collective emissions, placing the onus on the industry to determine how those commitments are met. The main difficulty with voluntary agreements is, according to the government, one of 'defining the baseline "business-as-usual" level of emissions against which savings can be agreed and monitored'.

As stated in Chapter 4, one of the main issues worthy of consideration relates to the extent to which the imposition of charges reflecting the full external costs of aviation would influence airline behaviour. For example, to be effective, a fuel tax would need to be very large, so that a system of tradable permits might be preferable. As stated, aviation, like other modes of transport, creates a number of external costs such as aircraft noise, local air quality problems and climate change. One of the difficulties, however, is that these environmental impacts are difficult to measure. It is certainly the case that in terms of the polluter pays principle any valuation of these environmental costs should be reflected in full in terms of the costs incurred by the aviation industry. Case Study 9.3 is based on a paper produced by the DTLR (2000) which reviews the valuation of aircraft noise, air quality and climate change based on estimates proposed by independent researchers.

CASE STUDY 9.3

The value of the external costs of aviation

The lack of clearly defined property rights is a major reason for problem of externalities, since it precludes the existence of a market for the external impacts. A number of studies, however, have attempted to place a monetary valuation on aircraft noise using the individuals' willingness to pay for a marginal reduction in aircraft noise. In addition, similar approaches have been used to place a value on the externalities in terms of air quality and climate change. Other impacts such as townscape, landscape, biodiversity, heritage and water have not been considered since there are a lack of relevant studies in this area.

Noise

Since there is no market in 'peace and quiet' then an indirect means of measuring a householder's willingness to pay for reduced noise is via their purchasing decisions. Known as *hedonic pricing* this approach has attempted to identify the premium, other characteristics being equal, which is paid for a quieter house, either in terms of rent or a purchase price. Hedonic pricing studies in terms of noise are often expressed in terms of a noise sensitivity depreciation index (NSDI) which provides a measure of the percentage change in house prices associated with a unit change in noise quantity measured in dBA Leq. It has been estimated that a 1dBA rise in the quantity of noise is likely to reduce house prices by between 0.5 and 1 per cent.

It needs to be remembered, however, that there are a number of sources of inaccuracy when measuring the effects of aircraft noise. One such factor is that the value for the willingness to pay is not likely to be uniform across the population, since there will be an element of self-selection with individuals less adverse to noise, as well as workers from the aviation industry, choosing to live near to airports.

Air quality

Poor air quality close to airports can lead to a number of effects on human health and the environment. Local air pollutants emitted from aircraft during landing and take-off include VOCs, CO_2, NO_x, SO_2, and indirectly ozone. There are the health impacts in terms of mortality and morbidity as well as the environmental effects on crops, forest damage, the damage to buildings and materials as well as the reduced visibility and effects on the ecosystems. In order to measure these impacts scientific and economic information is required in terms of:

- The nature of the relationship between concentrations of each pollutant and its associated health and environmental impact;
- The population exposed to the pollution or the stock at risk;
- The values the public place on each of the relevant health and environmental impacts.

It is important to stress that there are uncertainties in terms of quantifying many of the health and environmental impacts. It is the case that only a limited number of health effects can be considered to have sufficiently robust evidence to allow quantification. These include deaths brought forward and respiratory hospital admissions. There is limited empirical evidence as to the willingness to pay in order to reduce the mortality risks of air pollution. Those most affected by air pollution are mostly over 65 and may already be in a poor state of health with a reduced life expectancy. However, uncertainty over whether deaths are brought forward by just a few days or by months or years has led to a wide range of value of statistical life between £2,600 and £1.4 m.

Climate change

Aviation's contribution to climate change is through the production of CO_2 but there are also other emissions, most notably oxides of nitrogen, which result in the formation of ozone, particulates and water vapours resulting in the formation of contrails. There is, however, a greater degree of uncertainty in terms of the effect these 'other emissions' have on climate change. The concept of 'radiation forcing' has been used to measure the climate change effects attributable to the various emissions produced by aircraft. It has been estimated that aircraft accounted for 3.5 per cent of total radiative forcing from man-made sources in 1992 (excluding the effects of aviation on cirrus clouds).

Overall environmental cost

Table 9.11 is based on various estimates, including those of Pearce and Pearce (2000), and reveals noise and climate change environmental costs by aircraft type for short- and

Table 9.11 Estimated environmental costs per passenger and passenger kilometre (central estimates)

Aircraft type	Total £	Short-haul operations £ per passenger	£ per 000 passenger km
B 737–400	245	2.50	2.75
A 320	285	2.18	3.23
MD82	350	3.30	3.60
B 757	412	3.01	3.27
A 310	395	2.90	3.17

Aircraft type	Total £	Long-haul operations £ per passenger	£ per 000 passenger km
A 340	3,613	20.24	3.21
B 747–400	5,140	18.49	2.88
B 767–300	2,499	18.45	2.89
B 777	3,804	18.05	2.78

long-haul operations, excluding the damage costs from local air pollution. They are presented in terms of £ per passenger and £ per 1000 passenger kilometres.

Table 9.11 reveals environmental costs of approximately £3 per passenger in terms of short-haul operations and £20 per passenger on long-haul aircraft. On a cost per passenger kilometre basis, however, the marginal damage costs are roughly similar for short- and long-haul operations. Again it is important to note that these figures are subject to a high degree of uncertainty.

The central estimates of damage cost per passenger illustrated in Table 9.11 suggest that they would tend to increase short-haul fares by around $3^1/_2$ per cent and long-haul fares by about 6 per cent if they were fully passed on to passengers.

Source: Adapted from DTLR (2000).

Questions

1 Briefly outline the external costs of aviation.

2 Outline the difficulties encountered when measuring the external costs of aircraft.

In September 2001 a report was produced by AEA Technology and the Civil Aviation Authority for the Commission for Integrated Transport. It aimed to analyse the comparative environmental impacts of high-speed rail and short-haul air travel for regional journeys in Great Britain, namely from London to Manchester, Leeds, Newcastle, Edinburgh and Glasgow. The study aimed to assess the environmental impact for each route per passenger carried, based on average load factors of 33 per cent average seat occupancy for rail routes and 65–75 per cent for air routes. The emissions aspect of the Executive Summary are given in Case Study 9.4 below.

CASE STUDY 9.4

A comparative study of the environmental effects of rail and short-haul air travel

An explanation of the symbols and gases involved in this case study can be found in Chapter 13, page 321. PM_{10} refers to particulates.

Greenhouse gas emissions

Short-haul air journeys have higher CO_2 emissions, per passenger km, than high-speed rail

Domestic aircraft have CO_2 emissions per passenger km that are many times higher than that of high-speed rail. Domestic aircraft have emissions of 200–300 gCO_2/passenger km compared to around 40 gCO_2/passenger km for high-speed rail. The CO_2 emissions from aircraft landing and take-off are the same irrespective of journey distance and this increases the emissions per passenger km for shorter aircraft trips, i.e. from London to Leeds and Manchester...

Other atmospheric emissions

The comparison of the other main atmospheric pollutants (SO_2, NO_x, CO, PM_{10} and VOCs) shows that the two modes have different emissions of different pollutants. In summary:

High-speed rail journeys have higher emissions of SO_2, per passenger km, than domestic air

High SO_2 emissions from the UK electricity generating mix (from coal-fired generation) result in higher SO_2 emissions for high-speed electric trains than for domestic aircraft. SO_2 emissions from high-speed trains are likely to fall significantly in future years due to changes in the future electricity generating mix, and in the medium term (by 2020) high-speed rail and domestic aircraft will have similar emissions per passenger km (assuming no changes in future load factors).

Domestic aircraft have higher emissions of ground-level CO, NO_x and VOCs, per passenger km, than high-speed rail

The emissions from domestic aircraft, per passenger km, are highest on shorter trips, because of the emissions from take-off and landing. There was one exception to this. One rail route (London–Edinburgh) currently has a high proportion of high-speed diesel trains. These diesel trains have much higher emissions per km than high-speed electric trains. This increases the average emissions per passenger km for this route, so that emissions are greater than for the equivalent air journey. The diesel trains on this route will be phased out in the next few years. This finding is important as it shows there is a large difference according to train traction type (especially if looking to increase overall services of high-speed trains). Future emissions (beyond 2006) of CO, NO_x and VOCs per passenger km are likely to be even lower for high-speed electric trains relative to aircraft, as changes in the electricity generation mix lead to greater emissions reductions than occur from modern aircraft entering the fleet.

Emissions of PM_{10}, per passenger km, are broadly similar for both modes

The relative emissions of PM_{10}, per passenger km, vary on different routes because of different aircraft and trains in use. Electric high-speed trains have slightly lower emissions of PM_{10}, per passenger km, than aircraft. However, high-speed diesel trains have very high emissions of PM_{10}, and so domestic aircraft have lower PM_{10} emissions than for the east coast main line, which still has a proportion of diesel locomotives. The diesel trains on this route will be phased out in the next few years.

The emissions of PM_{10} from both modes are likely to fall in future years (2006 and beyond), due to reductions in the emissions from the electricity generation mix for rail and from modern aircraft entering the air fleet. In the medium term (by 2020) it is likely that PM_{10} emissions per passenger km will be slightly lower for high-speed rail compared to domestic aircraft. These benefits will be greatest on shorter trips (i.e. London to Leeds/Manchester). The relative balance of different pollutants from the two modes makes it difficult to conclude which has the lower burden for atmospheric emissions (which affect local and regional air quality). To make this judgement, the relative *impacts* of high-speed train and domestic air travel must be assessed, rather than the *burdens* (e.g. emissions) assessed here...

Emissions from surface access may be important

...It is clear that the choice of *surface access mode* is extremely important in the relative comparison of high-speed rail and domestic aircraft. For longer surface access trips by car, the emissions of most pollutants (especially CO, NO_x and VOCs) can be as large as the emissions from the regional journey itself. The reduction in car use for surface access is therefore a priority in reducing overall burdens from both modes. The inclusion of surface access emissions could change the comparison significantly. It is stressed that both short-haul air travel and high-speed rail have major emission advantages over road transport for domestic regional journeys (i.e. from London to the five cities).

For journeys from city centre to city centre, there will be additional surface emissions from short-haul aircraft, because of the location of the airports considered which are outside urban areas. Some data are available on surface access mode for passengers travelling to airports. This indicates that while the proportion of travellers using public transport is improving, the majority of surface access to regional airports, and approximately two-thirds of access to London airports, is by car. Data on surface access mode for passengers travelling to railway stations are available; however, data for passengers making specific high-speed rail journeys are not. The railway stations of interest for this study (King's Cross and Euston) are located in central London and the proportion of surface access journeys by car is likely to be low. The lack of data means it is not possible to assess in detail surface access emissions for high-speed rail and domestic aircraft, though the indications are that surface access emissions are likely to favour rail over air. In addition surface access emissions are more important (i.e. have higher emissions as a proportion of the total) on shorter trips from London to Manchester and Leeds...

Source: Watkiss, P., Jones, R., Rhodes, D., Hardy, A., Hardley, A., Hopewell, H. and Walker, C. (2001) *A comparative study of the Environmental Effects of Rail and short-haul Air Travel*, report published by the Commission for Integrated Transport, London.

Questions

1 Briefly compare the emissions from high-speed rail and domestic aircraft for regional journeys in Great Britain.

2 Outline the role played by surface access trips to airports and railway stations in terms of emission levels.

Now try the self-check questions for this chapter on the companion website
www.booksites.net/ison
You will also find up-to-date facts and case materials.

Key terms

Congestion Where additional drivers impose extra delays on every other road user on entering a road

External costs Costs imposed on others which may not be taken into account

Full marginal cost (marginal social cost) The addition to total cost (private plus environmental and congestion costs) resulting from an extra driver using the road – in the context of road transport

Marginal private cost The addition to total private costs

Market-based policy instruments Seek to use market prices to influence consumer and producer decisions (e.g. road user charging)

Non-market-based policy instruments Seek to use regulations and standards to influence consumer and producer decisions (e.g. licences)

Optimum flow Where marginal social cost equals the marginal social benefit so that 'social surplus' is a maximum

Road user charging Charging the motorist for road use

Subsidisation The use of subsidies to make a particular mode of transport more attractive

References and further reading

AEA Technology and the Civil Aviation Authority (2001) *A Comparative Study of the Environmental Effects of Rail and Short-haul Air Travel*, London, The Stationery Office.

Button, K. J. (1992) 'Road pricing as an instrument in traffic management', paper presented to Symposium on Road Pricing, Stockholm, Sweden.

Confederation of British Industry (1989) *The Capital at Risk: Transport in London Task Force Report*, London, The Stationery Office.

Department of the Environment, Transport and the Regions (1998a) *A New Deal for Transport: Better for Everyone*, Government's White Paper on the Future of Transport, Cmnd 3950, London, The Stationery Office.

Department of the Environment, Transport and the Regions (1998b) *Breaking the Log Jam: The Government's Consultation Paper on Fighting Traffic Congestion and Pollution through Road User and Workplace Parking Charges*, London, The Stationery Office.

Department of the Environment, Transport and the Regions (2000a) *Transport Statistics Great Britain 2000*, London, The Stationery Office.

Department of the Environment, Transport and the Regions (2000b) *The Future of Aviation: The Government's Consultation Document on Air Transport Policy*.

DTLR (2000) *Transport Statistics 2000*, HMSO.

DTLR (2000) *Valuing the External Costs of Aviation*, London, The Stationery Office.

Goodwin P. B. (1992) 'A review of the new demand elasticities with special reference to short and long run effects of price changes', *Journal of Transport Economics and Policy*, **26**, pp.155–70.

Grieco, M. and Jones, P. (1994) 'A change in the policy climate? Current European perspectives on road pricing', *Urban Studies*, **9**, pp. 1517–32.

Ison, S. (1998) 'The saleability of urban road pricing', *Institute of Economic Affairs*, **18**, pp. 21–5.

The London Congestion Charging Research Programme (1995) London, HMSO.

Maddison, D., Pearce, D. *et al.* (1996) *Blueprint 5: The True Costs of Road Transport*, Earthscan Publications Ltd.

National Economic Research Associates (NERA) (1997) 'The costs of road congestion in Great Britain', NERA Briefing Paper, London, The Stationery Office.

Newbery, D. M. (1990) 'Pricing and Congestion: Economic Principles Relevant to Pricing Roads', *Oxford Review of Economic Policy*, **6**, 2, Summer.

Pearce, D. W. and Pearce, B. (2000) *Setting Environmental Taxes For Aircraft: A Case Study of the UK*, Elgar.

Road Charging Options for London: A Technical Assessment (2000) London, The Stationery Office.

ROCOL Report (2000) *Road Charging options for London: A Technical Assessment*, London, The Stationery Office.

Royal Commission on Environmental Pollution (1994) Eighteenth Report, *Transport and the Environment*, London, The Stationery Office, Cmnd 2674.

Royal Commission on Environmental Pollution, (1997) Twentieth Report, *Transport and the Environment – Developments since 1994*, London, The Stationery Office, Cmnd 3752.

Royal Commission on Environmental Pollution (2000) Twenty-second Report, *Energy – the Changing Climate*, London, The Stationary Office Cm 4749.

Useful websites

For an up-to-date range of GB transport statistics: www.transtat.detr.gov.uk

Information on various modes (aviation, rail, road and shipping) and their environmental implications, see the government website: www.detr.gov.uk

Sources of information in relation to London's transport strategy including road-pricing: www.london.gov.uk

Environmental implications: www.environment-agency.gov.uk

Value/congestion pricing: www.hhh.umn.edu/centres/slp/conprice

Transport: (EC DGVII)

Environment: (EC DGXI)

Housing, households and the environment

House building can have a direct impact on landscape issues, such as the erosion of the 'green belt' surrounding urban areas, affecting flora, fauna, wildlife and other physical conditions. Volumes and patterns of house building will also play a major part in a number of environmental issues involving waste disposal and recycling; as noted in Chapters 1 and 6, they are part of the 'environmental perspective'. Building regulations for houses, offices and factories also play an important part in energy efficiency and energy conservation issues, and thereby feature in the environmental pollution/climate change debate. Housing availability and conditions also affect the more human-related (*anthropogenic*) perspectives of the environment in that they influence the growth and development of individuals and communities.

Nor is the direction of causation one way, namely from housing to the environment. Changing environmental conditions are themselves having important impacts on housing developments: for example, climate change is arguably increasing the risks of flooding in certain geographical locations (e.g. floodplains) and thereby influencing the prospects for building houses.

Housing, energy conservation and environmental pollution

In the UK, *domestic households* account for some 29 per cent of final energy consumption, second only to transport. In fact some 80 per cent of all the energy used in the household sector is for heating (Royal Commission on Environmental Pollution, 2000). Clearly the household sector offers considerable scope for energy savings, whether by better design for new housing or improvements to the existing housing stock. Savings in energy in turn imply less burning of fossil fuels and therefore less emission of the greenhouse gases associated with climate change (Chapter 7).

Such energy savings in the household sector can come from two main sources:

- *Increased energy conservation* via reductions in the amount of energy consumed (e.g. turning thermostats down, accepting lower room temperatures);
- *Increased energy efficiency* by deriving more useful output (e.g. heat, light) from each unit of energy input.

There has been a 10 per cent *fall* in the past 25 years or so in the absolute amount of energy consumed within the home by the *average UK household*. Increased heat retention by better insulation and draught-proofing and more efficient heating systems (gas central heating generates more heat per unit of energy input than coal-fired central heating or open coal fires) have played an important part in this absolute fall in household energy consumption. However, the decline in the average number of people per household over this time period has also played an important part.

Despite the reduction in average household energy consumption, *total* household energy consumption has continued to increase. This is because the increase in the number of households in the UK over the past 25 years has more than outweighed the recorded reduction in energy use per household. As projections for the number of future households continue to increase, this puts still greater pressure on the need to save energy in the 'average' household by increases in energy conservation and energy efficiency.

Fortunately, significant further savings on energy use can be made by simple modifications to the current housing stock in the UK. For example, Box 10.1 suggests that of the current 22.5 million houses and flats in the UK, a large number have low ratings using the government's **standard assessment procedure** (SAP) for energy efficiency. It is estimated that savings of between 25 and 34 per cent could be made on total current household energy consumption if every household employed a range of energy-saving equipment and techniques which are already available.

BOX 10.1

Standard assessment procedure (SAP) and energy efficiency

A flat or house's SAP rating is based on its estimated annual fuel costs for space and water heating, assuming standard heating patterns and a standard number of occupants. The rating is normalised for floor area so house size does not strongly affect the result (a large house might have higher energy bills than a small one, even though the former was more energy efficient). The rating runs from 1 (extremely poor) to 100 (highly efficient), and while a highly efficient house would achieve a rating above 100 the practice is to round the score down when this happens. The formula used is:

$$SAP = 115 - 100 \times \log_{10}E$$

where E is the dwelling's estimated annual space and water heating bill divided by its floor area in square metres. This estimate is made by taking account of the insulation levels in a dwelling's windows, walls, roofs and floors, its ventilation rate, the type of heating system and the unit price of the fuel it uses, the amount of solar heating the house will obtain through south-facing windows and sheltering by other buildings. A site visit by an energy surveyor lasting about half an hour is needed to gather the necessary data (although it can also be obtained by viewing a building's plans and specifications). This is then followed by a series of calculations – usually made using a computer program – based on the *Building Research Establishment's domestic energy model*. A house with an SAP rating of 20 would have heating bills about twice as high as a similar-sized dwelling with a 50 rating (slightly over the UK average) and four times as high as one with a 77 rating.

▶

Compliance with the 1995 *Building Regulations* requires the builder of a property to estimate its rating but not to pass the information to prospective purchasers, although the government intends to amend the regulations to require this. The government's *House Condition Surveys in England, Scotland and Northern Ireland* now include SAP surveys on a large sample of dwellings. Combining the findings from the three nations, a picture of the energy efficiency of the UK housing stock emerges.

SAP rating	Number of homes (millions)	%
0–20	1.8	8
20–39	6.1	27
40–59	11.4	51
60–79	3.1	14
80 plus	0.1	0
	22.5	

Analysis of SAP ratings from these surveys demonstrates that lower-income households – those who can least afford to waste energy – live in the most inefficient, hardest to heat property. In all three nations the privately rented sector has a lower rating than owner-occupied, council and housing association homes. There is also a strong correlation between age of housing and SAP ratings with pre-1919 housing (which generally lacks cavity walls) having an average rating of 37. A new gas-heated home conforming to current (1995) Building Regulations would achieve a SAP rating of about 75. This improvement over time reflects successive revisions to the Building Regulations, which have gradually set higher standards of energy efficiency.

Source: Royal Commission on Environmental Pollution (2000).

Demographic factors and housing demands

Before going further into these environmental issues it may be useful to review the demographic factors involved in the UK. A key driving force in housing demand has been the increase in household formation in the UK from 16.3 million households in 1961 to 23.9 in 2000 (Table 10.1).

While the population in the UK rose by around 50 per cent during the twentieth century from 38 million to almost 64 million, the number of households rose by around 300% during the same period from just under 8 million in 1900 to almost 24 million in 2000. A number of demographic and social factors lie behind this increase in household formations:

- Increased lifespan of individuals
- Trend towards living alone – particularly among the elderly
- Demand for separate, smaller accommodation units

Building Regulations and new housing construction

Building Regulations for houses, offices and factories also play an important part in energy efficiency and energy conservation issues, and thereby feature in environmental pollution/climate change debate. Box 10.2 examines the role of these regulations in more detail for the UK.

Table 10.1 Households by type of household and family: percentage of total households

Great Britain	1961	1971	1981	1991	2000
One person					
Under state pension age	4	6	8	11	14
Over state pension age	7	12	14	16	15
Two or more unrelated adults	5	4	5	3	3
One-family households					
Couple					
No children	26	27	26	28	29
1–2 dependent children	30	26	25	20	19
3 or more dependent children	8	9	6	5	4
Non-dependent children only	10	8	8	8	6
Lone parent					
Dependent children	2	3	5	6	6
Non-dependent children only	4	4	4	4	3
Multi-family households	3	1	1	1	1
All households (millions)	16.3	18.6	20.2	22.4	23.9

Source: *Social Trends* (2001).

BOX 10.2

Building Regulations

Building Regulations set the minimum legal standards for new or removed housing. Periodic revisions to these regulations over the past 30 years have progressively improved the quality of additions to the housing stock. The latest version is the *1995 Building Regulations* which made an explicit attempt to achieve a cost-effective level of energy conservation. The higher required standards for home insulation and design under the 1995 Building Regulations were estimated to reduce the energy consumption of a typical new house by 25–35 per cent while increasing the construction costs by 1.5–3 per cent. The Building Regulations Division of the then Department of Environment, Transport and the Regions estimated that these impacts represented a £130–£180 annual saving to the householder on energy costs while increasing construction costs by £675 to £1,350 (DETR, 2000). To the householder the 'payback period' for the extra housing investment/cost was estimated as only 5–7 years.

The same source estimated that further changes to the Building Regulations involving still higher standards for cavity wall insulation and double glazing, a switch to higher efficiency boilers for central heating systems and more effective insulation for lofts and water cylinders, would provide more cost-effective energy savings. A reduction in annual fuel bills of £130 for a typical semi-detached home could be achieved at an extra construction cost of some £1,200–£1,300, a 'payback period' below 10 years.

Innovative developments in *new housing construction* can also play a key role in energy conservation. This is particularly important when some 4 million new houses and flats have been projected over the period 1996–2021 in the UK. Case Study 10.1 indicates some of the energy savings now available in modern housing developments.

CASE STUDY 10.1

New low-energy housing

A pioneering development

The construction of the most ambitious low-energy housing development in the UK to date began in Sutton, south London, in March 2000. The 80 town houses, maisonettes and apartments in the high density, mixed Beddington Zero Energy Development will be heated mainly by sunlight streaming in through all-glass south-facing walls. Additional warmth is provided by the body heat of the occupants and by cooking and electric lighting. Warmth gained during the days will be retained through the nights, due to the large thermal mass of the development (its fabric stores heat) and high levels of insulation. The buildings, which also include offices, are well sealed to prevent cold air leaking in. Ventilation is supplied through large wind cowls on the roofs, which draw in external air. As this cool air flows down ducts into the buildings it is warmed by stale internal air rising up through another duct enclosed within.

The heat for hot water supplies is generated by a small (110kW) combined heat and power (CHP) station fuelled by wood chips derived from tree prunings from the streets and parks of the neighbouring borough of Croydon. Some of the heat is used to dry the wood chips. Each dwelling's hot water tank is uninsulated, but stowed in a well-insulated cupboard with louvres which can be opened to provide top-up space heating during particularly cold weather, or after the home has been left empty for some time. The electricity from the development's CHP station will be used for lighting and to power domestic and office appliances, all of which will meet high energy efficiency standards. Surplus electricity can be exported to the grid and power can also be imported when the CHP station is shut down or unable to meet peak loads.

The housing is being laid out on the site of an old sewage works, in seven parallel terraces running east to west. The homes will be on the south-facing, sunnier side with office accommodation on the north. The intention is to reduce the heating requirements to 10 per cent of those of a conventional home; they would achieve a SAP rating of well above 100. The office spaces, which also have high insulation and thermal mass and a passive ventilation system, will be kept at a comfortable temperature year round by exploiting the body warmth of the workers and the heat leakage from computers and other electrical equipment.

The transport-related CO_2 emissions associated with the BedZED should be considerably reduced compared to a conventional housing development of the same size. It is close to a station, a new tram line and four bus routes. It is hoped that some residents will work from home, or at the offices within the development. The developers plan to set up a car pool which will have several electrically powered vehicles, to be charged by photovoltaic panels on the roofs. Residents who keep a car on the site will pay a parking charge.

Despite this being a high-density development, every dwelling will have its own garden (many of which will be roof gardens). The great majority of homes will be for sale on long leaseholds but at least 15 per cent will be reserved for social housing; 300 potential purchasers had already expressed an interest before construction began. The BedZED is being developed by the Peabody Trust, one of Britain's oldest and largest housing associations, with architect Bill Dunster and a locally based environmental enterprise group, Bioregional.

A more conventional approach

Located 3km from the site of the BedZED, an ordinary looking home built by a volume house builder in Cheam, Sutton, uses about 40 per cent less energy than the typical new dwelling built to the energy efficiency standards of the 1995 Building Regulations and of equivalent size. The former has a SAP rating of 100; the latter would achieve about 75. One of the three-storey, 110m^2 town house's most important energy-saving features is that it is part of a terrace; this substantially reduces heat losses through the walls. The 75mm gap between the outer brick and inner masonry blocks is slightly wider than the industry norm and this cavity is filled with blown mineral fibre. There is also a layer of underfloor insulation. Space heating and hot water are provided by a high-efficiency gas condensing boiler. The remainder of the three-bedroom house's energy-saving features, such as double glazing and loft insulation, are typical of all new houses. The company estimates that the extra energy-saving features added £216 to the total construction costs.

Source: Royal Commission on Environmental Pollution (2000).

Questions

1 What extra environmental benefits might be obtained from these new developments as compared to implementing the 1995 Building Regulations (see Box 10.2)?

2 Can you suggest any problems for the BedZED type of development?

● ● ● ● Housing location and environmental impacts

An important environmental issue involves the location of the many new houses required to meet the demographic and lifestyle changes previously outlined. This is an important issue in the UK and in many other advanced industrialised economies (Chapter 12 considers urbanisation and housing-related issues in the developing economies).

Cycle of urban development

Before considering the contemporary debate on greenfield/brownfield development and environmental implications, it may be helpful to briefly review the so-called *cycle of urban development*. Figure 10.1 sketches out that cycle.

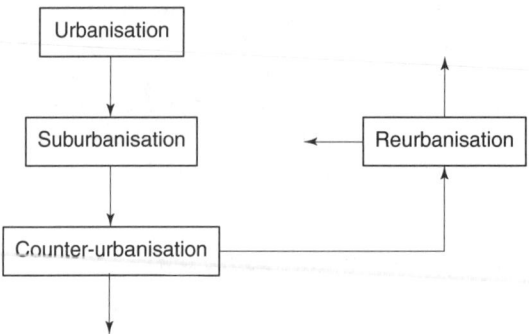

Figure 10.1 Cycle of urban development

● **Urbanisation**: the historical process involving the growth of *secondary sector* (manufacturing, construction, utilities) employment, often located in factory town and cities. Rural to urban migration was often involved in this process as people were attracted by the higher wages available in factory rather than agricultural employment. In the UK much of the urbanisation process occurred in and around the industrial revolution during the nineteenth century. Housing development tended to be concentrated in the central areas of towns and cities near to factory locations.

● **Suburbanisation**: the decentralisation of people and housing from central areas to town and city margins. Improved transport infrastructure played a part in this process with most jobs still located in the central areas of towns and cities. In the UK the most rapid expansion in suburbia took place in the 1919–39 period and resulted in measures being taken to control the spread of towns and cities (e.g. 'green belt').

● **Counter-urbanisation**: the movement of people, employment opportunities and housing developments to the small towns and villages outside the boundaries of the larger towns and cities. The rise of the *tertiary sector* (service-related employment) has been associated with counter-urbanisation, as have increasing population pressures in cities, adverse perception of urban (and positive perception of rural) life, increased car ownership, and so on.

● **Reurbanisation**: the movement of people and jobs *back* to areas of towns and cities which had been either abandoned during the process of suburbanisation or left derelict as manufacturing employment declined (deindustrialisation).

A particular housing-related issue of contemporary concern is whether the many new housing units needed should be built on 'greenfield' sites located *outside* existing settlements (perhaps by restricting the area designated as **'green belt'**) or *inside* existing settlements, especially the major towns and cities. The latter are often referred to as **'brownfield sites'** for housing developments.

'Greenfield' v 'brownfield' housing development

Planning regulations in the UK and many other countries have sought to restrict 'urban sprawl' (e.g. growth of suburbs) around towns and cities. In the UK this has involved the so-called 'green belt'.

'Green belt'

This is an area of rural or semi-rural land surrounding a city on which further urban development is to be prohibited or severely restricted. It was part of Howard's garden city idea and became law in the 1939 Green Belt Act. The original green belt was around London to check its growth and spread, but others have been created to keep two towns apart, e.g. Bath and Bristol or the Ruhr cities. In these cases it is not so much a belt as a buffer. Green wedges, corridors, hearts and zones also exist as variants on the same policy, and can help preserve the special character of a town and provide for recreational needs (Figure 10.2). Green belts are seen as restrictive by property developers who would like to use land for housing and out-of-town retailing. Restricting housing development in this way has been criticised for reducing the supply of building land, raising house prices and forcing out the local population in favour of the affluent commuter who then fights to maintain the green belt.

Examples of each of the types of 'green planning' in Figure 10.2 include:

1 Green belt, e.g. London;
2 Green wedge, e.g. Copenhagen;
3 Green corridors, e.g. Geneva;
4 Green buffer, e.g. Ruhr area;
5 Green zone, e.g. Paris;
6 Green heart, e.g. Netherlands.

The demand for some 4 million new homes in the UK and other industrialised economies is putting pressure on authorities to restrict these green planning areas

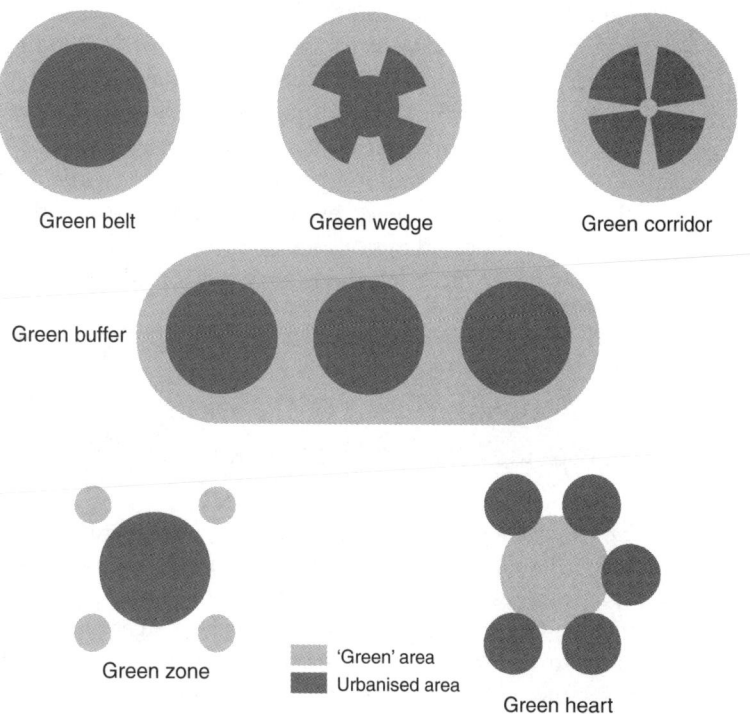

Figure 10.2 A classification of 'green' planning

and permit house building to occur on the greenfield sites released. However, there has been considerable resistance to this policy by 'environmentalists' opposed to adverse effects on landscape, rural economies and biodiversity.

The UK government has responded to such pressures by setting a target for 60 per cent of all new houses to be built on *brownfield* sites. The focus here is on reusing previously developed but now derelict sites for housing, converting empty buildings and offices to housing and making full use of infill sites in towns and cities. Local authorities in the UK have also been instructed to release land in urban areas previously reserved for employment purposes for housing, to pack higher housing densities into developments and reduce land earmarked for cars.

A problem for government in implementing such brownfield housing development is that large house builders prefer to build on greenfield sites, because brownfield sites are much more expensive to develop. For example, they are often contaminated with industrial wastes and may be owned by several parties. Assembling brownfield sites for housing development is often time-consuming and costly for developers. Critics have argued that unless the UK government gives regional development agencies and local authorities enhanced powers for compulsory purchase of brownfield sites in order to speed up the assembly process for developers, meeting the ambitious brownfield target of 60 per cent of all new houses will prove impossible. It has also been suggested that the UK government must remove the 17.5 per cent VAT on refurbishing or redeveloping existing buildings on brownfield house building to match the zero VAT rate on greenfield house building. A recent policy measure to support brownfield house building in 2000 was the 'sequential test' for housing developments, which instructed local authorities to use all brownfield sites available for housing *before* any greenfield site could be considered.

A particular problem for brownfield sites is flooding since, in the past, much industrial development has taken place alongside rivers. These rivers often provided sources of power and transport during the industrial revolution. However, climate change is increasing the risks of flooding (see pages 254–5). It has been suggested that the lower, more flood-prone areas of brownfield sites be allocated to nature conservation, open space or recreation areas, with the higher parts only of such sites being allocated to housing. Some of the risks associated with brownfield development of the more low-lying sites are considered in Case Study 10.2.

CASE STUDY 10.2

Living with a fear of flooding
From the Financial Times, January 2001

Ivor Wycherley began his career as an estate agent in Lewes in 1939, a year which saw serious flooding in the Sussex town. In 1960, when the town flooded again, he was out in a boat, rescuing people stranded in their houses and he was back doing the same thing in October 2000. As the Environment Agency and the insurance companies meet in the town's White Hart Hotel to estimate the likelihood of history repeating itself, his experience would seem as good a piece of evidence as any.

Lewes, along with nearby Uckfield, was one of the places worst hit by the first wave of flooding in autumn 2000. Four hundred homes and 200 businesses in the town were damaged. For those affected, the mess and worry drag on. For others, a second, longer-term issue has to be addressed about the viability of land for development. East Sussex faces problems common throughout south-east England: it has too little land to accommodate the 2,000 or so homes it needs to build every year to cope with its increasing population.

Two-thirds of the county is protected as an area of outstanding natural beauty. Of the few previously used brownfield sites in the remaining third, many have already been developed. Despite the best efforts of the local authorities, more than 50 per cent of the county's housing is being built on green fields.

Flooding has made the problem even more acute. What brownfield land there is tends to lie alongside the rivers which burst their banks in October 2000. One of the flooded sites in Lewes was a classic brownfield development of much needed social housing on formerly contaminated British Gas land. The county has to decide if it is worse to build houses on land that might flood, or whether to lose some more of its precious green-field land. 'It's a case of squaring the circle,' says Lindsay Frost, Lewes district council's director of planning.

Government figures show that 8 per cent of land in England is at risk from river flooding and 1.5 per cent at risk of flooding from the sea. That amounts to 1.3 million homes and business premises.

In its planning guidance following the 1998 Easter floods, the government acknowledged the tension between its desire to protect green fields and the need to avoid flood-prone areas. 'Because much past industrial development took place alongside rivers on suitable flat land, some brownfield sites will be potentially vulnerable to flooding,' it says. 'What was suitable for industry in the past may well not be suitable for housing today.'

Officials across the flood-hit areas are now weighing up their options. One consequence of the floods is that closer attention will be paid to advice from the Environment Agency on where and where not to build.

In East Sussex, the residents of Uckfield are among the first to witness the fall-out. Some of the new homes earmarked for their town now look more likely to be built in Polegate or Hailsham. The rain clouds that emptied on them at least had a silver lining.

Rural parts of the county are also likely to remain safe from development. The South Downs is on the way to becoming a national park. Government policy, which opposes car-dependent development, should protect villages. Craig Noel, planning expert at Strutt & Parker in Lewes, says the green fields most likely to be developed are farmland on the edge of towns.

He is one of several specialists who believe the best option for Lewes would be for development to continue in low-lying areas, but with developers making special adaptations to minimise flood risk. 'Developers are already subject to restrictions,' he says. 'They have been commonplace for the past 10 to 15 years'.

Lindsay Frost, Lewes chief planner, echoes that view. He says that by raising floor levels, improving surface water drainage and increasing flood water storage, houses can be built to withstand floods, without increasing flood risk elsewhere.

The floods have not deterred developers from seeking land in this part of Sussex. Craig Noel says they are paying £500,000 an acre for land with planning permission. The prices rise as you move towards London, reaching £1m. an acre in Horsham.

If developers are still paying the same for their land and having to spend more on flood defence systems, something else will have to give. Either they will build more cheaply, with aesthetic consequences, or prices will rise for the same quality.

Flooding is the latest factor to push the planning system further towards gridlock. Noel says it usually takes at least four years to go from identifying a piece of land to someone moving into a new home.

Meanwhile demand for housing continues to increase. James Bridgland of Strutt & Parker points out that short-term investors might be able to take advantage of this in Lewes. Properties in areas such as The Cliff are likely to be sold more cheaply while memories of the floods remain strong. Investors could do worse than to buy them up and let them to tenants who will pay the same rent regardless of the long-term risk.

Source: Financial Times, 13/14 January 2001.

Questions

1 Assess the environmental benefits and costs of building houses in Lewes on brownfield sites.

2 Consider the implications of recent flooding for this brownfield policy.

Settlement design

The current policies debate has moved beyond the greenfield/brownfield issue to focus more on developing 'sustainable settlements' (see Case Study 10.1). Advocates propose a shift towards high-density, well-designed housing areas, with workplaces, shops, schools and other facilities provided as close to people's homes as possible. The location of such settlements, whether on brownfield sites within towns and cities or on greenfield sites, is seen here as less important than the settlement design.

A key element in reducing pollution and conserving energy involves reducing the demand to travel for members of these high-density housing developments, especially to travel by car (see Chapter 9). Compact urban settlements can be designed to offer more work, educational and leisure facilities within safe walking and cycling distance from home. In addition, high-density housing populations are more attractive to public transport providers, with public transport requiring less energy input and emitting less pollution per passenger kilometre than private transport. Higher-density housing with shared walls is more efficient in retaining heat and can be designed to create wind shields. Shorter lengths of piping are needed for heat distribution networks in such developments, reducing heat losses and initial capital costs per house.

●●●● Flooding and floodplain developments: housing impacts

Flood risk issues have become an increasingly important aspect of the planning and development process in the UK and elsewhere, particularly as regards housing.

Flood risk and climate change

The global climate change effects outlined in Chapter 7 are widely accepted as increasing the susceptibility of land to flooding. The melting of the polar ice-caps in Greenland and Antarctica, extra meltwater from alpine ice and snow and thermal expansion of the oceans are, together, predicted to raise sea levels globally by some 210mm between 2000 and 2050. In the context of the UK, the rise in sea level will increase the expected frequency of high water levels in coastal areas by a factor of five by 2050 (i.e. occurring every 20 years on the east coast of England instead of every 100 years as previously).

Other than in coastal areas, climate change is also expected to increase flood risk inland. For example, the latest climate change scenarios reviewed in Chapter 7 suggest that annual rainfall in the UK is expected to increase by up to 10 per cent by 2050, with the largest increases in the north-west. The seasonal pattern of rainfall is also expected to change, with the UK receiving an extra 20 per cent of rainfall in the autumn and winter months. These projections also pointed to an increase in the number of rain days and in the average intensity of rainfall, together with a rise in average seasonal wind speeds. Overall the net effect of these changes is estimated to increase the inland flood risk in the UK for an unprotected area from once in 50 years to once in 10 years (PPG25, 2001).

Flood risk and housing development

Housing development has, historically, occurred in both river and coastal **floodplains** in the UK. *Floodplains* are level or near-level areas of land adjacent to watercourses (*fluvial* floodplains) or low-lying ground in coastal regions (*coastal* floodplains). They have often been delineated geographically by means of the statistical probability of a 'flooding event' greater than 1 per cent annual probability for fluvial floodplains and greater than 0.5 per cent annual probability for coastal floodplains.

Local planning authorities have responsibility in the UK for the control of housing developments in the floodplain and in the more extensive '**river catchments**'. *River catchments* are defined as the total area drained by a particular river, including areas away from the watercourse network. Altogether some 10,000km² (8 per cent of the total area) of land in England are estimated as being at risk from river flooding, including tidal rivers and estuaries, with a further 2,500km² (15 per cent of the total area) of land at risk of direct flooding by the sea. Expressed in terms of buildings this corresponds to some 1.7 million houses and 130,000 commercial properties in England.

The UK government has advocated the use of the '**precautionary principle**' by the regulatory authorities when deciding on planning applications for housing and other developments subject to flood risk (Box 10.3).

BOX 10.3

The precautionary principle

The *precautionary principle* is one in which action is proposed to avoid possible environmental damage where this may be substantial even when the scientific evidence for taking such action is currently inconclusive. The precautionary approach is characterised as recognising that:

● Human and environmental well-being has intrinsic value and legitimate status in achieving a better quality of life;

▶

- The environment should be passed on to future generations without further irreversible damage to its biological diversity and to its natural and built heritage;
- There are limitations in the ability of scientific knowledge to predict accurately the hazards which threaten the natural and built environment;
- Prudent action can be taken in advance of scientific certainty;
- There is a need for continued research, surveillance, monitoring and study of the environment to improve our understanding.

Although the local authorities will remain the arbiters of planning applications in the UK, it is now to be the responsibility of the *housing developers* to:

- Determine whether any proposed development will be affected by flooding and whether it will increase flood risk elsewhere; and
- Satisfy the local planning authority that any flood risk can be successfully managed with the minimum environmental effect to ensure the safe development and secure occupancy of any site.

Flood risk and house insurance

Planning authorities and house developers will be expected to give preference wherever possible to low-risk sites as regards house building. Where lack of land makes housing developments on higher-risk sites unavoidable, then adequate flood protection must be provided. The builders themselves will now be under much stronger legal requirements to provide and maintain flood defence works at new developments, and to undertake drainage measures to avoid increasing flood risks elsewhere (see Box 10.4).

BOX 10.4

Sustainable drainage systems

Sustainable urban drainage systems use techniques to control surface water runoff as close to its origin as possible, before it enters a watercourse. This involves moving away from traditional piped drainage systems to engineering solutions that mimic natural drainage processes. A wide range of sustainable draining options is available, from which designers, developers, planners, drainage specialists and civil engineers may choose in preference to piped drainage systems, including:

- *Preventive measures* – e.g. rainwater recycling, good-practice design and maintenance;
- *Filter strips and swales* – vegetated landscape features with smooth surfaces and a gentle downhill gradient to drain water evenly off impermeable surfaces, mimicking natural drainage patterns;
- *Filter drains and permeable and porous pavements* – permeable surfaces to allow rainwater and runoff to infiltrate into permeable material placed below ground to store water prior to discharge;

- *Infiltration devices* – below-ground or surface structures to drain water directly into the ground (soakaways, infiltration trenches, swales with infiltration and infiltration basins), which may be used at source or the runoff may be conveyed to the infiltration area in a pipe or swale;
- *Basins and ponds* – structures designed to hold water when it rains; basins are free from water in dry weather, ponds contain water at all times and are designed to hold more when it rains; examples include detention basins, balancing/attenuation ponds, flood storage reservoirs, lagoons, retention ponds and wetlands/reed beds.

Table 10.2 Potential Environment Agency risk-based advice to local planning authorities for proposed developments within floodplain zones

Nature of development	Inner zone[1] <100/200 years	Outer zone <1,000 years	Beyond
A Housing, hotels	Refuse[2]	Consult [3]	
B Workplaces <100 employees	Refuse[4]	Allow	
C Retail, community, leisure	Refuse[4]	Consult	
D Hospitals, schools, large examples of C, workplaces >100 employees	Refuse	Consult	Negligible risk of river/coastal flooding so no consultation with the Agency required except in relation to potential increased runoff
E Facilities of regional/national importance (e.g. major highways, railways, water/waste treatment)	Refuse unless appropriate adaptation or mitigation measures are adopted	Consult	

Notes:
[1] Inner zone refers to those areas at risk from events with return periods of up to 100 years (1% annual probability) for rivers and 200 years (0.5% annual probability) for coasts in the absence of any defences. Where there are existing or proposed defences to 100/200 year levels, the outer zone criteria should be applied.
[2] Infill housing should be permitted.
[3] Consult (for class A, C, D and E developments) will enable the Agency to be flexible, taking account of site and development-specific factors (size, proximity to inner/outer zone boundaries, existing developments etc.). It would also be possible to develop flood-proofing guidance (raising floor levels, air bricks, electrical fittings, etc.) enabling the Agency to judge the degree to which flood risk had been mitigated through design. Where extensive risk mitigation had been incorporated, the Agency could consider the application more favourably – but only for developments within the outer zone.
[4] Refuse on the basis that development in the floodplain should be judged in accordance with the Agency's existing guidelines (to advise against all development within the inner zone). However, sustaining an objection on risk grounds to class B and C developments within the inner zone could be problematic.

Source: PPC25 (2001a).

House insurance and flooding

The most recent analysis of flood risk (PPC25, 2001) has suggested the use of three zones for insurance purposes:

● *Inner zone* – areas at risk from flood events with return periods <100 years (1 per cent annual probability) for rivers or 200 years (0.5 per cent annual probability) for coasts;
● *Outer zone* – areas at risk from flood events with return periods of between 100/200 years and 1,000 years (0.1 per cent annual probability); and
● *Areas beyond the outer zone* – areas at a negligible risk of flooding from rivers or the sea.

Table 10.2 provides an example of the advice that the Environment Agency in the UK might give to local planning authorities.

> Now try the self-check questions for this chapter on the companion website
> **www.booksites.net/ison**
> You will also find up-to-date facts and case materials.

Key terms

Brownfield sites Housebuilding inside existing settlements

Counter-urbanisation Movement of people, employment opportunities and housing developments to small towns and villages outside the boundaries of larger towns and cities

Floodplains Level or near level areas of land adjacent to watercourses

Green belt Areas of rural or semi-rural land surrounding a city on which urban development is prohibited or highly restricted

Precautionary principle Where action is proposed because environmental risk is substantial, even if scientific evidence for that risk is as yet inconclusive

Reurbanisation Movement of people and jobs back to areas of towns and cities

River catchment Total area drained by a particular river

Standard assessment procedure (SAP) An official rating of energy efficiency, from 1 (extremely poor) to 100 (highly efficient)

Suburbanisation Decentralisation of people and housing from central areas to town and city margins

Urbanisation Historical process involving the growth of industrial population and employment, often located in towns and cities

References and further reading

DETR (2000), Building Regulations Division, May.

PPC25 (2001a), Planning Policy Guidance, *Development and Flood Risk*, Department of Environment, Appendix F.

PPC25 (2001b) Planning Policy Guidance, *Development and Flood Risk*, Consultation Paper, Department of the Environment.

Royal Commission on Environmental Pollution (2000), 22nd Report, *Energy – The Changing Climate*, Cm 4749.

Social Trends (2001) *Social Trends*, No.31, The Stationery Office.

Useful websites

Environment Agency

Scottish Environment Agency

Regional Policy: (EC DGXVI)

House Web (data on housing market)

Land Registry (house prices, etc.)

Rural economy and the environment

The impact of rural practices on the environment is touched on at various points of this book. For example, Chapter 12 outlines some of the environmental damage associated with the intensification of agriculture in the *developing* economies. This chapter, however, looks at the environmental issues and policy implications involving a wide range of rural activities within the *advanced industrialised economies* of the UK and other OECD countries.

Whatever the precise definition of the rural economy, there is no doubt that agricultural and related activities feature prominently within it. Table 11.1 might suggest a relatively restricted role for agriculture within the UK in which it accounts for only 2 per cent of all employment. Nevertheless the contribution of agriculture to national food security, the balance of payments, social and cultural life and to rural life in general is much more substantial than these figures might imply. The same holds true as regards the contribution of agriculture practices to a whole range of environmental outcomes, both favourable and unfavourable. We shall consider in some detail a number of agriculture-related issues which have major environmental implications, including traditional versus non-traditional farming methods, the use of genetically modified crops and the impacts of diseases such as foot-and-mouth and BSE.

Before turning to these specific issues it may be worth noting that the linkage between agriculture and the environment is very much a two-way process. Certainly agriculture affects the environment in a wide variety of ways:

- Agriculture can help maintain rural landscapes, preserve wildlife habitats and protect biodiversity as well as providing a carbon sink (e.g. trees and hedgerows) which traps carbon which would otherwise pollute the atmosphere as CO_2. Agricultural practices can also help in the sustainable management of water and soil resources and in the prevention of subsidence and flooding.
- Agricultural practices can also damage the environment by excessive use of fertilisers, pesticides and agrochemicals which can pollute and contaminate both surface and groundwater. Some farming practices can adversely affect natural habitats, threaten biodiversity and result in soil erosion.

However, the direction of impact can also be reversed, in that environmental standards and requirements can affect agricultural practices. For example, restrictions on permitted levels of nitrates in drinking water are influencing the application of fertilisers and other agrochemicals and thereby the volume and intensity of agricultural

Table 11.1 The 15 in the year 2000: some comparative statistics

Member country	Population (million)	Economically active population Agriculture (%)	Industry (%)	Services (%)	GDP per capita, euro (000 s)	Share of EU GDP (%)	Population (%)	Index of GDP per capita
Austria	8.1	7.2	33.2	59.6	24.6	2.4	2.2	110.3
Belgium	10.2	2.5	6.1	71.4	24.6	3.0	2.7	110.0
Denmark	5.3	4.0	27.0	69.0	26.3	1.7	1.4	117.0
Finland	5.2	7.1	27.6	65.3	23.1	1.4	1.4	103.7
France	59.4	4.6	25.9	69.5	22.5	15.9	15.8	101.0
Germany	82.2	3.3	37.5	59.2	23.8	23.3	21.8	106.8
Greece	10.5	20.4	23.2	56.4	15.1	1.9	2.8	67.2
Ireland	3.8	10.7	27.2	61.1	25.6	1.2	1.0	115.0
Italy	57.7	7.0	32.1	60.9	22.0	15.1	15.3	98.4
Luxembourg	0.4	2.8	30.7	66.5	44.2	0.2	−0.1	181.7
Netherlands	15.9	3.9	22.4	73.7	25.1	4 .7	4.2	112.4
Portugal	9.9	12.2	31.4	56.4	16.9	2.0	2.6	75.4
Spain	39.5	8.7	29.7	61.6	18.3	8.6	10.5	82.4
Sweden	8.9	2.9	26.1	71.0	22.7	2.4	2.4	101.9
UK	59.6	2.0	26.4	71.0	22.9	16.2	15.8	102.7

Sources: Various.

production. Similarly, increased consumer preferences for organic produce is beginning to influence farming practices (see Case Study 11.1).

●●●● Agricultural policies and the environment

In the UK and the EU a key influence on agricultural land use and farm practices has been the **Common Agricultural Policy** (CAP). Box 11.1 looks in more detail at its operation. However here we note that in recent times there has been a serious attempt to reform that policy by reducing price supports for agricultural produce and reducing subsidies for farm inputs. The results have in many cases led to less intensive forms of agricultural production, thus lowering the pressure on the environment, especially where such support had in the past encouraged unsustainable practices. In the crop sector, many farmers have responded to lower prices for their output and higher costs for their inputs by cutting down on the use of pesticides, fertilisers, machinery and irrigation water; in the livestock sector, such support reductions have led to smaller herds and lower stocking densities.

Lower prices for crops and higher costs for their inputs have also slowed down or brought to a halt the conversion of wetlands, forests and natural grasslands to agricultural use, thus preserving substantial areas of natural ecosystems. Where land susceptible to erosion has been afforested or its use shifted from cropping to grazing and forage production, the grass or tree cover established on this land has reduced erosion and helped restore degraded soil.

As already noted, a major criticism of the operation of EU agriculture has been the suggestion that high guaranteed prices to producers have led to excessive levels of crop production to the detriment of the environment. Box 11.1 reviews the basis for this criticism which tends to focus on the operation of the 'guarantee' system of the CAP.

BOX 11.1

Impacts of EU policies on farms and agri-businesses

The formal title for the executive body of the CAP is the European Agricultural Guarantee and Guidance Fund (EAGGF), often known by its French translation 'Fonds Européen d'Orientation et de Garantie Agricole' (FEOGA). As its name implies, one of its key roles is in operating the *guarantee system* for EU farm incomes.

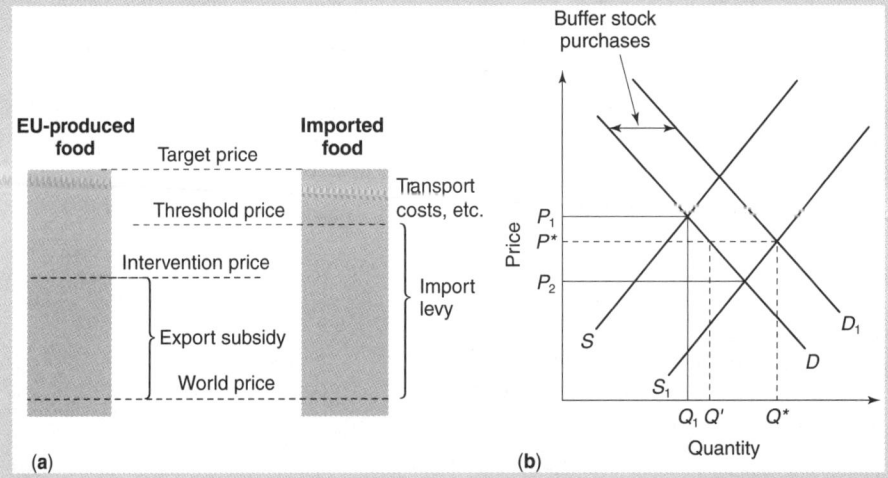

Figure 11.1 Common Agricultural Policy (CAP) of the EU: (a) CAP system: world price below target price; (b) guarantee system: maintaining the intervention price (P^*)

Different agricultural products are dealt with in slightly different ways, but the basis of the system is the establishment of a **target price** for each product, as in Figure 11.1(a). The target price is *not* set with reference to world prices, but is based upon the price which producers need to cover costs, including a profit mark-up, in the highest-cost area of production in the EU. The EU then sets an *intervention* or *guaranteed* price for the product in that area, about 7–10 per cent below the target price. Should the price be in danger of falling below this level, the Commission intervenes to buy up production to keep the price at or above the 'guaranteed' level. The Commission then sets separate target and intervention prices for that product in *each area* of the Community, related broadly to production costs in that area. As long as the market price in a given area (there are 11 such areas in the UK) is *above* the intervention price, the producer will sell his produce at prevailing market prices. In effect the intervention price sets a 'floor' below which market price will not be permitted to fall and is therefore the guaranteed minimum price to producers.   ▶

The 'guarantee system' becomes operative when the market price is in danger of falling *below* the intervention price. In Figure 11.1(b) we start with demand *D* and supply *S*, giving price P_1 and quantity Q_1. An increase in supply of agricultural products to S_1 would, if no action were taken, lower the market price from P_1 to P_2, i.e. below the intervention or guaranteed price, P^*. At P^* demand is Q' but supply is Q^*. To keep the price at P^* the EAGGF will buy up the excess supply $Q^* - Q'$. In terms of Figure 11.1(b), the demand curve is artificially increased to D_1 by the EAGGF purchase.

If this system of guaranteed minimum prices is to work, then EU farmers must be protected from low-priced *imports* from overseas. To this end levies or tariffs are imposed on imports of agricultural products. If in Figure 11.1(a) the price of imported food were higher than the EU target price then, of course, there would be no need for an import tariff. If, however, the import price is below this, say at the 'world price' in Figure 11.1(a), then an appropriate tariff must be calculated. This need not quite cover the difference between 'target' and 'world' price, since the importer still has to pay transport costs within the EU to get the food to market. The tariff must therefore be large enough to raise the import price at the EU frontier to the target price minus transport costs, i.e. **threshold price**. This calculation takes place in the highest-cost area of production in the EU, so that the import tariff set will more than protect EU producers in areas with lower target prices (i.e. lower-cost areas).

Should an EU producer wish to *export* an agricultural product then an export subsidy will be paid to bring his receipts up to the intervention price, as shown in Figure 11.1(a), i.e. the minimum price he would receive in the home market.

Reforms of the CAP over the past decade or so have modified this system which has proved an expensive method of supporting farm incomes. For example, **maximum guaranteed quantities** (MGQs) have now been set for most agricultural products. If the MGQ is exceeded, then the intervention price is cut by 30 per cent in the following year. In the cereals sector the intervention price has also been reduced by 15 per cent between 2000 and 2002 to set it closer to world levels. In the milk sector, the intervention price is to be cut by 15 per cent in three steps from 2005/6 onwards.

The system outlined above does not apply to all agricultural products in the EU. About a quarter of these products are covered by different direct subsidy systems, e.g. olive oil and tobacco, and some products, such as potatoes, agricultural alcohol and honey, are not covered by EU regulation at all.

Internalising environmental externalities in agriculture

Legg and Potier (1998) have pointed to the need for agricultural policies to help sustain the environment by providing more effective ways by which environmental costs and benefits can more readily enter into the production decisions of farmers. In some cases farmers in OECD countries are now charged for any damage caused by farming. For instance, some farmers are made to bear their share of the costs of polluting rivers through the application of the polluter pays principle (PPP) in agriculture. But farmers do not always bear the costs of the pollution they cause and are not always remunerated by the benefits they provide.

To distinguish between the beneficial and harmful effects of agriculture requires a reference point (benchmark). Such a benchmark can be *quantitative* (e.g. parts per million of phosphate in drinking water) or *qualitative* (e.g. desirable characteristics of the landscape). The identification and codification of 'good farming practices' can give guidance as regards the achievement of such reference points. The reference point represents what society expects farmers or landowners to provide – at their own cost – in their role as 'stewards' of the countryside. If society demands environmental benefits from agriculture (such as the maintenance of sustainable farming practices, the provision of habitats for wildlife or the prevention of soil erosion in fragile mountain areas) *above* the reference point, then farmers can reasonably expect government support for providing them.

Case Study 11.1 looks at the issue of pricing water to reflect its true environmental cost as a policy instrument. The aim is to help combat the excessive use of water for agricultural purposes which accounts for some 70 per cent of all water withdrawals.

CASE STUDY 11.1

Low water
From the *Financial Times*, August 2001

The world is getting drier. Climate change and irrigation have reduced Lake Chad, the African freshwater lake, to a twentieth of its size in the 1960s. Nine-tenths of the 'fertile crescent', the Mesopotamian marshlands near the confluence of the Tigris and Euphrates, have been lost through drainage and damming. The natural flows of rivers such as the Colorado, Yellow and Amu Darya (Turkistan) no longer reach the sea in the dry season.

For the world's water experts, who gathered in Stockholm for a symposium on water scarcity in August 2001, there is no doubt as to the gravity of the issue. Nearly a third of the world's expected population will live in regions facing severe water scarcity by 2025, according to findings released yesterday at the symposium by the International Water Management Institute.

The main reason for the global scarcity of water is increased demand. Growing the crops needed to feed the world's expanding population accounts for about 70 per cent of all water withdrawals. But increases in pollution are also taking a toll. In many parts of the world, rivers and lakes are so polluted that their water is unfit even for industrial use. In some countries, problems are likely to be exacerbated by future climate change.

Many observers believe there is a risk that future water shortages will lead to more famine and war. The message from the UN's Global Environment Outlook last year was stark: 'The world water cycle seems unlikely to be able to cope with the demands that will be made of it in the coming decades,' it said. Hans van Ginkel, UN under-secretary-general, has warned that conflicts over water could become 'a key part of the twenty-first-century landscape'.

Not everyone is so pessimistic. William Cosgrove, vice-president of the World Water Council, an international think tank, believes that the issue is about management of water, rather than absolute scarcity. 'There is a water crisis. But it is not about having too little water to satisfy our needs. It is just that we don't manage it well enough,' he says.

Tony Allan, professor of geography at the School of Oriental and African Studies in London, also finds some grounds for optimism. He says that there is sufficient water to satisfy people's personal needs almost everywhere. But agriculture is a different story. Growing food for an individual requires a thousand times as much water as it takes to meet that person's need for drinking water. Water-deficient economies balance their water budgets by importing 'virtual water' in the form of grain and other food staples, he says.

Many commentators remain sanguine about the world's continuing ability to produce enough food. Growth in food production substantially outpaced the growth in population between 1960 and 2000. The main problems will be experienced by arid countries, which are often extremely poor, that may be forced to move away from self-reliance in food production.

But some experts question the underlying sustainability of global food production. Attention is increasingly focused on groundwater, the water stored in underground aquifers, which is being depleted in parts of China, India and the western USA. Sandra Postel of the Worldwatch Institute, the US research group, believes farmers are over-pumping 160 billion m³ of groundwater a year – enough to produce nearly a tenth of the world's current grain supplies. The problem is worsening and 'represents one of the largest threats to future food production,' she says.

There are also concerns about the environmental and social costs of irrigation. It has inflicted significant damage on freshwater ecosystems, which provide sustenance for fish and other animals and millions of people. 'The protection of rivers and lakes is vital. Many people, especially in poor rural communities, depend directly on the food, timber and fish these ecosystems provide,' says Ger Bergkamp of the IUCN, the World Conservation Union.

Weighing the needs of agriculture against those of the environment is a complex matter, according to the organisers of the Stockholm conference. Agricultural scientists argue that farm water use, especially irrigation, must be increased by 15–20 per cent in the coming 25 years to maintain food security and reduce hunger and rural poverty. But environmental scientists say that water use will need to be reduced by at least 10 per cent to protect rivers, lakes and marshes.

As well as debating the conflicting needs of agriculture and environmental protection, the Stockholm conference will discuss practical measures to improve water use. The scope for improvements is significant. More than half the water entering irrigation distribution systems never makes it to the crops because of leakage and evaporation. Several techniques, such as the use of drip irrigation systems and precision sprinklers, can improve efficiency. Other innovations being developed include water-saving techniques for growing rice, the development of drought-resistant maize and low-cost irrigation technologies that produce higher crop yields because of more intensive cultivation.

Some water experts think the key to improved water management lies in setting prices that reflect the cost of supplying and distributing water. 'A major reason for growing water scarcity and freshwater ecosystem decline is that water is undervalued the world over,' according to a paper in *Science* by researchers at the World Resources Institute, a US think tank. The WRI acknowledges that pricing water to reflect its true cost is likely to run into stiff opposition from the public. But it argues that policy makers can win the support of farmers and urban residents if they offer a more reliable service.

There are already a number of agreements in which users make payments to preserve the source of their water. Since 1998, water users in Quito, Ecuador, have paid fees towards the protection of the high-elevation 'cloud forests', which extract water from the atmosphere.

Such deals may increasingly have to take place on an international basis. In the past 20 years, the number of river basins shared by more than one country has increased from 214 to 261, according to Peter Gleick of the Pacific Institute for Studies in Development, Environment and Security. He believes that water is likely to be a continued source of conflict and political tensions, even though it is rarely the sole source of violent conflict.

But some analysts think that there is exaggerated concern about the risk of conflict. In an article published by the International Committee of the Red Cross, Thomas Homer-Dixon of the University of Toronto argues that wars over river water are likely only in a narrow set of circumstances. The upstream country must be able to restrict the river's flow, there must be a history of antagonism between the countries and the downstream country must have sufficient military forces to think it worth starting a battle.

Such conditions apply in relatively few river basins. The most obvious is the Nile, where on several occasions Egypt has threatened military action to ensure an adequate supply of water. Even where there is the potential for international conflict, countries have tended in practice to opt for co-operation rather than conflict. 'My experience has been that once people begin to share information and look for ways to find solutions they will find them,' says Mr Cosgrove of the World Water Council.

But many of the experts meeting in Stockholm believe the world cannot afford to be too sanguine about the problems water shortages may bring. If water resources are managed badly, some parts of the world may experience an escalation in political tension, food shortages and environmental degradation. 'Pessimists are wrong but useful,' says Professor Allan. 'Optimists are right but dangerous because they allow politicians to treat water as a low political priority.'

Source: Financial Times, 14th August 2001.

Questions

1 Outline the causes and environmental costs of excessive water use.
2 What other costs might be identified?
3 What remedies might be proposed? Consider their advantages and disadvantages.

Legg and Potier (1998) suggest a number of other policy measures which might be used to provide appropriate incentives to farmers:

- *Economic instruments*, such as incentive payments, taxes and charges, or transferable permits, may be appropriate where farming practices affect the environment in a way that can be taken into account by farmers.
- *Cross-compliance measures* (which work by making the eligibility for income support conditional upon farmers taking specific actions, such as ensuring identified environmental outcomes) may be effective where income support is still important, and where practicable and enforceable environmental conditions can be identified.
- *Co-operative approaches* can be suitable for addressing specific local environmental issues, where farmers can apply their local expertise, and where collective action results in lower-cost solutions to environmental problems, as in the Australian 'Landcare' groups.

- *Information, advice and training programmes*, complemented by research and development incentives, can be very effective in enhancing the general awareness of farmers of how they can cultivate their land in environmentally sustainable and financially viable ways.
- *Regulatory measures* may be appropriate where environmental damage from a specific practice (the illegal or careless use of pesticides, for instance) could be severe and the resource loss irreversible and where rapid results are required.

It is increasingly recognised that policy measures and approaches intended to improve the environmental performance of agriculture must provide farmers with a set of appropriate incentives, which are then consistently applied.

It may be useful at this stage to review a number of agricultural issues which have major impacts for the rural environment and economy.

Climate change and agricultural practices

The global **carbon cycle** plays an important part in both releasing and absorbing CO_2, as noted in Chapter 6 (page 147). Forests, forest soils and wetland soils (e.g. peats) contain most of the carbon in terrestrial ecosystems. When forests are cleared and the soils cultivated or disturbed, much of the carbon in the soils is *released* into the atmosphere as CO_2 (methane is also released). On the other hand, trees growing to maturity *absorb* CO_2. Clearly land managerial practices leading to deforestation or afforestation will, respectively, increase or decrease the *net* amount of CO_2 (and methane) emissions contributing to global warming and climate change (see Chapter 7).

● ● ● ● Organic farming and biodiversity

A major report of the Soil Association (1999) stressed that the predicted move towards *organic farming* over the next decade could bring major benefits for the countryside. One obvious benefit from organic farming is the avoidance of fertilisers, pesticides and agrochemicals involved in more intensive non-organic methods of farming. Another involves the alleged benefits of organic farming for encouraging *biodiversity*.

Organic farming and biodiversity

Agriculture and appropriate farming practices are seen as essential elements in the conservation of farmland biodiversity. This is particularly important when, since the 1940s, farmland habitats in the UK have been eroded at an increasing rate (Table 11.2) with modern agriculture identified as a major cause.

Farmland bird populations have also been characterised by rapid decline, associated with the loss of these habitats. For example, over the past 30 years the following declines in bird population have been recorded in the UK (per cent): tree sparrow (89), grey partridge (82), corn bunting (80), turtle dove (77), bullfinch (76) and song thrush (73).

Table 11.2 Loss of UK farmland habitats since 1940s

Habitat type	% loss
Unimproved neutral grassland	97
Herb-rich meadow	95
Wetland	90
Calcareous grassland	80
Heathland	75
Broad-leaved woodland	50
Hedgerows	45
Ponds and ditches	30

The Countryside Agency (2000) in the UK has identified a number of environmental benefits of organic farming in terms of conserving biodiversity:

- *Mixed farming systems* – maintaining arable crops, pasture and livestock in close proximity;
- *Crop rotations* which provide feeding and breeding opportunities for farmland species;
- *Extensive livestock management* which supports the maintenance of permanent pasture, species-rich meadows and hedgerows;
- *Controlled stocking rates* which ensure sustainable grazing;
- *Maintaining soil fertility* with organic manures which encourages populations of earthworms and invertebrates in the soil, providing food for other farmland species;
- *Improving the water-retaining capacity of the soil* which reduces the demand for irrigation and thus benefits aquatic habitats and species.

Organic farming and the landscape

Organic farming is also seen as providing various benefits for the landscape:

- Crop rotations of organic systems maintain landscape diversity.
- Field boundaries tend to be better maintained and enhance biodiversity.
- Mixed organic farms contribute more beneficial landscape features than conventional farms – these include reduced field size, abundance of trees and sympathetic hedgerow management.

A Farm Environment Questionnaire was sent to 10 per cent of all Soil Association organic producers and 63 per cent responded. The results suggested that organic farmers had very positive attitudes towards wildlife and landscape conservation, particularly when compared with recent surveys of conventional farmers:

- 100 per cent of respondents stated an interest in wildlife on their farms.
- 68 per cent had received advice and training in wildlife management.

- 89 per cent were prepared to create wildlife areas on their farms if funding was available – 56 per cent were prepared to undertake the work irrespective of funding.
- 31 per cent had already prepared a Whole Farm Conservation Plan.
- 76 per cent found a biodiversity map an acceptable requirement.

Of course whether or not organic farming will grow as predicted and benefit biodiversity will depend in large part upon *consumer preferences* towards organic food and their willingness to pay a price premium in the early, more costly stages of organic food production. Case Study 11.2 looks at some of these issues in more detail.

CASE STUDY 11.2

Healthy food
From the *Financial Times*, August 2000

Iceland, the frozen food chain, announced in early 2000 it was 'going organic', at no extra cost to the customer. You might have expected the organic industry to have given unqualified support; instead it wavered. The Organic Farmers and Growers group expressed concern. The National Farmers' Union was worried. The Soil Association, it emerged, had already written to the frozen-food chain listing its reservations. 'Exciting, but flawed,' was the response of one of the association's directors; 'We have mixed feelings about this.'

This is because Iceland's scheme has revealed the British organic industry's predicament. Even as its advocates urge politicians, retailers and the public to embrace sustainable agriculture, they fear that any heavy-handed attempts to transform organic food from middle-class speciality to mass-market phenomenon could strangle the sector in its infancy.

However, recent studies show the organic food sector has great potential for expansion. Surveys show nearly 80 per cent of consumers, traumatised by a series of food-contamination scandals, would buy organic produce if it cost the same as conventional food. British production falls well short of meeting that demand. Although the present government is promising £140 m. over the next seven years, Britain remains one of only three EU countries not to offer organic farmers long-term 'stewardship grants' after they have converted to organic methods. Britain lies in only tenth place in terms of land given over to organic production, with less than 2 per cent, compared with Liechtenstein's 17 per cent, Austria's 8.4 per cent and Switzerland's 7.8 per cent.

As a result, Britain imported about 75 per cent of the £550 m. of organic food it consumed in 1999, much of that – humiliatingly – was root crops, cereals and dairy produce, all ideally suited to the British climate and soil. With the annual 40 per cent growth rate in British sales of organic foods likely to continue, and every supermarket now offering a range of products, local farmers have, belatedly, been queueing up to fill that vacuum.

Nevertheless organic farmers are worried that recent attempts by supermarkets to drastically reduce the 25 per cent premium on prices currently charged for organic products will be passed down the line to themselves. Many believe that if the price premium over non-organic products disappears, then it will be uneconomic for the many small organic farmers to continue production. The pity is that in the long term, organic producers argue, organic farming could supply the mass market relatively cheaply. Yields will gradually increase as the size of organic farms increases, crop rotation kicks in and soil fertility rises. The gradual transformation of what is, in effect, a cottage industry into a serious commercial concern will allow economies of scale, both technical and non-technical. Steady government support including aid that recognises the rural 'stewardship' provided by organic farmers would narrow the cost differences with conventional farming.

Only when a certain critical mass has been attained – and many organic advocates believe it must wait until 30 per cent of British land (2 per cent in 2000) and 20 per cent of British food is organic – can organic farm prices be expected to fall of their own accord. Until that point, their message will be: please buy organic, but be prepared to pay for it.

Source: Financial Times, 27th June 2000.

Questions

1 Consider the reasons why the frozen food retailer, Iceland, is seeking to support organic food.

2 What methods is Iceland using to support this strategy and what impacts are they having on Iceland itself?

3 Why are organic farmers fearful of Iceland's approach?

4 How might the government better support the growth of organic food consumption?

● ● ● ● Genetically modified (GM) crops

The use or avoidance of GM crops is a major issue for farming practice in both developed and developing economies and has serious implications for rural economies. Private sector research and development into GM crops had been boosted by a US Supreme Court decision in 1980 that extended patent protection to new types of plants and plant parts, including seeds, tissue cultures and genetic materials. After testing by the US regulatory authorities, GM crops were released for large-scale commercial use in 1996. By 2000, around half the US soyabean crop and a third of the corn crop were genetically modified. At the present time the USA, Argentina and Canada are the main producers of GM crops, with European countries currently trialling and testing before deciding whether or not to issue licences for their commercial production.

The incentives of GM crops for producers include reducing the problems of pest and weed control and soil protection. For example, a major US company developed soyabeans with a built-in immunity to that same company's herbicides. This herbicide could then be used without damage to the soyabean crop. Further, by being a strong and more effective herbicide it needed fewer applications than other more toxic weed killers. Similarly, a genetically modified strain of cotton contains an inbuilt toxin that minimises insect damage and reduces the need for chemical sprays.

Producers and consumers stand to gain, it is suggested, by lower costs and there-fore lower prices for GM crops and less exposure to pesticide and other toxic residues on GM crops. Indeed the GM crops can be further modified to contain additional nutrients such as vitamin A and iron, often lacking in the diets of poorer people.

In the UK and EU the situation is one in which the major current issue is whether, and to what extent, field trials of GM organisms should be undertaken to assess their respective benefits and costs. On the one hand we have environmentalists who argue that no field trial is worth the risk of releasing GM spores into the environ-ment to irrevocably 'cross-contaminate' other plants and species. By way of con-trast we have scientists and companies involved in developing GM organisms who argue that large numbers of field trials are essential to assess the risks scientifically (of course some argue that the environmental safety issue has already been resolved by testing in the USA!). Box 11.2 looks at the use of marginal analysis in approach-ing this issue.

BOX 11.2

GM field trials and marginal analysis

Chalkley (2000) addresses these perspectives, as can be seen in Figure 11.2.

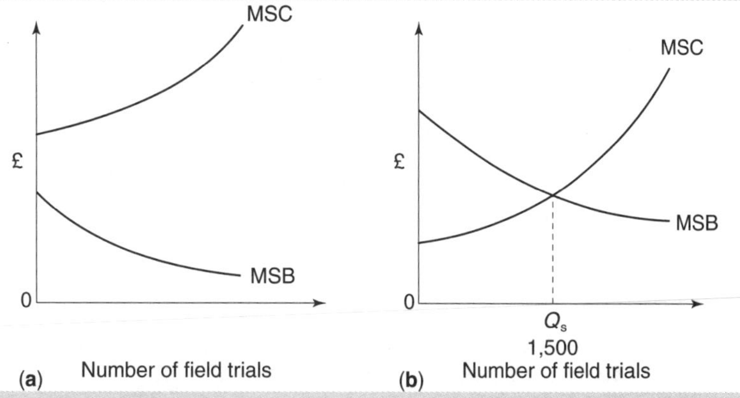

Figure 11.2 Opposing attitudes to trialling GM crops: (a) anti-GM crop trials; (b) pro-GM crop trials

Figure 11.2(a) reflects the first of these perspectives, namely that the marginal social cost (MSC) of trialling GM organisms is so high that it at all points exceeds any possible mar-ginal social benefit (MSB). On this perspective no trialling should take place. Figure 11.2(b) reflects the opposite perspective, namely a willingness to engage in as many as 1,500 field trials. The suggestion here is that the value of the marginal social benefit (extra information, etc.) of an extra field trial is deemed to be greater than the marginal social cost (extra risks to the environment) of an extra field trial at least up to a total of 1,500 such trials. Social surplus is a maximum where MSB = MSC, with Q_S (1,500) field trials. ▶

Clearly there is a subjective element involved in valuing the respective social costs and benefits which may be difficult to resolve, especially where opposing environmental perspectives are involved. However, any information gleaned from the early reporting of individual trials may be used to inform the debate as regards future trials. For example, information as to higher than expected probabilities of cross-contamination to greater geographical distances from trial sites will tend to shift the MSC curve upwards and to restrict the ultimate number of trials. However, information pointing in the opposite direction may shift the MSC curve downwards, increasing the number of trials, and so on.

● ● ● ● Farming and health issues

In recent years the farming sector and the rural economy in general have faced major problems in the UK, EU and elsewhere. Two major health issues involving animals and humans have involved the foot-and-mouth outbreak beginning in the UK in 2001 and the earlier outbreak of BSE.

CASE STUDY 11.3

The foot-and-mouth epidemic   FT

The foot-and-mouth virus is a highly infectious disease, which affects cloven-hoofed animals. The UK farming industry last suffered from the disease in 1967 but alarmingly a new case of foot-and-mouth was reported in February 2000. It has been suggested that the cause of foot-and-mouth disease (FMD) in the UK may have been via infected meat imported from East Asia, which ultimately found its way into the swill fed to pigs at a farm in Northumberland. FMD was then detected in pigs from this farm at an Essex abattoir. The disease can be spread over many miles by airborne particles and by the movement of infected or contaminated animals, vehicles or even people. The period of incubation is somewhere between 2 and 14 days in which time millions of FMD particles can find their way into food products such as milk and meat and into the saliva and urine of animals which can contaminate the environment. The clinical symptoms within animals are salivation, anorexia, depression, lameness and blisters on the tongue and lips. Here we review the extent of the virus and the likely economic costs.

The extent of FMD

According to the Department of the Environment, Food and Rural Affairs (DEFRA) as of 23th July 2001, 1,885 confirmed cases of FMD had occurred in the UK over a four-month period. In fact this figure stood at over 2,100 by early November of that year, having risen by an average of three cases per day over the previous three months.

The number of cases hides the fact that FMD has affected certain areas of the UK more than others. As can be seen in Table 11.3 certain counties, most notably Cumbria, have been disproportionately affected by FMD. In fact, over 40 per cent of all cases of FMD in the UK have been in Cumbria.

Table 11.3 Selected cases of FMD by county at 24 July 2001

County	Confirmed cases: overall
Berkshire	2
Cornwall	4
Cumbria	808
Derbyshire	8
Devon	173
Dumfries and Galloway	176
Northants	1
North Yorkshire	120
Oxfordshire	2
Northern Ireland	4

Source: DEFRA, 24th July 2001.

Table 11.4 reveals what all of this means in terms of the numbers of animals involved. It can be seen that over 3.5 million animals have been slaughtered. In early 2001 there were estimated to be around 44.4 million farm animals in the UK, comprising 10.9 million cattle, 27.6 million sheep and 5.9 million pigs. To date therefore around 8 per cent of the total UK livestock has been culled.

FMD is not confined to the UK. European countries, most notably France, the Netherlands and Ireland, have also experienced outbreaks. It is also found in other parts of the world with outbreaks reported in 34 countries the 18 months to July 2001. All of this has implications, not simply for the farming community but for other sectors of the rural economy, such as market traders and dealers, abattoirs, the horse racing and hunting fraternity and the tourist industry.

The economic costs associated with FMD

The cost of FMD can be looked at from a number of angles. This section deals with four aspects, namely the agricultural industry itself, tourism, the cost of government financial support and the cost of the clean-up required.

Agriculture

The slaughter of infected livestock has a direct economic impact on the farming community, but this is not the only impact of FMD. First, there is a loss of income

Table 11.4 Slaughter and disposal numbers at 17:00 Monday 23 July 2001

- 3,620,00 animals identified for slaughter
- 3,593,000 animals recorded as slaughtered. Of which:
  - 564,000 cattle
  - 2,895,000 sheep
  - 131,000 pigs
  - 2,000 goats
- 27,000 animals awaiting slaughter
- Of those animals slaughtered 11,000 remain to be disposed of

Source: DEFRA, 24th July 2001.

experienced by farmers until they can restock their culled animals. Second, farm- ers who have not suffered from FMD have been prevented from moving their livestock to market in order to facilitate their sale. This together with the fact that the animals which would have been sold have now required extra feedstuff, has resulted in serious cash-flow problems. Third, there has been a ban on the export of affected animals most notably in terms of lamb and pigmeat, which has repressed market prices.

Since FMD is not life threatening to adult animals then an important question to ask is why a slaughter policy is in place? Part of the answer lies in the fact that animals which have suffered FMD are not as productive. For example, cattle can experience a 50 per cent reduction in their milk yield in the year following infection and experience difficulty in regaining weight. Animals which have recovered may also still be carriers of the virus with the result that FMD-free countries ban the import of live animals, fresh meat and meat products from infected countries.

While farming represents a contracting sector, accounting for only around 0.9 per cent of the UK GDP and employing only 1.5 per cent of the workforce, the effects on agriculture are not to be underestimated. In saying this, however, the effect is likely to be less than that experienced by the tourist industry.

Tourism

Footpaths have been closed in many parts of rural England, as have National Trust properties and tourist attractions, all of which has an effect on the tourist industry. For example, a survey undertaken by the British Hospitality Association of approximately 500 UK hotels revealed that around 20 per cent of hotels located in rural towns had suf- fered a 25 per cent fall in business in April and May 2001. In addition, over 60 per cent of hotels were forecasting that business would decline further in the period June to September 2001.

The British Tourist Authority estimates that foreign tourists to Britain spent £12.5 bn in 1999 in addition to the £3.2 bn paid in fares. As can be seen in Figure 11.3, by far the biggest spenders are from the USA. It is widely accepted that potential US visitors to the UK have been put off by the images of dead and burning livestock regularly shown on US television.

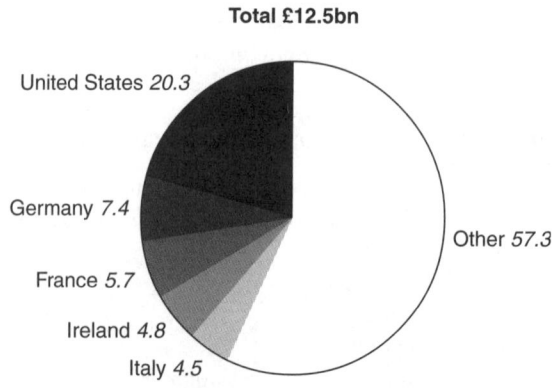

Figure 11.3 Overseas visitors' spending in Britain, 1999 (% of total)
Source: British Tourist Authority

In addition to foreign tourists, domestic tourism within the UK is highly important. PricewaterhouseCoopers have estimated a worst case scenario involving losses of at least £3–4 bn through a reduction in visitors to affected areas. It has been stated that in 2001 the foot-and-mouth crisis in Britain could impact tourism adversely by between £2.5 and £8 bn, which represents between 0.3 and 0.8 per cent of GDP (*The Economist*, 31st March 2001). In fact FMD has presented the tourist industry with its most difficult situation since the 1991 Gulf War. The British Tourist Authority estimates that the number of visitors and their associated spending could take up to four years to recover and the English Tourism Council estimates that FMD could cost the industry up to 250,000 jobs.

The clean-up cost

It has recently been estimated that the cost of clean-up of infected farms has been around £100,000 per farm on average, compared with a figure of 10 per cent of this cost in certain European countries and an average cost of only £30,000 in Scotland. At one point the clean-up budget was running at £2 m. per day. In mid-July the government temporarily halted the disinfecting of farms affected by FMD amid concern over this cost. As well as the clean-up cost there is also the cost of disposing of the 3.5 m. slaughtered animals.

Government support

On 11th July 2001 the government announced further financial support to businesses in rural areas hardest hit by FMD. The support will help councils to grant 100 per cent rate relief to small businesses, which are eligible for a period of up to one year. In addition, in a number of rural areas most seriously affected by FMD then central government will contribute 95 per cent of the cost of rates to larger businesses with a rateable value of up to £50,000. The remaining 5 per cent is paid by the relevant local authority.

Even though over 3.5 million animals have been slaughtered there is still the long-term threat that the virus can remain hidden, particularly among sheep. There have been outbreaks in areas unaffected by the disease. Vaccination remains an option but to use this would jeopardise the disease-free status of farming in the UK (afforded to countries who are not only free of FMD but have not resorted to a vaccination programme) and therefore the profitable export markets. Vaccination is expensive and needs to be repeated every 6–9 months. It may not prevent some animals from carrying the virus (while not developing the disease) and thus infecting livestock. What is clear is that FMD has severely affected the rural community and will continue to do so for some time to come.

Questions

1 Consider the environmental implications of FMD for the rural economy.
2 Outline the case for extensive government intervention in the rural economy in seeking to combat FMD.

BSE and the rural economy

Origins of the crisis

A useful survey of the origins of BSE was given by Goodman (1996). Bovine spongiform encephalopathy (BSE) was identified in the UK in 1986. It is similar in its effects on the brain to an ancient disease of sheep called scrapie, and to the very rare Creutzfeldt–Jakob disease (CJD) in mainly elderly humans. Around 200,000 cattle in the UK have been diagnosed as having BSE, mainly dairy cattle and mostly in England and Wales. The UK Government Advisory Committee concluded that the cause of BSE was the feeding of contaminated protein from scrapie-infected sheep to cattle, although many farmers never used such feed.

The UK government tackled the original BSE crisis with what most people now regard as lethargy. A Spongiform Encephalopathy Advisory Committee (SEAC) was set up. Affected cattle were slaughtered, a ban was imposed in 1988 on putting specified bovine offal (SBO) into human food and into animal feeding stuffs. The number of cases fell, but not as quickly as anticipated. In April 1995, the rules were tightened on SBOs, and again in August. In July 1995, exports of animals were restricted to those aged less than 30 months at slaughter. In February 1996, a compulsory test for protein in animal feed was introduced. Meanwhile, over 20 countries had introduced restrictions or prohibitions on the import of British beef and beef derivatives.

New variant CJD

By the end of February 1996, the beef market had settled down with steady prices and markets, and the initial consumer reaction against beef had largely disappeared to leave a small residual percentage decline in demand. On 20 March 1996, however, a government announcement hit the beef market and many associated farming and commercial activities like an earthquake – a classic 'economic shock'. A committee of experts, the CJD Surveillance Committee and SEAC found that there were then 10 cases of a variant of CJD which, unlike CJD itself which affects mainly the elderly, was affecting people whose average age was 27. Statements in the House of Commons and the subsequent press conference sought to reassure the public that there was no scientific evidence to prove that BSE could be transmitted to humans by beef but stressed the urgent need for more research. The main reassurance took the form of insisting that beef eaten since the SBO controls were introduced in 1989 was safe. However, this was somewhat undermined by persistent reports that these safeguards had not been fully observed in abattoirs. The European Union Standing Veterinary Committee immediately supported the imposition of a total ban on the export of all beef and beef products from the UK, which now extended to the EU countries which did not already have an import ban. There was an immediate collapse in demand for beef and hence cattle prices throughout the EU. Auction markets and abattoirs suffered a swift decline in business as supermarkets and fast food chains stopped selling British beef. Transport firms and meat processors began to lay off workers and cattle began to accumulate on farms. The loss of confidence in beef consumption was even greater in Germany and France which suffered the largest falls in demand as their beef consumption fell by 30 per cent between 20 March and July 1996, compared with a 15 per cent fall in the UK.

Schemes to deal with BSE

Four slaughter schemes were employed:

1 A calf scheme to reduce the number of cattle in the market.
2 A 30-month scheme where beef cattle must be killed before they reach that age.
3 A selective cull scheme of 80,000 cattle which were cohorts of BSE-infected cattle born after October 1990.
4 A voluntary accelerated slaughter of up to 67,000 cattle born in 1989/90.

This latter scheme was voluntary because keeping birth records of cattle was not mandatory before 15 October 1990. No one knew how many animals in this group were still alive. There were already serious delays in the slaughtering process, mainly because of the shortages of incinerator capacity, and the Ministry had to commission new cold stores to hold carcasses until they were destroyed. The auction price of beef cattle fell by about 26 per cent on average in the few months following the announcement of NVCJD but the retail price fell by less than 6 per cent. The supermarkets said that this discrepancy was because they were now only able to sell half the animal because consumers did not want items such as mince and sausages in the usual quantities. In July 1996, the sales of mince were at only 40 percent of the pre-crisis levels. There had also been a shift of consumption to chicken, lamb and pork.

The German and French governments introduced bans on the import of British beef and maintained these bans despite a European Court decision that they were illegal on the basis of 'flouting the single market rules'.

Impacts on the rural economy

The impacts of the BSE and NVCJD episodes on the rural economy of the UK and other beef-rearing countries in the EU have been substantial. The effective loss of the major part of the UK annual export market of beef to the EU of 190,000 t for much of the period since 1996 has depressed beef prices, seriously affected the income of beef farmers and the many other rural occupations closely linked to beef farming, for example those involved in the rendering, meat storage processing and distribution industries. In addition the export ban was extended to beef derivatives such as tallow and gelatine (the latter used in a wide variety of human food and confectionery), cattle embryos and bull semen. Although over £2 bn has been paid in compensation directly to beef farmers most of those involved in these related activities have received no such compensation. Over 100 known victims of NVCJD also received compensation in 2001, though the future projection of the disease across the population remains a matter of speculation.

The environmental effects of BSE involve changes in farm practices and land use patterns and therefore in the landscape. The human-related costs involve the depletion in incomes and employment opportunities for all those directly and indirectly involved in beef-related activities. Adverse health effects are, as yet, unquantifiable save for those already diagnosed as victims of NVCJD.

Nor have the rural impacts been confined to the UK. As cases of BSE were detected in cows in EU countries in 2000, sharp reductions in beef consumption have followed in those countries (27 per cent fall in beef consumption in the EU in 2001). In Germany the first BSE-infected cow was detected in November 2000, and a further 24 cows in the following three months. During that period beef eating fell by over a half and beef prices by over a third. The adverse environmental impacts on the rural economy already noted in the UK are repeating themselves in the EU.

However, arguably there are also a number of environmental benefits. Much greater effort is now being made to protect food standards across the EU countries. Under the 'Agenda 2000' farm reform approved by the EU, governments are now allowed to use up to 20 per cent of the direct farm supports they receive under the CAP (see page 262) to promote environmentally friendly farming and rural development. For example, Germany has set a target of using these funds to increase organic farming from the current 3 per cent of farm output to 20 per cent by 2010.

● ● ● ● Rural development policy (RDP)

The EU has sought to widen its rural perspective beyond reforming the CAP. Case Study 11.4 reviews the implementation of the RDP and some of its implications for environmental and other aspects of the rural economy.

CASE STUDY 11.4

Environmental implications of the RDP

The aim of the EU's RDP is to achieve the balanced development of rural areas; the promotion, creation and maintenance of employment; and the preservation of the environment and rural heritage. The 'measures', as they are called in EU terminology, come under seven headings, and member states have had to submit proposals within this framework. The seven headings are:

1 investments in farm businesses
2 human resources; young farmers, early retirement, training
3 less favoured areas and areas subject to environmental constraints
4 forests
5 processing and marketing of agricultural products
6 agri-environmental measures
7 various measures for general development of rural areas (13 are listed, for example promotion of tourism and crafts, land improvement, financial engineering, basic services for rural economies)

All the RDP initiatives are subject to *co-financing*, i.e. the Commission pays a proportion of the total cost of a scheme subject to the ceilings and conditions set in the Regulations (EC) 1257/1999 of 17 May 1999, and the member state pays the rest. The level of public aid is subject to a maximum which is expressed as a percentage of the total expenditure on the measure. This maximum can vary between different geographical regions of the EU and between different measures. For example, for *Tier 1* regions (i.e. where GDP per capita is below 75 per cent of the EU average) the maximum Commission support is 50 per cent for measures 1 (investment in farm businesses) and 5 (processing and marketing of agricultural products). For other regions of the EU, the maximum Commission support is only 40 per cent for measures 1 and 5.

If we take just two examples of the above measures, *less-favoured areas* (LFAs) (measure 3) and forests (measure 4), we can see how important the new RDP will be. Some rural areas are designated as LFAs because the farming conditions are more difficult due to natural conditions. These conditions tend to increase production costs, reduce yields and threaten the future of farming and the management of open spaces. The EU draws up a list of LFAs, based on submissions from each member country. The new RDP measures will pay farmers between €25 and €200 per hectare (€1 = £ 0.60 approx.), but the amount can go over €200 in some circumstances. Under the old policy, payments were based on the *numbers of animals*, which often led to overgrazing, so the new payments based on *area* are an improvement.

The EU also draws up a list of areas subject to environmental constraints such as mountainous areas, areas threatened with abandonment, areas where maintenance of the landscape is necessary, and areas where the continuation of agriculture is needed to ensure conservation or improvement of the environment, the management of the landscape or its tourism value. Farmers may also receive payments arising from these environmental constraints on their activities, covering any extra costs and loss of income, up to another €200 per hectare.

The second example, forests, is part of a new strategy aimed at ensuring the protection, sustainable management and development of EU forests. The new measures reflect the new EU buzzword, *multifunctionality*, which covers the role of forests in ecological, economic and social terms. The money allocated will help investments in forestry and forestry products and also other industrial processes using wood; it will help the creation of foresters' associations, the restoration of forests after natural disasters, and the development of preventative measures such as fire breaks. It will help pay for the afforestation of agricultural land subject to local conditions and the environment. Plantation of forests on agricultural land will attract an annual payment per hectare for five years to cover management costs, and an annual payment per hectare for up to 25 years to cover losses due to the afforestation. This latter payment can be up to €725 per hectare for farmers in associations and up to €185 per hectare for individuals. (The new CAP is keen to encourage co-operation between producers.)

The financial allocation to member states for the RDP and the CAP is given in Table 11.5. The UK will receive an average of €154 m. per year at 1999 prices; this is about 3.5 per cent of the total RDP allocation of the EU. The figure is relatively low compared

Table 11.5 EAGGF/guarantee section: annual support for rural development, 2000–6 (million euro, 1999 prices)

Member states	B	DK	D	GR	E	F	IRL	I
Annual average	50	46	700	131	459	760	315	595
%[1]	1.2	1.1	16.1	3.0	10.6	17.5	7.3	13.7

Member states	L	NL	A	P	FIN	S	UK	Total
Annual average	12	55	423	200	290	149	154	4,339
%[1]	0.3	1.3	9.7	4.6	6.7	3.4	3.5	100

Note: [1]Percentage of total RDP allocation by the EU going to each country.
Source: European Commission Director-General for Agriculture (1999).

with other members, although agriculture in the UK is itself a relatively smaller proportion of economic activity than the average for the EU (see Table 11.1).

The RDP in the United Kingdom

Each member state had six months in which to produce proposals for its own RDP and the UK government announced its EU-approved RDP schemes on 7th December 1999. The news was greeted by fierce criticism from the National Farmers' Union (NFU) in a press release on 7th December 1999 headed Rural Development funding 'a tax on farmers'. The Minister of Agriculture announced plans for England only because of Scottish and Welsh devolution and said a total of £1.6 bn would be spent over the years 2000–6, an increase of 60 per cent over the seven-year period. There are four sources of funding:

- The first source is the UK money already spent on existing schemes under the old version of the RDP.
- The second source will come from the EU's allocation of RDP money to the UK, about £100 m. (€154 m.) each year.
- The third, and very controversial, source, is from the redirection (or *modulation*) into the UK's RDP of a small percentage of the £1.6 m. paid in direct subsidies to UK farmers from the EU under the various CAP commodity regimes. The percentage to be redirected or modulated will be: 2.5 in 2001, 3.0 in 2002, 3.5 in 2003 and 2004, and 4.5 in 2005 and 2006. All money from this modulation will go into the UK's RDP and be spent in the UK.
- The fourth source is the United Kingdom government, which will match every redirected/modulated pound with money from the Exchequer.

The NFU is indignant about the modulation and regards it as a tax. It is angry because money that should be paid to them for growing crops and animals is being forcibly diverted from them into rural development. Only one other EU member state is using this method of financing the RDP.

Under its RDP proposals, the UK government plans to spend £1 bn on agri-environment schemes between 2000 and 2006, which is a doubling in expenditure over the period. Of this, £500 m. will be allocated to the *Countryside Stewardship Scheme* and £140 m. to *organic farm conversion*, £85 m. will be spent on *woodlands on farms*, £40 m. on *better marketing and processing*; £30 m. for the *growing of energy crops*, £22 m. for *training to improve the skills of farmers and workers relating to environmental land management and other aspects of diversification*.

There will be a new *Rural Enterprise Scheme* to promote rural development on and off the farm. The old Hill Livestock Compensatory Allowance will be replaced to help farmers in LFAs and the details will be settled after consultation. Administrative arrangements for some CAP payments will change. The UK has chosen not to adopt the measures allowed for in the RDP for compensating the early retirement of farmers and farm workers aged over 55. In other member states farmers may receive up to €150,000 and farm workers up to €35,000 over 10 years if they retire early.

Policies such as the RDP take time to make a noticeable difference especially if, as in the United Kingdom, there is a history of lukewarm acceptance of the principles behind them and a reluctance to match EU funds with UK money. In other member states, previous versions of the RDP have been applied with enthusiasm and some elements have had a major effect upon rural prosperity and diversification. Given the recent parlous state of UK farming with farm incomes falling dramatically, it would be a sensible long-term investment if the new RDP were applied with greater vigour.

Source: Goodman (2000).

Questions

1 How do supporters of the EU's RDP expect it to benefit the environment?

2 What particular environmental issues are raised when applying the RDP reforms to the UK?

Now try the self-check questions for this chapter on the companion website
www.booksites.net/ison
You will also find up-to-date facts and case materials.

Key terms

Carbon cycle The processes involved in the release and absorption of CO_2

Common Agricultural Policy (CAP) The mechanism by which the EU seeks to influence agricultural developments. Involves a 'guarantee system' of price supports and a 'guidance system' seeking to support those leaving agriculture

Cross-compliance measures Used to make the eligibility of farmer for income support conditional upon taking specified actions (e.g. environmentally 'friendly' actions).

Intervention (guaranteed) price That price at which the Commission intervenes in order to prevent it falling further

Maximum guaranteed quantities (MGQs) Quotas for products beyond which penalties are applied if exceeded by farmers

Target price The price producers need to cover costs, including a profit mark-up, in the highest cost area of production in the EU

Threshold price The price used to calculate import tariffs to protect EU farmers

References and further reading

Chalkley, M. (2000) 'Genetically modified economics', *Economic Review*, **18**, 1, September.

Countryside Agency (2000) 'The Organic Farming Environment', *Research notes*, Issue CRN 10, April.

Countryside Agency (2001) *The State of the Countryside 2001*, London, The Stationery Office.

European Commission Director-General for Agriculture (1999) *CAP Reform: Rural Development*, 3rd edn.

Goodman, S. (1996) 'Beef Wars: The Impact of the BSE crisis', *British Economy Survey*, **26**, 1, Autumn.

Goodman, S. (2000) 'CAP reforms: the Rural Development Policy (RDP)', *British Economy Survey*, **29**, 2.

Legg, W. and Potier, M. (1998) 'Reconciling agriculture and the environment', *OECD Observer*, No. 210, Feb.–March.

MAFF (2000) *Our Countryside: The Future. A Fair Deal for Rural England*, DETR, London, The Stationery Office.

Royal Commission on Environmental Pollution (2000), 22nd Report, *Energy – the Changing Climate*, Cm 4749.

Soil Association (1999) *The Organic Farming Environment: An Assessment of the Agronomic Impact, Biodiversity and Landscape Benefits of Enhanced Organic Conservation Standards*, Soil Association.

Useful websites

World Economic and Social Survey (2000)
www.foodfuture.org.uk
www.foe.co.uk/realfood/index.html
Full details of the measures under the RDP and their financing can be found via:
http://europa.eu.int/comm/dg06index.htm
Food and Agricultural Organisation
Friends of the Earth
Agriculture: (EC DGVI)
Environment: (EC DGXI)
Regional Policy: (EC DGXVI)
MAFF

Developing economies and the environment

As we shall see, the term 'developing economies' is something of a catch-all phrase which can legitimately be extended beyond those countries which are widely recognised as being among the 'less developed countries' (LDCs), although the latter are certainly included. The focus of the chapter will move beyond the LDCs alone to cover the situations in other 'developing' economies which also play a key role in determining global environmental outcomes. The environmental impacts of attempts to raise the standard of living in developing economies by increasing both industrial and service sector output and, as a result, the degree of urbanisation will be carefully considered.

The chapter begins by reviewing conventional criteria for classifying countries, including those regarded as 'developing' and 'transitional'. An analysis of the major features of these economies will shed some light on the pressures facing national policy makers which must be fully addressed by those seeking developing country compliance with international environmental agreements. The issue of 'sustainability' (see also Chapter 5) is reviewed in the particular context of the developing economies. Particular attention is also paid to definitions of 'well-being' in such economies, using broader indicators than national income per head. This reflects the human-related (**anthropogenic**) perspective we applied to definitions of the 'environment' in Chapter 1. The role of technological change in helping sustainable development in these low-income economies is also addressed.

The chapter concludes by reviewing a number of policy approaches directed towards environmental improvements in developing economies. Some of these focus on building 'positive links' between economic development and the environment, whereas others seek to break down existing 'negative links' between economic development and the environment.

●●●● Who are the developing economies?

It may be useful to note at the outset that there are a number of ways of classifying countries in a world economy which consists of over 6 billion people, living in 181 nation states and with an estimated average annual income of around $4,500 per person.

IMF classification

One widely used method for classifying economies is that of the International Monetary Fund (IMF), which uses three broad groups:

- *Industrial countries*: this covers the 23 highly industrialised countries, including the so-called Group of Seven or G7 economies (Canada, France, Germany, Italy, Japan, UK and USA), 14 other European economies and Australia and New Zealand.
- **Developing countries**: this is an extremely broad group of 130 countries covering the Middle East and Africa. It has been criticised as covering too wide a range of countries, from rural countries in extreme poverty to those close to being classified in the group of industrial countries. In an attempt to address this issue a subgroup of *newly industrialising countries* (NICs) has been separately identified within the 'developing countries', including countries such as Hong Kong, South Korea, Singapore and Taiwan.
- **Transitional economies**: these are the 28 countries that have emerged from the former Soviet Union (e.g. Ukraine, Belarus) together with the countries of Central and Eastern Europe which were closely allied with the former Soviet Union (e.g. Poland, Hungary).

World Bank classification

The World Bank and a number of other bodies use annual gross national product (GNP) per head to identify three broad groups of countries, one of which is further subdivided, making four groups in all:

- *High-income economies*: countries with an annual GNP per head of $9,361 or more (in 1998 values).
- *Middle-income economies*: countries with an annual GNP per head from $761 to $9,360 (in 1998 values). Because this group is so broad it has been subdivided into:
    (i) *Upper-middle-income economies*: annual GNP per head from $3,030 to $9,360
    (ii) *Lower-middle income economies*: annual GNP per head from $761 to $3,029
- *Low-income economies*: countries with an annual GNP per head of $760 or less (in 1998 values)

Official GNP figures place China (just) and India within the low-income economies. However, we will often present separate data for these two countries; first, because they make such a significant individual contribution to this grouping in terms of population size and share of GDP, second, because their pattern of development (especially that of China) has tended to run counter to that of other members of the low-income economy grouping.

Economic development and environmental impacts

Before considering the particular problems of LDCs, transitional economies and other country categories, it may be useful to consider the more general concerns of environmentalists as to increased levels of national income worldwide.

Using the World Bank classification, any country currently in one income category clearly aspires to move upwards to the next category. The data in Table 12.1 give an immediate impression of rising energy use and CO_2 emissions as such progression occurs. Such data have led many policy makers to focus on environmental impacts associated with attempts to raise real national income per head (standards of living) in developing economies. Indeed Figure 12.1 shows how energy consumption in developing and transitional economies is forecast to outstrip industrial country consumption.

Table 12.1   GNP, energy use and CO_2 emissions by income group

Country category	GNP per capita (US$ 1998)	Energy use (kg of oil equivalent per capita, 1996)	CO_2 emissions (t per capita, 1996)
Low-income countries	520	640	0.9
Lower-middle-income countries	1,710	1,763	2.6
Upper-middle-income countries	4,860	1,861	4.0
High-income countries	25,510	5,346	12.3
China	750	902	2.8
India	430	476	1.1

Source: Adapted from *World Development Report* (2000)

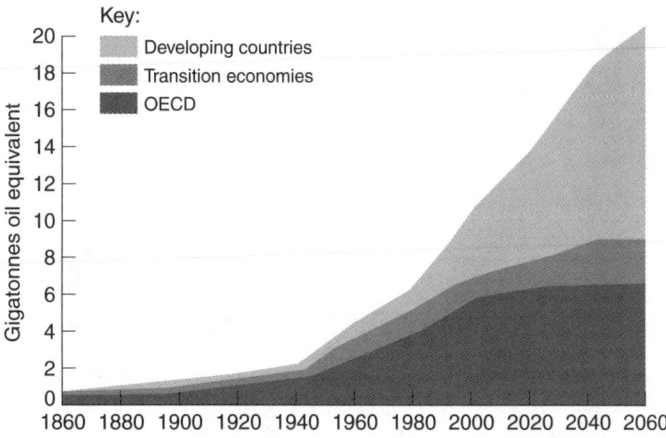

Figure 12.1   Energy consumption in developing and developed economies. Data for the period 2000–60 show a scenario of future energy consumption based on current trends
Source: World Development Report (2000)

As we noted in Chapter 7, industrial countries have historically been responsible for most of the increase in man-made greenhouse gases in the atmosphere but, as Figure 12.1 indicates, before the middle of this century the energy consumption of the developing countries is forecast to be more than twice that of the industrial OECD countries. This is despite the fact (Figure 12.2) that high-income countries currently use, and in the foreseeable future will continue to use, much more energy per capita than lower-income countries.

We might briefly review the factors behind such forecasts, which have been a driving force for those seeking the inclusion of the developing countries in international environmental agreements such as the Kyoto Protocol (see Chapter 7).

Income–environmental 'trade-off'

A dilemma facing the developing economies can usefully be illustrated in Figure 12.3 which uses production possibility curves to indicate a negative trade-off between national income and environmental quality; in other words, these curves suggest that a rise in national income can only be attained by some sacrifice of environmental quality. However, the production possibility curve for the developing economies is shown as lying inside that for the developed economies, suggesting that any given increase in national income can only be attained in the developing economies by a still larger sacrifice of environmental quality. For example, an increase in national income from N to N_1 requires a sacrifice of $E_1 - E_2$ for the developing economies but only $E_2 - E_3$ for the developed economies. The excess of environmental degradation from any given increase in national income would be still larger in the case of the developing economies if the base level of national

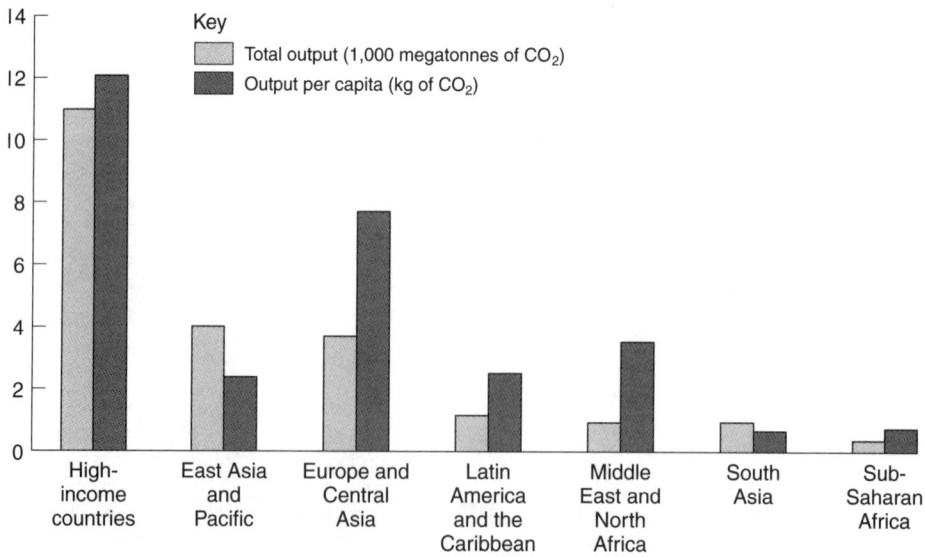

Figure 12.2 High-income countries use energy more intensively than countries in low-income regions
Source: World Bank (2000)

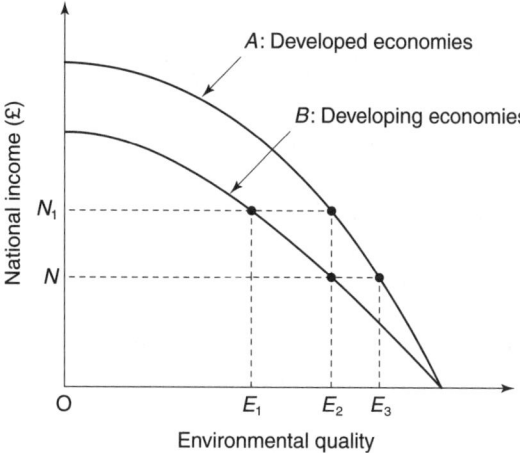

Figure 12.3   National income/environmental quality trade-off: developed and developing economies

income from which the change takes place was shown in Figure 12.3 as being lower for the developing economies (rather than as being identical at N).

Field (1997) quotes Robert Dorfman, a well-known environmental economist, to amply illustrate this point:

> …the poorer countries of the world confront tragic choices. They cannot afford drinking water standards as high as those the industrial countries are accustomed to. They cannot afford to close their pristine areas to polluting industries that would introduce technical know-how and productive capital and that would earn urgently needed foreign exchange. They cannot afford to bar mining companies from their exploited regions. Nor can they afford to impose anti-pollution requirements on these companies that are as strict and expensive as those in richer industrial countries. They should always realise that environmental protection measures are financed out of the stomachs of their own people; the multinationals cannot be made to pay for them.

Developing countries, according to this view, are less well placed than developed countries to be able to afford to utilise expensive but 'clean' technologies and to set exacting environmental standards to offset the environmental degradation invariably associated with a rise in economic development.

The 'Janicke' effect

The previous argument of a diminishing income–environmental trade-off associated with rising standards of living was given further impetus by the work of Janicke (1989). Janicke's study of 31 Eastern and Western industrialised countries from 1970 to 1987 related changes in GDP per capita to environmental impacts associated with the energy, steel, cement and transport sectors. For high-income economies such as Denmark, France, Germany and the UK, Janicke concluded that there had even been an 'absolute decoupling' of national income growth from environmental degradation, in the sense that various environmental impact indicators actually improved as national income continued to rise. This is shown in Figure 12.4 as occurring at just over $10,000 per capita in the values used at the time of the study.

As Janicke puts it, the mature, post-industrial societies are experiencing 'the environmental gratis effect' where the usage rate of those factors that have a detrimental environmental effect remains below the growth rate of GDP. The now dominant service and knowledge-based sectors are seen as providing a whole range of technological improvements and environmental benefits to a society which is increasingly environmentally aware and which chooses to spend a higher proportion of its extra income on environmentally 'friendly' goods and services. Put another way, these environmentally 'friendly' goods and services are deemed by consumers to fall in the 'luxury' categories that become available to consumers and economies only when levels of real income pass beyond some income threshold, giving us the 'inverted U' diagram of Figure 12.4.

A note of caution may be useful here. The environmental impact data used in Janicke's study tended to be rather narrow, concentrating on the known environmental hazards of the four sectors identified. If a broader range of environmental indicators had been used, no such 'inverted U' diagram may have been derived since many of these extra environmental indicators (such as municipal waste, deforestation, biodiversity, CO_2 emissions, etc.) are known to deteriorate as national income rises.

Nevertheless this is an area worthy of further study. For example, Turner (2001) found some evidence of an 'inverted U' relationship between energy use and GNP per capita, using data on 131 economies. He found that although CO_2 emissions tended to rise consistently with higher energy use across countries, energy use itself reaches a peak at a GNP per capita figure (in 1997 terms) of $25,000 before actually falling back at still higher levels of income.

A number of factors have been suggested as 'explaining' the increasing contribution to environmental degradation which allegedly can be attributed to the low-income developing economies:

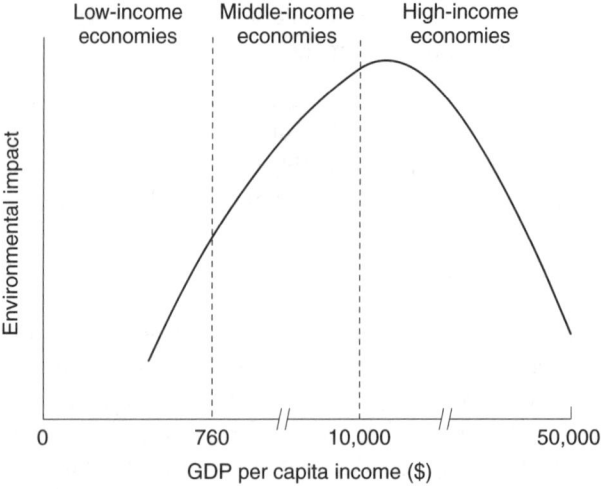

Figure 12.4 The 'Janicke effect'

- More rapid growth of manufacturing and industrial output in the developing countries
- Less utilisation in the developing countries of the more expensive but 'cleaner' technologies now feasible in many sectors of industrial activity
- Less emphasis on devising and enforcing environmental standards and regulations
- More extensive rural–urban shift patterns in the developing countries
- More rapid population growth in the developing countries

Of course many of these possible 'explanatory' factors may be interconnected. Nevertheless it may be useful to look at such factors separately and to consider their environmental impacts not only in terms of energy use and greenhouse gas emissions but also in broader environmental terms.

Industrialisation and environmental impacts

The **economic maturity argument** suggests that, as countries develop, the dominant share of national output and employment will progressively shift from the primary (agricultural and extractive) sector to the secondary (manufacturing and industrial) sector. Further development will then result in 'deindustrialisation' as the tertiary (service) sector becomes pre-eminent in both output and employment. Indeed some now argue that the advanced industrialised economies are becoming quaternary or post-industrial economies, dominated by information-handling activities.

For many of the low-income, developing economies there is certainly some evidence of a growth in share of industrial output and employment at the expense of the previously dominant agricultural and extractive industries over the period 1980–98. For example in Table 12.2, while agriculture fell by 10 per cent from 31 per cent of 1980 GDP to 21 per cent of 1998 GDP in the low-income economies, industry increased its share by 3 per cent over the same period, rising from 38 to 41 per cent. However, even in these low-income countries the

Table 12.2   % of GDP by country/income group and economic sector, 1980–98

Country/income group	Agriculture		Industry		(of which manufacturing)		Services		Average annual % growth of GDP
	1980	1998	1980	1998	1980	1998	1980	1998	
Low income	31	21	38	41	27	29	30	38	9.9
Middle income	13	9	41	36	25	21	46	56	1.9
High income	3	2	37	14	25	19	59	65	1.7
China	30	18	49	49	41	37	21	33	13.4
India	38	25	24	30	16	19	39	45	5.9

Source: Adapted from *World Development Report* (2000).

past two decades have seen a still more significant rise in the share of the service (tertiary) sector within total economic activity, rising by 8 per cent from 30 to 38 per cent over the same period. When we look at the main low-income economies of China and India separately, China confirms this picture as, to a lesser extent, does India.

When we look at the middle- and high-income economies, the expected pattern (via the economic maturity argument) of continued agricultural decline, deindustrialisation and further growth of the service sector is clearly evident from the data.

Of course we must remember that in the low-income developing economies, a higher percentage of a growing national income being involved in industrial activities is, in *absolute terms*, still more significant for industrial output and employment. Indeed, even for the middle- and high-income countries, a smaller percentage of GDP for the industrial sector within rapidly growing national incomes over a prolonged period (1980–98), may represent in *absolute terms* a considerable increase in industrial activity.

Industrial output and environmental quality

Historically a more industrial (and urbanised) world has produced ever greater quantities of common pollutants such as household waste and sewage, pesticides, heavy metals, dioxins, polychlorinated-biphenyls (PCBs), radioactive discharges, and so on. Figure 12.5 indicates the much more rapid growth in waste volumes projected for low-income developing countries as they industrialise over the years to 2025.

A major assumption behind such estimates is that the developing economies will be unable to afford to install the more advanced technologies capable of decoupling economic growth from environmental degradation. Nor will they be in a position to devise and enforce the higher environmental standards of the developed

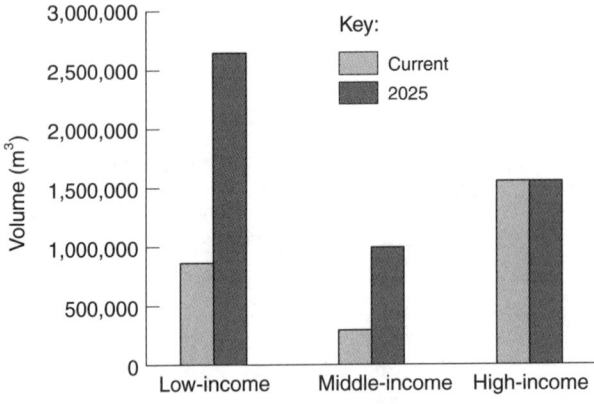

Figure 12.5 Total waste volumes generated by low-, middle- and high-income countries (per day)

Source: Hoornweg and Thomas (1999, p. 11)

economies. The increased use of 'clean' technologies and application of more rigorous environmental standards in the high-income economies has reduced the environmental damage inflicted per unit of raw material consumed.

Figure 12.6 shows that the growth path of damaging pollutants has to some extent been successfully **decoupled** from the growth path of production in the high-income EU countries. Sulphur dioxide and nitrogen oxide emissions have fallen significantly since 1990 relative to the index of production, though less progress has been made in reducing CO_2 emissions. A similar pattern has been observed over a longer period in the high-income OECD countries. For instance, since 1970 the GDP of the OECD countries has risen by over 80 per cent, yet sulphur dioxide emissions have fallen by 38 per cent, particulate emissions by 60 per cent and lead emissions by over 85 per cent. While more can still be done, technological change and the application of more rigorous environmental standards have certainly helped the high-income economies to change the ratio between economic growth and adverse environmental impacts.

Of course the invention and application of clean technologies are not without cost. Improvements such as those shown in Figure 12.6 have been achieved as the result of *annual* expenditures on anti-pollution policies equivalent to 0.8–1.5 per cent of GDP since the 1970s, with half of these expenditures incurred by the public sector and half by the private sector. To expect such sustained government and private sector expenditure by low-income developing economies with per capita incomes averaging some $520 per head (see Table 12.1) is clearly unrealistic.

Pollution haven hypothesis

The **pollution haven hypothesis** is another reason why 'decoupling' in the manner suggested by Figure 12.6 is likely to be more problematic for the developing

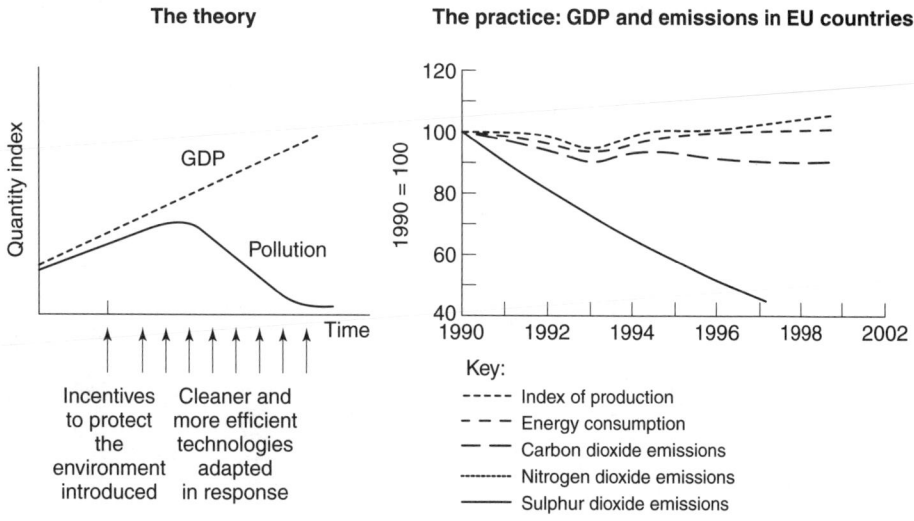

Figure 12.6   Breaking the link between growth in GDP and pollution

Source: Adapted from World Bank and European Environment Agency (2000)

economies. The suggestion here is that an increasingly important factor in the decisions by multinational firms to locate production facilities in the developing economies is the absence of the strict environmental controls applied in the developed economies. In this sense the developing economies are acting as 'pollution havens', proving particularly attractive to firms in the more toxic-intensive industries which release relatively large amounts of toxic chemicals per unit output.

With many variables involved in locational decisions by multinationals, testing this hypothesis by establishing the significance of the single explanatory variable (environmental standard avoidance) is clearly difficult. Some studies do, however, claim to have found evidence that the more toxic-intensive industries have grown most rapidly in the developing economies (Lucas *et al.*, 1992; Low and Yeats, 1992).

Nevertheless we should note that a major time-series study of the pollution haven hypothesis over the period 1960–95 by Mani and Wheeler (1998) came to a different conclusion. The period 1960–95 was one of rapid economic development, particularly in countries pursuing relatively open economic policies. Given the increased environmental awareness since the 1960s which also led to a rapid tightening of pollution regulation in the developed economies, the hypothesis would predict a more rapid growth of toxic-intensive industries in the unregulated (developing) economies that were open to international trade. The study concludes that no such evidence could be found over this time period.

Urbanisation and environmental impacts

'Urban areas' are usually defined in terms of concentrations of non-agricultural workers and non-agricultural production sectors. Although individual country

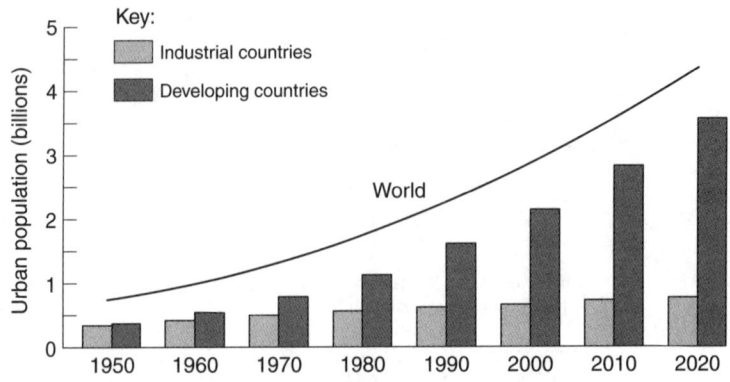

Figure 12.7 Most urban dwellers reside in developing countries
Source: UNDIESA (1998).

definitions differ, most countries regard settlements involving 2,500–25,000 people as urban areas. Larger urban areas are often termed 'metropolitan areas' as they involve networks of geographically adjacent urban areas, including towns and cities (the latter defined in terms of legal status within countries rather than pure size).

Increased urbanisation is clearly associated with the transfer of workers from agricultural and rural activities to new industrial and service sector employment in towns and cities. Around 50 per cent of the world's population currently lives in areas classified as urban, a rapid increase on the 34 per cent recorded in 1975. However, as Figure 12.7(a) indicates, by 2020 over 4 billion people (around 60 per cent) of the world's population will live in towns and cities, with the developing countries being the major contributor to this continued growth in urbanisation. The rate of urbanisation has passed its peak in the middle- to high-income industrial countries, but is far from its peak in much of Asia and Africa, as can be seen in Figure 12.8. The more rapid pace and less regulated nature of the urban growth in the developing economies has created a number of environmental problems, as indicated for a variety of cities in Table 12.3.

Urban living conditions such as crowding, sewage connections, waste collections and water access tend to be far inferior in cities with lower levels of average household incomes. Box 12.1 pays particular attention to the issue of sanitation in the context of urbanisation within developing economies.

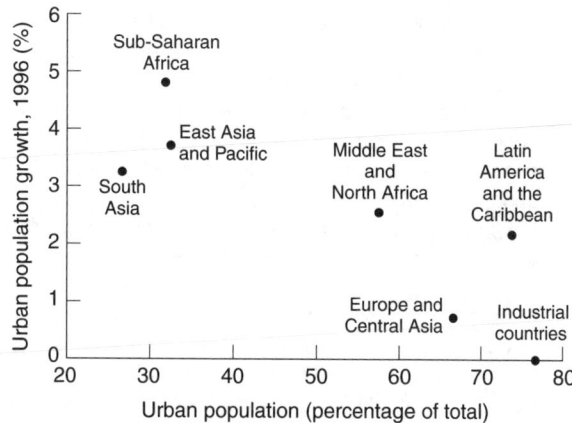

Figure 12.8   Asia and Africa are just beginning the urban transition
Source: World Bank (2000)

Table 12.3 Urbanisation and selected environmental impacts

City	Urban population (000)	Average household income ($)	Income differential (ratio of top to bottom quintile)	Crowding (m of floor space per person)	Households with sewage connections (%)	Households with waste collection (%)	Households with water access (%)
Dhaka (Bangladesh)	7,500	478	6.9	2.7	44	50	5
Lagos (Nigeria)	5,968	492	18.2	5.5	2	8	75
Recife (Brazil)	1,503	815	28.7	15.5	38	95	95
Delhi (India)	1,196	1,196	11.4	6.9	40	77	92
Jakarta (Indonesia)	13,048	2,460	6.6	15.0	37	84	75
Amsterdam (Netherlands)	724	21,687	5.2	38.3	100	100	93
Paris (France)	9,319	20,899	14.7	30.0	98	100	100
Melbourne (Australia)	3,023	30,216	12.0	55.0	99	100	

Source: Adapted from UN Human Development Report (2001).

Despite such problems there are a number of factors which make urbanisation so attractive to firms in both developing and developed economies. These are briefly reviewed below.

BOX 12.1

Sanitation and urbanisation

As already noted in Figure 12.5, as the low-income developing countries industrialise over the next 25 years, progressively larger discharges of wastewater and solid wastes can be expected in total and per capita. Inadequate investments in waste collection and disposal mean that large quantities of waste enter both groundwater and surface water. Groundwater contamination is less visible but often more serious because it can take decades for polluted aquifers to cleanse themselves and because large numbers of people drink untreated groundwater.

More environmental damage occurs when people try to compensate for inadequate provision. The lack or unreliability of piped water causes households to sink their own wells, which often leads to overpumping and depletion. In cities such as Jakarta, where almost two-thirds of the population rely on groundwater, the water table has declined dramatically since the 1970s. In coastal areas this can cause saline intrusion, sometimes rendering the water permanently unfit for consumption. In, for example, Bangkok, excessive pumping has also led to subsidence, cracked pavements, broken water and sewerage pipes, intrusion of seawater and flooding.

Inadequate water supply also prompts people to boil water, thus using energy. The practice is especially common in Asia. In Jakarta more than $50m. is spent each year by households for this purpose – an amount equal to 1 per cent of the city's GDP. Investments in water supply can therefore reduce fuelwood consumption and air pollution.

Effects on health

The health benefits from better water and sanitation are substantial: diarrhoeal death rates are typically about 60 per cent lower among children in households with adequate facilities than among those in households without such facilities. Improved environmental sanitation has economic benefits. Consider the case of sewage collection in Santiago, Chile. The principal justification for investments was the need to reduce the extraordinarily high incidence of typhoid fever in the city. A secondary motive was to maintain access to the markets of industrial countries for Chile's increasingly important exports of fruit and vegetables. To ensure the sanitary quality of these exports, it was essential to stop using raw wastewater in their production. In just the first 10 weeks of the cholera epidemic in Peru in the early 1990s, losses from reduced agricultural exports and tourism were estimated at $1 bn – more than three times the amount that the country had invested in water supply and sanitation services during the 1980s.

Agglomeration economies and urbanisation

Why is it that economic activity is so often concentrated in large, urban areas where land prices are often more than 50 times higher and the cost of living four or five times higher than they are in smaller urban or rural areas, less than 80 km away? From the firm's point of view the answer must involve the perceived benefits more than outweighing the additional costs. Many of these benefits are often grouped under the heading *agglomeration economies*, which refers to the alleged synergies which benefit firms from increases in urban size:

● *Localisation economies* – firms benefit from locating close to other firms in the *same* industry since this expands the pool of specialised workers and inputs. Henderson (1998) shows that in Brazil and the Republic of Korea, if a plant moves from a location shared by 1,000 workers employed by firms in the same industry to one with 10,000 such workers, output will increase by some 15 per cent on average.

● *Urbanisation economies* – firms also benefit from locating close to firms in *different* industries. The presence of a common pool of labour, materials and services provides benefits for all firms, whatever their sector of economic activity. Geographical proximity to other firms can, for example, help in the more rapid diffusion of knowledge, as in the case of 'information spillovers' via firms observing what others are doing, whatever the activities involved. Glaeser (1997) shows, using patent citations, that information flows increase with geographical proximity and deteriorate with geographical distance. 'Transaction costs' also fall when there is a higher degree of industrial concentration, e.g. the lower search costs now involved in matching workers with employment opportunities.

● *Diversification economies* – large urban areas are less vulnerable to business cycles because of their more diversified economic base.

● ● ● ● Population issues and environmental impacts

Population growth is occurring fastest in the developing countries (Table 12.4), with demographers expecting 97 per cent of all population growth in the next 25 years to occur in these countries.

The developing economies are by no means homogeneous in terms of demographic trends. The LDCs are characterised by much higher population growth than are the transitional economies, with the latter projected to experience an absolute decline over the period 1999–2015. The LDCs have experienced a more rapid rate of growth of urbanisation (although at a lower absolute level), have populations containing a much higher proportion of young people (and lower proportion of old people) and have much higher total fertility rates. Clearly policies which seek to address some of the environmental problems facing developing economies must be fine-tuned according to the needs of individual countries (or groups of countries) within this broad category. We return to these policy issues later in the chapter.

These population patterns and trends in the developing economies have a number of environmental implications. For LDCs these are usefully illustrated for Ghana by Case Study 12.1.

Table 12.4   Demographic trends in country/income groups

Country/income group	Annual population growth rate (%)		Urban population (% of total)			Population under 15 (% of total)		Population 65 years + (% of total)		Total fertility rate (per woman)*	
	1975–99	99–2015	1975	1999	2015	1999	2015	1999	2015	1970–75	90–2000
Developing economies											
LDCs	2.6	2.4	25.9	38.9	47.6	33.1	28.1	3.1	3.4	6.6	5.4
Transition	0.5	− 0.2	57.7	65.9	69.6	21.4	15.9	11.5	12.9	2.5	1.5
High income	0.7	0.4	75.0	78.7	82.2	18.6	15.8	14.5	18.3	2.1	1.7
Middle income	1.5	0.9	34.8	49.5	57.6	27.8	22.2	6.5	8.5	4.6	2.2
Low income	2.2	1.7	21.9	31.2	40.2	37.2	32.3	4.4	5.2	5.7	4.0

* Average number of children a woman would bear if age-specific fertility rates remained unchanged during her lifetime.

Source: Adapted from UN Human Development Report (2001).

CASE STUDY 12.1

Population explosion in Ghana

In 1921 Ghana had just 2 million people. That doubled in the next 27 years. Between 1948 and 1970 it doubled again. The 2000 census showed population at 20 million, a 500 per cent rise in 50 years. The crude birth rate is falling but Ghanaian mothers still bear 4.4 children on average. With medical advances, the mortality rate is falling even faster than the birth rate. Almost one in five Ghanaians are now under 5, half are under 15 and 62 per cent under 25. The momentum in this country of the young is unstoppable, and will define Ghana in the twenty-first century.

At best, the government can reduce the long-term numbers but it expects there to be 30 million by 2025, perhaps as many as 38 million. The national plan is to reduce the birth rate to 4.0 by 2003 and then bring it, as fast as possible, down to 3.5. That does not sound difficult but it represents a Herculean task in educating people and providing contraception. The culture in the countryside, where 70 per cent of people live, is still to see children as assets, conferring status, wealth and recognition.

The national rate of population increase is falling but birth control is only practised by 15 per cent of couples. Many believe that there is no problem with the growing numbers if the economy and the environment on which people depend keep up with the needs. It is a big 'if'. More than 12,000 teachers should be employed just to cope with today's burgeoning school numbers. Training colleges for the next generation of professionals must be built soon, the country needs to invest in infrastructure, education, health and agriculture now to avoid massive problems later.

It cannot. Ghana may be one of Africa's most economically successful and peaceful countries, but the average wage is just over £600 a year, and it depends heavily on US and Japanese aid for help with population control. Social services are falling behind and unless the economy picks up, the future is rocky. It is hard enough to service a population of 20 million, and 18 million more over the next 20-odd years means work must be found for millions more when a third of the country is even now unemployed. So people leave the villages, adding to pressures on the cities. Accra is now bursting out of its boundaries, 10 times the size it was 40 years ago and a magnet for thousands of illiterate people every year.

Questions

1 Outline some of the causes and consequences of population pressure in Ghana.

2 Suggest some environmental implications of this pressure.

The relevance of population size and growth to environment impact analysis can usefully be represented, though in a somewhat oversimplified form, by the following expression.

Total environmental impact = Environmental impact per person × Number of persons

We noted earlier (e.g. Table 12.1 and Figure 12.2) that a number of adverse environmental impacts per capita recorded in the low-income developing economies are below those recorded in the high-income developed economies. Nevertheless the more rapid population growth rates in many low-income developing economies are more than outweighing this differential (e.g. Figure 12.1).

However, this type of analysis is highly partial, focusing on specific industrial sectors (e.g. energy) and adverse environmental by-products of those sectors (e.g. greenhouse gas emissions). It also tends to use a single measure of economic and social welfare, namely GDP per capita. A broader-based approach which applies the perspective of sustainability (see Chapter 7) to the low-income developing economies will give a much fuller insight into emerging environmental patterns, issues and policy options.

● ● ● ● Sustainability and the developing economies

We have already considered the idea of sustainable development in Chapter 5. Sustainability has been broadly defined as development that meets the needs of its present generation without compromising the ability of future generations to meet their own needs. Put another way, sustainable development involves a country securing increases in 'well-being per capita' that last over future generations. A key question is therefore to seek to estimate current 'well-being per capita' and to project it over future generations.

Sustainability 'rules' and developing economies

Both the 'strong' and 'weak' sustainability rules outlined in Chapter 5 are extremely difficult for developing economies to achieve. Even the 'weak' sustainability rule is associated with total savings within the economy being sufficient to cover the total depreciation of capital assets (man-made capital, human capital). Few developing countries can generate total savings which come anywhere near the level needed to meet this 'general savings rule'.

In fact the debate as to 'sustainability' in the developing economies tends to focus on more realistic parameters, such as **carrying capacity**. This refers to the adequacy of the resource base of the system to support the population (current and projected) at the minimum standard of living necessary for survival. The idea of 'carrying capacity' is entirely different from the 'optimum population' considered in Chapter 8. The focus here is entirely on subsistence rather than on achieving any 'best possible' standard of living.

In a situation where, say, the potential food production of the agricultural system can generate Y calories, and where each person need $Y/1,000$ calories to survive, then the carrying capacity of that system is 1,000 persons:

$$\text{Carrying capacity} = \frac{\text{total calories}}{\text{Calories per person for subsistence}} = \frac{Y}{Y/1000} = \frac{1000Y}{Y} = 1000.$$

While food supplies have actually doubled over the past 25 years, it has been estimated that global food supplies will need to double again over the next 35 years if the carrying capacity of global agriculture is to be adequate to sustain the projected growth in world population over this time period. Of course it is not merely the volume of global food production but its distribution and accessibility which will ultimately determine the numbers sustainable within any particular geographical area.

Human Poverty Index (HPI)

A further step in this direction has been taken by the UN in 1997 with its introduction of the **Human Poverty Index** (HPI). This seeks to measure the extent of deprivation in terms of the percentages of people *not* expected to attain specific target levels for various economic and quality of life indicators. In this sense the HPI measures the proportion of people who are 'left outside' certain minimum standards for a country or a community.

The HPI incorporates three indicators, P_1, P_2 and P_3, the last of which is a composite of three separate items:

- (P_1) percentage of people not expected to survive to age 40
- (P_2) percentage of adults who are illiterate
- (P_3) percentage of people who fail to attain a 'decent living standard'

This latter indicator (P_3) is subdivided into three (equally weighted) separate items:

- (P_{31}) percentage of people without access to safe water
- (P_{32}) percentage of people without access to health services
- (P_{33}) percentage of people with underweight children

The P_3 indicator is then calculated as a simple average of these three separate items:

$$P_3 = \frac{P_{31} + P_{32} + P_{33}}{3}$$

The HPI is then calculated by the following formula:

$$\text{HPI} = \left[\frac{1}{3} \left(P_1^{\ 3} + P_2^{\ 3} + P_3^{\ 3} \right) \right]^{1/3}$$

Although rather complex, this formula gives an index number which is usually expressed as a percentage from 0 to 100. The closer to 0 per cent the HPI is, the smaller the degree of deprivation in terms of the three indicators. The closer to 100 per cent the HPI is, the greater the degree of deprivation in terms of the three indicators. Box 12.2 considers the HPI in rather more detail.

BOX 12.2

Applying the human poverty index (HPI)

We can illustrate the idea of the HPI by considering the values of the three indicators for Egypt (Table 12.5).

Table 12.5   Deprivation indicators for Egypt (%)

	P_1	P_2	P_{31}	P_{32}	P_{33}
Egypt	13.0	48.6	13	1	15

To calculate P_3 we take the simple average of the three separate items:

$$P_3 = \frac{13 + 1 + 15}{3} = \frac{29}{3} = 9.67 \ percent$$

HPI can be calculated as follows

$$HPI = \left[\frac{1}{3} \left(13.0^3 + 48.6^3 + 9.67^3 \right) \right]^{1/3}$$

$$= \left[\frac{1}{3} \left(2{,}197.0 + 114{,}791.3 + 904.2 \right) \right]^{1/3}$$

$$= \left[39{,}297.5 \right]^{1/3}$$

$$HPI = 34.0 \ percent$$

Broadly speaking, we can interpret this figure as suggesting that some 34.0 per cent of people in Egypt suffer from 'poverty', in the sense of being deprived of a minimum standard of entitlement in one or more of the three poverty indicators.

Table 12.6 shows the extent of poverty as measured by the HPI in the poorest 41 out of 77 developing countries for which data were available. For Niger some 62 per cent of people suffer from 'poverty' in terms of the HPI. In fact 32 countries have an HPI in excess of 33 per cent, implying that for these countries at least one-third of their people suffer from human 'poverty', with five countries having an HPI in excess of 50 per cent.

Table 12.6   Human Poverty Index (HPI) for the 41 poorest countries

	HPI (%)	HPI rank	HPI rank minus HDI rank
El Salvador	27.8	37	4
Oman	28.9	38	25
Guatemala	29.3	39	8
Papua New Guinea	29.8	40	− 1
Namibia	30.0	41	11
Iraq	30.1	42	3
Cameroon	30.9	43	− 1
Congo	31.5	44	4
Ghana	31.8	45	0
Egypt	34.0	46	14
India	35.9	47	− 3
Zambia	36.9	48	− 7
Lao People's Democratic Republic	39.4	49	2
Togo	39.8	50	− 4
Tanzania	39.8	51	− 8
Cambodia	39.9	52	1
Morocco	40.2	53	16
Nigeria	40.5	54	2
Central African Republic	40.7	55	− 7
Democratic Republic of the Congo	41.1	56	3
Uganda	42.1	57	− 10
Sudan	42.5	58	− 6
Guinea-Bissau	42.9	59	− 10
Haiti	44.5	60	− 6
Bhutan	44.9	61	− 2
Mauritania	45.9	62	4
Pakistan	46.0	63	14
Côte d'Ivoire	46.4	64	7
Bangladesh	46.5	65	9
Madagascar	47.7	66	5
Malawi	47.7	67	− 1
Mozambique	48.5	68	− 2
Senegal	48.6	69	4
Yemen	48.9	70	10
Guinea	49.1	71	0
Burundi	49.5	72	− 1
Mali	52.8	73	− 1
Ethiopia	55.5	74	2
Sierra Leone	58.2	75	− 2
Burkina Faso	58.2	76	1
Niger	62.1	77	1

Notice that the ranking of countries by the earlier Human Development Index (HDI) and the HPI differs, at times considerably so. Arguably the HDI measures progress for the country as a whole, but the HPI measures the proportions of people in that country who are excluded from that progress. So, for example in Table 12.6, out of the 77 developing countries ranked in terms of HPI and HDI, Oman is ranked 25 places lower on HPI than on HDI. This suggests that the average achievements in Oman in terms of HDI are less evenly distributed among its population than is the case elsewhere (hence its lower ranking in HPI than in HDI). On the other hand, Uganda is ranked 10 places higher on HPI than on HDI, suggesting that its average achievements in terms of HDI are more evenly distributed among its population than is the case elsewhere.

Although not shown in Table 12.6, China has an HPI of 17.1 per cent and an HPI ranking of 16 out of the 77 countries. The HDI calculated for China and Egypt turned out to be very similar, yet Egypt's HPI is much higher at 34 per cent, a ranking of 46 out of 77 countries. This implies that, although the average achievements in terms of the HDI are quite similar in China and Egypt, they are more inequitably distributed in Egypt than in China.

Measuring 'well-being' in developing economies

Tables and diagrams in this chapter have, until this point, used GNP (or GDP) per head values as a measure of economic well-being. Although this value gives an average figure for income (or output) per head of population, it is particularly unhelpful for measuring 'well-being' in developing economies.

(a) Inappropriate exchange rates

Converting the value of GNP expressed in the local currency into a $ equivalent using the official exchange rate may misrepresent the actual purchasing power in the local economy. This is because the official exchange rate is influenced by a range of complex forces in the foreign exchange markets and may not accurately reflect the purchasing power of one country's currency in another country. A more accurate picture is given if we use purchasing power parities (PPPs) rather than official exchange rates when making this conversion (see Table 12.5). Purchasing power parities measure how many units of one country's currency are needed to buy exactly the same basket of goods as can be bought with a given amount of another country's currency. On this basis the Mozambique figure rises from $90 to $959 per capita and the Switzerland figure falls from $44,320 to around $24,881 per capita using 1998 purchasing power parities.

(b) Differing degrees of non-market economic activity

GNP per capita only includes the money value of recorded (market) transactions involving goods and services. Non-market transactions are excluded. For example, the output of subsistence agriculture, whereby farmers grow food for their own consumption, is excluded from GNP figures. In many less developed economies where there is often a greater degree of non-market economic activity this fact may lead GNP figures to underestimate the true living standards.

(c) Varying levels of inequality

GNP per capita gives an indication of the 'average' standard of living in a country. However, this may reflect the experience of only a small number of people in that country because its income distribution may be highly unequal, being skewed in the direction of the wealthier sections of society. For example, instead of using the arithmetic mean for GNP per capita, the median might be a more useful measure of the 'average', i.e. that figure for which 50 per cent of the population has a higher GNP per capita, and 50 per cent has a lower GNP per capita.

(d) Incidence of externalities

Externalities occur where actions by an individual or group impose costs (or benefits) on others which are not fully 'priced'. Increased pollution is a by-product of many industrial processes, reducing the quality of life for those affected. However, this negative externality may not be reflected in the GNP calculations. Similarly, the GNP figure makes no allowance for the depletion and degradation of natural resources and for the social costs these may impose, e.g. deforestation as a factor in global warming.

For these and other reasons (differing accounting conventions, economic and social practices, etc.) there has been a move towards the use of indicators other than the GNP per capita figure to reflect the 'true' standard of living in developing countries, using various 'quality of life' indicators such as life expectancy, medical provision, educational opportunities, etc. The United Nations has published a *Human Development Report* since 1990 in which a new method of classification is presented, namely the *Human Development Index* (see Chapter 8), which incorporates both quality of life indicators and GNP per head data.

Environmental policy and developing economies

Many reports have pointed to the key role in environmental policy of providing incentives and institutional structures to encourage environmentally sustainable practices by local populations. Two broad sets of policies are needed to attack the underlying causes of environmental damage:

- Policies that seek to build on the positive links between economic development and the environment. These might involve supporting best practice, correcting or preventing policy failures, improving access to resources and technology, and promoting equitable income growth.
- Policies which seek to break down negative links between economic development and the environment. These might involve introducing regulations and/or incentives needed to force decision makers to take account of environmental values.

Arguably each set of policies is necessary, but neither is sufficient by itself.

Building positive links

We first consider a number of policies directed towards building positive links between economic development and the environment.

Supporting adaptation

Case Study 12.2 looks at policies which seek to support *adaptation* – namely strategies that encourage the rural poor to avoid actions which might have adverse environmental impacts in favour of alternatives which have positive environmental impacts.

Supporting technological change

The contribution of cleaner technologies to 'decoupling' adverse environmental impacts from economic development has already been noted (e.g. Figure 12.6) as has its contribution to sustainability (Figure 5.3). Of course the developing economies and international agencies may need to be *selective* in choosing the technologies likely to yield the greater benefits. These may not always involve overtly 'environmental' policies. Economic development and rising standards of living are associated with greater, not less, concern for environmental improvements.

CASE STUDY 12.2

Rural poverty and adaptation

Near a Bengali village, peasant families searching for firewood pick a local forest patch clean. A refugee from wartorn Rwanda flees to Tanzania where he poaches game in a national park to feed his family. A poor Kenyan family continues to cultivate their small farm plot in spite of severe erosion and exhausted soil. These are the typical images of the rural poor – people hugely dependent on ecosystems, unable to afford sound management practices, and caught in a vicious cycle of overusing already fragile and degraded resources.

A more nuanced view has emerged, however, that recognises that the poor may have limited resources and great dependence on the environment, but they also have considerable ability to protect their ecosystems, when given the opportunity. Research is bringing to light abundant examples of adaptation – strategies that the poor use to lessen the impacts of environmental, economic or social change on their resources. Adoptive measures include innovative land-use practices, the adoption of new technologies, economic diversification and changes in social organisation.

Who are the poor?

Approximately 1.3 billion people, one-quarter of the world's population, live on about $1 a day. In addition to encompassing insufficient financial assets, poverty often means a lack of education, mobility, employment opportunities, or access to basic services such as safe water, and physical isolation in remote villages. Limited access to land is another key aspect of poverty; 52 per cent of the rural poor have landholdings too small to provide an adequate income, and 24 per cent are landless.

The vulnerability of the poor is often exacerbated by a lack of political power to defend their rights to environmental resources or defend themselves against outright oppression. In South and South-east Asian countries, for example, many governments consider forest-dependent people to be squatters who are illegally using state-owned resources. They can be arbitrarily displaced, often with state sanction, no matter how long they have occupied the forest. War and civil conflict in Central and Eastern Europe, Somalia, the Congo, Lebanon and other countries have torn people from their land and plunged them into poverty.

Urban poverty is a growing phenomenon, but the largest numbers of poor people in developing countries still live in rural areas – as much as 80 per cent. Many struggle to subsist on lands variously described as 'poverty traps', 'less favoured' or 'marginal'. These tend to be areas of high ecological vulnerability (such as subtropical drylands or steep mountain slopes) or low levels of biological or resource productivity combined with high human demands. There may also be twice as many poor living on marginal lands as on favoured lands in developing countries – 630 million compared to 325 million. If current trends in poverty and natural resource degradation persist, by 2020 more than 800 million people could be living on less favoured lands, places like the upper watersheds of the Andes and the Himalayas, the East African highlands, and the Sahel (Hazell and Garrett, 1996).

Protecting their ecosystems

It is increasingly evident that the poor can fight back against environmental degradation. In some places they have been fighting back for centuries, using adaptive measures whenever ecosystem changes have demanded them.

One example of adaptation can be found in the highlands of Papua New Guinea, where the Wola people grow crops on slopes cleared of native forests by means of slash and burn techniques. Instead of accelerating soil exhaustion and furthering deforestation, as traditional models would predict, the Wola have maintained soil fertility by constructing mounds of soil using rotting vegetation as compost. They select strategically what crops to plant, using a variety of crops in the first years of cultivation when soils are rich. In later years when soil fertility declines, the Wola plant only sweet potatoes, a crop that can thrive without many nutrients (Batterbury and Forsyth, 1999, p. 8).

The Mossi people in Burkina Faso offer other examples of successful adaptation. As rapid population growth and frequent droughts have degraded their soils, Mossi farmers have responded by creating compost pits and building diguettes – semipermeable lines of stone placed at right angles to the slope to prevent erosion (Batterbury and Forsyth, 1999, pp. 9–10).

The significant number of Mossi who have migrated to cities of the neighbouring country of Côte d'Ivoire for wage employment during the dry season is also an adaptive response that reduces pressures on the land and food supply, provides remittances for families, and diversifies income sources. Like all adaptations, however, these local strategies have their limitations. Severe drought or a shortage of non-farm job opportunities can undermine the Mossi's successes

Adaptation is not confined to rural areas. In cities the poor supplement their diets and income by transforming vacant lots, rooftops and the lands along roadsides and other rights-of-way into highly productive plots of vegetables, fruits and trees. As food and fuel are the largest household expenses for low-income urban populations, urban agriculture can be a first line of defence against hunger and malnutrition. Shanty-town dwellers who mobilise to secure access to water and sanitation and improve their environments are engaging in another form of adaptation. But adaptation can be more difficult in cities, where a community's response may be more dependent on access to and support from local and state governments, corporations or international agencies. In addition, many environmental risks are relatively new or beyond the experience of the urban poor, or difficult to detect, such as solvent or lead poisoning (Forsyth and Leach, 1998, p.26)

Governments, NGOs and development agencies can help the poor respond positively to natural resource management challenges by working with local residents – supporting locally designed adaptations and community-based institutions, creating employment opportunities and providing new knowledge, technical and marketing assistance, training and credit. Those institutions can also hinder adaptations and progress against poverty. Limiting the voice of the poor in resource management decisions or denying local people security of tenure and rights of access to resources are among the most

Table 12.7   Methods of adaptation

Country	Rainfall (mm)	Population density (per km²)	Indigenous soil and water conservation techniques
Burkina Faso	1,000–1,100	35	Stone bunds in slopes, network of earth bunds and drainage channels in lowlands
	1,000	35 – 80	Contour stone bunds on slopes, drainage channels
	400–700	29	Stone lines, stone terraces, planting pits
Cameroon	800–1,100	80 – 250	Bench terraces (0.5–3 m high), stone bunds
Cape Verde	400–1,200 (uplands)	> 100	Dry stone terraces (walls 1–2 m high), rectangular basins (approx. 2 × 4 m)
Chad	250–650	5 – 6	Water harvesting in drier regions; various earth bunding systems with upslope wingwalls and catchment area
Niger	300–500		Stone lines, planting pits
Nigeria	1,000–1,500	110 – 450	Stepped, level benched stone terraces, rectangular ridges, mound cultivation
Mali	400 500–650	20 – 30 13 – 85	Pitting systems Cone-shaped mounds, planting holes, terraces, square basins, stone lines, bunds or low walls
Sierra Leone	2,000–2,500	38	Sticks and stone bunding on fields and drainage techniques in gullies
Togo	1,400	80	Bench terraces and contour bunds, (rectangular) mound cultivation

detrimental factors. Without recognition of traditional tenure rights and grants of control over resources, the poor have less incentive and capacity to adapt.

Experiences of the people of Sukhomajri, India, illustrate the difference that stable tenure systems can make in the health of an ecosystem. Twenty years ago, the forest department granted villagers the right to harvest the grass in the watershed for a nominal fee, rather than auctioning the grass to a contractor who, in turn, would charge the villagers high rates for the grass (Agarwal and Narain, 1999, p.16). With the assurance that they would reap the benefits of increased biomass production, villagers identified ways to protect the watershed – regulating livestock grazing, investing in the construction of water tanks for increased crop production, and sustainably harvesting wood from the forest that lies within the catchment. By the mid-1980s, Sukhomajri was no longer importing food but exporting it. The result – a once degraded watershed is today a wetter, greener, more productive and prosperous area.

Source: World Resources (2001, pp. 28–9).

Questions

1 What environmental benefits might result from supporting adaptive responses by the rural poor in developing countries?

2 How can international institutions support such adaptive responses?

Box 12.3 shows how two technological breakthroughs have made a significant contribution to economic and environmental improvements, namely oral rehydration therapy and vaccines better adapted to conditions in developing countries. Deaths from major childhood diseases and from diarrhoea-related illnesses in developing countries were cut by some 3 million between 1980 and 1990 alone. Under-five-years mortality rates fell between 1970 and 2000 from 170 per 1,000 people in developing countries to less than 90 per 1,000 people.

Many other policies could also be attributed to the first set of policies seeking to build positive links between economic development and the environment. For example, improved education, skills and training are key ingredients for the widespread adoption of environmentally sound agricultural technologies, most of which are more knowledge intensive than those they replace. Better nutrition, family planning, promotion of competition, improving the transport infrastructure, clarifying legal structures and property rights, can all play a role in this respect.

Breaking down negative links

The second set of policies involve creating or strengthening environmental guidelines and/or removing incentives towards actions which are associated with environmental damage. This lack of accountability by decision makers for outcomes which involve adverse environmental impacts, has often been cited as a major problem, especially in developing countries. Indeed there are many cases of subsidies

---

BOX 12.3

Oral rehydration therapy and vaccines

When oral rehydration therapy was developed at Bangladesh's International Centre for Diarrhoeal Disease Research, the *Lancet*, a leading medical journal, hailed it as possibly the most important medical discovery of the twentieth century. Until then the only effective remedy for dehydration caused by diarrhoea was providing sterilised liquid through an intravenous drip – costing about $50 per child, far beyond the budgets, facilities and capacities of most developing country health centres. But scientists found that giving a child sips of a simple sugar–salt solution in the right proportions led to a 25-fold increase in the child's rate of absorption of the solution compared with water alone. During the 1980s packets of oral rehydration salts were manufactured by the hundreds of millions, with most selling for less than 10 cents apiece.

Adaptation to developing country conditions of vaccines for the killer communicable diseases – measles, rubella, whooping cough, diphtheria, tetanus, tuberculosis – was another major breakthrough. The antigens to tackle these six diseases had long been known. But they required sterile conditions and a reliable cold chain – a system of well-maintained refrigerators and cold transport from the point of vaccine production to clinics and village health centres thousands of miles away. Important advances came with technological improvements: a polio vaccine that requires only a drop on the tongue, freeze-dried and more heat-stable vaccines that do not require refrigeration and the development of vaccine cocktails in a single shot.

For both oral rehydration therapy and new immunisation methods, advances in technology had to go hand in hand with advances in organisation. Massive campaigns were developed to spread awareness. Politicians, churches, teachers and NGOs were enlisted to underscore the facts and help organise the efforts.

---

and governmental supports in developing countries which arguably encourage adverse environmental impacts. For example, logging fees in developing countries have been found to be less than a third of the costs of replanting trees, with irrigation charges less than a fifth of the costs of supplying the water directly. Similarly energy subsidies in the various 'transition economies' were estimated at over $230bn a year in the early 1990s, with more than half the air pollution recorded in the former Soviet Union and Eastern Europe attributed to such market price distortions.

Here the main focus will be on introducing or strengthening regulations or incentives needed to induce decision makers in developing countries to take account of environmental values. Policy options to encourage decision makers in developing countries to take more account of environmental values include the following:

- Establishing or clarifying property rights (see Box 12.4).
- Using 'market-based' policy instruments (e.g. taxes or charges) where these are able to 'internalise' any negative externalities (see Chapter 4).
- Using 'command and control' policy instruments where 'market based'

(regulations and standards) instruments are deemed ineffective or where they are insufficient by themselves (see Chapter 4).

● Using regulations and standards which are realistic and enforceable and which are consistent with the overall policy framework. For example, the Brazilian government sought to restrict fishing off the Bahia coast during the 1980s while at the same time providing subsidies for fishermen to purchase new, more efficient nylon nets.

● Improving information for decision makers. Access to accurate data on the environmental costs and benefits of alternative policies can play an important role here. For example, studies in Thailand showed that curbing lead and particulate emissions created more environmental benefits per dollar spent than curbing other emissions. Case Study 12.3 also reinforces the importance of better information for local decision makers.

● Enhancing institutional arrangements to strengthen national and international capacities for environmental management.

BOX 12.4

Property rights and the environment: Jakarta's kampung residents

Land rights in Indonesia are complex, combining informal traditional rural processes with a modern registry system. Large tracts of land in the Jakarta Utara harbour area, particularly in the low-income kampungs, have often been held by families for some generations in traditional housing developments. Typically residents do not have a registered claim of ownership – they owned the land before titles were registered. They have possessory rights, so generally they cannot be displaced without some compensation. They can strengthen their claims to ownership by paying property taxes and having their claims recognised by kampung officials. But paying taxes can be difficult, since some tax officials refuse to accept payments precisely to avoid strengthening residents' ownership claims. Land without a secure title changes hands among local residents at prices that are estimated to be 45 per cent below the costs of securely titled land of the same quality.

In a dynamic developing city, informal property rights foster spatial mismatches and hinder urban redevelopment. In Jakarta the pattern of industrial growth under globalisation is moving low-skill manufacturing jobs to distant suburban locations. Jakarta has also made street vending illegal, severely restricting the informal food-processing and service industry. Many low-income residents would be financially better off selling their land and moving to the suburbs where jobs and business opportunities are located. The city would also be better off, because Jakarta needs upscale, mixed-use land development in the harbour area. But the system of land rights prevents this natural market exchange. ▶

Since kampung residents typically lack secure titles to the lands their families have lived on for generations, they cannot sell their land to developers for new uses. They are literally trapped in the kampung areas. The result is a spatial mismatch between business and employment opportunities in the suburbs and residents stuck in the inner city. Many workers must make a long commute to the suburbs each day, and many others remain under- or unemployed. The result is a no-win situation for both workers and the city.

To deal with the situation, the city government has proposed the Jakarta Water Development Programme. To find space for the needed mixed-use developments, the city will build out into the existing harbour, a process requiring expensive and environmentally risky land reclamation. Kampung residents would be asked to yield their lands voluntarily in return for new public housing accommodation in the harbour area. But this plan would only make the spatial mismatch worse. A more plausible solution is to give traditional kampung residents full title to their land, allowing them to sell it and move to the suburbs to seek employment. With the money they receive for their land, the residents would have the capital they need not only to relocate but also to seek new business opportunities.

CASE STUDY 12.3

A weather eye on African farmers

Kelly Sponberg's Washington office could scarcely be further removed from the desert villages of Niger in central West Africa. Yet Mr Sponberg is a vital link in a chain that provides some of the most isolated people on the planet with their first real weather news.

Mr Sponberg is technical manager of Ranet, an international project to make climate and weather-related information more accessible. Ranet combines information from global weather banks in the USA with local African reports and distributes it via digital satellite, receiving stations, computers and wind-up radios.

Getting their first real weather data may help farmers and herders in Niger, the world's second poorest nation, to decide when to plant crops and where to find water for their animals.

'This is a hopeful development for Africans and vulnerable people everywhere who don't get weather forecasts that we take for granted in the industrial world,' says Professor Peter J. Lamb, a climatologist at the University of Oklahoma who oversees the US involvement in Ranet. 'It's an absolute first for Africa and for the developing world.'

Ranet also demonstrates how cheaply and easily advanced nations can share their weather know-how with poor people who lack telephones, television and electricity.

It also gets round the problem that, in Africa, many national meteorological services have not shared forecasts with the people.

The programme is the brainchild of Mohammed Boulahya, an Algerian meteorologist. A decade ago Mr Boulahya started the African Centre of Meteorological Applications for Development (Acmad) in Niamey, Niger's capital, to train African meteorologists. Once Acmad was up and running, Mr Boulahya had another inspiration: why limit the sharing of African data to meteorologists? Mr Boulahya asked for help from the US National Weather Service, which is part of the National Oceanic and Atmospheric Administration. The NWS arranged that Professor Lamb's institute, at the University of Oklahoma, run jointly with NOAA and known as the Co-operative Institute for Mesoscale Meteorological Studies, would get $834,000 (£591,000) to help launch Ranet in Niger and five other countries. The funds come from the US Agency for International Development's Office of Foreign Disaster Assistance, since the countries to be served by the pilot programme are so prone to drought and other disasters.

Thus, three years ago, Mr Sponberg who works for NOAA, was asked to find a way of transmitting weather data from Africa to Washington and back. He canvassed US and foreign sources for the data Mr Boulahya wanted, put it on a server and has been adapting and updating it ever since.

An important requirement was that the data feed to Africa be small enough to run on the old personal computers commonly used there. The whole database had to be just 60 Mb and the outgoing stream only 4 Mb. Mr Sponberg's job is to transmit each of the 5,000 files at different times of the day and week. 'I'm like the disc jockey playing African climate's greatest hits,' he says.

Mr Sponberg's feed goes by fibre-optic sea cable to a WorldSpace Corporation digital satellite dish in Johannesburg and from there to its Afristar satellite, which beams it all over Africa. Anyone with a WorldSpace receiver hitched to a computer can use Ranet multimedia graphics, maps and text.

The broadsheets can also be received on the ground by receiver-transmitters, built for desert use by Wantok Enterprises of Canada and connected to computers powered by solar batteries. Mr Boulahya insisted that the receiver-transmitters had to be as simple to operate as sewing machines, one of the few mechanical devices familiar to those in remote parts of Africa.

At receiving stations, villagers translate information into local languages to create local broadcasts. They beam it to people who hear it on wind-up radios up to 25 km away from towns. Mr Boulahya says when he demonstrated how simple the radios were in one village, 'within a few minutes 25 ladies asked me if they could use it'.

Using the radios, made by the FreePlay Foundation of London, herders can learn where to find water without having to bring their herds to a village every day or so. That can double the radius of their forage. Farmers can stay on their plots and receive news and planting information.

The potential for reversing the rise in population movement and land stress is huge. Niger is being overrun by an 'avalanche of sand', says Barbro Owens-Kirkpatrick, US ambassador to the country. She says Niger's government supports Ranet because it realises rural development is crucial to hold people on the land, get them to plant effectively, retain plant cover and hold back the sand.

Niger has the world's highest birth rate and infant mortality rate. The UN Food and Agricultural Organisation has issued warnings for famine, as everyone waits, anxiously, for the rainy season. The USA plans more support, Ms Owens-Kirkpatrick says. Ranet will add 15 more village receiving stations. The radios receive health and agriculture programmes, as well as weather. 'The radio's long-term effects are important,' says Ms Owens-Kirkpatrick. 'This country is at the edge of human civilisation.'

Source: Financial Times, 2nd July 2001

Questions

1 Outline some of the environmental benefits of improved access to information in Niger.

2 What implications does this case study have for international development institutions?

Now try the self-check questions for this chapter on the companion website
   www.booksites.net/ison
You will also find up-to-date facts and case materials.

Key terms

Anthropogenic   Human-related aspects (of the environment)

Carrying capacity   Adequacy of the resource base of the system to support the population at the minimum standard of living necessary for survival

Decoupling   Breaking the link between growth of real national income and environmental degradation of one form or another

Developing countries   Defined in various ways by different international bodies. Using the World Bank classification of 'low-income economies', it refers to countries with an annual GNP per head of $760 or less (in 1998 values)

Economic maturity argument   This suggests that, as countries develop, the primary sector and secondary (industrial) sector of economic activity will progressively diminish and the tertiary (service) sector progressively grow, as a share of total output and employment

Human Poverty Index   A measure of the extent of deprivation of people not expected to attain specific target levels for varying economic and quality of life indicators

Janicke effect   The suggestion that environmental indicators actually improve as real national income rises above a threshold level

Pollution haven hypothesis   The suggestion that as environmental regulations 'tighten' in the developed economies, multinationals will progressively seek to locate production facilities in less regulated developing economies

Transitional economies   The 28 countries that emerged from the former Soviet Union together with those countries in Central and Eastern Europe previously closely allied with it

References and further reading

Agarwal, M. and Narain, S. (1999), 'Community and household water management: the key to environmental regeneration and poverty alleviation', Paper presented to EU-UNDP.

Batterbury, S. and Forsyth, T. (1999) 'Fighting back: human adaptations in marginal environments', *Environment*, **41**, 6 pp. 6–11, 25–30.

Field, B.C. (1997) *Environmental Economics: An Introduction*, McGraw-Hill, Singapore, especially Chapter 19.

European Environmental Agency (2000) *Environmental Signals 2000*, No. 6, Copenhagen.

Forsyth, T. and Leach, D. (1998) *Poverty and Environment: Priorities for Research and Policy: An Overview Study*. Prepared for the UNDP and European Commission, Sussex, UK: Institute of Development Studies, August

Gilpin, A. (2000) *Environmental Economics: A Critical Overview*, Wiley, especially Chapter 10.

Gaeser, E. (1997) 'Learning in Cities', *Discussion Paper 1814*, 1–23, Harvard Institute of Economic Research, Cambridge, Mass.

Hazell, P. and Garrett, J.L. (1996) Reducing poverty and protecting the environment: The overlooked potential of less-favoured lands, 2020 Brief 39.

Henderson, J. (1998) 'Externalities, location and industrial deconcentration in a Tiger economy', Working Paper, Department of Economics, Brown University, USA.

Human Development Report 2001 'Making new technologies work for human development', United Nations Development Programme, OUP, Oxford

International Fund for Agricultural Development (2000), OUP, Oxford.

Janicke, M. (1989) 'Economic structure and Environmental Impacts: East-West Comparisons', *The Environmentalist*, **9**, 3.

Low, P. (ed.) (1992) *International Trade and the Environment*, World Bank Discussion Paper, No. 59, Washington DC.

Low, P. and Yeats, A. (1992) 'Do Dirty Industries Migrate?' in Low, P. (ed.) *op. cit.*

Lucas, R., Wheeler, D. and Hermanala, H. (1992) 'Economic Development, Environmental Regulation and the International Migration of Toxic Pollution, 1960–1988' in Low, P. (ed.) *op. cit.*

Mani, M. and Wheeler, D. (1998), 'In search of pollution havens – dirty industry in the world economy, 1960–1995', *Journal of Environment and Development*, Sept., La Jolla

Turner, P. (2001) 'Energy demand, carbon dioxide emissions and GNP', *The Economic Review*, **18**, 3, Feb.

UNDIESA (1998) *World Urbanization Prospects*.

World Bank (2000), 'Entering the 21st Century' *World Development Report 2000*, OUP, Oxford.

World Development Report 2002 'Building Institutions for Markets', The World Bank. OUP, Oxford.

World Resources (2001) *People and Ecosystems*, Elsevier Kidlington, UK.

Useful websites

Department for International Development
Environment Agency
Food and Agricultural Organisation
International Monetary Fund (IMF)
OPEC

World Bank
World Health Organisation
United Nations
United Nations Industrial Development Organisation
Friends of the Earth
Jubilee 2000
Oxfam
European Bank for Reconstruction and Development (EBRD)
World Trade Organisation (WTO)
United Nations Development Program

See also:
UNICEF
NAFTA
MERCOSUR
ASEAN

Practical environmental policy making in the EU

In this chapter we look in some detail at cases of actual policy making in the environmental field, in the particular context of the European Union. The chapter begins by reviewing some of the procedures and institutions involved in general policy making within the EU as well as the stages involved in the EU developing an environmental policy and the principles guiding that policy. The focus then moves to three detailed case studies in which the principles, processes and outcomes of environmental policy making are examined in some detail, namely:

- Developing an EU-wide policy for reducing auto-related toxic emissions and improving fuel efficiency (The EU Auto-Oil Programme);
- Reforming the Common Agricultural Policy (CAP) of the EU to achieving a more 'sustainable' system;
- Establishing formalised environmental management and audit systems within EU organisations (EMAS).

EU legislative process

The European Commission plays the central role in the legislative procedures of the Community. Figure 13.1 sets out the legislative process involved, before a Commission proposal becomes a Regulation or a Directive.

- *Regulations.* Once adopted by Council, regulations will be binding in their entirety and are applicable as they stand to all member states. If, for example, there is agreement in Council on a new Regulation concerning permissible limits for car exhaust, the agreement will be published in the *Official Journal* and will immediately become part of national law in all 15 member states.
- *Directives* are different from Regulations in that, although they are binding on member states, the form and method of their implementation are left to the discretion of the national authorities.
- *Decisions* are similar to Regulations but may not apply to all Community states. There are also Recommendations and Opinions, but these have no legal force and are in effect advice to governments.

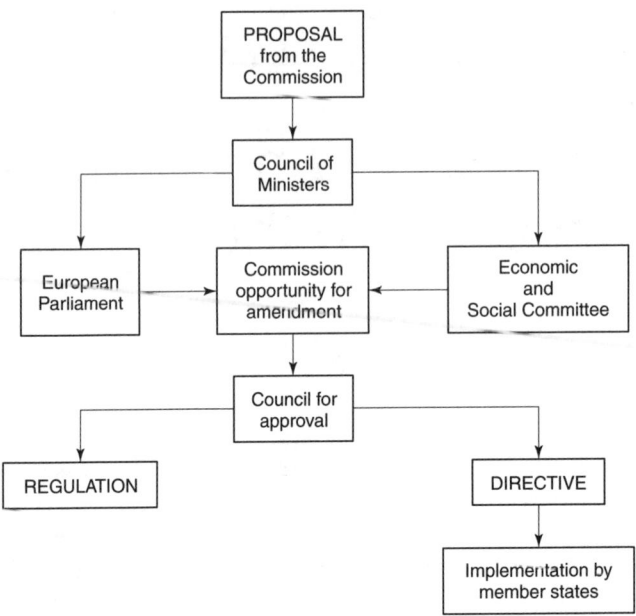

Figure 13.1 The consultation procedure in the EU

It is perhaps useful to consider a hypothetical case and follow it through the legislative process of the EU. Let us say that the Commission wishes to propose a Directive on the transport of nuclear waste. The first step is to produce a draft paper. This would be written by the staff in DGXI, the Directorate-General responsible for nuclear safety. They would work closely with their colleagues in the DGs for transport, energy, the environment, the Internal Market, industrial affairs, and possibly others on an ad hoc basis. They would meanwhile inform and seek the views of national governments, road haulage, rail and shipping concerns, environmental groups, and industry and trade union representatives. Interested parties would thus have the opportunity to make their views on the proposed legislation known at an early stage in the drafting process.

The DGXI staff would then produce a revised paper for approval by the Commission. This proposal would then be sent to the Council for comment. After comments and amendments had been received the final draft would be sent to the Council for approval. When the Council approves the draft the Directive is then sent to national governments and becomes law.

Institutional context of EU policy making

Three *supranational institutions* play a key role in EU policy making and are independent of the national governments:

- The European Commission (EC)
- The European Parliament (EP)
- The European Court of Justice (ECJ)

European Commission (EC)

Since 1995 the European Commission has consisted of 20 commissioners appointed by the national governments. On appointment they are expected to act independently of national interests. The five larger member states (France, Germany, UK, Spain and Italy) have two commissioners each and the 10 other member states each have one commissioner. The EC is divided into 35 separate Director-Generals (DGs), each of which deals with specific policy areas.

The European Commission is often regarded as the 'pillar' of the EU in the economic policy domain. Bulmer (2001) identifies the functions of the European Commission as:

- Proposing legislation;
- Mediating between governments to achieve agreement on legislation;
- Managing technical details of policy;
- Representing the EU in commercial policy negations (e.g. with the World Trade Organisation);
- Acting as the defender of the EU's collective interests;
- Acting as guardian of the treaties by ensuring that EC law is upheld.

European Parliament (EP)

The European Parliament consists of members (MEPs) who, since 1979, have been directly elected by member states on a five-year mandate. It has the power to dismiss the European Commission, and can therefore exert considerable influence on the latter at times of crisis. For example, in 1999 the EP insisted on the Commission appointing a special investigating committee to inquire into alleged irregularities, which it secured under the threat of it dismissing the Commission. Nevertheless its main influence is on the *legislative process*, within which its procedural authority varies depending on the particular policy area:

- *Consultation procedure* (Figure 13.1): here the EP merely gives an opinion and has no effective sanction over the central decision-making agency, the Council of Ministers (see below).
- *Budget treaties*: here the EP has important powers, including that of rejecting the budget in its entirety.
- *Single European Act* (SEA): here the EP must give its assent to the accession of new member states and for Association Agreements with third countries.
- *Co-decision procedure (Article 251)*: here the power of the EP extends to 37 separate policy areas, in each of which the EP can reject legislation coming before it. In effect, the EP is now a co-legislator with the Council of Ministers.

European Court of Justice (ECJ)

This consists of 15 judges and 9 advocates-general. The ECJ does not formulate policy but its rulings on matters referred to it involve the interpretation and application of EC law and these play a key part in the implementation and effectiveness of policy proposals over time.

As well as these three supranational institutions, another body, the Council of Ministers, also plays a key role in the policy-making process.

Council of Ministers

This consists of the ministers of the member states. The actual ministers involved depend on the policy areas in question; for example the agricultural ministers will meet when the policy area is the CAP. There are some 100 meetings of the Council of Ministers each year, with the Council of Agricultural Ministers, the Council of Economics and Finance Ministers (Ecofin) and the Council of Foreign Ministers having the most frequent meetings. Meetings are chaired by the minister from the member state which holds the current 'presidency' of the Council for a six-month period. National civil servants support their ministers in these meetings.

Decisions of the Council can use *qualified majority voting* (QMV) in many areas, though *unanimous voting* is required in certain areas (e.g. tax policy). A decision by QMV requires 62 of the 87 votes, distributed according to a weighting system (e.g. France, Germany, Italy and the UK have 10 votes each, Belgium, Netherlands, Portugal and Greece 5 votes each, and so on).

Another key body is the *European Council*, comprising the 15 heads of state, 15 foreign ministers, EC president and vice president, meeting at least twice yearly. This is responsible for political and strategic decision making. However, it is to environmental policy making within the EU that we must now turn.

Environmental policy in the EU

The original Treaty of Rome (1957) failed to mention the environment, largely because at that time environmental concerns had little public prominence. However, by the late 1960s and early 1970s debates involving finite human and environmental resources and infinite human wants, had raised the profile of the environment, as in the Club of Rome's publication *Limits to Growth* in 1972. Shortly afterwards the EU adopted its first *Environmental Action Programme* (EAP) in 1973. The focus of the first EAP was on environmental principles and policies, with each of the subsequent EAPs following particular themes (see Box 13.1).

BOX 13.1

Environmental Action Plans (EAPs)

First EAP 1973–76
Defines basic principles of environmental policy and sets out general goals as:

- Prevention better than cure
- Environmental impacts should be taken into account very early on in decisions
- 'The polluter pays' principle
- Actions in one member state should not affect the environment in another Member State
- Subsidiarity*
- Co-ordination of national policies

Second EAP 1977–81

- Repeats earlier goals
- Focus on preventative action

▶

- Priority to water and air pollution and noise nuisance
- Environmental impact assessment
- First discussion of eco-labels
- Protection of nature and biodiversity

Third EAP 1982–87

- Make most economic use of natural resources
- Harmonise national policies
- 'Polluter pays' principle again
- Reduce pollution at source
- Subsidiarity principle restated

Fourth EAP 1987–92

- Environment and economic development to be made compatible
- Identify environmental problems from Single Market
- Environmental protection can create jobs
- Pollution issues require a multimedia approach

Fifth EAP 1992 – towards sustainability

- Sets sustainable development as the goal
- Targets climate change, acid rain and air pollution, urban quality of life, coastal resources, waste, protection of biodiversity, and management of natural resources
- Emphasises the role of market-based instruments

* The suggestion that decision making should remain decentralised and with Member States wherever possible unless strong reasons exist for doing otherwise.

Pearce (2001) identifies some of the key principles spanning these various EAPs:

- Prevention is better than cure.
- Environmental impacts should be taken into account very early on in the decision-making process.
- The polluter pays principle.
- Actions in one member state should not affect the environment in another member state.
- The Community should act as one in international negotiations.
- Policy should be enacted at the appropriate level: some is best suited to action at the Community level, some at national level (the 'subsidiarity' principle).
- There should be co-ordination of national policies in the interests of avoiding competitive distortions.

The focus on environmental policy within the EU is a relatively recent phenomenon.

Single European Act (SEA)

The *Single European Act* (SEA) in 1987 provided the first formal and legal recognition of environmental policy within the EU. Article 130R on the 'Environment' stated that the EU's goals would include:

- preserving, protecting and improving the quality of the environment
- contributing towards protecting human health
- ensuring a prudent and rational utilisation of natural resources

Such a broad set of goals could clearly embrace a wide range of issues and policies, potentially opening them up to EU legislation in order to achieve the stated environmental goals.

Treaty of the European Union (Maastricht Treaty)

The *Treaty of the European Union* in 1992 (the *Maastricht Treaty*) took the legal recognition of environmental policy within the EU still further. Whereas the original Treaty of Rome had sought 'continuous and balanced expansion', this was now re-expressed as 'sustainable growth respecting the environment'. Environmental perspectives were now to be integrated into all policies as a matter of *explicit injunction* to policy makers rather than, as previously, merely being one attribute of 'good policy making'.

The *precautionary principle* (PP) was now to be used in guiding environmental policy; namely that where significant environmental risks are involved, any lack of scientific evidence as regards cause and effect must not be cited as a reason for avoiding taking appropriate corrective action. The 'polluter pays' principle had already been outlined in the First Environmental Action Programme (Box 13.1), but was reiterated in the clause dealing with the precautionary principle.

> Community (environmental) policy ... shall be based on the precautionary principle and on the principle that preventive action shall be taken, that environmental damage should as a priority be rectified at source and that the polluter should pay. Environmental protection requirements must be integrated into the definition and implementation of other Community policies. (Maastricht Treaty, 1992)

Article 130R of the SEA (1987) was amended at Maastricht to extend the EU's environmental role into global policy making. The article now referred to the EU's responsibility for 'promoting measures at international level to deal with worldwide environmental problems'.

Clearly environmental outcomes and implications were, from 1992 onwards, to be considered in all aspects of EU economic activity and policy formation. The three case studies which now follow give some useful insights into the complexities of real-world environmental policy making in the EU. At the end of *each* case study, ask yourself the following questions (responses can be found at the end of the book, on pages 356–7).

1 Which of the environmental principles outlined in Box 13.1 are, or are not, being implemented?

2 Does the EU's approach involve selecting market-based or non-market-based policy instruments? Look for the reasons behind the policy instrument chosen.

3 Could the environmental problems have been tackled in any other way? Comment on possible alternative approaches.

4 Examine the environmental costs and benefits to:

(a) EU member states, and

(b) Non-EU member states

from the policies adopted.

CASE STUDY 13.1

The European Auto Oil Programme

Total emissions from motor vehicles are decreasing around the world. The environmental performance of vehicle and fuel technologies, encouraged by emissions and fuel quality regulations, has been improving significantly and will continue to do so at least in the medium term. Further tightening of these regulations as regards pollution emissions and fuel quality has become still more important, given the projected increases in road traffic and therefore in the vehicle kilometres travelled. It is in this context that the EU has sought to develop its *Auto Oil Programme* (Peake, S. 1997). Box 13.2 explains some of the technical terms which appear frequently in this case study.

Box 13.2

Useful technical terms

CH_4	Methane
CO	Carbon monoxide
CO_2	Carbon dioxide
HC	Hydrocarbons – compounds containing hydrogen and carbon (see also VOCs 1)
HDV	Heavy duty vehicle
LCV	Light commercial vehicle
LDV	Light duty vehicle. These include passenger cars and LCVs
NMVOCs	Non-methane volatile organic compounds. As VOCs, minus methane (CH_4)
NO	Nitrogen monoxide
NO_2	Nitrogen dioxide
NO_x	Nitrogen oxides
N_2O	Nitrous oxide
O_3	Ozone
OBD	On board diagnostics
VOCs	Volatile organic compounds – these include hydrocarbons, but also aromatic compounds. Used often to refer to the hydrocarbon emissions which evaporate from the vehicle in operation (see NMVOCs)

Pre-Auto Oil developments

At the end of several clashes of fundamental aims and differences of technical opinion between the Commission, the European Parliament and industry, Europe finally backed

Table 13.1 Stages in emission legislation in Europe by vehicle type and implementation date of compulsory type approval

	Cars	LCVs	HDVs
Stage I	1993	1993	1993
Stage II	1997	1996	1996
Stage III	2000	2000	2000
Stage IV	2005, indicative proposals	Not announced	Not announced
Stage V	Not announced	Not announced	Not announced

Source: European Commission.

catalyst technology in 1991 with the adoption of *Directive 91/441/EEC*. The effective requirement to fit catalytic converters to new cars from 1 January 1993 marked *Stage I* of Europe's current emission control programme. From 1991 onwards the situation in Europe moved rapidly and progressively in the field of emissions regulations to encompass all categories of vehicles. For example, in March 1992 the Commission adopted *Stage II* of its strategy for developing an emissions reduction policy. For cars, Stage II meant the requirement to comply with new emission limit values by 1997 and for other light commercial vehicles (LCVs) and heavy duty vehicles (HDVs) to comply with these emission limit values a year earlier. These pre-Auto Oil developments are shown in the first two rows of Table 13.1.

The European Auto Oil Programme

The *European Auto Oil programme* was initially about defining still tighter emission limits for *Stage III* for all classes of vehicles, as well as bringing about further improvements in fuel quality. The importance of what became known as the 'Stage III' Auto Oil package for reducing projected emissions of pollutants is indicated in row three of Table 13.1, together with the then provisional approaches to *Stages IV* and *V*.

These projections were based on an emissions model, FOREMOVE, which therefore played a crucial supporting role within the European Auto Oil Programme. FOREMOVE was used to predict the change in total emissions from EU vehicles under assumptions about changes in vehicle emission technology and fuel quality as well as the application of different policy measures at different strengths. A *base case scenario* for future emissions was developed from a set of assumptions about future vehicle and traffic growth, incorporating the influence of already agreed legislative measures to reduce emissions from road vehicles. These base case trends for CO, HC and NO_x are shown in Table 13.2, both 'without Auto Oil' and 'with Auto Oil'. Clearly major health benefits were envisaged as following from the significant reductions projected for these air pollutants under the Auto Oil Programme.

Table 13.3 outlines the contribution of the various *vehicle types* to three important pollutants in the EU countries as at 1990. It was information of this type which resulted in the separate treatment of these vehicle types in the Auto Oil Programme. Clearly cars were the major source of two out of the three pollutants, but with heavy trucks making the major contribution to NO_x emissions.

Table 13.2 Results from FOREMOVE, showing effect of Auto Oil package on top of the effects of already agreed measures

Pollutant	1990 (100)	1995	2010 without Auto Oil	2010 with Auto Oil
Urban NO$_x$	100	100	62	39
Total NO$_x$	100	95	52	34
Urban particulates	100	110	56	34
Urban CO	100	80	47	24
Urban benzene	100	87	49	25
Total VOCs	100	90	44	24

Source: Adapted from Peake, S. (1997).

Key aspects of how the Auto Oil approach differed from previous legislative exercises include:

● For the first time, new regulations were to meet environmental goals in a *cost-effective* way rather than be based solely on the principle of *best available technology* (or some political hybrid). This was in line with the broader strategy and approach to environmental policy outlined in the EU's Fifth Action Programme on Environment and Sustainability:

● For the first time, the ultimate objective was to meet environmental goals, defined by air quality targets.

In June 1996 the European Commission announced its proposals for Stages III and IV emission limits for passenger cars and for a new fuel quality directive. Proposals for LCVs and HDVs were made in early 1997.

The key elements of the European Commission's proposals for Auto Oil legislation included:

● Proposals for new passenger car (gasoline and diesel) emission standards for the year 2000 and further proposals for 2005;
● A revised test cycle for passenger cars and LDVs eliminating the 40-second cold start allowance;
● New gasoline and diesel fuel quality standards;
● Indicative emission limits for 2000 for LCVs and HDVs.

The passage of legislation for passenger cars and fuel quality was expected to take at least 18 months (see Box 13.3), given the stages involved in implementing an EU decision.

Table 13.3 Estimated shares (%) of global motor vehicle emissions by vehicle type, 1990

%	Heavy trucks	Light trucks	Cars	Motorcycles	All vehicles
CO	4	0.5	92	3.5	100
NO$_x$	50	6.5	42	1.5	100
HC	7	2	77	14	100

Source: Adapted from Peake, S. (1997).

BOX 13.3

Five stages in implementing an EU decision on vehicle emissions

Adoption	Passage of vehicle emission legislation in the EU is governed by a (*co-decision*) procedure involving possible amendments and final agreement from the European Parliament and Council of Ministers
Transposition	From the date of adoption EU governments have a maximum of six months to transpose EU legislation into national laws
Optional implementation	Member states may implement standards ahead of mandate
Entry into force for *new* vehicles	All new vehicle types must be type approved to the new standards
Entry into force for *all* vehicles	Typically one year later than for type approval on new vehicles. All vehicles sold must be type approved to the new standards

Gasoline and diesel passenger cars

The specific vehicle and fuel specifications for gasoline and diesel passenger cars are summarised in Tables 13.4 and 13.5 respectively.

Light commercial and heavy duty vehicles

Limit values for Stage III were to be an extrapolation of limit values on passenger cars, as indeed were to be many of the provisions including OBD, recall, improved test procedures for evaporative emissions and separate limits for HC and NO_x.

Table 13.4 The European Commission's Auto Oil proposals for gasoline passenger cars

Pollutant (g km^{-1})	Stage II 1996/97[1] corrected values	Stage III 2000 regulatory values	Stage IV 2005 indicative values
CO	2.7	2.3	1.0
HC	0.341	0.2	0.1
NO_x	0.252	0.15	0.08

Note:[1] On a test-cycle equivalent basis with Stage 2000.

Table 13.5 The European Commission's Auto Oil proposals for diesel passenger cars

Pollutant (g km^{-1})	Stage II 1996/97[1] corrected values	Stage III 2000 regulatory values	Stage IV 2005 indicative values
CO	10.6	0.64	0.50
HC + NO_x	0.71/0.91	0.56	0.30
NO_x	0.63/0.81	0.50	0.25
Particulate matter	0.08/0.10	0.05	0.025

Note:[1] On a test-cycle equivalent basis with Stage 2000.

Table 13.6 Increased cost per vehicle to meet the Stage III (2000) and Stage IV (2005) Standards: 1995 Ecus (1 Ecu = £0.60 approx)

	Gasoline	*Diesel*
Cost of Stage III		
Small car	200	–
Medium car	225	380
Large car	290	520
LCV		145–290
HDV		530–1,620
Cost of Stage IV		
All cars (on average)		150–200

Source: Adapted from peake, S. (1997).

Estimated vehicle and fuel costs for the Stage III and IV proposals

The European Commission's estimates of increased vehicle costs associated with the tighter emission limits contained in the Stage III and IV proposals are shown in Table 13.6. The Commission estimated that the increased fuel cost, in 1995 Ecus, to drivers would be:

- *For gasoline* – 2 Ecu per 1,000 litres, or 2.3 Ecu for the average European motorist driving 12,600 km a year at an average fuel consumption of 8.6 litres per 100 km.
- *For diesel* – 1.8 Ecu per 1,000 litres, or 1.7 Ecu per year for the average European motorist driving 12,600 km a year at an average fuel consumption of 7.6 litres per 100 km.

Clearly, these additional fuel costs were very small indeed and well below the likely effects of normal price variations – seasonal and random – within fuel product spot markets. Indeed these extra costs were well below the likely effects of the annual (above inflation) tax increases which were commonly imposed on fuel in Europe at that time. In fact they were regarded as so insignificant for the motorist, that it led the EU's energy commissioner, Christos Papoutsis, to make his celebrated quote: 'That's about as much as it costs for a couple of beers or a couple of cups of coffee. It's not even as much as the cost of a packet of cigarettes.'

International comparisons: passenger vehicle emission legislation in Europe, the USA and Japan

Prestige, jobs and profits are associated with environmental leadership in emissions control standards and technologies. However, international comparisons of vehicle emission legislation are becoming increasingly complex. As limit values for emissions move towards zero, the differences in *test cycles* and *durability requirements* become still more important in assessing which countries and vehicles really meet the toughest (i.e. most stringent) conditions.

Vehicle manufacturers view 'stringency' as a multifaceted concept involving the full range of limit values, test cycle attributes, conditions and legislative requirements. Manufacturers look at the:

- legislated limit values for emissions
- explicit or implied durability factors
- shape of the speed curve in the test cycle(s)

Table 13.7 Characteristics for the key light duty vehicle test cycles in Europe, the USA and Japan

	Europe (current)	Europe (for Stage III)	USA	Japan
Cycle name	NEDC	NEDC-40s	FTP-75	10/15 mode
Cycle distance (km)	11.01	11.01	17.84	4.16
Duration (seconds)	1,220	1,180	1,877	660
Maximum speed (kph)	120	120	91.2	70
Average speed (kph)	33.6	33.8	34.3/41.8	22.7

- test cycle protocol – the way the test is carried out – how many cycles are driven, what the averaging and weighting procedures are between cycles
- local reference fuel that must be used
- existence of corporate averaging requirements

As the official limits for emissions standards fall across countries, a true comparison depends very much on how the testing of vehicles with regards to those limits takes place. These *test cycle* characteristics for light duty vehicles in Europe, the USA and Japan are compared in Table 13.7.

Clearly there are significant differences. The way vehicles with different types of emission control technology react to two different test cycles can be very different from one another. Put another way, test cycle results are themselves sensitive to vehicle technology. For light duty vehicles, the new European driving test cycle is probably tougher than the US FTP-75 and certainly tougher than the Japanese 10/15 test cycle.

Ford took an empirical approach with one test and tested the same vehicles over the European Stage III and US FTP-75 test cycles. Figure 13.2 shows that emissions over the European Stage III cycle (the NEDC-40s cycle) are recorded as being significantly higher for both the Mondeo and a town car, and means that for these cars, the European test cycle is in fact the more stringent. This comparison shows that it is not in fact a simple matter to answer the question: which is the toughest standard – Stage III in the EU or

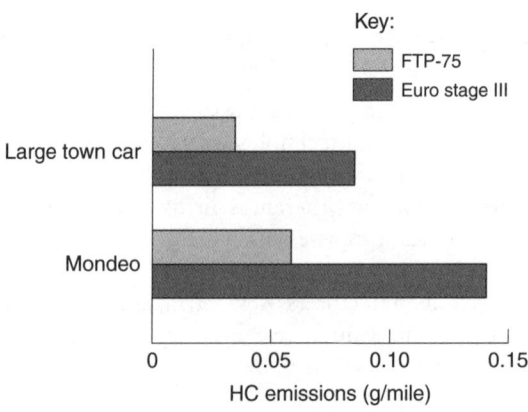

Figure 13.2 Comparison of the European Stage III and US FTP-75 test cycles
Source: Ford Motor Company

Table 13.8 European and US gasoline passenger car emission standards

	CO	HC/NMOG	NO_x
Limit values (g km^{-1})			
Stage III (EU)	2.3	0.2	0.15
Stage IV (EU)	1	0.1	0.08
ULEV (USA)	1.06	0.02 (NMOG*)	1.12

Note: *NMOG refers to non-methane organic gases

ULEV in the USA? Table 13.8 would imply more stringent emission limits for two of the three pollutants in the USA. However the FTP-75 test cycle in the USA is less demanding than that in the EU, making it easier for the tested vehicles to comply in the USA.

Pressure for harmonising test cycles is likely to continue to grow. There is now a global test cycle for off-road vehicles and an international cycle for HDVs is being discussed. Cars are next, although they represent the most complex and politically sensitive case. There is no doubt that the size of vehicle emission limit values around the world is taken as an indication of the progressiveness of environmental legislation. However, the true stringency of emissions legislation depends not only on the 'headline' emission values, but also on a range of factors, including notably the characteristics of the test cycle and durability conditions in each country (see Box 13.4).

BOX 13.4

How vehicle manufacturers ensure that vehicles will meet durability requirements

It would be extremely expensive and slow to have to test the durability of every vehicle/engine design in real test and driving conditions. In developing sufficiently durable systems, manufacturers need a number of aged catalysts to perform different tests on the emissions control system. The goal is to be able to develop fake dynamometer aged catalysts in much less time and at much less expense. First, a real test over a real driving period is needed to be able to provide a model for the fake aged catalysts.

A car is taken round a test track and subjected to a drive cycle so tough on the vehicle, that only one drive in 20 could punish the vehicle more (in emissions terms). The vehicle is driven for 80,000 km (50,000 miles) and its emissions are tested every 16,000 km. The real test gives the catalyst efficiency at the end of the 80,000 km (and by implication the rate of degradation of the emissions control system).

Once the catalyst efficiency is known at the end of 80,000 km, fake dynamometer aged catalysts can be quickly developed (on a bench in around a full day) with similar levels of degradation. The dynamometer aged catalysts are used in the calibration of the vehicle. The calibration is done so that the emissions will be at least one standard deviation below the legal requirement. How the standard deviation is calculated is another complicated story involving end-of-line test results and customer in-use data.

At the end of this, the vehicle manufacturer is confident that it will provide the customer with a product that meets the durability requirement and beyond in two main ways. First, the whole thing was done on the worst one out of 20 drive cycles, and secondly, at one standard deviation, there is only a 16 per cent chance of being above the durability threshold. The combination gives the probability that not more than two vehicles in a thousand would not meet the durability requirements – enough to meet the durability test criteria.   ▶

Ford estimates that a typical passenger car calibration requires approximately:

● 2.5 years
● testing in a range of temperatures and altitudes (− 29 °C to + 40 °C and up to 3,000 m altitude)
● many specialist qualified and skilled engineers
● a vehicle fleet driven for 50,000 km

Ford estimates that the inclusion of OBD legislation, for example, increases the requirements for testing and skilled manpower by 60 per cent. The lead time for calibration requires firm legislation at least three years before the introduction date.

Auto Oil and air pollution

Early indications of results of the Auto Oil Programme are rather encouraging. Figure 13.3 shows the long-term trends in emissions from road transport in Europe. The diagram shows a significant decline in projected emissions of carbon monoxide, nitrogen oxides, particulate matters from diesel, volatile organic compounds, benzene and sulphur dioxide. However, Figure 13.3 clearly shows that the challenge of reducing CO_2 emissions remains.

In broad terms, emissions from road transport are projected to fall by 70–80 per cent between 1995 and 2010. Emissions are set to fall further as new technologies begin penetrating the vehicle market from 2005 onwards.

In the absence of the Auto Oil measures, road transport emissions would have been 50–100 per cent higher than those shown in Figure 13.3. The Commission maintains that these projections suggest that it is possible to break the link between economic growth and this kind of environmental damage. Moreover 'improvements in technology above all else appeared to be capable of staying ahead of the effects of traffic growth'.

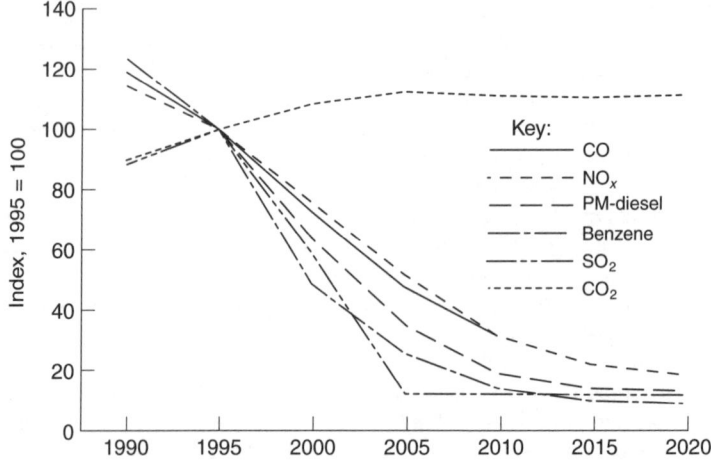

Figure 13.3 Road transport emissions in Europe

Source: European Commission (2001)

Monetary estimates of the benefits of the Stage III Auto Oil directives were in the range of 3–16 billion ECU per year (1995 ECU). Much of this valuation derived from an analysis of the health benefits of reduced exposure to pollution.

Health impacts of air pollution

The health effects of air pollution are generally difficult to measure, except during extreme pollution episodes – and there are still many uncertainties in the link between poor air quality and adverse health effects. Nevertheless, in the USA and Europe, air quality objectives drive vehicle emissions and fuel quality regulation.

The World Health Organisation has developed air quality guidelines for 28 air pollutants which influence many jurisdictions' air quality standards, including Europe's. The health effects of the five 'classical' air pollutants are summarised in Table 13.9.

Table 13.9 Health effects of classical air pollutants

	Pollution level	*Affected groups*	*Effects*
Ozone	Short-term exposure to 120–240 $\mu g\,m^{-3}$	Children, adolescents and young adults	Pulmonary function decrements. Symptoms, especially coughs, have been associated with ozone levels as low as 300 $\mu g\,m^{-3}$
Nitrogen dioxide	30-minute exposure to 380–560 $\mu g m^{-3}$	Asthmatics	Change of about 5% in pulmonary function and increase in airway responsiveness to bronchoconstrictors
		Children 5–12 years old	20% increased risk of respiratory systems and disease for each increase of 28 $\mu g\,m^{-3}$ in the average NO_2 weekly concentrations
Sulphur dioxide	24-hour average, 200–250 $\mu g m^{-3}$ in the presence of PM and other pollutants	Children	Small changes in lung function
Particulate Matter	Any – no threshold yet found	Everyone, but particularly the elderly and those with pre-existing heart and lung disease	Two studies have concluded that life expectancy may be shortened by more than a year in high versus low PM communities
CO		Normal person engaging in relatively heavy work	Exposure guidelines are given so that a carboxy haemoglobin (COHb) level of 2.5% is not exceeded. At 0–10% COHb there are generally no signs or symptoms of illness. However, COHb levels may quickly rise in response to exposure. Athletes have suffered from epidemic CO poisonings in indoor ice areas. Headaches occur at around 10–20% COHb and death within less than an hour above 80%

Table 13.10 Pollutants and air quality targets in the EU

Pollutant	Air quality targets
NO_2	200 μg m^{-3} as maximum hourly value
Carbon monoxide	10 mg m^{-3} as maximum 8-hourly value
Benzene	10 μg m^{-3} as an annual mean
Particulates	50 μg m^{-3} as a 24-hour rolling average
Tropospheric ozone	180 μg m^{-3} as a 1-hour 99th percentile value

Following this, Table 13.10 outlines the critical air quality targets underpinning the European Auto Oil Programme.

Critique of the Auto Oil Programme

Auto Oil represented a new approach in Europe to developing motor vehicle emissions regulations. The Auto Oil philosophy is distinct, for example, from the previous approaches based on the principle of best available technology (BAT) or best available technology not entailing excessive cost (BATNEEC). The explicit alignment between the Auto Oil Programme and air quality targets represents a step in the direction of 'closed loop' environmental policy making – where actions are appropriate and proportional to desired outcomes.

For the European Commission, Auto Oil is regarded as a success. Indeed, the EU environment commissioner presiding over the process, Ritt Bejjregard, has stated that with some modifications to improve transparency, Auto Oil serves as a model for Community policy in the field of environmental regulation and acts as a good example of implementing the ideas incorporated in the European Commission's Fifth Action Programme on environment and sustainability.

Other aspects of the Auto Oil philosophy are dictated by the nature of the air quality problem; the ideas of the Fifth Action Programme; and the usual subsidiarity issues relevant to any field of EC policy making. From the European Commission's point of view, the result is a six-point framework underpinning the basic principles behind the Auto Oil process. The framework is that Auto Oil outcomes should:

- incorporate ambitious objectives
- recognise differences between countries in air quality
- be proportional and subsidiary
- incorporate shared responsibility and partnership
- be based on cost-effectiveness
- allow European member states to pursue environmental policy objectives more ambitious than Community rules

The objective of respecting air quality targets by the year 2010 was certainly ambitious, and allowance within the final package of measures was made for particularly severe and unique air quality problems in southern Europe and Athens in particular. However, it is less clear that the programme lived up to all its aims.

The key regulatory innovation behind Auto Oil was the notion of linking emissions standards to air quality targets, as opposed to fuzzier concepts like 'best available technology' or costed hybrid versions. Auto Oil also for the first time formally recognised the vehicle-fuel system as a whole, and attempted an open and transparent cost-effectiveness analysis.

The outcome of Auto Oil is that Europe will adopt stringent emission limits for all classes of road vehicle in two stages for 2000 and beyond. Fuel quality will also be addressed, and all the indications are that the mild fuel technology forcing for Stage III will give way to proposals for further legislation to make fuels significantly cleaner. Europe's plans for Stage III and IV mean that the USA is no longer the clear leader in the global vehicle emissions control race. Europe's Stage IV passenger car CO and NO$_x$ limits are appreciably tougher than ULEV, while the new European driving cycle (NEDC) is itself tougher than the FTP-75.

Prestige, jobs and profits are associated with environmental leadership in emissions control, as the Californian experience shows. However, as we have seen, international comparisons of vehicle emission legislation are becoming more complex. As limit values move towards zero emissions, differences in test cycles and durability requirements become increasingly more important to the question of which legislation is the toughest.

While there are systematic differences between different test cycles – differences in length, duration, maximum and average speeds, operating temperatures and soak conditions – other differences are less straightforward to compare, as they may depend on technology. The way vehicles with different types of emission control technology react to two different test cycles can be very different from one another. Pressure for harmonising test cycles is likely to continue to grow. There is now a global cycle for off-road vehicles and an international cycle for HDVs is being discussed. Cars are next, although they represent the most complex and politically sensitive case of harmonisation yet.

Questions

Review the case study in the light of the questions posed earlier on pages 320–1.

CASE STUDY 13.2

Common Agricultural Policy (CAP): reforming the system

In reviewing the materials for this case study, to avoid repetition reference is made to Chapter 11 and in particular to Box 11.1 on the operation of the 'guarantee' system of the CAP and Case Study 11.4 on the EU's Rural Development Policy.

Historical background

When the Treaty of Rome was signed in 1957 over 20 per cent of the working population of the 'Six' were engaged in agriculture. In the enlarged EU of today that figure is only 3.9 per cent, ranging from the UK with 2.0 per cent to Greece with over almost 20.4 per cent. Since one in five of the EU's workers were involved in agricultural production in 1957, it came as no surprise that the depressed agricultural sector became the focus of the first 'common' policy, the CAP, established in 1962. The objectives of this policy were to create a single market for agricultural produce and to protect the agricultural sector from imports, the justification being to ensure dependable supplies of food for the EU and stability of income for those engaged in agriculture.

Both the demand for, and the supply of, agricultural products are, for the most part, inelastic, so that a small shift in either schedule will induce a more than proportionate change in price. Fluctuations in agricultural prices will in turn create fluctuations in agricultural incomes and therefore investment and ultimately output. The CAP seeks to stabilise agricultural prices, and therefore incomes and output in the industry, to the alleged 'benefit' of both producers and consumers.

There are, of course, a number of ways of achieving such objectives. Prior to joining the EU, the UK placed great emphasis on supplies of cheap food from the Commonwealth. The UK therefore adopted a system of 'deficiency payments' which operated by letting actual prices be set at world levels, but at the same time guaranteeing to farmers minimum 'prices' for each product. If the world price fell below the guaranteed minimum, then the 'deficiency' would be made up by government subsidy. Under this system the consumer could benefit from the low world prices while at the same time farm incomes were maintained. Although the UK system involved some additional features, such as marketing agencies, direct production grants, research agencies, etc., it was by no means as complex as that which has operated in the UK since 1972 under the CAP.

Method of operation

The formal title for the executive body of the CAP is the European Agricultural Guarantee and Guidance Fund (EAGGF), often known by its French translation 'Fonds Européen d'Orientation et de Garantie Agricole' (FEOGA). As its name implies, it has two essential roles: that of guaranteeing farm incomes, and of guiding farm production. We shall consider each aspect in turn.

Guarantee system

Different agricultural products are dealt with in slightly different ways, but the basis of the system is the establishment of a 'target price' for each product. The target price is not set with reference to world prices, but is based upon the price which producers would need to cover costs, including a profit mark-up, in the highest-cost area of production in the EU. Box 11.1 reviews the key elements involved in operating the guarantee system of the CAP.

Guidance system

The CAP was, as originally established, a simple price-support system. It soon became obvious that agriculture in the 'Six' required considerable structural change because too much output was being produced by small, high-cost, farming units. In 1968 the Commission published a report called *Agriculture 1980*, more usually known as the 'Mansholt Plan' after its originator, the commissioner for agriculture, Sicco Mansholt. The plan envisaged taking large amounts of marginal land out of production, reducing the agricultural labour force, and creating larger economic farming units. The plan eventually led to the establishment of a Common Structural Policy in 1972, which for political reasons was to be voluntary and administered by the individual member states. The import levies of the EAGGF were to provide funds to encourage small farmers to leave the land and to promote large-scale farming units.

Reform of the CAP

The relative failure of the guidance policy has meant the continued existence of many small, high-cost producers in many agricultural areas of the EU, with correspondingly high 'target' prices. High target prices have in turn encouraged excess supply in a number of products, requiring substantial purchases by the Guarantee section of the EAGGF, resulting in butter and beef mountains, wine lakes, etc. The net effect of the CAP has therefore been, via high prices, to transfer resources from the EU consumer to the EU producer. At the same time the CAP has led to a less efficient allocation of resources within the EU in that high prices made the use of marginal land and labour-intensive processes economically viable. Arguably, resource allocation has been impaired both within the EU and on a world scale, in that the system of agricultural levies distorts comparative advantages by encouraging high-cost production within the EU to the detriment of low-cost production outside it. Finally, through its import levies and export subsidies the CAP introduces an element of discrimination against Third World producers of agricultural products, for whom such exports are a major source of foreign earnings.

The growth of agricultural spending in the early 1980s placed increasing pressure on the EU's 'own resources'. By 1983 the 1 per cent VAT ceiling had been breached and even the steady growth in imports (providing CET (Common External Tariff) revenue) was not sufficient to meet the demands on the budget. The member governments were forced to agree to special additional payments to meet deficits which arose in 1983, 1984, 1985 and 1987. With no agreement on reform during the late 1980s, the CAP began to expand rapidly and the Council was forced to agree a series of 'supplementary' budgets.

The breakthrough occurred at the Brussels Heads of Government meeting in February 1988 during which a further, new source of finance was sanctioned (up to 1.2 per cent of GNP) in return for legislative limits on the CAP. In 1988 the CAP was limited to a fixed sum of 27.5bn Ecu and from then onwards could only expand, in future years, by three-quarters of the average rate of growth in EU GNP (see Table 13.11). Other significant limits were placed on the CAP in the form of a ceiling on cereal production (160 million t), a cut in producer prices of about 3 per cent and a new 'co-responsibility' levy of 3 per cent on larger farmers.

The reform of the CAP took a further step forward in June 1992 when the so-called 'McSharry proposals' for reform were adopted. The purpose of the reforms were, first, to control agricultural production which had been artificially stimulated by the CAP; second, to make European agriculture more competitive by reduction of support prices; third, to discourage very intensive agricultural methods while still maintaining high employment on the land and supporting more marginal and vulnerable farmers.

Table 13.11 CAP spending as proportion of the EU budget

	% of EU budget
1984	65.4
1988	65.0
1990	59.4
1992	53.3
1994	55.7
1996	50.4
1998	49.0
2000	39.5

To achieve these aims, support prices for cereals were to be reduced by some 30 per cent. Also, arable land was taken out of production or 'set aside', with farmers receiving payment based on average yields for what is not produced. Livestock farmers were limited to a maximum head of cattle per hectare of available fodder. Other elements of the reform involved direct income support for farmers in Less Favoured Areas (LFAs) and for those who use environmentally sound methods of farming. Finally, an early 'pre-pension' scheme was introduced to accelerate the retirement of farmers who operated unviable holdings.

Agenda 2000

In July 1997 the European Commission published Agenda 2000 which analysed the EU's past policies and considered certain long-term future trends. As far as agriculture was concerned, it recognised the need to extend the agricultural reforms of 1992. The recommendations of 1997 were designed to continue the post-1992 trend of reducing price support to farmers (through the intervention buying system) and providing more money payments direct to producers. For example, in the cereals sector the intervention price would be reduced by 15 per cent between 2000 and 2002 to set it closer to world levels (see Figure 11.1(a)). In the milk sector, the intervention price will be cut by 15 per cent in three steps from 2005/6 onwards, although output quotas will be raised by 1.5 per cent in three steps from 2000 onwards (from 2003 in the UK) to try to alleviate the problems resulting from a lower intervention price.

The EU's Rural Development Policy (RDP)

Finally, a new *Rural Development Policy* (RDP) was introduced in January 2000 to boost a variety of restructuring schemes directed towards easing these changes in agricultural policy (see Case Study 11.4). This is to be the 'second pillar' of EU agricultural policy and is designed to help stimulate investment in farming business, develop forestry and forestry products, improve training for young farmers, and provide help for those older farmers wishing to retire. In the UK, expenditure on the RDP will amount to £1bn between 2000 and 2006, and it will certainly be needed to support hard-pressed farmers given the drop in their incomes resulting from lower intervention prices.

The pressure for agricultural reform has come from many sides – such as consumers who worry that the CAP encourages higher prices, ministers afraid of the spiralling budget costs of agricultural subsidies, policy makers aware of the need to shift resources from an EU farming community of 7 million in order to help the 18.5 million Europeans who are unemployed, and supporters of the single currency who accept the need to cut member states' budget deficits in order to meet the Maastricht criteria. Agricultural reform has also been accepted as necessary by supporters of EU enlargement who recognise that if price supports are not decreased, then the enlargement of the EU to include Eastern Europe will cause severe budgetary difficulties. This is because farm prices in the potential new entrants are already 20–40 per cent below the EU level and would require extensive (and costly) support to be raised to the EU levels. Such increases in agricultural prices to EU levels could, of course, also cause financial hardship for the consumers in those lower-income countries, as well as giving a cost-push stimulus to inflation.

Questions

Review the case study in the light of the questions posed earlier on pages 320–1.

CASE STUDY 13.3

The EU Eco-Management Audit Scheme (EMAS)

EMAS is a continuation in the European context of a movement towards environmental management systems which began in the mid-1980s in the USA. An *environmental management system* (EMS) is a transparent, systematic process which clearly delineates environmental goals, policies and responsibilities for the company, establishes procedures to implement these policies and stipulates regular auditing of the environmental outcomes of these policies. An important focus here is the phrase 'transparent, systematic process': it is emphatically not an ad hoc approach to environmental concerns by a firm.

Epstein and Roy (1998) stress the particular importance to multinational corporations (MNCs) of a regularised framework within which they can address environmental concerns. They are constantly facing the tension in the environmental field of whether to adopt local (often lax) environmental standards in low-wage economies to the benefit of corporate profits or whether to adopt higher, more generally acceptable environmental standards. Some managers would see a trade-off between environmental standards/business ethics and profits, others would see them as complementary (see Case Study 1.2).

Without a clear framework within which to proceed, the corporate response to a particular environmental problem is likely to be shaped by some combination of *internal* and *external* pressures on the management of the MNC at a given point in time (Figure 13.4). An inappropriate response by senior managers to these pressures can lead to unwanted pressures on MNCs: for example, boycotts of products by protestors at, say, using child labour, paying poverty wages in developing economies, using ecologically 'unfriendly' practices.

Some, more proactive, companies had, during the 1980s and early 1990s, established more standardised processes and procedures for dealing with environmental issues. A further impetus was given to the corporate role in fostering environmental protection by the 'Earth Summit' in Rio in 1992 (see Chapter 7, page 176). Shortly after this the European Union devised an *Environmental Management and Auditing System* (EMAS) which was launched in April 1995. At around the same time the *International Standardisation Organisation* (ISO) set up a committee to develop an environmental management system which might be applied globally. In 1995 this committee

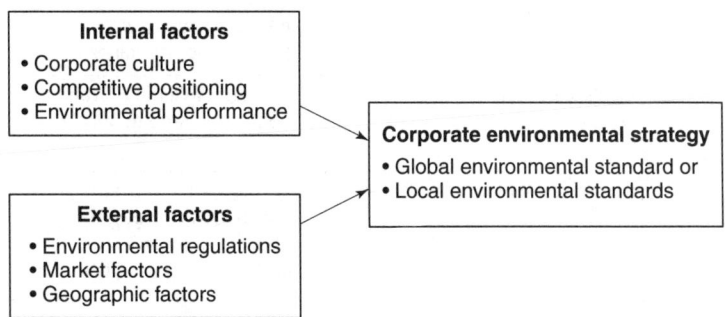

Figure 13.4 Evolution of an environmental management system driven by internal and external factors

established ISO 14001 (see below). It may be useful at this point to compare the two systems.

EMAS compared to ISO 14001

The Eco-Management and Audit Scheme (EMAS) is a voluntary scheme to promote continuous environmental improvement among its member organisations. Some of the key elements of EMAS are outlined in Table 13.12 and compared with the *International European Standard for Environmental Systems* (ISO/EN ISO 14001). While both systems share the same objective of improving environmental management, there are a number of differences. EMAS arguably imposes greater rigour on member organisations by requiring them to:

- undertake an initial environmental review to identify existing environmental procedures and practices in the organisation (review to be validated by an independent government-accredited verification)
- actively involve employees in implementation of EMAS
- make the environmental information available to the public and to other interested parties

EMAS is open to any organisation in the public and private sector within member states of the EU and the European Economic Area (Norway, Iceland and Liechtenstein). An increasing number of candidate countries are also implementing the scheme in preparation for their accession to the EU.

Table 13.13 indicates how these two standardised environmental management systems have spread rapidly across the world since 1995. EMAS is clearly based within

Table 13.12 EMAS and ISO 14001 compared

	EMAS	ISO/EN ISO 14001
Preliminary environmental review	Verified initial review	No review
External communication and verification	Environmental policy objectives, environmental management system and details of organisation's performance made public	Environmental policy, made public
Audits	Frequency and methodology of audits of the environmental management system and of environmental performance specified	Audits of the environmental management system (frequency or methodology not specified)
Contractors and suppliers	Required influence over contractors and suppliers	Relevant procedures are communicated to contractors and suppliers
Commitments and requirements	Employee involvement, continuous improvement of environmental performance legislation	Commitment of continual improvement of the environment management system rather than a demonstration of continual improvement of environmental performance

Table 13.13 Geographical coverage of organisational registrations for EMAS and ISO 14001 as at June 1999

EU ('EMAS') country	EMAS registration	ISO 14001 certification
Germany	2,085	1,400
Austria	189	200
Sweden	155	645
Denmark	102	350
UK	70	947
Norway	58	72
France	33	285
Spain	23	234
Netherlands	20	443
Finland	18	191
Italy	9	150
Belgium	7	130
Ireland	1	82
Luxembourg	2	6
Portugal	1	8
Greece	0	6
Iceland	0	1
Liechtenstein		1
Japan		2,124
Taiwan		506
USA		480
Korea		463
Switzerland		370
Australia		300
China/Hong Kong		81/42
Thailand		121
Malaysia		101
Canada		100
Brazil		90
Singapore		80
Argentina		67
India		60
Hungary		53
Mexico		50
Indonesia		48
Turkey		45
Czech Republic (CZ)		36
Philippines		30
South Africa		30
New Zealand		28
Other non-EU		113

Europe, and especially in the German-speaking countries, while ISO 14001 has a more global presence.

Effectiveness of environmental management system (EMS)

Environmental goal setting

Steger (2000) has reviewed the empirical evidence as regards the environmental impacts of the various EMS. He notes that EMS require – some more explicitly (EMAS), some more implicitly (ISO 14001) – corporations to set ecological goals (e.g. emission reductions) in a transparent way, both at the corporate and the unit/plant level. But many companies had already set targets long before they formalised their EMS. The majority of companies surveyed argued that the implementation of (standardised) EMS had *not* resulted in dramatic changes in goal setting. Management systems can help management to achieve its goals more effectively, but do not necessarily lead to a change in the goals themselves (as some proponents of EMS have been hoping). A majority of the companies, therefore, maintain that they would have achieved their environmental goals anyway, regardless of the EMS.

Steger notes two main outcomes of his empirical studies of EMS:

- First, there was no visible or measurable difference in environmental performance between EMAS, ISO 14001 or company-specific systems. The goals were very similar and depended much more on the companies' specific situations, expected legislation or corporate history than on the chosen variety of EMS. However, whereas EMAS requires the *explicit* setting of environmental goals and their continuous improvement, ISO 14001 does not (mainly due to opposition from the USA, where there were concerns about potential liability risks resulting from such a provision).
- Second, companies implementing EMAS in effect ignored the complicated provisions for deducing their environmental goals from an in-depth analysis of the environmental impacts of their activities. The verifiers accepted this approach and validated the environmental goals whenever any such goals were referred to at all, admitting implicitly the impracticality of the provision.

Steger's review of the (quantitative) environmental goals revealed that many companies were already operating above compliance targets in their emission standards and were reducing their pollution continuously anyway. The main impacts of the standardised system seem to be in the area of *legal compliance*, which has increased with the introduction of a (standardised) EMS. Both ISO 14001 and EMAS require a careful checking of legal compliance and the documenting of all relevant regulations. Companies maintain that most of the violations they discovered were of a formal nature (e.g. the expiration of a permit, or not exceeding emission limits). There was little evidence in Steger's surveys of companies changing their environmental goals by adopting either EMAS or ISO 14001.

Economic cost–benefit analysis

Steger found that among organisations there were no common definitions of the elements that count towards estimating the cost of an EMS. Some companies counted only the cash cost, others included the cost of follow-up actions triggered by a discovery of an environmental 'lapse' during the process of establishing the EMS. He also noted that whereas the costs are immediate and (at least in principle) measurable, the benefits are partly long term and therefore more difficult to measure.

With these qualifications in mind, Steger reported that the cost estimates for companies acquiring EMAS ranged from 15,000 to 2 million euro, with a cluster around 50,000–100,000 euro. The environmental declaration cost estimates within this total varied between 10,000 and 45,000 euro. The cost estimates by companies acquiring ISO 14001 certification also centred around 50,000–100,000 euro.

On the benefit side, most firms reported cost savings and some reported some extra market opportunities. Resource efficiency and pollution prevention ranked high on the list of 'win–win' potential reported. Some companies also reported higher motivation of employees, more transparent and effective organisation, lower risk of environmental liabilities, improved allocation of responsibilities and information flows for all environmental issues.

Integrating EMAS with ISO 14001

It has become increasingly clear to the EU regulatory authorities that ISO 14001 could become a useful stepping stone on the way to EMAS certification. The EU authorities have therefore revised EMAS to make it more compatible with ISO 14001. For example, EMAS originally applied to a small number of site-based organisations in the chemical sectors. It now encompasses all organisations (including local authorities) and economic sectors, in line with the broader reach of ISO 14001.

Figure 13.5 outlines the now more 'streamlined' approach by which an organisation which already has ISO 14001 can be EMAS accredited.

Box 13.5 outlines the incremental guidance given by the European Commission to organisations already possessing an ISO 14001 designation.

BOX 13.5

Modifications to ISO/EN ISO 14001 to meet EMAS requirements

1 *Environmental policy* – ISO/EN ISO 14001 includes a commitment, but not a provision, to comply with relevant environmental legislation. Your organisation must strengthen its statement of commitment included in its environmental policy to make provision for regulatory compliance. If more than one site is registered under EMAS then continual improvement must be demonstrated on a site-by-site basis.

2 *Planning* – EMAS has very specific requirements on the type of environmental aspects that may need to be addressed within the environmental management system, while ISO/EN ISO 14001 is less prescriptive in this area. Your organisation should ensure that in identifying its environmental aspects in the planning stage of ISO/EN ISO 14001, it has addressed the items listed in Annex VI, which are applicable. Your organisation should also ensure that all the elements of the initial environmental review, detailed in Annex VII, have been considered and incorporated where necessary in the ISO/EN ISO 14001 process.

3 *Implementation* – one of the requirements of EMAS is the active participation of employees in the environmental improvement programme. This may be achieved in a variety of ways: an environmental committee, suggestion book, environmental representatives. Your organisation should also take steps to ensure that any suppliers and contractors used also comply with your organisation's environmental policy. ▶

4 *Checking and corrective action* – since the frequency of the audit cycle is not specified in ISO/EN ISO 14001 it is necessary for your organisation to check that the frequency of the audit cycle is in compliance with Annex II of the EMAS Regulation and takes place at intervals of no longer than 3 years. In addition to the EMS being audited your organisation's environmental performance must also be addressed annually to demonstrate continual improvement.

5 *Certification of ISO/EN ISO 14001* – in order to comply with the requirements of EMAS, the ISO/EN ISO 14001 certificate must be issued under one of the accredited procedures recognised by the European Commission.

Source: European Commission.

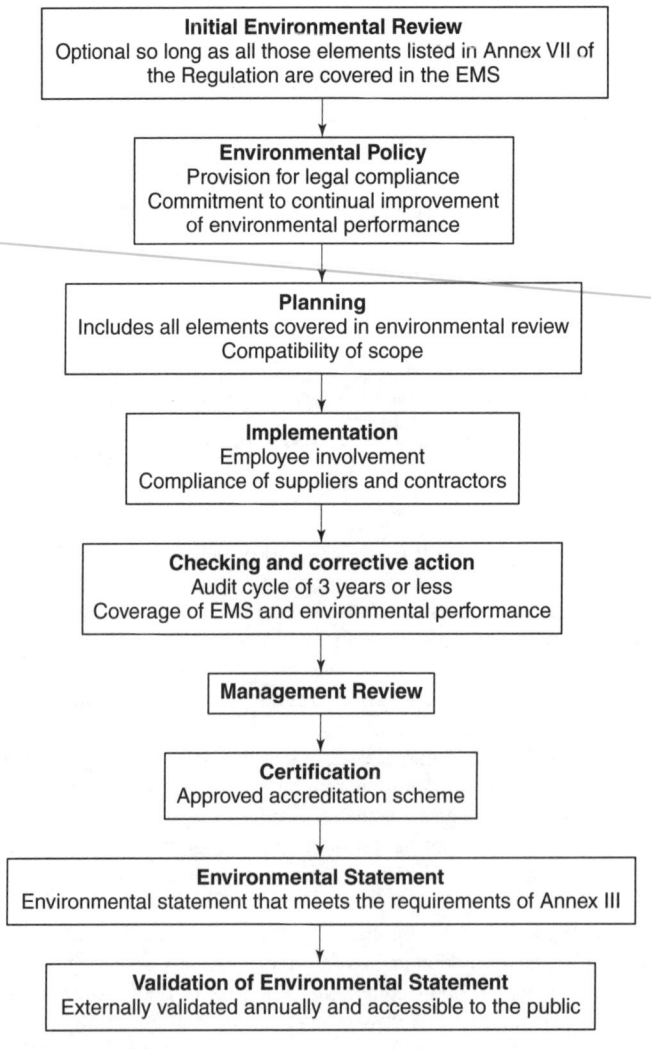

Figure 13.5 EMAS implementation route for an ISO/EN ISO 14001 certified organisation

How effective is EMAS?

EMAS has been criticised for focusing on internal EMS, rather than on key environmental aspects of products and services. As already noted (page 338) it seems to have had little impact on the environmental goals of organisations. Box 13.6 outlines some different stakeholder perspectives.

BOX 13.6

Different stakeholder perspectives

Industry's points of view

- Costs of implementation are immediate, potential benefits are more long term and less clear cut.
- If member states want EMAS to expand significantly, then governments are going to have to provide incentives for organisations to voluntarily sign up (e.g. tax breaks, faster track approaches to other regulatory and legal processes).
- EMAS does not add anything to ISO 14001.

Member States/ EU points of view

- Believe EMAS goes further than ISO 14001 because e.g. EMAS requires a public statement.
- There are differences in terminology around legal compliance with environmental regulations.
- The emergence of ISO 14001 has helped EMAS in terms of raising general awareness of environmental management schemes, with the two systems complementary but with EMAS more rigorous in some areas.
- EMAS continues to be seen as more prestigious than ISO/EN ISO 14001 in many member states.

NGO points of view

- NGOs generally welcome schemes such as EMAS, but want it to be much stronger.
- Enthusiastic about the environmental statement component of EMAS.
- Worried that companies will cheat and that verifiers and certifier are not doing a good enough job.
- Would like to see more focus on environmental outcomes rather than only procedures.

Source: Unstead-Joss, M. (2001)

We might note that environmental audits are expensive. A typical manufacturing site might take six people a full week to audit, amounting to 30 person-days. EMAS might be considered more effective by industry if it helped reduce the amount of time and resources that are necessary to devote to the auditing and verification of EMS. Another critical aspect of EMAS is that it deals simply with environmental impacts of products during their manufacture. Such impacts can be very small compared with the environmental impacts of *using* products.

According to the European Partners for Business website: 'Stakeholders have highlighted that EMAS focuses solely on environmental management at the site level and neglects both the life-cycle aspects of products and the social dimensions of sustainability.'

Figure 13.6 The EMAS logo
Source: European Commission

In an attempt to reinvigorate EMAS, the following regulatory changes were made in 2001 (Regulation EC76/2001):

● the extension of the scope of EMAS to all sectors of economic activity including local authorities
● the integration of ISO 14001 as the environmental management system required by EMAS
● the adoption of a visible and recognisable EMAS logo to allow registered organisations to publicise their participation in EMAS more effectively (Figure 13.6)
● the involvement of employees in the implementation of EMAS
● the strengthening of the role of the environmental statement to improve the transparency of communication of environmental performance between registered organisations and their stakeholders and the public
● a more thorough consideration of indirect effects including capital investments, administrative and planning decisions, procurement procedures, choice and composition of services (e.g. catering)
● the need to provide more explicitly for legal compliance

Question
Review the case study in the light of the questions posed earlier on pages 320–1.

Now try the self-check questions for this chapter on the companion website
   www.booksites.net/ison
You will also find up-to-date facts and case materials.

References and further reading

Bulmer, S. (2001) 'History and institutions of the European Union' in M. Artis and F. Nixson (eds.), *The Economics of the European Union: Policy and Analysis*, 3rd edn, OUP.

Epstein, M. and Roy, M-J. (1998) 'Managing corporate environmental performance: a multinational perspective', *European Management Journal*, **16**, 3, Elsevier.

Peake, S. (1997) *Vehicle and Fuel Challenges Beyond 2000: Market Impacts of the EU's Auto Oil Programme*, Financial Times Automotive Publishing, London.

Pearce, D. (2001) 'Environmental policy' in M. Artis and F. Nixson (eds.), *The Economics of the European Union: Policy and Analysis*, 3rd edn, OUP.

Steger, U. (2000) 'Environmental Management Systems: Empirical Evidence and Further Perspectives', *European Management Journal*, **18**, 1.

The Auto-Oil II Programme: a Report from the Services of the European Commission, October 2000.

Unstead-Joss, M. (2001) 'Different stakeholder perspectives', mimeo.

Useful websites

http://europa.eu.int/comm/environment/autooil/
http://europa.eu.int/comm/environment/emas/
http://www.epe.be/
MAFF
Agriculture: (EC DGVI)
Transport: (EC DGVII)
Environment: (EC DGXI)

Outline responses to Case Study Questions

Chapter 1

Case study 1.1

1 To associate itself with more 'positive' images (environmentally friendly renewable energy, etc.) and avoid associations with more negative features (hydrocarbons associated with pollution). Also to better reflect the expanding product portfolio. Petrol associations create poor brand images (BP is 58th in a survey of recognised product names), and so on.

2 Rebranding is a widely used and successful strategy and there would seem to be some factual basis to support BP's new approach. It has shifted many of its operations towards natural gas and renewable energy sources, and its revamping of petrol stations is making use of high-technology approaches, etc. However, there is some danger of the new approach being too vague – so that consumers do not really understand what message is being communicated.

Case study 1.2

1 Consumers (aided by pressure group activity) are increasingly aware of the positive and negative environmental attributes of various products and activities (e.g. increase in demand in recent times for those known to be GM free, and decrease in demand for those known to contain GM ingredients). Increased demand is usually associated with higher revenues, which may more than offset any higher costs to the company from using more expensive but 'environmentally friendly' inputs, thereby raising profitability for the company.

2 There are many possibilities here. It may be useful to consider further the extra costs, the cost savings and the revenue benefits from ethical policies identified by other companies. Perhaps some discussion could include how 'hard' you might consider the various valuations to be.

3 Again there are many possibilities here. Esso (Exxon-Mobil) have been threatened with a global boycott in view of their links with funding the Bush presidential campaign and their support for abandoning the Kyoto treaty and for other alleged anti-environmental activities (e.g. supporting oil drilling in Alaska); BP and Shell have moved in the other direction, deliberately seeking a more 'green' image, with the former rebranding itself as 'Beyond Petroleum' and both investing heavily in renewable energy sources.

Case study 1.3

1 Some possible examples are:

(a) *Macroeconomic*: 'Advance Brazil' seeking to open up Amazonia with new roads and waterways for the (alleged) benefit of the whole economy.

(b) *Microeconomic*: individual businesses (e.g. Rosa Group) seeking certification by the Forest Stewardship Council (FSC) as to its meeting certain standards for sustainable forestry. The belief is that such certification will increase consumer demand for its timber products by environmentally conscious consumers.

(c) Seeking to balance achieving 'legitimate norms' such as extra employment opportunities via deforestation with breaching other 'legitimate norms' such as loss of biodiversity. These tensions arguably correspond to 'moral free space' in the social contract theory approach to ethical behaviour.

(d) Encouraging riverbank dwellers (*ribeirinhos*) that adopting certain cultivation practices is in both their short- and long-term interests ('long-term orientation'). Or seeking to encourage a 'less individualist' and 'more collectivist' approach (i.e. less 'masculinity' and more 'femininity') to using and valuing the rainforests.

(e) Political issues may involve types of government policy instruments adopted, e.g. keeping or changing incentives to deforestation via tax/subsidy system. Political perspective may also involve views as to how the Amazonian rainforest should be developed, e.g. whether greater access via road/waterway, and how to establish jurisdiction over the rainforest, e.g. federal government versus state authorities. Other legal issues involve property rights, e.g. private sector 'stealing' publicly owned forest in the absence of a central land register. A law creating a land register has now been passed to rectify this issue.

2 Some potential areas of conflict ('trade-off') between some of the environmental considerations (a)–(e) have already been identified in the responses to question 1. As a further example, political/legal consideration have resulted in many benefits being given to large, influential landowners engaged in deforestation via taxes (e.g. using deforested land as tax breaks) and subsidies. Yet the practices which followed from these incentives could arguably be shown to be counter-productive at both the microeconomic (individual) and macroeconomic (group) levels. These practices could further be shown to be unsustainable and to lead to losses of biodiversity, arguably breaching ethical norms.

3 In various ways you might show that a more integrated, coherent set of policies is needed to bring about sustainable forest development. These must provide appropriate incentive structures at the micro and macro level and be supported by credible political/legal institutions involved in monitoring and enforcing rules and regulations. Chapter 5 considers the policies and practices consistent with environmental sustainability in still more detail.

Chapter 2

Case Study 2.1

1 More attention could be paid to explicitly environmental impacts such as changes in levels of noise or emissions of various pollutants, changes in amenity value (e.g. aesthetic

appearance of countryside) impacts on local, regional and national economy via changes in output/employment, etc. These could be evaluated on the cost or benefit side of the 'account'. More accurate ways could also be sought to value working and leisure time (e.g. rather than simply assuming leisure time to be 40 per cent of the value of working time). More 'scenarios' could also be used other than the 'do minimum' and 'do something' scenarios currently in use. The discount rate used for calculating NPV might be made more sensitive to individual projects. For example, a higher discount rate might be used for more 'risky' (here in terms of environmental impacts) projects.

2 Placing monetary values on many of these more environmentally specific costs and benefits faces many of the problems already considered in earlier discussion of expressed preference and revealed preference methods.

Case Study 2.2

1 Even the retrospective cost – benefit analysis for the Columbia Basin Project does not support it using a 10 per cent discount rate, despite adopting two 'favourable' assumptions as to benefits.

2 Costs might have been increased (or benefits reduced) by incorporating adverse environmental impacts in terms of displacement of people, damages to the ecosystem and to cultural heritage, and loss of water availability to other uses (opportunity costs). However, benefits might be increased (or costs reduced) by incorporating more favourable environmental impacts in terms of economic impacts on local, regional and national economies via more plentiful (and cheaper) electricity inputs, more employment opportunities (tourism and construction), etc.

3 It takes into account the fact that costs and benefits are spread over time and therefore gives a more representative value when comparing costs–benefits with different time profiles.

Case Study 2.3

1 Some nearby residents were given grants to help minimise the impacts of noise pollution on their homes during construction and a noise barrier constructed along the edge of the airport. A higher profile was also given to reducing noise pollution from both the airport and other uses once the airport was operational. Other beneficiaries would seem to include residents subjected to less airborne pollutants via better monitoring (though little detail given as to enforcement!). Some biodiversity protection (e.g. Romer's tree frog) as well as special treatment procedures for hazardous materials. Administrative machinery established to liaise more effectively on environmental and other matters with the local community. Other beneficiaries include those no longer adversely affected from an environmental standpoint by the airport in its previous location and those who would have been adversely affected by expansion of air travel in that location.

On the other hand 'losers' might include those villagers relocated, those still subject to increased pollution from noise, airborne and other pollutants and hazardous materials, those subject to adverse environmental impacts from constructing and operating the infrastructure projects supporting the new airport. Some biodiversity losses of flora and fauna species.

2 Impacts on people in the local economy could perhaps be dealt with in a broader context; e.g. extra employment, income and output from employment during the construction process and when the airport was operational. Additional prospects for tourism. In other words, a more anthropogenic (human-oriented) view of the environment might touch on a wider range of issues.

In a cost/benefit type of analysis more attention would be given to seeking to derive monetary valuations for the various beneficiaries and losers.

Chapter 3

Case Study 3.1

1 Clearly the marginal social cost of providing the new heavy crude oil pipeline will be greater than the marginal private cost faced by OCP Ecuador. The loss of biodiversity in terms of the cloud forests affected, loss of jobs associated with the rainforest and environmental damages from landslides are all 'costs' *external* to OCP. In terms of Figure 3.2 the marginal social cost curve (MSC) will lie above the marginal private cost curve (MPC). The result will be more deforestation via the private sector mechanism than would be appropriate if social surplus (rather than private surplus or profit) was the key objective. In terms of Figure 3.2 'output' will be higher than is optimum from society's perspective.

2 Figure 3.2 perhaps fails to capture marginal social benefits which are also 'external' to the firm. It assumes that marginal private benefits (MR) are the same as marginal social benefits (MSB). In fact as well as generating income for OCP Ecuador, the heavy oil pipeline is clearly stimulating Ecuador's economy (2.5 per cent a year extra growth in GDP to 2020), 52,000 new jobs (directly and indirectly), extra inward investment, and so on. Arguably the analysis in Figure 3.2 should show the MSB curve *above* the MR curve, since the extra oil output is benefiting others in society as well as privately benefiting OCP Ecuador.

Case study 3.2

1 Marginal social cost (MSC) is no longer zero and must therefore intersect marginal social benefit (MSB) from road use *above* the horizontal axis. Social utility is a maximum where MSB = MSC, which means that instead of the zero price for a 'pure public good', the optimum price for the (congested) road is greater than zero.

2 Clearly the target 'output' (road use) will be less than in the case of a zero price.

3 Substantial monetary valuations are given to time losses, extra vehicle costs, etc. for both individual firms, motorists, passengers and households. Other 'costs' include making congested areas less attractive to people and firms.

Case study 3.3

1 Many possibilities here. Endorsements of nuclear power by the new Bush (Republican) administration. Deregulation (a political decision) is giving opportunities to run the nuclear plants with commercial objectives. Licences to run *existing* nuclear plants extended beyond their original limits (e.g. beyond 40 years). Granting of subsidies to nuclear industry over many years, limitations placed on the liability of nuclear plants in the event of accidents and subsequent clean-ups, etc.

2 Higher costs in the absence of these various subsidies and supports would raise the price of nuclear energy relative to other energy forms, reduce demand and therefore reduce target levels of output and use of nuclear energy.

3 Environmental benefits include less use of alternative (e.g. fossil) fuels which are more damaging to the environment (e.g. CO_2 and other greenhouse gas emissions). Environmental costs include problems of disposing of highly radioactive wastes, risks of major environmental disasters involving nuclear plants or the transport of nuclear materials.

Non-environmental benefits include national security of supply (e.g. not having to depend on overseas supplies of fossil fuels) and allegedly lower energy prices via lower operating cost. Low energy prices can also help increase real incomes and therefore consumer expenditure, stimulating output and employment nationally. Non-environmental costs include high capital costs in nuclear plants and losses of output and employment in alternative (more labour-intensive) energy industries. A high proportion of the R & D budgets involving energy supplies is taken up by the nuclear industry at the expense of other energy industries.

Chapter 4

Case study 4.1

1 The case *for* a carbon tax includes penalising fossil fuels which have a greater carbon content and therefore face a higher tax rate (thereby reducing CO_2 and greenhouse gas emissions). Other possible benefits include giving incentives to substitute other fuels with little or no carbon content for those with higher carbon content. Technological research and development will in these ways be given market incentives to be directed towards replacing high carbon content fuels and products.

The case *against* includes higher fuel costs and therefore higher prices for products. Such inflationary impacts may reduce real incomes and discourage output and employment. Higher fuel prices are also regressive, taking a higher proportion of the income of poorer households.

2 Many possibilities here. Some products have *less price elastic demands* (see Figure 4.11), so that producers are better able to pass higher costs on to consumers as higher prices; vice versa for products with *more price elastic demands*.

Case study 4.2

1 This is a colloquial expression for 'carbon sequestration' credits which give their holders the right to emit the levels of CO_2 indicated. Many CO_2 emissions are a by-product of combustion engines with their association with heat – hence trading in 'hot air'.

2 Many points can be raised here. Arguments for include 'efficiency' arguments with those better able (lower costs) to reduce CO_2 emissions given incentives to cut emissions by selling permits no longer needed to those less able to cut them (higher costs). This was claimed to have been demonstrated in the USA by the earlier market in tradable permits for sulphur dioxide. Less disruption to output, employment and real incomes of nations when tradable permits are used to meet the Kyoto targets. Otherwise the recessionary impacts on the world economy of achieving these targets are likened to a doubling or tripling of the world oil prices.

Arguments against include attempts to circumvent genuine reductions in greenhouse gases by allowing countries experiencing deindustrialisation to be given permits on the basis of past emissions (grandfathering) – which are then available for future trading. Countries buying these are then adding to total emissions of these gases.

Case study 4.3

1 If marginal abatement cost curves differ between sectors, then a non-uniform reduction in CO_2 emissions will be appropriate rather than a uniform 50 per cent cut across all sectors (see Figure 4.10).

2 The suggestion here is that environmental taxes provide the least-cost method of securing a given reduction in CO_2 emissions. A tax on CO_2 emissions provides a 'price signal' to which all producers of electricity can respond in the way most appropriate to themselves. Such decentralised decisions are thought likely to be more 'efficient' than 'command and control' (centrally directed) decisions.

3 The MAC curves still have to be estimated for each economic sector if an 'appropriate' tax rate is to be devised (i.e. one which achieved the intended overall reduction in CO_2 emissions). In Figure 4.10 any other tax rate than the one shown will equalise the MACs in each sector but will not achieve the intended overall reduction OO′ in CO_2 emissions.

Chapter 5

Case study 5.1

1 By specifying more carefully how exporters' costs and profits should be measured, the WTO will make it less easy for importing countries to use contrived figures to claim that 'dumping' is occurring. In other words, exporters will have greater freedom to argue that their lower costs are part of their competitive advantage in open trade, rather than a distorted and unfair means of securing access to overseas markets.

2 On the one hand the ruling may help many poorer countries to benefit from greater access to overseas markets. Higher standards of living in those countries then help encourage better environmental practices (often associated with higher real incomes – see Chapter 12). On the other hand the ruling may encourage employers paying poverty wages, using child labour, etc. Some poor countries themselves may be disadvantaged by having to open up their own protected markets – reducing further already low standards of living. However, if open trade really is associated with growing world standards of living, restricting the use of 'dumping' allegations as a protectionist measure will support sustainability worldwide – especially when we use the more human-centred (anthropogenic) perspective of sustainability.

Case study 5.2

1 Support the current global economy with its inequalities; too 'hard' on the poor (e.g. tough conditions imposed on countries receiving help); pay little heed to environmental / ecological / human rights issues, etc.

2 They support the expansion of global trade and investment, which is arguably the most effective means of helping the poor. The evidence for standards of living of the 'poor'

(bottom 20 per cent of the population) rising in line with average incomes worldwide, for greater 'economic openness' being associated with higher productivity, higher income levels and lower inequality suggest that supporting the growth of international trade and investment may have benefits for the disadvantaged.

Chapter 6

Case study 6.1

1 It suggests that market-based policy instruments such as environmental taxes or tradable permits allow a flexibility of response which will often allow a given environmental target (e.g. pollution reduction) to be achieved at the lower total abatement cost.

2 Minimising *abatement costs* is not necessarily the same as minimising *damage costs* for the environment. In the case study, in situations in which river 2 imposes less environmental damage per unit of pollutant than river 1, minimising total abatement costs results in less pollution from river 2 and more from river 1. From an *environmental damage* point of view, a social optimum solution would be more pollution from river 2 and less from river 1 within any total of pollution reduction.

3 Market-based policy instruments may be useful for achieving least-cost outcomes but not necessarily least environmental damage outcomes. Where local knowledge is important, regulators with such knowledge may be better able than (impersonal) market incentives to allocate resources in ways which minimise environmental damage costs.

Case study 6.2

1 Support might come from a recognition by environmentalists that landfill has been overused as a means of waste disposal. This is because the firms and authorities involved have only considered their private costs and largely ignored the (negative) environmental externalities associated with landfill. The landfill tax seeks to remedy this situation by raising the relative cost of this means of disposal, i.e. 'internalising the externality'.

Criticisms might include the failure of the tax to influence household decisions as to the reuse and recycling of waste. This is because the tax is levied on those depositing the (given) amount of waste to be disposed of.

2 The BPEO scheme at least seeks to consider environmental externalities explicitly for each method of waste disposal. The 'waste hierarchy' ensures that the method which, on average, is estimated as usually providing most benefits/least costs on waste disposal is considered first. Movement down the hierarchy of methods only occurs when a previous environmental option is disqualified (e.g. 'unacceptable cost' or 'lack of proximity').

Alleged weaknesses with BPEO might include the inflexibility of this approach. For individual waste disposal issues a full costing (private and social) of different alternatives would arguably yield a more socially acceptable decision. The 'waste hierarchy' might lead to a choice being made in a particular case before all the alternative methods had been fully appraised. The policy document only lays down general principles – it does not provide for policy instruments (e.g. taxes) which might generate specific outcomes.

Case study 6.3

1 The landfill tax supports the 'polluter pays principle' in seeking to charge the full value of external costs to organisations dumping waste in landfill sites. Critics argue that it is set at too low a level to cover the full costs and to encourage the use of more environmentally friendly alternatives – e.g. recycling by contractors. Critics also point out that the landfill tax duty does not impact on households and there-fore does not influence reuse or recycling behaviour.

2 As applied, the ranking system used ('waste hierarchy') inhibits a full cost–benefit assessment of all methods before selecting that method with the greatest net benefits to society. Only when a higher-ranked method is rejected is a lower one evaluated. On the other hand, waste disposal, which has arguably been overused in the past, is at the bottom of the 'waste hierarchy'.

Chapter 7

Case study 7.1

1 Benefits include a longer growing season in previously colder northern climates. Also more rapid rates of crop growth via increased CO_2 concentrations in the atmosphere. However, in this summary of the report many more potentially adverse effects are involved, including increased air pollution, increased exposure to extreme weather con-ditions, rise in sea levels and associated flooding, etc.

2 The UK would experience a warmer climate, with a longer growing season and presum-ably new varieties of crop/wildlife/biodiversity features, etc. However, coastal and inland flood risks would rise, forests would be at increased risk, air pollution would increase with associated health hazards (e.g. exposure to extra UV radiation via ozone depletion).

Case study 7.2

1 Changes in fuel supply away from coal and towards gas-fired electricity generation in Germany and the UK especially have made an important contribution to green-house gas emission reductions. So too have tendencies involving the rise of service-related (less energy-intensive) industries throughout the EU and reduced importance of industrialised output (deindustrialisation). Many of these changes are now largely complete, so further emissions reductions must come from other sources.

2 Quite a comprehensive list is presented. However, little emphasis is placed on mar-ket-based policy measures, such as increased taxes on carbon or energy content to discourage households from consuming energy (pollution) intensive products.

Case study 7.3

1 Various ways – some of the *adverse* environmental impacts have already been cata-logued in the earlier Case Study 7.1.

2 Lack of financial resources and infrastructure to develop appropriate adaptive responses.

3 Many possibilities here, e.g. reluctance of developing countries to inhibit economic/industrial growth by restricting the use of cheaper/more plentiful fossil fuels, levels of financial support available to help developing countries make adaptive responses to climate change; benefits to developing countries of participation as partners in the 'clean development mechanism' (CDM), etc.

Chapter 8

Case study 8.1

1 Shortcomings aside, the agreement is laudable. It formally acknowledges the interests of watershed residents and stresses the need to implement watershed protection plans fairly and equitably. Elements of the New York City watershed agreement may serve as a model for other communities. There is a growing recognition that filtration, by itself, is no panacea. It can reduce the threat of water-borne pathogens, but it cannot completely eliminate the threat, especially if the source water is poor. Watershed protection offers a cost-effective approach to clean drinking water, and benefits the environment as a whole.

2 The challenge in the case of New York City is the need to compel many people and communities to work together, putting aside self-interest, towards the twin goals of saving the watershed and saving money.

Case study 8.2

1 Increase in the total cost-effective resource available from onshore wind power above 6.5 GW, currently some 16 per cent of total UK electricity (6.5/41 GW).

2 Reductions in the contribution of onshore windpower below the current 16 per cent contribution to electricity generation.

3 A higher discount rate would reduce the present value of any given amount of electricity generated in the future from *all* sources. It might not, therefore, impact the *relative* attractiveness of different energy sources to electricity generators.

4 This might lead to recalculations of existing projections in favour of wind power. For example, a more favourable (smaller) discount rate might be applied to future revenues associated with onshore wind power.

Case study 8.3

1 It does not have enough supply of generating power to provide for its customers' needs (3,000 MW less power than the 11,000 MW demanded).

2 Rationing supply availability by command and control methods (non-market based instruments) e.g. insisting on 5–10 per cent cuts per annum from large utilities, but an effective 100 per cent cut from the aluminium smelting industry. The proposed huge price increases in the new contracts for electric power to aluminium smelting if a 'voluntary' withdrawal for two years is not agreed, are alleged to be impossible for them to meet and stay in business.

3 Benefits could include the smelting industry developing its own generating power, using more efficient and cleaner fuels. Conservation of scarce energy resources for future generations via rationing or higher prices in renewed contracts. Costs could

include unemployment and human deprivation associated with disrupting an important local and national industry.

Chapter 9

Case study 9.1

1 Charging motorists a price which captures the true costs to society of their activity.
2 Benefits include the application of the 'polluter pays' principle so that individuals/firms take account of the full costs they impose on the environment and on others. Also useful revenue raised to be used in a variety of potentially beneficial ways. Also benefits by switches to now cheaper, less environmentally damaging, transport sources (e.g. underground). Difficulties include technological problems with implementing the system. There may also be major problems in achieving public acceptance of road use charging.

Case study 9.2

1 Fuel cells, electric batteries, liquid fuels, etc.
2 Fossil fuels have higher energy density and power density – important in transportation. Some 99 per cent of energy used for transport is oil-based – difficult to change this substantially in the near future. The merit in replacing oil-based energy sources is the pollution emission reductions from these alternative fuels for transport.

Case study 9.3

1 These include noise, air pollution, illness and death, ecosystem damage directly via toxic emissions and indirectly via climate change.
2 Placing a monetary value on adverse impacts often requires indirect measurements, e.g. house price variations (for a given type) in relation to proximity to an airport – the hedonic pricing method. Some impacts are long term and difficult both to measure in physical and in monetary terms e.g. climate change. When assessing the monetary values placed on illness or death via aircraft externalities (pollution, noise, etc.), again statistical problems often arise (see Chapter 2).

Case study 9.4

1 High-speed rail has advantages in respect of emissions of certain greenhouse gases per passenger km, namely carbon dioxide (CO_2), carbon monoxide (CO), nitrogen oxides (NO) and volatile organic compounds (VOCs). Short-haul air travel has the advantage in terms of sulphur dioxide (SO_2) with little difference in terms of particulates (PM_{10}).
2 The shorter the distance travelled by passengers to rail terminals and airports (especially by car) the fewer pollutants emitted. On balance the evidence favours rail transport in this respect, since railway stations tend to be more central and nearer to centres of population from which most journeys start or end.

Chapter 10

Case study 10.1

1 More heat retention in BedZED by better design and insulation: less energy requirements needed to generate heat. Recycled materials used as fuels. Less travel-related
energy and pollution involved than in conventional housing developments. Higher
SAP ratio in Cheam development (100) than in houses conforming to the 1995
Building Regulations (75); also 40 per cent energy efficiency gains.

2 The facilities provided may not cover all the needs of residents, and home working
may not grow as rapidly as enthusiasts predict. Therefore travel cost/time in savings
and pollution benefits may be overestimated. If there is economic recession and/or
structural change in the economy, empty office space in the midst of a housing development may give an impression of dereliction. Dependence on new forms of energy
and power may be neither as economical nor efficient as expected.

Case study 10.2

1 Environmental benefits include preserving more greenfield sites, with landscape
and biodiversity benefits. Renovating old, derelict sites in the town centre benefits the environment, with the extra local population housed in and round the
centre creating additional demands for goods and services. A more buoyant urban
economy may result. Environmental costs include flood risks since many factories
and much derelict urban land is built near watercourses. Also other toxins and
contaminants may affect brownfield sites.

2 Brownfield developments will now be more expensive to build as housing developers
have to provide better flood defences. Unless house prices rise sufficiently to offset
these higher costs, there is a risk of lower quality, less environmentally 'friendly'
housing being built. There may also be renewed pressure on greenfield site developments where these are less prone to flood. Planning delays will grow even longer as
flood risks for new developments must be carefully assessed.

Chapter 11

Case study 11.1

1 Causes include climate change, increased demand via population growth and
increased food requirements, and poor water management (e.g. excessive use in irrigation).

2 Increased risks of political and economic conflicts among nations. Less self-reliance
on food production in more arid countries.

3 Remedies include better water and land management practices. Use of drip irrigation
sprinklers can increase water efficiency, as can improved crop-growing techniques
and the development of crops requiring less water intake. Setting prices for water use
to reflect the true (private + external) costs of its use has also been advocated.

Case study 11.2

1 Evidence suggests that demand for organic food is extremely price sensitive, e.g. surveys showing around 80 per cent of consumers would buy organic if prices were sim-

ilar to conventional foods. Currently prices are 25 – 30 per cent higher. Organic food demand is growing even now at 40 per cent per annum – at lower prices even more growth potential.

2 Cutting price to that for conventional foods but promising not to cut the price they pay to producers. This will cut Iceland's profits by some £8 m. per year.

3 Rivals to Iceland will be forced to cut their organic prices and are likely to pay less to suppliers. Eventually Iceland itself may follow this path. Costs of organic producers are currently higher than for conventional producers – need the incentive of higher prices.

4 It could offer the higher value and longer-term 'stewardship' grants, as in other EU countries. It could offer extra grants for covering the costs of converting to organic (e.g. two-year conversion cycle) and other aid thereafter. Only when some 30 per cent of British land is organic (currently 2 per cent) can various scale economies allow lower prices via lower costs of production, so that few government supports will be necessary.

Case study 11.3

1 In Chapter 1 we noted that the 'environmental' perspective can be broad-based, including impacts on humans. Therefore as well as impacts on animals, landscape, flora and fauna, account can be taken of impacts on output and employment in farms and other rural activities.

2 Negative externalities (see Chapter 3) involve 'market failure' which is often used to justify government intervention. Certainly the marginal social cost of FMD is widely regarded as exceeding estimates of marginal private costs. For example, if farmers are unable or unwilling to kill (or vaccinate) infected animals, the costs imposed on others (e.g. adjacent farms, other animals, flora and fauna, other human activities) will be substantially greater than the costs imposed on themselves. Only governments can help rectify such situations using interventions such as regulations, subsidies and grants, other resources (e.g. military).

Case study 11.4

1 By redeploying some of the European Commission's budget away from the CAP (with its tendencies to intensification of agriculture and overproduction) and towards a more balanced and broad-based support of rural activities. Many of the latter involve practices favourable to the environment.

2 Modulation (redirection) of monies from farm supports in the UK to broader-based rural development activities, has attracted criticism. However, others argue that it will have a favourable environmental impact. Countryside stewardship, organic farm conversion, woodland and other RDP schemes would seem to be providing support for environmentally sustainable activities.

Chapter 12

Case study 12.1

1 Causes include medical advances reducing death rates. Even though birth rates are falling, the death rate is falling even faster.

2 Environmental implications include increasing pressure on an already stretched infra-structure, increasing poverty, unemployment and other indicators of human depriva-tion. The tendency to move to towns and cities is placing the urban environment under greater pressures.

Case study 12.2

1 In developing economies most (around 80 per cent) are still rural poor – with sup-port they will adopt more environmentally sustainable agricultural practices (see Table 12.7). Although more difficult in cities, some environmental benefits have been seen there when adaptive support is given to the poor.

2 Granting property rights, providing education and training, helping introduce appro-priate agricultural practices and crop varieties. Governments, both national and local, and international institutions may need to monitor and regulate health standards where individuals (especially in towns/cities) are unable to intervene on their own account.

Case Study 12.3

1 Better animal husbandry and better land management practices result from local peo-ple having better access to weather-related and other information. Higher crop yields and more sustainable agricultural practices are occurring, as are better health and nutrition services for people.

2 Relatively low-cost, environmentally appropriate and locally devised programmes can have important environmental and social benefits. Better information access is important to the poor as well as to the rich.

Chapter 13

Case study 13.1

Certainly environmental principles of sustainability, targeting climate change and asso-ciated impacts are present in the Auto Oil Programme, all part of the Fifth EAP (Box 13.1). Other elements of earlier EAPs would appear to be present, e.g. belief that envi-ronmental protection can save jobs (Fourth EAP).

The approach involves mainly non-market-based instruments, via regulations. The impacts on consumers via increases in driving costs discouraging travelling, were regarded as negligible. It could be argued that environmental taxes on road users might reduce emissions by curbing travel, though this would have serous economic implica-tions for many sectors of the economy. There was an *implicit* market element in the belief that cleaner technologies would enhance future sales – helping bring industry 'on board' for the programme. In any case it was recognised that emission limits would be progressively reduced, closing global markets to high-emission vehicles. Arguably, the costs of non-participation in Auto Oil for EU Member States and their vehicle-related industries would be greater than compliance.

Case study 13.2

The CAP reforms are certainly in line with a number of the environmental principles outlined in Box 13.1 and elsewhere. For example, moving away from producer subsidies which were arguably unsustainable in both environmental and budgetary senses. Attempts to broaden the base of EU support to a broader range of rural activities, many with positive environmental associations, are also in line with a number of the principles of various EAPs in Box 13.1.

The EU's approach is a combination of market and non-market-based instruments. For example, market-based initiatives involved reducing EU support for maintaining artificially high prices in the market for foodstuffs, thereby helping these prices fall closer to world market level. However, a range of regulations and standards and central directives also feature in various parts of the CAP reforms.

Some would argue the need for a more radical overhaul of the CAP, removing supports for various products more rapidly and completely to let prices return to world levels and using the large agricultural budget for other EU purposes. Others favour the more gradual approach adopted.

The budgetary costs to the EU of the guarantee system (see Box 11.1, page 262) are considerable – but the 'opportunity cost' of not providing such supports would also be considerable – lost farm employment, change of and diminished rural communities, etc. To non-EU members there is a significant cost of the EU protecting itself from their agricultural exports to the EU – especially the developing economies. Removing these EU barriers to international trade (including subsidised EU food exports) is an important objective for these non-EU countries.

Case study 13.3

EMAS would certainly be seen by supporters as implementing some of the principles outlined in Box 13.1, such as supporting sustainability by improving and regularising EMS in organisations. It may then have many favourable indirect effects on other environmental outcomes listed in Box 13.1 and elsewhere.

The EMAS approach would seem to be mainly non-market-based, in that adherence to a set of standards is the means of certification. However, an implicit market-based element can arguably be cited in that new market opportunities (and less market risks) may result from EMAS participation. ECO labelling may help in this respect.

A criticism is duplication of effort with a more global (though arguably less rigorous) standardised system already available in ISO 14001. This alternative could have been supported and strengthened by the EU, rather than duplicated! The balance of costs and benefit would seem unclear at present, with companies citing the immediacy of compliance cost but the longer-term, less tangible nature of benefits. Companies registered in non-EU Member States may feel 'pressure' to adopt EMAS when operating in the EU, even though they may already be certificated via ISO 14001.

Index

Note: Page references in *italics* refer to figures or tables.